FUGITIVE IRELAND

FUGITIVE IRELAND

European Minority Nationalists and Irish Political Asylum, 1937–2008

DANIEL LEACH

FOUR COURTS PRESS

Typeset in 10 pt on 13.5 pt Sabon by
Mark Heslington Ltd for
FOUR COURTS PRESS LTD
7 Malpas Street, Dublin 8, Ireland
e-mail: info@fourcourtspress.ie
and in North America for
FOUR COURTS PRESS
c/o ISBS, 920 NE 58th Avenue, Suite 300, Portland, OR 97213.

A catalogue record for this title is available
from the British Library.

ISBN 978-1-84682-164-6

SPECIAL ACKNOWLEDGMENT

Publication of this work was assisted by a publication
grant from the University of Melbourne.

Printed in England
by MPG Books, Bodmin, Cornwall.

Contents

Illustrations

appear between pages 160 and 161.

Abbreviations

AVV-VVK	Alles voor Vlaanderen – Vlaanderen voor Kristus, 'All for Flanders–Flanders for Christ'
BNNS	Breton National News Service
BUF	British Union of Fascists
CBL	Comité national de la Bretagne libre, 'National Committee of Free Brittany'
CCB	Comité consultatif de la Bretagne, 'Consultative Committee of Brittany'
CIC	Counter-Intelligence Corps (US Army)
CNB	Conseil national breton, 'Breton National Council'
CNV	Comunión Nacionalista Vasca, 'Basque Nationalist Communion'
DEA	Department of External Affairs (Ireland)
DIAS	Dublin Institute of Advanced Studies
DSSO	Democratic Scottish Self-Government Organisation
ETA	Euskadi ta Askatasuna 'Basque Country and Freedom'
FFI	Forces françaises de l'Intérieure, 'French Forces of the Interior'
FFL	Forces françaises libres, 'Free French Forces'
FLB	Front de Libération de la Bretagne, 'Liberation Front of Brittany'
FO	Foreign Office (UK)
FTP	Francs-tireurs et partisans français, French communist Resistance fighters
FWA	Free Wales Army
G2	Irish military intelligence
HO	Home Office (UK)
IP	Interparty (government) (Ireland)
IRA	Irish Republican Army
IRO	International Refugee Organisation
LVF	Légion des Volontaires français contre le Bolchevisme, 'Legion of French Volunteers against Bolshevism'
MI5	British domestic intelligence service
MP	Military police; Member of Parliament (UK)
NATO	North Atlantic Treaty Organisation
NDH	Nezavisna Država Hrvatska, 'Independent State of Croatia'
NPS	National Party of Scotland
OSS	Office of Strategic Services (USA)
OT	Organisation Todt (Nazi engineering and construction service)

PC	Plaid Cymru, 'The Party of Wales'
PCF	Parti communiste français, 'French Communist Party'
PNB	Parti national breton, 'Breton National Party'
PNV	Partido Nacionalista Vasca, 'Basque Nationalist Party'
PPF	Parti populaire français, 'French Popular Party'
RAVSIGUR	Ravnateljstvo za javni red i sigurnost, 'Directorate for Public Order and Security' (Croatia).
RG	Renseignements généraux, French internal security intelligence service
SARE	Sociedad Argentina Recepción Europeos, 'Argentine European Reception Society'
SD	Sicherheitsdienst, 'Security Service' (Security/intelligence service of SS)
SDF	Scottish Defence Force
SIM	Scottish Independence Movement
SLA	Scottish Liberation Army
SNG	Siol nan Gaidheal, 'Race of the Gaels' (Scotland)
SNL	Scottish Neutrality League
SNLA	Scottish National Liberation Army
SNP	Scottish National Party
SOE	Special Operations Executive (UK)
SP	Scottish Party
SRA	Scottish Republican Army
SS	Schutzstaffel, 'Protection Squad' (Nazi party paramilitary)
SSP	Scottish Socialist (1940) Party
STO	Service du Travail obligatoire, 'Compulsory Labour Service' (France)
TD	Teachta Dála 'Assembly delegate' (Member of Irish lower house)
UCD	University College, Dublin
UCG	University College, Galway
UNS	Ustaška Nadzorna Služba (Ustaša Surveillance Service)
URB	Union régionaliste bretonne, 'Breton Regionalist Union'
USM	United Scotland Movement
USSR	Union of Soviet Socialist Republics
VNV	Vlaamsch Nationaal Verbond, 'Flemish National League'

Notes on the text

Ireland, Éire and the Republic
'Ireland' refers to the 'Twenty-Six Counties' (as opposed to the 'Six Counties' of Northern Ireland), known as the Irish Free State (Saorstát Éireann) from 1922 to 1937; Éire from 1937 to 1949; and finally the Republic of Ireland.

Breton orthography
Unless from a quotation, Breton usage corresponds to 'KLTG'/*peurunvan* orthography. Under this system, Breiz Atao becomes Breizh Atav. The original spelling is used when referring to the nationalist publication of 1919–39.

Dutch versus Flemish
'Dutch language' refers to Nederlands as spoken in Flanders and the Netherlands. Although Flemish usage is distinctive, linguistic conformity with the Netherlands was adopted by the Flemish Cultural Council in 1973.

Placenames
Placenames follow English usage, except Euskadi, which is generally preferred to the more cumbersome 'Basque Country'.

Translations of source material
Translations from Breton and French are by the author. My thanks to Guillaume Legros for his assistance with the latter. Translations from Dutch are by the author, except where noted. My thanks to Toos de Boer for her work on *Ierland en het Iersche Volk*. The translation of *Aiséirí Flóndrais* from Irish is by Anna Heussaff. My thanks also to Kintilla Heussaff. Translations from Spanish are by *mi hermano*, Michael Leach. The author assumes responsibility for any and all errors.

Acknowledgments

THIS WORK WAS CONCEIVED in 2003. Secondary research was conducted principally at the University of Melbourne and State Library of Victoria, Melbourne, between 2003 and 2005. My thanks to the Inter-Library Loans staff at the former, who were obliged to request incomprehensible titles on my behalf.

Archival research was undertaken in summer 2005 at the Irish Military Archives and National Archives of Ireland, Dublin; the National Archives of Scotland, Edinburgh; the National Archives, Kew, England; the Archives du Ministère des Affaires étrangères and the Archives nationales, Paris; the Centre des Archives diplomatiques de Nantes; and the Archives de l'État en Belgique, Brussels. Exile and autonomist publications were researched during the same period at the National Library of Ireland, Dublin; the Bibliothèque nationale, Paris; the British Library, London; and the National Library of Wales, Aberystwyth.

Archival material relating to Flemish exiles was provided in 2006 by Luc Boeva and Ann van Gastel of the Archief, Documentatie en Onderzoekcentrum voor het Vlaamse Nationalisme in Antwerp. Staff at ADVN forwarded my name to Keith Farrell of Tile Films, producer of the *Ireland's Nazis* two-part documentary aired on RTÉ One in January 2007. Keith kindly provided me additional material, connections and other assistance throughout 2006.

Correspondence with exiles, their families and associates has been a continuous process. Interviews with these generous individuals took place in summer 2005. See bibliography for details.

A version of Chapter One appeared in *Irish Studies Review,* 15 (4), November 2007, pp. 425–49. Parts of Chapter Five appear as 'Bezen Perrot: the Breton nationalist unit of the SS, 1943–5', *e-Keltoi: Journal of Interdisciplinary Celtic Studies,* 4 (Nationalism), pp. 1–38, http://www.uwm.edu/Dept/celtic/ekeltoi/volumes/vol4/4_1/index.html; published 6 February 2008. Parts of Chapter Six appeared as '"Repaying a debt of gratitude": foreign minority nationalists and the fiftieth anniversary of the Easter Rising 1966', *Éire–Ireland*, 43 (3–4), Fall–Winter 2008, pp. 267–89.

To all who assisted me in seeing this project to fruition, I say: *Thank you:* Kath Wilson, Elizabeth Malcolm, P.B. Brennan, Peter Berresford Ellis, Gillian Cooper, Andrew Eastham, Michael Farrell, Keith Farrell, James McLeod, Patrick O'Sullivan; *Merci beaucoup*: Armelle Goulet-Conway, Charles 'Chips' Sowerwine, Guillaume Legros; *Trugarez vras*: Louis Feutren, Per Denez, Yann Fouéré, Gwennig Helloco, Trystan Mordrel, Jos Ollitrault, Rozenn Fouéré Barrett; *Buíochas le*: Anna Heussaff, Kintilla Heussaff, Piaras Mac Einri, Brendan Hennessy, Eamon Ó Ciosáin, Róisín Bean Uí Chuill ... and the late Bríd Heussaff, whose hospitality is fondly remembered; *Dank U wel*: Alexander Colen, Staf van Velthoven, Bruno de Wever, Dirk Folens, Paul van Cauwelaert, Alexandra Colen, Ann van Gastel, Luc Boeva, Toos de Boer; *Diolch*: Mair Piette; *Eskerrik asko:* Iker Gallastegi; *Muchos gracias*: Michael Leach; *Hvala*: Rad Artukovic, Marko Attila Hoare.

Finally, I am grateful to Mr Gerry Higgins and the Higgins Trust. The financial assistance provided me as inaugural holder of the Gerry Higgins Postgraduate Scholarship in Irish Studies at the University of Melbourne made this research possible.

Introduction

Historians [...] have been reluctant to accept that raisons d'état *have motivated Ireland.*[1]

IN DUBLIN ON EASTER MONDAY, 1949, a former newspaper editor watched celebrations marking the declaration of the Republic of Ireland 'with an emotion mixed with melancholy'.[2] His was not the only equivocal reaction to the proceedings. Fianna Fáil had instituted a nationwide boycott, while many supporters of the ruling Interparty coalition felt the declaration either went too far in terminating Commonwealth membership, or not far enough concerning Partition.[3]

But the former editor had other cause to view the celebrations with ambivalence. For a start, Yann Fouéré was not Irish. He had in fact been resident for only a year. Unless he wanted to spend the rest of his life in prison, however, there was currently no indication he would ever be allowed to return to the land of his birth. Perhaps inevitably, though, on that thirty-third anniversary of the beginning of the Easter Rising, 'watching the flags rise and the army parade, listening to the bagpipes and brass sound', Fouéré found himself not in Dublin but back home in Brittany, imagining 'the *Place du Parlement* at Rennes, [or] that of the *Château des Ducs* at Nantes [...] equally adorned and packed with crowds, celebrating under our unfurled flags the return of our liberty ...'[4]

In the years following the Second World War (the 'Emergency' in Ireland), Dublin granted political asylum to various European ethnic minority nationalists, many of whom were wanted for war crimes, collaboration with Axis powers, or attacks upon the 'territorial integrity' of Allied states. They came discreetly and in small numbers, and their hosts sought largely to conceal their presence. Bretons of varying autonomist shades, including pro-Vichy regionalists like Fouéré, leaders of the proscribed Parti national breton (Breton National Party), or separatists of the SS-uniformed Bezen Perrot (Perrot Unit); Flemish veterans of German forces or collaborationist parties; even a high-ranking war criminal subsequently dubbed the 'Yugoslav Himmler'[5] – all were granted temporary or permanent refuge in postwar Ireland.

Many professed an Irish inspiration to actions that led them on the path to exile. Some returned home at the earliest opportunity, or used Ireland as a staging post for emigrations further afield. Others still remained, sometimes rising to considerable prominence. Albert Folens arrived from Belgium in 1948 and founded a textbook publishing firm that achieved near ubiquity in Irish education. Yann Goulet fled France in 1947 and became a sculptor of Irish memorials. Yann Fouéré developed an export trade in lobsters based in Connemara, and remained a leading figure in autonomist politics in his native country. Alan Heusaff became general secretary of the Celtic League. Each of these men, and many more like them, built new lives and raised families in Ireland. Each also arrived as a fugitive, fleeing retribution for his wartime political or military activities. What brought them to Ireland? Who helped them arrive? And, most importantly, what was the attitude of Irish governments toward them?

That Ireland sheltered these fugitives at a time when Nazism was defeated and reviled appears suggestive at best of an insular mentality out of step with global realities; at worst, it suggests that in the heart of Irish government lurked the very sort of pro-Axis proclivity Allied press had long accused Dublin of harbouring. As Carter comments, Allied citizens were led to believe that:

> Ireland crawled with spies, that German subs refueled off the Irish coast with help from Irish dissidents, that Eamon de Valera [...] would do anything to hurt Britain, and that if Ireland had permitted the British to use her ports the Allied war effort would have been greatly facilitated.[6]

It is an image that persists to this day – even within the Republic. In the wake of the two-part documentary *Ireland's Nazis* broadcast in January 2007, the *Sunday Independent*'s Eoghan Harris described the asylum granted to Axis fugitives as an expression of Irish 'Anglophobia' and 'an ambivalence about Nazi Germany which persisted until well after the war'.[7]

Such interpretations, however, are based upon mistaken presumptions. No previous study has investigated the arrival of these fugitives, the circumstances of their flight, and the attitude with which they were regarded by Irish authorities. Attitudes toward nationalist exiles resident during the Emergency itself, moreover, have been almost entirely unexplored. The scant attention that *has* been paid to either has focused upon successful entries; cases in which the Irish government opposed, refused or deterred embarrassing arrivals have been overlooked or inadequately contextualised, contributing to an uncritical paradigm of an 'open door' for pro-Axis fugitives, or of a sympathetic sanctuary for those engaged in minority nationalist struggle.

This study reveals that asylum for foreign nationalists was not determined by such abstractions. Instead the determinants were the same *raisons d'état* that shaped wartime neutrality: sovereignty, national security, and, in key cases, a desire to contribute discreetly to the defence of Western interests without formally allying with Britain. The friction between these imperatives generated an apparent pro-Axis proclivity readily exploited by opponents of Irish policy, but this was as misleading after 1945 as it had been during the Emergency.

Neutrality and the Emergency

It is now well established that characterisations of a pro-Axis or even strictly neutral Ireland during the Emergency ignore its 'friendly neutrality' towards the Allies, in particular the intelligence contacts that existed between G2 (Irish military intelligence) and British MI5. These were established in 1938 following the surrender of the Treaty Ports to Irish control.[8]

Ireland's neutrality, however, was never guaranteed by the Allies.[9] Their wish to regain use of the ports resulted in intense pressure on Dublin throughout the early years of the Second World War. Neutrality was, however, of strategic utility to Germany.[10] For many in Dublin, therefore, the most significant invasion threat was posed by Britain, which could have seized the ports without serious opposition from poorly-armed Irish forces.[11]

De Valera's challenge was therefore, Lee argues, to ensure Britain's security did not become so imperilled that Irish ports would be seen as crucial to its national survival.[12] The economic and strategic relationship also meant Dublin would have to act favourably towards its neighbour.[13] By the terms of the 1938 agreement, Ireland had undertaken not to provide a base for attacks upon the UK, including subversion against British interests.[14] Suppression of Republicans was therefore stepped up: during the Emergency six IRA men were executed, and hundreds interned, under the Emergency Powers and Offences against the State Acts (1939).[15]

Co-operation with Britain could not be publicly acknowledged, however, for fear of the reaction among nationalists. Ireland's 'unneutrality' was therefore expressed in discreet ways: repatriation of downed Allied aircrew; broadcast *en clair* of German submarine sightings; and absence of legal impediment to the stream of Irish volunteers for British forces and industry.[16] Even MI5 acknowledged that, as a partner in all but name that did not require defence by British forces, 'Éire neutral was of more value than Éire belligerent would have been.'[17]

But if Irish neutrality was 'friendly' towards the Allies, why did Dublin join with fascistic European outcasts like Spain, or Latin American autocracies like Argentina, in providing sanctuary to Axis collaborators who had (in the words of Frederick Boland of the Department of External Affairs), 'donned the uniform of the invading forces' during the recent conflict?[18]

Neutrality and sovereignty

Although committed to assisting the Allies without declaring war – a position at least the Canadians acknowledged – neutrality allowed de Valera to realise two crucial objectives. First was to avoid direct alliance with Britain, the 'occupier' of the northern Six Counties, which would antagonise Republicans and possibly provoke renewed civil war.[19] Strict accordance with the protocols of neutrality was therefore backed by rigid censorship, which kept hidden from the Irish public not only secret pro-Allied actions but also the ideological dimensions of the global conflict.[20]

Most importantly, as the only Commonwealth country to remain aloof from the war, Éire was in this way able to assert its independence and sovereignty. Neutrality was, in Lee's phrase, the 'supreme assertion' of independence.[21] Fisk similarly notes that 'Dev' considered 'any tiny qualification of the principle of sovereignty a denial of that principle'.[22] Impending Allied victory forced changes in the way this principle was applied, however. Once Irish ports ceased to be regarded as vital to Allied prosecution of the war, the Americans in particular began to take a hard public line upon Ireland's neutrality. As the threat of German triumph receded, so too did the imperative of secret Allied-Irish co-operation in the spheres of security, surveillance and border control. In this changing context, the Irish objective of asserting sovereignty remained, but the means employed would become very different.

Between 1944 and 1947 a group of 'aliens' was used to assert this sovereignty vis-à-vis the Allies, but they were not minority nationalists. As Chapter Three discusses, the fate of Germans resident in Ireland – 'Hitler's colony in Éire',[23] as the Allies called them – was determined by a very public struggle between Dublin, Washington and London, in which de Valera sought to balance Irish sensitivities against the political liability of the individuals in question. This issue has been extensively examined by historians, but the largely simultaneous entry of fugitive Bretons, Flemings and Croats has not.[24] How, if at all, are these arrivals to be understood differently?

Postwar Axis fugitives

In addition to Germans on the run after 1945, there was a considerable number of collaborators from countries that had been occupied by, or allied to, the Third Reich, including French fascists, Dutch Nazis, Croatian Ustaše and Belgian Rexists. Many had supported Hitler's 'New Order', and had taken up the 'crusade' against communism either on the Eastern Front, or in their home countries, with a zeal comparable to any in Berlin. For those unable to flee to sympathetic destinations such as Spain or Argentina, the alternative was harsh vengeance at the hands of post-Liberation governments or the very Resistance fighters they had formerly hunted so ruthlessly. The term 'refugee' hangs awkwardly on such characters, connoting as it does flight from unjust persecution. As a Lithuanian exile in the US himself wondered, 'How many ran not from persecution but from justice?'[25] 'Fugitive' seems a more suitable term, although a 'refugee' is literally only 'one who seeks refuge'. These fugitives found asylum in a variety of countries – many of which, unlike Ireland, had actually declared war upon the Axis.

There was a further sub-stratum of Axis fugitive at this time. Embracing collaboration with Nazi Germany or its cohorts, their objectives differed from major collaborationist parties. These were members of nationalist movements in the ethnic minority regions of Europe, who collaborated in the hope of gaining independence under German aegis. They comprised a diverse range of views, from regionalists to autonomists to separatists, from conservative Catholic anti-communists to racists, anti-Semites and enthusiastic Nazis. Many found inspiration in the Irish struggle for nationhood, and had applied 'the old Sinn Féin formula' that the difficulty of their governing state – whether France, Belgium, Yugoslavia or the USSR – was their nationalist opportunity.[26] The collapse of this bargain with the forces of Nazism – and, in many cases, the animosity of their own compatriots – forced them into exile. This story, so much as it provides a background to those who found asylum in Ireland, is therefore one of defeat and execration; of those whose obsession with independence led them into accommodations with one of the most murderous regimes in history. The reasons behind their flight and why they should have chosen Ireland are complex and at times surprising; the motivations behind the Irish state's acceptance of them are perhaps more surprising still.

'Who better to grant asylum?'

An introductory article on the wartime Breton movement introduced me in 2002 to two Bretons: Alan Heusaff and Yann Goulet. These, in Doody's imperfect summation, had been 'granted asylum in Ireland and continued to lead militant Breton nationalist factions from exile'.[27] Brief mentions of exiled Bretons or others could be found in works of contemporary Irish history,[28] yet these, plus obituaries of exiles like Goulet, rarely explored the reasons why Ireland granted asylum.[29] Those few that ventured an explanation were qualified and uncertain. Farrell observes that de Valera was 'firm to the point of obtuseness on the question of political offenders', yet confines his analysis to the speculation that this was 'probably a reflection of [his] rigid interpretation of wartime neutrality'.[30] Keogh explores the issue of inter-departmental disputes concerning the rumoured arrival of Belgian collaborator Léon Degrelle.[31] Illuminating as this is regarding Irish attitudes toward Catholic 'proven anti-communists', Degrelle never actually travelled to Ireland, as Keogh recognises. The phenomenon of asylum for European minorities appeared otherwise to be almost entirely unstudied. The implication seemed to be that this asylum was in some way axiomatic; that Ireland was a logical refuge for foreign nationalists. This in turn was bolstered by Ireland's history of struggle, diaspora and exile, and indeed its own experience of nationalist 'collaboration' from the Wild Geese in French and Spanish service to Roger Casement's 'Irish Legion' in German POW camps of the First World War. As the only Western European state born of nationalist armed struggle in the twentieth century, the presumption appeared to be that Ireland was in some way predisposed to sympathy for those who sought to emulate that struggle. 'Who better to grant them asylum?' commented a professor at the University of Melbourne upon learning of my nascent research project. I soon learnt he was not alone in presuming Ireland held a conception of its revolutionary heritage that, while perhaps not explicitly encouraging of foreign nationalist movements, would at the very least welcome their fugitives on the basis of nationalistic sympathy and solidarity.

Pan-Celticist historiography

From the opposite side of the Celtic Sea, much Breton nationalist historiography carries identical assumptions. There is a wealth of literature in French examining the inspiration Breton nationalists found in the Easter Rising of 1916, the establishment of the Irish Free State in 1922, and the general concept of Irish self-determination. Olier Mordrel, one-time second-in-command of the PNB and editor of its journal *Breiz Atao* (Brittany Forever), traced bullet holes in the walls of public buildings during a pilgrimage to Dublin in 1925 and fantasised with his comrades about creating a Breton analogue to the Rising: 'A thousand times we went to sleep dreaming of being in combat at the General Post Office in Rennes, transformed into a *blockhaus,* and we slept happily.'[32] *Breiz Atao*, on the nineteenth anniversary of Easter 1916, celebrated Irish independence and established an explicit connection between it and Breton nationalist aspirations. Bretons saw in the Irish Free State, it claimed, a 'new sun shining over the land of Brittany'.[33]

Perhaps because of this, the attention paid by Breton historians to the question of Irish asylum is considerably greater than that paid by Irish scholars themselves – even after *Ireland's Nazis*. With few exceptions, however, most accounts cease at the point of flight. The admission of Bretons to Ireland is frequently presented without analysis, again implying its axiomatic character.[34] Implicit in this historiography, therefore, is a pan-Celticist interpretation of Ireland's revolutionary heritage and its attitude to foreign struggles; a Breton expectation of fraternity projected upon the Irish state. Lebesque is most explicit in this view, asserting that militants of the Bezen Perrot were immediately 'furnished with passports' in postwar Ireland owing to 'interceltic solidarity'.[35]

The most overt assertion in English of the role of pan-Celticism is to be found, perhaps unsurprisingly, in a history of pan-Celticism itself. Although Ellis' *The Celtic Dawn* accentuates the pan-Celtic credentials of both de Valera and Interparty External Affairs Minister Seán MacBride, it does acknowledge there was generally more inspiration than assistance flowing from Dublin to the other countries of the Celtic Fringe. Pan-Celticist sentiments both in that region and in the broader Irish diaspora were also exploited for domestic political ends. Conradh na Gaeilge (The Gaelic League) actually opposed pan-Celticism for nationalistic reasons, Ellis notes, and its utility in Ireland had always been limited. In fact, many saw it as a diversion from nationalism.[36]

The truly significant inter-Celtic exchange in the early twentieth century was in fact between the Welsh and Breton movements. As Chapter Four discusses, the assistance for fugitive Bretons provided by Welsh activists of Plaid Cymru (the Party of Wales) contrasts starkly with Irish state attitudes, and this assistance had significant impact upon the Breton flight to Ireland.

The postwar influx of Bretons, combined with their own conceptions of Celtic fraternity and the literature implying their ready acceptance by the Irish state, has contributed to the presumption that pan-Celticism determined asylum policy. This interpretation has influenced English-language sources as well, including Scottish nationalist and Irish Republican literature. The presence of high-profile Bretons such as Goulet, Fouéré, the 'physical force' extremist Célestin Lainé and others serves to heighten this perception, as does the topic's neglect in Irish academic research.

In reality, the allure of Ireland as a preferred destination for Breton fugitives is overstated, as Chapter Five details. Even so, for the two dozen or so who did gain entry, there is no doubt that the country's revolutionary heritage (as they understood it) was a prime factor in their election to flee there. But did that heritage or anything like it determine Irish acceptance of them?

Revolutionary heritage and asylum

Asylum has always been a political tool. It may be used to shelter dissidents from a rival state for political advantage. More broadly, it can assert aspects of identity, especially a revolutionary heritage. Revolutionary France granted citizenship to European republicans in the late eighteenth century (including Irishmen), and again in 1958 guaranteed asylum to any refugee 'persecuted for his activities in the cause of freedom'. Cuba famously sheltered fugitive members of Western Hemisphere revolutionary movements, and Article 38 of the Fundamental Law of the USSR declared in 1977 Moscow's willingness to afford 'the right of asylum to foreigners persecuted for upholding the interests of working people [...] or for participation in a revolutionary and national liberation movement'.[37] In the young state of East Timor, refusing asylum to any member of a foreign national liberation movement would likewise be unconstitutional.[38]

'Asylum' connotes the shelter of persecuted innocents, but the Institute of International Law defined it in 1950 as simply 'the protection accorded by a State [...] to an individual who comes to seek it.' While those persecuted on the grounds of race, ethnicity or religion commonly become refugees, the term equally encompasses those who refuse to live under a particular form of government, or those accused of offences of a political character who have fled abroad. Before the 1951 UN Convention on the Status of Refugees and the 1954 Caracas Convention on Territorial Asylum, the 'right of asylum' under international law was simply the prerogative of states to grant or deny it as they saw fit.[39]

When Irish governments sheltered foreign nationalists they were therefore acting within international law. But were they consciously expressing a revolutionary heritage? The Irish struggle always had wider implications for the British, who kept a nervous eye upon India in particular.[40] There is some emerging literature on the inspiration Indian nationalists derived from the Irish experience,[41] yet surprisingly little investigating Irish attitudes toward those movements most likely to find encouragement in Irish statehood. This lack of awareness of the international aspects of their struggle was recognised by Hubert Butler. Most Irish nationalists, he noted, were 'insular'. Significantly, when he himself professed solidarity on a nationalistic basis it was not with European minority movements but with the 'Successor States' of Central and Eastern Europe after 1918.[42]

The fact that Éire was governed during the Emergency by a surviving commandant of the Easter Rising and former head of anti-Treaty forces in the Civil War also contributes to the assumption that sympathy for exiled nationalists could be expected in official circles. 'Dev', fellow cabinet members such as Frank Aiken – even their successor Seán MacBride – had themselves known imprisonment or exile in the name of nationalist struggle. But did this necessarily determine their formulation of policy once at the helm of state, especially at the beginning of the Cold War? And if pan-Celticism was the major determinant, why was an equal number of nationalists admitted from Flanders, Croatia and other non-Celtic regions?

Catholic anti-communism

By the time the Interparty government took power in February 1948, Dublin was looking towards the Vatican as never before. One of the first actions of the new government in that polarising atmosphere of the early Cold War was to profess its 'filial loyalty' to the Holy Father.[43] Perhaps Butler, as a Protestant and Republican, was less able to perceive that there were indeed profound international aspects to Irish nationalism, but they were not concerned with 'Successor States', Celts nor minority movements. What appealed to Irish sympathy was Catholicism, and nothing guaranteed solidarity more than the threat posed by a force diametrically opposed to its teachings and power. That force was communism.

The influence of Catholic anti-communism upon Irish international relations in the early postwar period is a subject of considerable research. In the asylum sphere, elements of the attitude toward putative or actual applications from fascistic, anti-communist figures have been examined, including prominent cases like those of Degrelle, Oswald Mosley and Otto Strasser. Hubert Butler also examined Irish attitudes to the postwar repression of Catholic identity in Croatia and Hungary, and traced the entry into Ireland of the former Interior Minister of the Croatian Axis puppet state, Andrija Artuković.

Ireland's identity as a profoundly Catholic country, professing allegiance both to the Vatican and the West in the burgeoning stand-off with the Eastern Bloc, forms the backdrop for most asylum entries. Keogh especially has researched how anti-Semitism in Ireland contributed to a discriminatory asylum posture regarding Jewish refugees. Conversely, Dublin's attitude towards 'proven anti-communists' was one in which their wartime actions were elided or ignored in the name of combating the 'greater evil' of communism. Partition may have militated against Irish alliance with Britain in the North Atlantic Treaty Organisation – just as it had in 1939 – but Irish governments left little doubt in the minds of diplomatic observers as to which side the country would support in any future conflict.

Just like many of its wartime actions, Irish postwar asylum was in many ways in secret accord with the Western Allies. This study places the various postwar escape routes to Ireland within the corpus of literature on the 'Ratline' and other networks that operated with the complicity of the Catholic Church and Allied intelligence services. It argues that Irish involvement in these networks was part of an international Catholic enterprise fuelled by anti-communism; a collusion between the Vatican, Washington and London designed to stymie the Soviet march in the East and the rise of communist parties in the West. How precisely did these networks operate, and who employed them? Who assisted the fugitives at both Continental and Irish ends of the line? Employing first-hand accounts from many of the fugitives themselves, this study adds an important chapter to the story of Axis escape networks and foreign complicity in them.

As historical adviser for *Ireland's Nazis*, I argued that Catholic anti-communism should receive the prime focus, and in this regard the documentary series successfully contextualised Ireland's role within that grander ideological enterprise. There was, however, insufficient contextualisation in other areas. Interestingly, the programmes did not address pan-Celticist interpretations nor those based upon presumed nationalistic sympathy, which only underscored the fact that Irish conceptions of foreign struggles rarely operate upon these bases. More importantly, while there was some discussion of wartime neutrality, there was no attempt to examine Dublin's attitude toward foreign nationalists resident *during* the Emergency itself. Had there been, commentators such as Harris may have found it difficult to explain how supposed Irish sympathy for the Axis manifested itself only *after* German defeat.

This story begins, therefore, during the Emergency. The attitude of the Irish government towards the first significant influx of foreign nationalist exiles reveals the extent to which relations with Britain took precedence over supposed anti-Allied or pan-Celtic 'sympathies'. These exiles came not from Catholic Brittany nor Flanders under Nazi occupation, but significantly closer to home.

CHAPTER 1

The unwelcome brothers: Scottish nationalists in Irish exile during the Emergency

SHORTLY AFTER THE OUTBREAK of war in September 1939, the yacht *Ron Bhan* put in at the Irish town of Athlone. On board was a family of sorts: a striking man of theatrical bearing, his wife, sister and adult daughter. The party claimed they were on their way to the French Riviera, but the outbreak of hostilities had obliged them to put into the Shannon.[1]

As British subjects, their arrival elicited only passing interest. They enjoyed a legal right to reside in Éire, and would not have to report regularly to the Garda Síochána (the Irish police), as other foreigners were required to do under the provisions of the Aliens Act (1935).[2] The family bought a little cottage at Bray, and a second residence where the man 'resided with his entourage for various periods'.[3] It seemed a harmless idyll – a wealthy British family waiting out the war in sleepy, neutral Ireland. Yet as the war progressed and the threat of invasion frayed nerves in Dublin, both G2 and the Garda determined to have a closer look at their guests' backgrounds and activities. Then came some disturbing reports.

He 'hopes to do for Scotland what Padraig Pearse did for Ireland,' reported G2 in November 1940. Even the *Ron Bhan* had been procured 'to do in Scotland what Erskine Childers did in Howth'.[4] The man in question went by the name of Ronald MacDonald Douglas, and he was a well-known militant Scottish nationalist.

Douglas was one of several Scots militants who fled to Ireland on the eve of the Second World War. Others were in the country already, legacy of their participation in the War of Independence and Civil War. While they do not constitute a mass migration or diaspora – the total number of such militants was probably less than a dozen – those involved were among the major advocates of 'physical force' nationalism at a time when the mainstream Scottish National Party was in crisis over its attitude to conscription and the defeat of fascism. These individuals, and their reasons for decamping to Éire, reveal much about the inspiration Scots nationalists found in the Irish fight for independence. Conversely, Irish records concerning these exiles reveal a great deal about the security relationship between Dublin and London. This had significant impact upon Irish attitudes toward those Scots engaged (as they saw it) in a struggle inspired by their wartime hosts. For, although they comprised the first significant influx of foreign nationalists to the independent Irish state, the presence and activities of these militants produced not solidarity and sympathy, but alarm and disquiet.

Perhaps more than other cases of minority nationalist flight to Ireland, the literature regarding exiled Scots is scant indeed. What few mentions exist fail entirely to explore Irish state attitudes. Solange and Christian Gras write simply that 'some members [of the SNP] went to Ireland once war was declared.' [5] The Scottish nationalist group Siol nan Gaidheal (Race of the Gaels) likewise limits its discussion of Douglas' exile to the observation that he 'slipped over to Ireland where he was to stay for over thirty years.' [6] The implication is that the Irish government must have looked at least with toleration upon these fugitive Gaelic militants. The reality, however, was one in which an avowed Scottish 'incorruptible republican nationalist and enemy of the British Empire'[7] could cause as much consternation in Dublin as he did in London and Edinburgh.

In some cases these Scots militants had maintained subversive contacts in Ireland for many years. But for all of them it was their reaction to policy decisions of the British government that forced them on the path to ultimate exile. From their perspective, the most crucial of these took place in the wake of the German invasion of Poland in 1939.

Scottish nationalism in 1939

In December of that year, the SNP held a conference to determine its attitude to the war declared three months earlier. The central question for party members was whether London had the right to declare hostilities and conscript Scots without the approval of a Scottish parliament. Some had earlier declared 'to refuse to serve with any section of the Crown forces until the programme of the SNP has been fulfilled.' [8] Other groups such as the Democratic Scottish Self-Government Organisation (formed in 1933 by the independent nationalist Wendy Wood), maintained that conscription without the assent of such a parliament was in violation of the Treaty of Union.[9] Belief that the Treaty had been abrogated by England was a common view in nationalist circles: Oliver Brown, an SNP propagandist, provocatively condemned 'the *Anschluss* of 1707, whereby the former nation of Scotland was incorporated into the English *Reich*'.[10]

Realising their stance on conscription was at odds with Scottish public opinion, the SNP, as Finlay explains, began 'desperately seeking a strategy which would free them from the contradictions of their previous policies.' As war neared in May 1939 the party relaxed its stance, provided that conscripts were used only for the defence of Britain.[11] This was moderated again in October in a manifesto that declared Scotland's willingness to fight alongside England for ideals appealing to the Scottish people.[12] Finally, at the December conference, the SNP settled upon a policy of 'acquiescence' in the war, arguing that Germany had trampled on the freedom of three small nations already, and that a free Scotland would 'inevitably' have declared war against it anyway.[13]

Each concession precipitated defections from the party and the foundation of splinter movements. The Scottish Neutrality League maintained solid opposition to British conscription, charging that 'England would fight to the last Scot' in the coming conflict. Indeed, it is largely through loss of members, Webb observes, that the SNP became a more ideologically streamlined party.[14] Formed from a union of the radical National Party of Scotland and the aristocratic Scottish Party in 1934, the SNP soon began shedding members on both its right and left wings. It counted only 2,000 members in 1939.[15] 'You'd expel Wallace!', Wendy Wood is said to have exclaimed after a divisive party meeting.[16] 'I bitterly regret the day when I compromised the unity of my party by admitting a second member,' Oliver Brown drily remarked.[17]

'Acquiescence' in the war, and the various expulsions and defections it precipitated, marginalised dissenters in the Scottish movement. Given that the general public largely ignored the SNP's view on the war, anyway, it is not difficult to estimate the level of support more radical stances commanded.

These coalesced around the concept of objection to military service. While some dissenting nationalists were pacifists in a manner similar to that found in the Welsh movement, many more supported the line championed by Douglas Young, a tutor in Greek at the University of Aberdeen and chairman of his local SNP branch. Young held to the original line on conscription, insisting only a Scottish parliament could order Scots to war or to obey 'industrial conscription' laws drafting workers into English industry. The December 1939 conference attempted to assuage this tendency by resolving that the definition of conscientious objection should be broadened to include 'profound political conviction',[18] but the British government would not recognise this defence. Young disaffiliated his branch from the party once the mainstream line began to moderate.[19]

Other tendencies were at play in the margins of Scottish nationalism at this time. Militant nationalists may have shared Young's conviction regarding conscription, but their beliefs did not necessarily contain themselves to conscientious objection. As with many minority nationalist movements of the inter-war period, the rise of ideologies such as communism, fascism and Nazism excited interest and exerted influence upon Scottish nationalism. Of course, 'great power' nationalism was not immune to these influences either, as the rise of Mosley's British Union of Fascists attests.

But as a burgeoning force dedicated to reorganisation of the European order – especially the boundaries and ethnic composition of nation-states – fascism and Nazism exerted considerable attraction in minority nationalist circles. 'Mussolini points the way,' declared the *Scots Independent* in 1929.[20] *Volkisch* notions likewise held appeal for nationalists struggling to define their particularism on linguistic lines, which were of low or diminishing relevance to most of their compatriots. Ideas of 'Celtic race' allowed nationalists like Ruairidh Erskine to turn from Gaelic language revival among the elite to a broader appeal including the 'English-speaking Celt' of the Lowlands.[21] Such 'blood and soil' tendencies in Scottish nationalism did not go without notice in the intelligence services of Britain's major Continental rival.[22]

In 1936 and 1937, Dr Gerhard von Tevenar of the German Society of Celtic Studies visited Scotland as part of a tour of the Celtic Fringe. Von Tevenar could already boast of links with the PNB, and was on close terms with some of its leaders.[23] He also enjoyed a close relationship with Admiral Wilhelm Canaris, head of the Abwehr (German military intelligence), owing to the fact that he was employed by its Second Department, responsible for 'utilis[ing] indigenous subversive movements' in foreign countries for German ends.[24] While in Scotland he introduced himself to SNP members on the pretext he was researching a thesis on Celtic culture.[25] Once welcomed into party counsels, he reportedly engaged in confidential discussions with a view to enlisting support in the coming struggle against Britain.[26]

The German found few co-conspirators in Scotland.[27] Many nationalists were not only repelled by the notion of Nazi assistance, but realised such contacts could be exploited by British intelligence in its effort to discredit them. 'The temper of our own people was strongly opposed to Nazism [...] and if the Scottish National Party were to take any stand which laid us open to the charge of being lukewarm in the cause of European freedom we should lose all chance of increasing our strength,' wrote SNP secretary John MacCormick.[28]

The nearly unanimous rejection of German approaches did not mean all nationalists rejected militancy. There was a much closer source of inspiration in anti-British struggle: one that had engaged in successful armed conflict with the British state, with which numbers of Scots had directly participated. For many marginalised militants, Ireland was the most powerful influence.

Scottish nationalism and the Irish

The SNP was, as noted, an amalgam of radicals and moderates dating from 1934. By the mid-1930s, however, the party was 'sliding toward [...] anti-Catholic racism'.[29] This owed as much to nativist reaction to Irish immigration as it did to the origins of the upper-class SP. While the NPS owed its origin to Irish-inspired groups, the SP represented the social elite of nationalism,[30] and was heavily influenced by the Church of Scotland. As such, it viewed Irish immigration as a threat to Scottish Protestant mores, especially as the Catholic vote was gravitating to Labour.[31] After the merger, the former activists of the NPS, who had been more sympathetic to pan-Celticist and Irish Republican ideas,[32] soon realised their position was being marginalised by a Protestant backlash among ordinary Scots, who were better represented by the SP wing. This backlash was sectarian – not nationalist – in character,[33] increasing adherence to Unionist parties and rendering the NPS faction's 'Free State, Sinn Féin' elements a profound electoral liability. What at first appeared an unlikely alliance became a more streamlined party,[34] not only through defections, but also through a retreat from radicalism by most of the NPS wing. As Marr observes, 'Any attempt to move the SNP to the mainstream right would sooner or later [have] come up against the Irish question.'[35]

Of course, many former NPS activists held to their pan-Celticist views. Hugh MacDiarmid welcomed Irish immigration as a means of sustaining 'the ancient Gaelic commonwealth'.[36] But increasingly those who professed commonalities with Ireland were seen as out of touch with contemporary Scots, and those who sought to emulate the Free State solution became even more marginalised within the SNP. This was best exemplified by the appearance of a section entitled 'The Green Terror' within an SNP pamphlet of 1937, in which Nationalists 'sympathised' with the average Scot in his fear that 'Scotsmen will be dispossessed of their own country by immigrants and their children.'[37] Regulation of Irish immigration was therefore a nationalist issue, and one with which England, with its strictly materialist concerns, could not be trusted. It is also worthy of note that the SNP disdained notions of Gaelic kinship:

> It is certain that, unless measures are taken to arrest and control immigration and to put into the hands of the Scottish people the key to the racial destiny of their country, there will inevitably be a race-conflict of the most bitter kind.[38]

Many nationalists had therefore been marginalised by the SNP by the time war was declared and the party adopted its 'acquiescent' attitude in December 1939. Objectors had been sidelined or expelled as the average Scot expressed support for war against Hitler; and those looking to Éire were reviled in a climate of sectarian animosity towards Irish Catholic immigrants, to which the

SNP inevitably pandered. These marginalised, radical, Sinn Féin-inspired nationalists obviously looked to Éire as a logical place of refuge. Whether the Irish authorities would look upon them with the same sympathy remained to be seen.

Actor on the margins: Ronald MacDonald Douglas

'WOOD called DOUGLAS an English spy and completely lost control of herself. DOUGLAS in turn attacked her and called her a "dangerous woman".' So reads a Special Branch report on a meeting of the Scottish Defence Force on 4 October 1933. Turning to the forty-odd members present for support:

> DOUGLAS, who in his appeal engaged in a virulent attack on England, eventually burst into tears, which induced the majority to exclaim emotionally: 'A Douglas! A Douglas! A Douglas!' (this having reference to ancient history).

Three months earlier in Glasgow, when she first introduced him to DSSO members and 'leading officials of the Irish republican movement in Scotland', no-one could have guessed that Wendy Wood's association with Ronald MacDonald Douglas would end in tears. Wood's organisation, which its bulletin *Smeddum* declared was not communist, did 'not recognise the so-called National Party' and was 'most emphatically not Fascist!', did however stand for 'complete separation from England and the creation of a workers' state with an economic policy definitely anti-capitalist'. It also rejected London's right to conscript Scots for foreign wars. Owing to this left nationalist position DSSO members had been threatened by both communists and Protestant 'Billy Boys', but Wood assured members they 'will soon have a remedy for these political gangsters'. She called for volunteers to effect this plan: men who 'must be prepared to go out and do what Ireland has done'. This force already had a leader, she said. With this, Douglas was introduced to the gathering. Resplendent in Mackenzie tartan kilt, he predicted war with England 'in a year or two'. 'Nothing will be got from England without fighting for it,' he intoned, instancing, once again, the case of Ireland.[39]

Douglas' commitment to pan-Gaelic ideas would become well known. In 1936 he published *The Irish book: a miscellany of facts and fancies, folklore and fragments, poems and prose to do with Ireland and her people.* It was not a heavyweight political treatise on the Irish model of national liberation, as its cumbersome title indicates. In structure it followed the light, folkish 'miscellany' the author had perfected in *The Scottish book,* published the previous year. But the reader needed to look no further than the foreword to discern Douglas' political sympathies and vision for Scotland:

> To do whatever I can in my small way to re-unite in some fashion the related but severed peoples of Ireland and Scotland is one of the ardent desires of my life.

Waxing lyrical, Douglas imagined fashioning a literary 'claymor' in the service of this pan-Celtic goal:

> the names of Éire and Alba close entwined in the metal of its hilt, and it engraved in the Gaelic with 'Repeal the Union' on the one side of its blade, and with 'Remember Arbroath' on the other.[40]

Following the break with Wood, Douglas declared he would establish a new political organisation to complement the fighting arm of which he was leader. Launching it, Douglas 'quoted Irish republican literature' and announced, 'As the Scottish Defence Force is being modelled on the lines of the Irish Republican Army a "political" movement, similar to Sinn Féin, has been started. It is called the Scottish Independence Movement.' He then distributed cards which declared the movement's non-sectarian nature, and (oddly for a 'political' movement) the fact that it was 'entirely non-political'.

Attention was paid by the Special Branch to those in the SDF with IRA or other radical connections. An 'advocate of force' named Clark, an IRA member named McQuillan and a former communist named Melville were singled out, as it was learned they were planning to acquire arms. 'It is understood that the arms in contemplation will be brought from Ireland.' A report on an SDF route march at Strathblane early in 1934 noted the absence of another 'officer', Duncan McDougal, 'who, it was learned, was due to leave for Ireland the following day'. Douglas' attire was again noteworthy on this occasion, having traded his kilt for a 'military officer's tunic, dyed green, and Sam Browne belt'.[41]

Cutting a fine figure was second nature to Douglas. Not only was he a produced playwright on top of his political talents, he had also reportedly trod the boards with John Gielgud and Claude Rains.[42] No doubt this added dramatic flair to his political meetings. 'You are a spy. Clear out of this hall or I'll fling you through the window!' he threatened a man at an SDF meeting at Holm Street, Glasgow. Protesting 'treachery' he promptly resigned as the movement's leader, but turned up again as its 'Commandant-General' the following month.[43]

SNG considers the SDF 'a network of highly motivated Scots' ready to fight for independence. Unfortunately (as Special Branch reports confirm), 'their small force was infiltrated [...] and they were smashed before they had their opportunity to make history.' [44] In reality, intelligence reports concluded that the SDF was of 'little or no importance' and was, for example, 'practically non-existent' in Edinburgh; in other words, outside the Irish Catholic areas of Glasgow where most meetings took place. The Procurator-Fiscal at Edinburgh concluded there were no grounds for action as the movement was too small and would only profit from the exposure.[45] It was the group's links to the IRA that concerned British authorities.

Over the sea to Éire

The events leading to Douglas' flight to Ireland in 1939 are disputed. For SNG, the story begins after his split from the DSSO and the creation of his new Scottish Independence Movement. Despite his supposed Irish Republican connections and their vaunted arms sources, SNG has Douglas in Geneva late in 1935 on a secret ordnance-buying trip. This, like most of his nationalist ventures, was funded by his 'personal fortune'.[46] This was not the last time Douglas' financial affairs would be of significance.

According to SNG, Douglas was snatched by 'British/English' agents in Switzerland, taken to a 'safe house' and there beaten 'quite efficiently'. His assailants took pains to break his fingers, suggesting to him that this was 'specifically to lessen his enthusiasm for pulling triggers'.[47]

Carn, the journal of the Celtic League, takes up the tale in its 1984 obituary of Douglas. Again in Alpine Europe in 1938, Douglas accepted an invitation to visit the Brown House, Nazi headquarters in Munich, where he met Rudolf Hess. On his journey back to Scotland he was reportedly tailed by unnamed (but presumably 'British/English') agents, 'and his movements subsequently closely watched'.[48]

Both *Carn* and SNG concur that a legal case was then brought against Douglas. The former contends this was on the basis of evidence provided by an 'agent provocateur' (perhaps the author of the Special Branch reports detailed above) within the SDF. SNG is more precise: the charge was high treason, punishable by death.[49] Both are certain that the authorities were concerned by Douglas' alleged Nazi connections: the audience with Hess in Munich and the visits by von Tevenar. They were even aware of a brief connection with Mosley's BUF. Douglas had reportedly abandoned links with the BUF several years before,[50] and Wood at least was arrested on one occasion for attempting to disrupt a Blackshirt rally in Edinburgh.[51] But it seemed the authorities felt there was still enough in the way of compromising fascist connections to have Douglas sent to 'the concentration camp on the Isle of Man'[52] for those harbouring Nazi sympathies, even if the other charges should be unproven.

According to SNG, the Lord Advocate of Scotland paid Douglas a visit while on remand. Not wanting to create a Scottish nationalist martyr at a time when 'certain tensions' were mounting, it would be better if Douglas went into exile, he explained. The Lord Advocate would arrange for his release pending further investigation into the charge of high treason. Douglas should take advantage of this opportunity if he was keen to avoid the alternative. He did as suggested and 'slipped over to Ireland'.[53]

For *Carn,* the story is rather different. The prosecution dropped their case against the SDF leader for lack of evidence, but his advocate Harald Leslie nonetheless advised his client to flee to Ireland rather than risk being interned in the aforementioned Manx camp. Douglas reportedly accepted this 'bad advice'. He is said to have regretted this action, realising he should have 'stayed in Scotland and fought the issue to the bitter end'.[54]

Divergent though these accounts are, both are united in their silence regarding the Irish state's attitude to their fugitive guest, his activities in Ireland, and indeed upon each and every aspect of his extended stay in this supposedly fraternal Celtic haven. Both move directly from Douglas' flight to Ireland to his later re-entry to Britain, as if to suggest Irish exile was as unproblematic as it was axiomatic, the Irish authorities figuring not at all in the equation other than to stamp cheerfully and unquestioningly the passports of fugitive Celtic militants. Available evidence from the Emergency period paints rather a different picture of Irish state attitudes.

'His deportation is recommended'

'He is clearly an adventurer and intriguer and potentially dangerous, and his deportation is recommended,' wrote Colonel Liam Archer of G2 in a report to the Garda dated 27 November 1940. Douglas' reported avowal of Pearse and Childers as revolutionary models might be thought complimentary to his Irish hosts, but the sentiment was clearly not appreciated. There was to be no revolutionary sympathy or Celtic solidarity forthcoming from Irish intelligence. Indeed, for G2, Douglas' Scottish nationalism was 'the sole' reason he warranted surveillance, owing to the 'probability of his enthusiasm in this connection linking him up with subversive organisations in this country.' The prospect of an IRA-backed Scottish rising supplied from Ireland while Britain faced Nazi invasion clearly sent alarm bells ringing in Dublin. Information was therefore desperately sought (they were fast becoming inseparable threats in G2's view) on Douglas' 'Fascist-IRA activities'.

Yet Douglas had done nothing illegal. The authorities were monitoring his mail and telephone calls, but had to concede it was 'difficult to form any conclusions as to his possible subversive activities'. Despite his entourage having reportedly 'taken up the Scots cause', Douglas had not, by the time of a major G2 report of 13 September 1944, undertaken one activity or produced one publication in its support. The sole incriminating incident had been in 1940, when

Douglas funded the defence in Scotland of one Matthew Somerville, who had been charged with larceny of gelignite supposedly on behalf of the IRA. Douglas had given Somerville's lawyer £80 when the latter visited Ireland. This was not sufficient to convict Douglas of subversive activities and deport him, as the Department of Justice wanted. His private affairs were not beyond investigation, either, and there were allegations concerning the real nature of his relationships with the women of his household. If he was not an active subversive, G2 reasoned, he was, at the very least, an 'immoral adventurer'. Among other things, it was noted that the money made available for Somerville's defence had been 'in the form of a cheque drawn by Frances MacLennon' – supposedly Douglas' sister – leading to questions as to whether Douglas was not exploiting the women's Scottish nationalist fervour to 'extract' funds from them.[55]

Ronald MacDonald Douglas wasn't even his real name, reported G2, but the stage name of one Ronald Edmonston. He was not unknown in Ireland, having run a theatre in Dún Laoghaire for two years from 1930. Demonstrating their ignorance of Scottish politics, G2 also doubted his nationalist bona fides, as he seemed to have 'no connection' with the SNP, nor did the party 'have [any] use for Douglas.' Most significantly, G2 contended he was twice arrested for breaches of the peace in Inverness in the late 1930s – the latter incident, in 1938, for stabbing a Royal Air Force officer with a dirk. He was then remanded in the care of a mental specialist for seven months in Edinburgh, coming to Ireland 'following his residence at the nursing home'.[56] While strikingly different to the SNG and *Carn* accounts, in this the British state still offered something of a deal to Douglas: '[T]he attitude of the Scottish Authorities toward him at the time appeared to be that they would be glad if he stayed out of Scotland.'[57]

Widening suspicions: Colm MacClean

Similar material was gathered on the potential threats posed by other Scots in Ireland at this time. Colm MacClean was working at Clonmel Industries when he became of interest to G2.[58] He was known as a Scottish nationalist, although again not a member of the SNP, but of 'the younger University Scot. [*sic*] Gaelic group'. A native of 'one of the islands' and fluent in Gaelic, MacClean appeared in Ireland in 1939 'principally to avoid conscription', according to G2's informant.[59] Although this informant 'never heard him discuss any subjects of interest to us' and he expressed no affiliation as far as Irish politics were concerned, MacClean appears to have been monitored owing simply to his connections and a presumption that he was 'as "Nationalist" as this country would care [him] to be'.

The manager at Clonmel Industries was Seamus Horan, himself suspected of IRA affiliations, somewhat assuaged by his reported conversion to Fianna Fáil. By 1944 MacClean was also known to be friendly with members of the local branch of Ailtirí na h-Aiséirí (Architects of the Resurrection), but his level of interest in that fascistic, pro-German organisation was unknown. To complete the array of potential threats, MacClean's brother, a poet, was known to be 'an avowed Communist'.

'Actively in touch with the Scottish Nationalist movement', G2 further noted that MacClean, born into a Presbyterian family 'of the extreme conservative type', had converted to Catholicism since his arrival. This confessional choice would itself have marginalised him from mainstream Scottish nationalism. Even so, MacClean was moved to remark to G2's informant in March 1943 that 'things were going well in Scotland';[60] probably a reference to the reinvigoration of the SNP under Douglas Young.

Dublin takes action: Duncan McDougal

Reflecting its importance in Scottish nationalism, conscription is a frequent theme in Irish surveillance reports. Duncan McDougal, it may be recalled, was the SDF officer whose absence was noted by the Special Branch at the Strathblane route march in 1934, owing to his imminent trip to Ireland. He turned up in Ireland again as a known associate of MacDonald Douglas, drawing commensurate G2 interest. McDougal had reportedly been arrested alongside Douglas in 1938 after the RAF officer was stabbed in Inverness, had come to Ireland the following year, and was even engaged to Douglas' daughter, Deirdre. G2, however, assessed his nationalist objection to British army service with rather unsympathetic scepticism:

> McDougal may have been a genuine Scottish Nationalist [...] and he has stated that it was against his principles to join the British Army. It is still open to question as to whether McDougal was genuine or merely dodging conscription.[61]

This was an interesting question for G2 to pose, as soon after his arrival McDougal had found gainful employment: he joined the First Battalion of the Irish army. Clearly he was no pacifist or anti-militarist. Was Irish military intelligence suggesting he was cravenly seeking to avoid action by joining their own armed forces? If so, G2 could have no argument with those Irish soldiers who deserted their posts to join the British army – as around 4,000 allegedly did.[62]

Notwithstanding their doubts regarding his opposition to conscription, the potential embarrassment posed by the Irish state arming and training a militant Scots nationalist with possible Republican connections was not lost on the military authorities. His connections to MacDonald Douglas were apparently enough to prompt action, even without hard evidence. Liam Archer took such action in November 1940, promising Patrick Carroll of the Garda that:

> In view of the character of MacDonald Douglas I have decided that we should get rid of Private McDougal of the 1st Battalion, who is associated with MacDonald Douglas in former reports.[63]

Connections to domestic subversives were viewed with concern by Irish authorities. The possibility that Scots nationalists might co-operate with these elements and co-ordinate efforts was an even greater danger, as such militants using Ireland as a base for attacks upon the UK at such a critical wartime juncture could clearly be employed as justification for British retribution, or even a *casus belli.*

Scots nationalist to Irish republican: George Kemp Scott

Such concerns persisted even beyond the Emergency era. The nationalist objection that brought George Kemp Scott to Ireland was still being questioned by G2 head Dan Bryan in 1949, who again remarked that he was one of those Scots who came 'ostensibly because their convictions would not allow them to fight for Great Britain, but, in the opinion of some, merely to avoid conscription.' Lacking hard evidence of IRA links, Bryan was however 'reliably informed' that in 'private discussions' following meetings of the Anti-Partition Organisation (an unofficial group of which Scott was secretary), 'he consistently advocates a policy of war against Northern Ireland' by means of guerrilla attacks that would broaden to include both Irish states.[64] Scott, possibly another former SDF officer,[65] appears therefore to have abandoned immediate plans for his homeland's liberation and adopted purely Irish Republican objectives.

There was of course another source of potential subversion afoot in Ireland during the Emergency, and one that excited even greater alarm. As has been seen, the possibility that a Scottish nationalist might link up with local Republicans was frequent justification for close surveillance. The risk that either or both could connect with Nazi agents was potentially disastrous. Any person who had the potential to link these three subversive forces would doubtless be subjected to particularly close scrutiny; close enough that something especially significant would be revealed in their files.

'Something secret': Seamus Reader

It is known that G2 intercepted the shortwave transmissions of various diplomats in Dublin,[66] and kept foreign missions under visual surveillance.[67] This included the German, Italian, Japanese, Spanish and American legations, and Dan Bryan himself is reported to have undertaken a nightly 'mooch' past the residence of the Vichy French minister, Laforcade.[68] The Irish agency, fulfilling its unusually powerful brief of both domestic and foreign intelligence, also monitored postal communications, maintained press censorship and, with the assistance of the Garda, kept aliens under surveillance.[69] Information on the electronic surveillance of foreign missions is less known, but is gradually coming to light.[70]

On 1 December 1942, G2 logged the first of several 'rather mysterious telephone calls' to the German and Italian legations. The caller was at a public callbox and asking to speak to Herr Eduard Hempel, German Minister in Ireland. Questioned as to the nature of his call, the caller answered in German: 'Something secret.' He was promptly told to call at the legation in an ordinary way if he had legal business.

Nine days later, G2 logged another call. The same caller wanted to speak with the Chancellor. 'Half past five here,' was the reply without discussion. He called again at 5.36pm, wanting to know if 'somebody' was there. After querying, 'Is it safe?' he agreed to come as arranged. Finally, at 6.28pm – perhaps after the arranged meeting, or in lieu of it – the same caller rang again. The Chancellor was not there, he was told. Come back tomorrow morning at eleven.

In the German cases, the caller's name was heard as Schneider or Ryder. To the Italian legation, sometimes as Schneider, but most often as Raeder. Whoever it was sounded very nervous, supporting the notion that the suspect 'stood to lose much by involvement in any subversive activity'.[71] This made sense to G2, which had already formed a good idea of who the mystery caller might be: a Scottish-born messenger for Dáil Éireann (the lower house of parliament) and former IRA man by the name of Seamus Reader.

Known also as Jim Reeder[72] or Seamus Mac Ridire,[73] Reader was born in Glasgow in 1898 to an Irish mother.[74] He joined the Fianna Éireann, an Irish Republican youth organisation also known as the Sinn Féin Boy Scouts, in 1914.[75] The following year he made several trips to Ireland ferrying munitions for the use of Irish Volunteers in Belfast and Dublin.[76] He was unable to take part in the Easter Rising, having been arrested in Glasgow after a smuggling mission in January 1916, remaining in custody until an amnesty was declared the following Christmas Eve.[77] More than fifty Scottish-born militants (including James Connolly) did, however, take part in the rebellion. Many of these had first come to Ireland – as MacDonald Douglas and others would a generation later – to avoid conscription.[78] At the time of his arrest the 18-year-old Reader was already, according to Republican Sinn Féin, 'official representative to Dublin of the Scottish Divisional Board of the Irish Republican Brotherhood'.[79]

Reader soon got his chance to participate actively in the Irish struggle. By the time the War of Independence broke out in 1919, Reader was head of the Scottish Brigade of the IRA.[80] He continued the Republican struggle into the Civil War, being 'attached to the IRA up to the cessation of hostilities'.[81]

Reader's activities after the Civil War are less clear. Nan Milton claims he was one of the founders of the 'abortive' Scottish Republican Army, which attempted to replicate the Irish struggle in Scotland.[82] Little is known about this movement, and there is doubt it ever carried out meaningful operations. Another source has Reader as an officer of the 'Glasgow Brigade' of Douglas' SDF in the 1930s.[83] But by 1944, when G2 drew up an assessment of his case, Reader was living with his family at Howth Road, Dublin, supplementing his military pension with parliamentary messenger work. The Ceann Comhairle (parliamentary speaker) interviewed him personally for this position and was 'satisfied as to his bona fides'. G2 were not so easily assured. To them, Reader embodied a frightening array of threats: 'In addition to his old IRA activities, he is reported as having been associated with Scottish Nationalism, with the present day IRA and with Nazi organisations, and is stated to be an avowed pro-German.'

A Republican background like Reader's might have led to internment in the Curragh even without such connections. But G2 noted also that a certain W. Ahearne, thought to have been Commanding Officer of the IRA in Britain until 1927, had telephoned Reader in January 1942, seeking to renew their acquaintance. Evidently Reader's home telephone was being monitored as well. Reader had also been implicated as a potential go-between for Matthew Somerville's solicitor to obtain funds from MacDonald Douglas in 1940. And then there were sightings of Reader attending early meetings of the Cumann Náisiúnta,[84] also known as the Irish Friends of Germany – a tiny, Nazi-leaning group which attempted to recruit members of the Irish armed forces.[85] Fear of the Cumann's influence via this connection may have contributed to Liam Archer's recommendation that Duncan McDougal be discharged from the service.

And then of course there were the 'mysterious telephone calls' to Axis legations by a German-speaker with a name similar to Reader's. G2 knew of his maternal ancestry and his pan-Celtic sympathies. They also knew his father was German, and that the family name had originally been either Roeder or Raeder. Could this paternal influence not also lead to 'avowed pro-German' sympathies? G2 was not sure, but extremely nervous:

> Reader is reputed to be very deep and cunning and is generally somewhat of a mystery man. It seems on the face of it that he has so much to lose that he would be unlikely to indulge in

any subversive activity but the information available regarding him is hardly reassuring and seems to establish him as a worthy subject of future attention.[86]

Meanwhile in Scotland: the police raids of May 1941

London, too, claimed the potential of Scottish nationalism linking up with German intelligence was a serious security threat. In 1941, assisted by SNP secretary John MacCormick,[87] the police raided premises associated with the 'extremist' United Scotland Movement, leading to minor charges against several but a month's preventative detention under Defence Regulation 18B for its leader, Arthur Donaldson.[88] 'That is because Donaldson, like other Quislings, uses a local Home Rule movement as the basis of his subversive activities,' explained the Crown Office.[89]

Authorities also targeted the Scottish Socialist (1940) Party, founded by Jem Wheeler, another former SDF man.[90] The maverick tutor in Greek, Douglas Young, was hauled from his bed, as was Roland Muirhead, honorary president of the SNP.[91] Of particular interest were members of the Nationalist Mutual Aid Committee,[92] which aimed to assist 'Nationalists who are in straits as the result of war conditions, such as Nationalist objectors and their dependents'. Among the incriminating items unearthed during searches were posters declaring 'No national service until Scotland gets Home Rule'; fascist and Nazi propaganda and correspondence, including a letter Muirhead had allegedly sent to the Abwehr agent von Tevenar before the war; and a copy of Dorothy Macardle's *The Irish Republic*.[93] One Iain Haig had authored the only overtly seditious item found: a letter to his nationalist objector friend, George Hay, in which he allegedly stated, 'I wish more than ever now that Germany would win this war and create a hell of a change in this bloody country.'[94]

A member of the SSP claimed authorities had been anxious to 'discover the extent of our associations with the Irish and Indian National Movements.'[95] But perhaps the most significant find was evidence of a network dedicated to assisting nationalist objectors evade military service. A map indicating hide-outs at 'various places in Argyllshire and Perthshire' had been found at the home of one Walter Ross, leading to the subsequent arrest of the fugitive George Hay. But the most important evidence had been found among Muirhead's papers, in a subfile entitled 'Conscientious Objectors Assisted'. Objectors were not only being helped to hide in Scotland – 'Muirhead has, at least, assisted one person in obtaining a passport to enable him to travel to Ireland for the purpose of evading military service.'[96] Muirhead stated that he had 'no alternative but to assist [objectors] in their stand against conscription', as the SNP had resolved to oppose it in 1937. Even if the party had since reversed that decision, it was still 'virtually responsible for the attitude taken up by these young persons'.[97] The SNP refused to denounce the search of Muirhead's premises, although it did hasten to state that none of those arrested was a current party member.[98]

Foreign representatives in Ireland

What was the likelihood of foreign representatives co-ordinating subversive activity with local elements in Ireland? Much has been written about Hempel's scrupulous conduct towards the Irish government during the war, as its neutrality operated in Germany's strategic interest, even if it was 'friendly' to the Allies.[99] Germany's leaked plan for Irish invasion, 'Operation Green', is now considered to have been a ruse,[100] and the IRA's own 'Operation Kathleen' scheme to invade Northern Ireland with German assistance was dismissed as amateurish by both Wehrmacht (German armed forces) and Abwehr. Attempts to co-ordinate action between the Abwehr and IRA nearly all ended in failure, as did German efforts to carry out missions in Britain with the help of Welsh and Scottish militants, using Ireland as a base.[101]

According to Duggan, the German minister was 'particularly sensitive to approaches from the Scottish Independence Movement' owing to fears of 'British provocation'.[102] This accords with the view that Hempel was opposed to espionage efforts in Ireland for fear its neutrality would be jeopardised, but whether these 'approaches' were the Reader/Schneider telephone calls, were made by the SIM that Douglas founded in October 1933 – or whether they even originated in Ireland – is unclear.

A reluctant host?

The question arises as to why the Irish state allowed persons posing such threats to reside in their country. British authorities had been prompted into action, uncovering evidence of the Scottish end of a nationalist escape route to Ireland. Across the Irish Sea, the deportation of MacDonald Douglas at least had been considered by both G2 and the Department of Justice, and pre-emptive action without hard evidence had been recommended in the case of McDougal's military discharge. It is not beyond reason to imagine Irish authorities would have seized any opportunity to deport foreign nationalists suspected of subversive activity. Yet it is known Douglas, for one, did not return to Scotland until 1967.[103] Reader, too, was still in Dublin in 1968.[104]

First, there is the possibility that British authorities preferred the most militant nationalists out of Scotland. G2 believed this had been the attitude of

Scottish police when Douglas left in 1939. We know also of the high-level contacts that took place between British and Irish intelligence. Although this sharing had its limits – G2 was under strict orders not to discuss details of IRA planning it obtained[105] – the intelligence assessments of Scots exiles are likely to have been discussed, given that they concerned British subversives and their alleged contacts with Axis agencies. It is evident also that Irish intelligence was as efficient as it was intrusive, especially in its surveillance of aliens – a task relatively simple amongst a small, nearly homogeneous population as was the Éire of the 1940s.[106] Considering its 'friendly neutrality' towards the Allies and its effort to thwart Republican subversion – and of course the legal difficulties in deporting a British subject without firm evidence of wrongdoing – it is conceivable that Ireland might acquiesce to British requests to leave them in the country. While MI5 doubtless understood such militants to be on the margins of the Scottish movement, it is also certain that the impotence of exile for such individuals held greater attraction for British authorities than potential espionage in Nazi service or rabble-rousing in Glasgow. Anti-conscriptionists especially could disrupt a major source of recruitment for the British war effort, and not all of them were satisfied with constitutional action: in December 1939 – immediately following the SNP conference in which opposition to conscription was reversed – a bomb had been found at Edinburgh's National Service Offices. Responsibility for the unexploded device had been claimed by a previously unknown 'Scottish Republican Brotherhood'.[107]

A more important determinant in the continued presence of Scottish militants in Éire is that the Irish government had little choice in the matter. As British subjects, Scottish nationals enjoyed a legal right of abode. It is also likely that men of Irish descent like Reader had Irish citizenship, ruling out deportation altogether. This meant that Dublin could sidestep embarrassing questions regarding asylum for Scots militants; such individuals could reside in Ireland without the government making a legal or political judgement regarding their struggle. Antagonisation of the country upon which the Irish economy depended could thus be avoided and the presence of such individuals blamed on enduring constitutional connections.[108]

This is not to suggest there was no extradition mechanism in place between Éire and Britain. In fact, this was a relatively simple procedure under the terms of the British Indictable Offences (1848) and Petty Sessions (Ireland) (1851) Acts, which were adjudged still to be in force after 1922 under Article 73 of the Free State Constitution. Under a procedure known as 'endorsement and execution of warrants', warrants issued by British magistrates were enforceable in Ireland once endorsed by the Commissioner of the Garda or his deputy. There was therefore no conventional extradition agreement with Britain, whereby a *prima facie* case would first have to be established before a local magistrate, nor any need for a formal extradition request. More importantly, there was no political exception clause, in contrast to the Extradition Act (1870), which governed extradition to third countries and specified 'no person is to be surrendered if his offence is one of a political character'.[109] It is significant, therefore, that despite a legal framework so favourable to their return, no evidence of a warrant being served upon nor even sought for Scottish nationalists in wartime Ireland exists. Once again, it would appear British authorities were pleased to be rid of the likes of Ronald MacDonald Douglas. It is also possible, however, that both governments preferred not to hand Scottish exiles the publicity opportunity of putting the Petty Sessions Act to the test; the enforceability of Northern Irish warrants (as opposed to mainland British ones) had been successfully challenged by fugitive IRA men from Belfast in 1927.[110]

The unwelcome brothers

Those few Scottish militants who fled to Ireland to escape British rule did not do so as refugees welcomed by the Irish state. Their presence was a legacy of the constitutional relationship that persisted between London and Dublin since the creation of the Irish Free State in 1922. Moreover, as surveillance records show, their activities were closely monitored for fear that their dedication to radical politics in Scotland could bring their hosts profound embarrassment, imperil internal security or, at worst, provoke British retaliation. In this regard their activities were seen as connected with, and as threatening as, domestic Republican subversives. Possible German connections, personified by Seamus Reader, added further danger. The story of Irish Republican links with the German secret service is now well known, and G2 was aware of the Abwehr's attempts to liaise with other Celtic nationalists in Britain. Such operations, if conducted from an Irish base, would have been taken very seriously in Whitehall. As discussions regarding MacDonald Douglas' deportation indicate, such threats were taken seriously by the Irish authorities, too. That Scottish militants were not deported during the Emergency indicates of course that they may have been innocent of any subversive activity. The G2 reports record suspicions and allegations, not proven crimes. However, as Duncan McDougal's military discharge demonstrates, the authorities were not unwilling to act upon mere suspicion of subversion.

For the Irish state, the presence of Scots militants served only to antagonise a relationship with Britain already strained over Partition and neutrality. Those who did make the journey across the Northern Channel were on the margins of Scottish nationalism: admirers of an Irish Republicanism that set them at odds not only with the mainstream SNP, but also with the majority of Scots who supported Unionist parties. Irish pan-Celticists and Republicans no doubt made them welcome, but it is the attitude of Irish authorities towards such exiles that is of prime importance. It is significant in this context that, while some Welsh volunteers fought for the IRA during the War of Independence,[111] there is no evidence of Welsh militants fleeing British justice and seeking sanctuary in Ireland, either before or during the Emergency. The Protestant mainstream around which Welsh culture – and the Welsh language movement in particular – revolved was equally opposed to Irish influences or attempts to emulate the Irish struggle. Saunders Lewis, one of the founders of Plaid Cymru, claimed he was hounded from the party's leadership for his Catholicism. His successor, Jack Daniel, was similarly ousted when his wife converted to the Roman Church in 1943.[112] It would be many years after 1945 before a Welsh militant sought sanctuary in Ireland – even then, his stay would be as brief as it was discreet.[113]

Professing the Catholic faith was no guarantee of wartime Irish favour, either. In addition to recent converts like Colm MacClean, there were other foreign nationalists resident in Ireland during the Emergency who, despite their Catholicism, also found themselves suspected of shadowy connections with the IRA and German intelligence. In a further challenge to pan-Celticist interpretations of Irish policy towards such exiles, these were natives of the Celtic region of Brittany. By contrast, the Irish state would demonstrate its goodwill towards another nationalist exile of non-Celtic origin but manifestly pro-Allied sympathies.

CHAPTER 2

Two Bretons and a Basque: pan-Celticism, Axis sympathy or raisons d'état?

IT MAY BE PRESUMED THAT, owing to the peculiar exigencies of the Anglo-Irish relationship, only Irish Republicans and Celts from regions under British rule would be regarded with the level of suspicion shown Scots exiles during the Emergency. Exiled nationalists from Brittany – the only Celtic region not under such rule (excepting Éire itself, of course) – would presumably present little security threat, either in the Irish or British purview. The number of such militants residing in Éire at this time would, moreover, be negligible.

It comes as something of a surprise therefore to learn that the Irish authorities did indeed regard Breton nationalist exiles as serious threats to national security during the Emergency. This seems remarkable given that there were only two such exiles known to be in the country. More remarkable still is the contrast between the suspicion with which these men were regarded, and the goodwill and assistance shown another foreign nationalist in Ireland; a nationalist who, although a great admirer of the Irish struggle for national liberation, was certainly no Celt.

The first of these suspect exiles had been living in Ireland since 1914, and attracted suspicion because of the major role he played in inspiring Breton nationalists with tales of Irish rebellion. The other was a potato merchant.

Louis Le Roux and the Irish example

For Breton nationalists coming of age before the Second World War, there were a number of key texts. Most were familiar with the journal *Breiz Atao* (Brittany Forever), organ of the Parti national breton, which appeared from 1919 until its prohibition in August 1939.[1] There was also the fascistic *Stur* (Tiller), edited by the PNB's Olier Mordrel, and *Breiz Atao*'s wartime successor *L'Heure bretonne* (The Breton Hour), a weekly which appeared during the German occupation and benefited from the 'goodwill' of the Nazi authorities.[2]

But for many Breton militants the greatest inspiration was to be found in stories of Ireland's fight for independence. Dan Breen's memoirs appeared in Brittany as *Mon combat pour l'Irlande,* translated by Robert Kadig, pseudonym of the militant Hervé 'Bob' Helloco.[3] But by far the most influential work appeared in 1932: Louis Le Roux's *La vie de Patrice Pearse* (The life of Patrick Pearse).

Louis Le Roux (his middle name was Marie; he changed it to 'Napoléon' allegedly out of 'megalomania')[4] was born in 1890. He and the poet Camille Le Mercier d'Erm founded the first incarnation of the PNB in July 1911. This was Brittany's first avowedly separatist party,[5] rejecting the conservative regionalism of the Union régionaliste bretonne (Breton Regionalist Union) and declaring Brittany 'an original nation, enslaved and oppressed like Poland and Ireland'.[6] In a parallel with the Scottish movement, the 'First PNB' upheld the primacy of the 1532 Treaty of Franco-Breton union.[7] This, they argued, had been unilaterally abrogated by France in 1789, when Brittany's autonomous parliament was abolished and administration replaced by five *départements* controlled by Paris. Most significantly, Breton nationalists of Le Roux's period (such as the poet Jean-Pierre Calloc'h) drew inspiration from Irish Fenian models, especially ideas of exploiting great power rivalries to achieve nationalist objectives.[8] When war broke out with Germany in 1914, these Breton nationalists – marginalised in the atmosphere of exuberant French loyalism, and with virtually no electoral support – had already imagined a future in which independence would be restored by the only means imaginable: destruction of French power by foreign invasion or domestic revolution. In d'Erm's words, they 'adapt[ed] the celebrated Irish Sinn Féin formula ... [and] hoped that one day "France's difficulty would be Brittany's opportunity".'[9]

Virtually all Breton nationalists obeyed the national call-up in August 1914. Many – including Calloc'h, who once declared *'Ned on ket Gall evit ur blank!'*[10] (I'm not French for a penny!) – fell in battle *pour la France.* Virtually all nationalists, that is, except Louis Le Roux, who made for the United Kingdom – supposedly to learn other Celtic languages,[11] but in all likelihood to avoid service in accordance with his separatist conscience.

Like other militant nationalists such as Ronald MacDonald Douglas, Le Roux's life story varies considerably with the sources. He does not appear to have travelled straight to Ireland,[12] but did claim involvement in the Easter Rising and to have been secretary to Patrick Pearse.[13] These claims are almost certainly fanciful. Fant Rozec 'Meavenn', who visited Ireland on an unsuccessful mission to obtain IRA support in 1931, considered Le Roux 'overvalued' (*surfait*) and given to outlandish claims.[14] Ó Ciosáin notes, however, that his *Vie de Patrice Pearse* was edited by Desmond Ryan, who had known Pearse, and who imparted the biography greater verisimilitude.[15] According to the *Irish*

Press, France requested Le Roux's extradition in 1916, but this was refused on the grounds of his proven political convictions.[16]

The 'political exception'

The 'political exception' in extradition law has a long history. Many of its earliest beneficiaries were Irish rebels who fled to France or other countries in the eighteenth century, such as James Napper Tandy. The first codification in Britain of relief from extradition on political grounds featured in a treaty with Belgium in 1852, and later in the Extradition Act (1870), which stipulated 'no person is to be surrendered if his offence is one of a political character'. There were limitations to the 'political exception', of course: if a state made a formal extradition request, the accused would have to prove to a British magistrate that his or her actions in that state had been part of a wider effort to seize political power. If proven, the magistrate would issue a writ of habeas corpus, granting relief from extradition.[17] Among other exceptions to extradition are offences relating to purely military law, such as desertion or evasion of conscription.[18] This may have been the determination in Le Roux's case, especially if he was not sought by Paris for any specific separatist offence.

Le Roux is said to have obtained British citizenship,[19] and to have served for over a year in the British army before being discharged in September 1917 on medical grounds.[20] He later contributed articles for *An Phoblacht* (The Republic), where he reportedly became acquainted with Frank Ryan. MI5 claimed he received Irish citizenship in 1936; Ó Ciosáin contends this was obtained four years earlier.[21] But it was his work on Pearse – the first of an intended series of biographies on all seven signatories of the Republic proclamation in 1916 – that was to immortalise him and become 'the bible of Breton autonomism'.[22]

> The heroes of Easter Week and particularly P. Pearse became our heroes alongside the Breton heroes of the past: more real since they were our contemporaries. Easter Week was for us a sign of Resurrection and its martyrs died for us too, and if the heroes of Easter Week came to replace our own long dead heroes in our minds we owe it to that great book of L.N. Le Roux.[23]

Le Roux's Republican connections drew attention from security services during the war. But fears of Celtic nationalist-Nazi liaison were this time largely confined to British intelligence. Le Roux had moved to London to work at an egg import firm in 1940 along with his Irish wife, Marion Murphy.[24] He denied being a member of the IRA, but his connection with figures such as Dan Breen and Sean Russell did not allay doubts. Le Roux was even known to have addressed meetings of the Republican-leaning National Party of Scotland as far back as 1931,[25] and to have described himself as a 'Breton Sinn Féiner'.[26] He was killed in a V2 rocket attack on London in 1944.[27]

Leon Mill-Arden: nationalist, Abwehr liaison, potato merchant

Breton nationalists' enthusiasm for the IRA had significant, unintended consequences. In its regular monitoring of the post, G2 noticed Breton nationalist propaganda in packages postmarked Brussels, Amsterdam and Milan. The material might have been overlooked had it not 'paid particular attention to IRA activities'. Concerned, Irish authorities placed one Leon Mill-Arden of Dollymount, Dublin, under surveillance and opened postal warrant no.33/40 upon all his correspondence.[28] In this way, perhaps the most important link between German intelligence, domestic Republicans and foreign Celtic nationalists came to be exposed.

The facts, as far as they can be assessed, are these: Léon Victor Millarden was born at Rennes in 1905.[29] As was common with Breton names at this time, his *état civil* (civil status, such as appears on official documents like birth certificates) was registered under the more Gallic 'Millardet'.[30] He studied medicine, taking after his father who taught at the medical school in the Breton capital,[31] before switching to agricultural commerce at Guingamp. He entered the potato trade in 1927.[32] The following year he undertook compulsory military service at Brest with the 2e Regiment d'Infanterie Coloniale. Here he was observed in a local café attending a small gathering of Breton autonomists infiltrated by police. 'He insisted on the need to organise groups that would later compose a Breton army,' their report read.[33] Millarden had been associated with Breton nationalism since 1922,[34] and was known as one of the most ardent militants in the movement: 'keenly alert and intelligent [...] almost fanatically pro-Breton and anti-French'[35] and 'always ready to pass over into direct action.'[36] Mordrel describes him as among the 'first wave' of the movement nationalists came to call *Emsav*,[37] from the Breton *en em sevel*, or 'raising myself up'.[38] To others, nationalists were simply *'Breiz Atao'*. This movement's accommodation with Germany was the motive for Millarden's move to Ireland.

Foreign assistance and the Breton movement

If France's difficulty was to be Brittany's opportunity, Breton nationalists would have to prove their utility to powers hostile to France. The PNB's Fañch Debauvais is reported to have considered inviting Britain to establish a '*petit Gibraltar*' at Brest,[39] but the power with the greatest interest in undermining France during the inter-war years was Germany. The extremist wing of the movement understood this very early: Célestin Lainé, head of the small 'physical force' group Gwenn-ha-Du (White and Black, the Breton national colours) sent 'Meavenn' to Ireland to contact the IRA in 1931, but he also sent Hervé 'Bob' Helloco to Germany to meet with the Abwehr. Ireland and Prussia were the 'two bases' for Breton nationalism, according to Lainé.[40] While the former inspired Bretons with tales of the Easter Rising and IRA flying columns, the latter was powerful enough to provide actual assistance, and had an interest in destabilising the hereditary foe on its western frontier. As 'Meavenn' discovered, the IRA was in no position to help any 'fraternal' foreign movement in the 1930s, with many of its members in prison and a concomitant focus upon defeating domestic enemies, be they in the 'six' or 'twenty-six counties'.[41] But German material help would have to be handled carefully as well, as French commentators were already describing Gwenn-ha-Du's actions as 'German attacks'.[42]

The prospect of a resurgent Germany creating an independent Brittany from a dismembered France thrilled separatists. The PNB was unlikely to overthrow French power by constitutional means: its electoral performance (such as at a by-election at Guingamp in 1930, when its candidate Goulven Mazéas won only 349 of 13,872 votes cast),[43] was uninspiring to say the least. Even Gwenn-ha-Du's operations were arguably more in the nature of spectacular propaganda than guerrilla warfare.[44] The first and greatest of these was on 6 August 1932, 400th anniversary of Franco-Breton union, when Lainé bombed the monument commemorating that event at the Hôtel de Ville in Rennes – the hated *'monument de la Honte nationale'* (monument of national dishonour).

While the 'Irish example' clearly exercised influence upon Breton nationalism, several Breton historians have noted that attempts to import Irish methods and tactics wholesale were destined to fail. Bretons, it is argued, have rebelled against unfair taxation, the anti-clericalism of revolutionary Jacobinism or the inflexibility of Parisian centralism,[45] but Franco-Breton relations were never marked with the sectarian hostility or 'genocide' that characterised much of British rule in Ireland.[46] Accordingly, many ordinary Bretons supported symbolic actions which publicised concerns about unemployment, underdevelopment or the plight of the Breton language, but rejected blood being shed in pursuit of these goals. Gwenn-ha-Du's propaganda triumph in destroying *'la Honte nationale'* owed much, therefore, to Lainé's insistence upon remaining in the square at Rennes before detonating his device to ensure no bystanders were injured.[47]

It has been suggested that Millarden fled to Ireland to avoid arrest in connection with Gwenn-ha-Du's activities,[48] but since the destruction of the monument at Rennes in 1932 was the group's first attack this seems improbable. Millarden first came to Ireland (to Killarney, where he later returned after a long period in Dublin) in 1931.[49] The French police did suspect an Irish connection after the *'Honte'* attack, however, arresting among others one Pierre Leroux. They had confused him with the exile Louis Le Roux.[50]

Once in Dublin Millarden set up the Agricultural Produce Company on O'Connell Street.[51] Now 'Hibernicising' his name Leon Mill-Arden,[52] the import-export business required travel between Ireland, London and the Continent, including Brittany and Germany.[53] As such, it was the perfect front for business of another kind. This was seemingly proven to an already wary G2 when the name 'Mill' was found on a list of contacts for the fugitive German spy, Hermann Görtz, in May 1940.[54]

This list was found at the house of Stephen Held, an IRA man.[55] Later piecing the puzzle together, G2 and MI5 determined that Mill-Arden and his Breton nationalist associate at Brussels, Paul 'Fred' Moyse, had first facilitated contact between German intelligence and Irish Republicans.[56] This three-way contact enabled the Breton movement to downplay German support while emphasising pan-Celticist solidarity. When a boatload of weapons and propaganda was transferred to Helloco's yacht off Locquirec in August 1939, for example, the rumour that this was active assistance from the IRA was encouraged. In fact the cargo was of purely German origin, and Irish Republican involvement was limited to the inspirational: the operation's codename was 'Casement'.[57] What Moyse termed 'active pan-Celticism'[58] on the part of Breton nationalists was therefore limited to the role of intermediaries. Held entered Germany via Moyse's Brussels residence in April 1940, whereupon he presented the 'Kathleen' plan to the Abwehr.[59] Mill-Arden acted as courier for IRA man Jim O'Donovan in 1939,[60] and Moyse delivered a codeword for the use of German agents in Ireland.[61] Moyse had also been chosen to accompany Sean Russell on the German U-boat that was to deliver him back to Ireland;[62] his eleventh-hour replacement by Frank Ryan, liberated from Spanish jail, is said to have caused him 'great disappointment'.[63]

G2's surveillance was stepped up when Mill-Arden moved to Killarney in 1941.[64] The signs were not encouraging. Among his papers was a letter from Seamus Reader on Clonmel Industries letterhead – the same firm run by Seamus Horan, he of suspected IRA affinities. Horan himself had been receiving Breton nationalist literature for some years, including the famous Easter Rising commemorative edition of *Breiz Atao*, as he later confirmed to the Garda in interview. There were reported visits in 1937 and 1938 from the *éminence grise* of the Abwehr, Dr Gerhard von Tevenar, as well as clumsily-coded correspondence from Moyse, asking if Mill-Arden still had 'relations with your old clients in the west of France'.[65]

In September 1942 the Garda interviewed an associate of Mill-Arden's, the Kafkaesquely-titled 'K', who reported that they had talked about 'obviously German agents' before discussing a plan to spirit one of these, referred to as 'Neymer', out of the country. Another informant opined that Mill-Arden could not possibly afford his lifestyle, a view shared by the Killarney Garda in their reports to G2. Mill-Arden and his wife, Northern Ireland-born Bridie, née McMahon, were turning out 'more respectably dressed than for some time back'. He was known to pay cash for all local purchases, but '[t]he volume of business indicated by [his bank] account is so small that it would suggest the existence of another source of income ...'[66]

Some studies ignore Mill-Arden's extracurricular activities while manager of the Agricultural Produce Company.[67] Other, more recent works charge that the company was funded by the Abwehr, either entirely or in part, as a front for espionage and liaison with subversive elements.[68] But one aspect of Mill-Arden's role in Ireland has remained unexplored: that of para-diplomatic representative of the PNB in Ireland.

'Officious Breton consul in Ireland'

> It is our deep desire [...] that we should get in direct touch with [...] the Governement [*sic*] of the first Celtic Country who has recovered a National Statute, with a view to be represented there in a true and proper way, [...] and so to be in a position to avoid in the same extent an official representation which misrepresents our people and ignores its interests.[69]

So reads a letter found among Mill-Arden's papers dated 27 June 1936, addressed to the President of the Executive Council of the Irish Free State, Eamon de Valera. It is signed by PNB leaders Olier Mordrel and Fañch Debauvais (or 'Deb' as he was known to party comrades, in the style of 'Dev'), and appoints Mill-Arden *'da Gannad ar Vrezoned en Iwerzon'* – representative of Bretons in Ireland.[70] It continues, emphasising the pan-Celtic connection:

> The Bretons know, better than any people on the Continent, that the Irish are not English or not even British [...] They should be pleased that, in return, the Irish consider the existence of the National awakening of Celtic Brittany, whose aims are identic [*sic*] to those of the original Sinn-Fein [*sic*].

It is not clear whether this letter was ever presented, nor its companion from the Breton Catholic association Bleun Brug (Heather Bloom) led by Abbé Yann-Vari Perrot, which inadvertently disparaged Mill-Arden's social skills in supporting his appointment as 'officious Breton consul in Ireland'.[71] It is probable that Mill-Arden understood the Irish government would never accept his 'appointment' and kept the letters to himself. As for that 'official representation' which ignored Breton interests, wartime recognition of the Vichy government was to last until the Liberation in 1944, when the French minister Laforcade finally switched allegiance to de Gaulle.[72]

Another significant letter among Mill-Arden's papers was addressed to 'the Fuehrer of the German Reich'. It asked Hitler not to collaborate with France but to liberate Brittany.[73] Evidently it was composed around the time of the Montoire agreement of October 1940, when Marshal Pétain's decision to collaborate with the occupiers put an end to Breton nationalist hopes of an independent Brittany under German aegis.[74] As Moyse described it in one of his coded letters, 'The authorities upon which we relied were [now] engaged in new politics'.[75] Elements of the Wehrmacht and Abwehr had favoured a weakened France and the establishment of a Breton client state, but Foreign Minister Joachim von Ribbentrop and the German diplomatic service favoured enticing France into the war against Britain and securing the Reich's flank in the west and North Africa.[76] Hitler was reportedly undecided on the issue.[77] Vichy's entrance onto 'the path of collaboration' at Montoire was therefore, according to le Boterf, strongly influenced by a desire to thwart German plans in Brittany and 'secur[e] the unity of France'.[78] Mill-Arden was aware of the strategic attractions of Breton independence for Germany: 'Brittany outside France would be a check that hardly any weakening in France's eastern side could equal,' he wrote in his letter to the German Führer. Although the letter mentions how it would be handed to the German representative in Éire, there is again no evidence that this was actually done, or that Hempel would have forwarded it to Berlin had it been delivered. It could, perhaps, have been interpreted as yet another Allied 'provocation' designed to embroil him in intrigue.

Once again, it is abundantly evident that Irish authorities were not moved to consider Mill-Arden's Celtic nationalism as justifying contact with German intelligence services or Republican subversives. By war's end they had confiscated his private papers, intercepted his mail, received detailed information on his personal meetings from informants, and interrogated him at length. Interestingly, they decided not to intern him, as this would jeopardise their source – perhaps the mysterious 'K'. Furthermore, it was 'felt he served a more useful purpose outside, under surveillance';[79] a lightning rod of sorts for all manner of Axis, Republican and foreign nationalist subversives. In a clear demonstration of the close intelligence-sharing relationship between G2 and MI5, reports arising from this surveillance were shared by Irish intelligence with their British counterparts for comment and analysis. MI5 discussed the information coming from 'Dan' in Ireland, and noted in a briefing sent to Dublin that, according to G2 reports, there would obviously be 'considerable difficulty in getting anything out of [Mill-Arden], or at least, any truth out of him.'[80] 'Mill-Arden is the most difficult, shifty and evasive person [we] have ever had to deal with,' G2 confirmed in a testament to the Breton's composure under interrogation, no doubt honed by earlier encounters with French police. '[H]e could lie without qualm, was most evasive under questioning and showed consummate skill in avoiding the issue on any question.'[81]

Eli Gallastegi and the contrast of Basque exile

While the pursuit of independence led some minority nationalists in France, Britain and other countries to court fascist and national socialist regimes in the inter-war years, the reverse was true in Spain. Here, the Basque and Catalan movements were at the forefront of action against Franco's Nationalists and their Italian and German backers during the Spanish Civil War.[82] Because of the guaranteed refuge provided by France, few Basques fled to Ireland after the fall of the autonomous government of Euskadi (the Basque Country) in August 1937.[83] Those few who did benefited from a demonstrably different attitude from the Irish authorities, however. In assessing the influence of both pan-Celticist sympathy and supposed pro-Axis proclivity upon Irish asylum policy, it is of supreme significance that those exiles *not* subjected to intense scrutiny and suspicion during the Emergency were actually non-Celts, and were of manifestly pro-Allied sympathies. The most significant of these was Eli Gallastegi, *aka* 'Gudari' (Warrior).[84]

Gallastegi arrived in Ireland in September 1937, at the height of intense Irish debate concerning the Spanish Civil War. Like MacDonald Douglas, he was an uncompromising nationalist on the radical fringe of the movement in his home nation, although rather less marginal a figure. Both his arrival and subsequent exile in Ireland are in stark contrast to that experienced by Scottish militants, however – not least because of the official assistance and goodwill extended him by key figures in the Irish government. The reasons for this contrast are to be found not only in the nature of the Basque struggle itself, but also in the nationalist activity pursued by Gallastegi and his avowed solidarity with the Irish movement – in particular, with the practical form that solidarity would take.

'Gora Irlanda askatuta!'[85]

Born in Bilbao in 1892, Gallastegi joined Basque Youth, the junior movement of the Partido Nacionalista Vasca (Basque Nationalist Party), at the age of fifteen. By 1916 he was writing articles for the movement's newspaper, *Eusko Deya* (Basque Voice).[86] Like many minority nationalists, the events of that year were to have a profound impact upon him, and eventually lead him into exile.

When the Easter Rising broke out in Dublin, the PNV newspaper *Euzkadi* affirmed its support for the British presence on the island.[87] The party had moved away from the separatist impulses of its founder, Sabino Arana y Goiri, and now sought a simple restoration of the *fueros,* the ancient statutes that had guaranteed the autonomy of the various Basque provinces but had been abolished by the liberal, centralising government in Madrid after the Second Carlist War of 1873–4.[88] The PNV's reaction to Easter Week may have been designed to allay fears of similar violence breaking out in Bilbao, but the party was also now controlled by a conservative españolista (Spanicist) wing.[89] This move toward conservative regionalism was exemplified by the rebranding of the party in 1916 as the Comunión Nacionalista Vasca (Basque Nationalist Communion), which incorporated Carlist, clerical overtones.[90]

Inspired by Irish courage during Easter Week, younger, more radical members of the Basque movement rejected the españolistas and advocated full independence for Euskadi. These converged around the new publication *Aberri* (Fatherland) and became known as 'Aberrianos'. Gallastegi, adopting the *nom de plume* 'Gudari', began publishing articles on the Irish struggle soon after Easter 1916, assisted in great measure by his Irish-Argentinian friend Ambrose Martin, a member of Sinn Féin in Dublin.[91] Irish nationalists 'offered the world a great example of heroism and dignity',[92] and 'astonishe[d] the world for a week with [their] heroism', he wrote.[93] England's dismissal of Irish demands at the Versailles Conference likewise demonstrated that the sacrifices of those who followed the moderate John Redmond to the Great War, hoping that Britain would reward them with Home Rule, were in vain.[94] The intended lesson for the españolistas was clear.

By 1921 Gallastegi had joined Luis Arana y Goiri, brother of Sabino, and other 'intransigent'[95] Aberrianos in creating a new PNV after their battles with the CNV led to rancorous schism.[96] *Aberri* carried Gallastegi's articles concerning the Irish War of Independence, castigating English hypocrisy as it talked loftily of Belgian and Polish freedom at the peace conference while letting loose the Black and Tans upon Irish civilians. When the Anglo-Irish Treaty was signed in December of that year, Gallastegi emphasised that this was a 'transitory' compromise that did not abrogate Ireland's right to complete independence. Again, the lesson was for the CNV's digestion: 'Let us learn, Basques.'

The new PNV's solidarity with the Irish movement pre-dated co-ordinated action between movements under Spanish rule. Only after the rise of *Aberri* did Basque nationalists give thought to supporting Moroccan independence, for example; Gallastegi's vocal opposition to the Rif War being yet another point of contention with mainstream Basque nationalism.[97] Growing awareness of the value of co-ordinated action led to the establishment in 1923 of the Triple Alianza (Triple Alliance) of Basque, Catalan and Galician nationalists,[98] but in September of that year General Primo de Rivera seized power in Madrid. Centralist reaction unleashed by this *coup d'état* forced both moderate and radical Basque organisations into clandestinity.[99] It was during this period that the Gallastegi family had its first experience of exile.

The well-worn path of Basque exile: France and Mexico

In May 1925, Gallastegi held an illegal political meeting at a Bilbao restaurant. The pretext was a bachelor party for his upcoming wedding. While he was addressing the crowd of over 500 guests, Spanish police burst in, making wholesale arrests. Gallastegi managed to flee the scene, and, learning that prosecutors were seeking a sixteen-year sentence should he be captured, he and his wife decided to flee across the Pyrenees to France. It was here in North (French-administered) Euskadi that his first son Iker was born in April 1926.

The following year saw the family in Mexico, home to a sizeable expatriate Basque community. Here, between 1928 and 1931, Gallastegi published the first five issues of *Patria Vasca* (Basque Fatherland), a journal which he distributed gratis.[100] In this publication, Gallastegi once again 'proclaim[ed] the solidarity of nationalism with all peoples who fight for their freedom', especially the Irish.[101]

While he was in Mexico, the PNV and CNV resolved their differences. By the time Primo de Rivera and his successors were ousted in March 1931, the two parties had agreed to reunite, against Gallastegi's insistence that they combine forces but remain separate entities.[102] Significantly, although committed to a rejection of the autonomist compromise, Gallastegi was similarly opposed to the breakaway Acción Nacionalista Vasca (Basque Nationalist Action), a leftist group that split from the reunited PNV at this time. His was an uncompromising adherence to what he saw as Arana's original vision: racial and cultural separation that would erect a bulwark against anti-Catholic, liberal and 'morally degenerate' Spanish ideas. This did not mean that Gallastegi shied away from social and labour questions (sometimes to the alarm of mainstream PNV figures),[103] but he and other radical Basque nationalists had no truck with Spanish labour unions, let alone concepts of internationalism or class warfare. They rejected deals with Madrid and were 'only mildly anti-clerical'.[104]

The family returned to Bilbao in time for the declaration of the Republic in April 1931. In the elections that followed, a PNV–Carlist alliance triumphed in Euskadi while the rest of Spain opted for the left. The Basque alliance was itself sundered the following year, when the PNV struck a deal with the Republic concerning an autonomy statute. The Carlists rejected such bargains with 'anti-clerical' forces.

For Gallastegi, 1932 brought two developments that would eventually see him flee to Ireland. The first was his rejection of the PNV's deal with the leftist, secular Republic. The second was an important business connection he established with his old friend Ambrose Martin.

Jagi-Jagi and Euskadi at war

Inspired by Sabino Arana's vision of a unique mountain people unsullied by Latin or Moorish influences,[105] Gallastegi had been a key figure in the Mendigoxale Batza (mountaineers' groups) that were bastions of integral nationalism. Dismayed at the mainstream PNV's acceptance of a promise of mere autonomy, 'Gudari' began publishing once again: this time at the head of the groups' new journal, *Jagi-Jagi* (Upward). Again the Irish experience was invoked, particularly as division between autonomists and independentists had led to open warfare in that country – encouraged, he argued, by Britain in the same way Spain was arming autonomists against separatists in Euskadi and Catalonia.[106] In honour of both the Easter Rising and the PNV's profound Catholic orientation, the inaugural Aberri Eguna (Fatherland Day) was held on Easter Sunday, 1932.[107] It remains the national day of Euskadi.

Despite the promised autonomy statute, the PNV's alliance with the Republic was not painless. For those espousing the creed of Jaungoikua eta Lagi-Zarra ('God and the Old Laws'),[108] conservative Catholic and monarchist forces held greater appeal than the anarchist and socialist militias of the Republic. Vizcaya and Guipuzcoa remained loyal to the government when the Nationalist rebellion broke out in July 1936, but Navarre and parts of Alava – bastions of conservative Carlism – defected to General Francisco Franco.[109]

For Gallastegi and *Jagi-Jagi,* collaboration with the Republic was a dishonourable 'politics of breadcrumbs'.[110] Only full independence would suffice. Behind the scenes the Basque government was considering offers (communicated through Vatican and Italian intermediaries) to jettison the 'anti-Catholic' Republic and join the rebellion, but the centralist factions within Franco's forces soon eclipsed conservatives committed to a return to traditional regionalism. As distasteful as the alliance with the Republic was, it was the only means of attaining greater autonomy. The alternative would be brutal repression by a rightist, centralist Madrid.

But even those PNV members who accepted the autonomy deal were ambivalent about supporting the Republic. When fighting erupted – often against fellow Basque *requetes* from Carlist Navarre –the PNV sometimes pulled operational punches,[111] and the Eusko Gudaroztea (Basque Army) focused upon building up its own forces and acting independently of Republican command.[112]

The Basques and Irish perceptions of the Spanish Civil War

While groups allied to *Jagi-Jagi* contributed three battalions to the defence of Euskadi,[113] Gallastegi's anti-Republican stance nevertheless had crucial bearing upon his later acceptance in Ireland. For the *Independent*, the Civil War in Spain was a 'battle between Christianity and communism in which there can be only one victor'.[114] Others viewed it as a reflection of the Free State's own combat against the IRA: the forces of conservative Catholic nationalism ranged against Marxist-inspired Republicanism.[115] Significantly, while General Eoin O'Duffy mustered more than 700 men to his ill-fated Irish *bandera* of the Nationalist Spanish Foreign Legion, leftist Republicans joining Frank Ryan in the International Brigades numbered only around 150.[116]

While the average Irish person regarded all who supported the Republic in Spain as 'Reds', figures better briefed about the situation understood that many conservative Catholic nationalists from Catalonia or Euskadi chose to oppose Franco. If these figures were themselves former fighters for Irish independence – as Taoiseach Eamon de Valera and Defence Minister Frank Aiken, to name but two, were – they could be expected to regard such militants with sympathy, or at least understanding. The fact that de Valera's Fianna Fáil government had evolved out of anti-Treaty forces in the Irish Civil War might also predispose them towards this view, especially as the major opposition party, Fine Gael, was so closely associated with General O'Duffy's Blueshirts and the first ruling party of the Free State, the pro-Treaty Cumann na nGaedheal.[117]

The opposition had already attempted to paint the government as 'Red' over its official neutrality in the Spanish war.[118] Fianna Fáil was, however, moving away from secular Republicanism itself – a move indicated by the new constitution of 1937.[119] The Church's recognition in that constitution, and the press hysteria concerning Marxism and anti-clericism in Spain, meant any large-scale influx of Spanish Republican refugees would be politically disastrous for the party. As has been noted, though, hundreds of thousands of Spanish Republicans found ready asylum across the Pyrenees. For Basques and Catalans, this would not necessarily require leaving their native homelands, so was obviously a more attractive option than countries further removed.

In an attempt to correct Irish perceptions of Basque involvement in the war, Father Ramón Laborda, a Basque priest, visited Ireland in January 1937.

Making an address at the Gaiety Theatre, Dublin, Laborda refuted the charge that supporting the Republic made the PNV 'Communists', indicating furthermore that Catholicism was alive and well in Euskadi. He also challenged the notion that Franco's forces were defending Catholicism in Spain:

> When I read recently that the Catholics of Ireland were offering men and money to fascist Franco, the personification of the most brutal imperialism, I exclaimed indignantly: 'It is impossible.' Ireland could not do that unless she had been miserably deceived.[120]

It is fair to say, however, that the appearance of such comments in *The Worker* (organ of the Irish Communist Party) were unlikely to assuage conservative Catholic concerns about Basque defenders of the Republic.

Euzkerin and Irish-Iberian

Gallastegi's pro-Irish proclivities had led him to establish links beyond the political. Keen to support the fledgling and impoverished Irish state in practical ways, Gallastegi established in 1932 an import-export company, Euzkerin (Euskadi-Erin) which traded between Bilbao and Dublin. Trade became especially brisk during the Anglo-Irish Trade War (or 'Economic War'), with Spanish citrus fruit and tools among the chief exports. At the Irish end, Ambrose Martin and others set up Irish-Iberian, which received Euzkerin's exports and shipped out Irish goods in return. It is said that, owing to the company's efforts, it was possible to enjoy a pint of Guinness in the Basque Country of the 1930s.[121]

Practical economic assistance of this kind was favourably regarded by the Irish Department of Industry and Commerce, irrespective of attempts by Patrick Belton TD to condemn Martin as 'one of the most pronounced and prominent Communists in this country' and Irish-Iberian as nothing but a front for propping up Republican Spain.[122] But the links between the two companies exercised an even more persuasive influence upon Gallastegi's case: the war in Spain prevented Irish-Iberian from making cash payments to Gallastegi in Bilbao, and this money was piling up in Dublin.[123] Therefore, when the Basque government finally fell to the Nationalists, Gallastegi assessed the options for his family: remain in France, to which they had once again fled a few days earlier; or head to Ireland, the land that had inspired his struggle, where he had friends and business associates, and where a large sum of money awaited him. In this period of Economic War with Britain and large-scale annual emigration, Industry and Commerce exercised a significant influence over immigration approvals, including refugee admissions.[124] There was fear new arrivals would worsen the unemployment situation, so the Aliens Act (1935) had empowered immigration officers to turn away those lacking employment prospects, or those deemed incapable of independent support.[125] Conversely, those with significant assets or wealth were looked upon favourably. The Gallastegi family therefore found Ireland most responsive to their applications, and they arrived in September 1937.

The Gallastegis of Gibbstown

The Gallastegi family settled in Gibbstown, Co. Meath. The Land Commission had resettled Irish-speaking families from Kerry, Mayo and Donegal here in preceding years in order to assist the resurrection of the language and alleviate poverty in the country's west.[126] As a consequence the Gallastegi children – Iker, his brothers Lander and Unai, and sisters Ninbe and Argiñe – became fluent in Irish, the language of instruction at the local national school. No doubt utilising the funds built up by Irish-Iberian, the family took up residence in the town's 'Big House', which was soon put to extensive cultural use, as Iker explains:

> Our house [...] was a sort of Museum of the Basque Country and, for many years, [Eli] acted as a guide and explained to many at a time [...] Basque history, sports, dances and answered all sorts of questions which youngsters are prone to make.

The wealth owed to Eli Gallastegi must have been considerable, as in addition to the family home-cum-museum he was able to donate land for the construction of a Gaelic Hostel, which functioned as an Irish-language summer school.[127] Of course, preservation of threatened languages is a major motivation for minority nationalists, and is in many cases the chief reason for their embrace of politics. That exiled militants would continue this commitment in their adopted country is perhaps not surprising, but it is noteworthy how often exiles chose to marry Irish-speakers, school their children in Irish, or otherwise engage with the Irish language. For the Gallastegis, integration with the culture of their hosts went further still, with Ninbe and Argiñe winning prizes at *feisanna* (Irish dancing competitions) and Lander playing rugby for University College, Dublin.[128]

There are no known G2 or Garda surveillance records concerning Gallastegi. There are several likely reasons for this. Primarily, following the fall of the Spanish Republic in April 1939, Basque, Catalan and other Spanish Republican refugees were considered implacable opponents of fascism and Nazism, given that the German Condor Legion and Italian troops had supported Franco's Nationalists. The German air contingent in particular had destroyed the Basque town of Gernika (or Guernica) in April 1937. Many gudaris followed their government into exile in France and, after June 1940, to Mexico, the United States or London, where a Basque National Council was established.[129] Around 150,000 Spanish refugees settled in southern France,[130] many joining the Resistance from 1940 and becoming some of the most dogged anti-fascist fighters of the Maquis.[131] A Basque unit of the Forces françaises à l'Intérieure (French Forces of the Interior), the Gernika Battaloa (Guernica Battalion), later fought in some of the final battles of the war, dislodging pockets of German troops from fortresses along the French Atlantic coast.[132] De Valera's government recognised Franco's regime two months before his victory, but many expected that the collapse of both Italy and Germany presaged similar Allied efforts against Spain. The intelligence links between the American Office of Strategic Services (forerunner to the Central Intelligence Agency) and the PNV government-in-exile of José Antonio Aguirre were particularly strong.[133] In this climate, goodwill towards Basque exiles and their organisations could be seen as yet another manifestation of 'friendly neutrality' towards the Allies.

This favourable attitude towards Basques in Ireland was in starkest contrast to that shown the Scots, Mill-Arden et al. following the German invasion of France in June 1940. At a time when G2 was drafting its first reports on the suspicious activities of Ronald MacDonald Douglas, a French fishing boat arrived at Cork. On board were eleven Basques who had begun their exodus in St Jean de Luz, a seaside town in North (French) Euskadi. The Irish immigration authorities were perplexed by the unexpected arrivals, especially when they applied for political asylum and claimed, as a vouchsafe of their status, that they were friends of Eli Gallastegi *aka* 'Gudari'. Remarkably, according to Iker, the Basques were then shown how accommodating Ireland could be to refugees who were not considered threatening to national security, were pro-Allied and unlikely to jeopardise Anglo-Irish relations:

> [T]he Irish Minister for Home Affairs phoned us saying that [the eleven Basques] claimed to be friends of my father's, so when we confirmed it he sent them all in three taxis to Gibbstown. Some of them later joined the Free French forces and others more or less settled in Ireland until the end of the war and then returned to their homes.[134]

The Basques' willingness to serve the Allied war effort was one mark in their favour; their eagerness to return to France at war's end and not settle permanently in Ireland was no doubt another.

As for Gallastegi himself, he is said to have had 'very little engagement in Basque politics' after leaving Euskadi in 1937. Apart from showing visitors through his unofficial Basque museum in Gibbstown and playing host to Basque nationalist leaders on their occasional visits, he would no longer 'interfere directly' in the politics of his homeland until his return there, to St Jean de Luz, in the mid-1950s.[135] It is not to be assumed, however, that 'Gudari' had lost interest in such matters while in Ireland; directions to cease political agitation against the state of origin are common conditions of asylum, although most commonly for diplomatic considerations rather than any requirement under international law.[136] The mundane necessities of life no doubt also demanded attention. Assisted by Irish-Iberian capital, by war's end Gallastegi had entered into a gainful new business – running a local sawmill.[137] Unlike Ronald MacDonald Douglas, Gallastegi's financial independence and industriousness ensured he was not considered a potential 'nuisance' by Irish authorities.

Conclusion

National security concerns, not pan-Celticism or anti-British sentiment, were the chief determinants of Irish asylum for foreign nationalists during the war years. The treatment of Gallastegi and other Basques thought hostile to the Axis stands in stark contrast to the detailed surveillance of Scottish exiles detailed in Chapter One, and to the extensive surveillance and interrogation of Leon Mill-Arden. Unlike Louis Le Roux, who, it seems, was granted asylum by the British government before Irish independence, Mill-Arden had not sought official asylum at any stage. His presence in Ireland was ostensibly commercial, and he furthermore married a woman from Northern Ireland. It is important to remember, however, that G2 first became concerned about Mill-Arden owing to the pro-IRA orientation of the Breton nationalist literature he received; in other words, overt expressions of pan-Celticism and anti-British proclivity did not cause the government to look upon him favourably, but rather marked him as a 'person of interest' to be closely monitored.

Some sense of how such treatment outraged pan-Celticists can be found in Bridie Mill-Arden's impassioned appeal on behalf of her husband to Frank Aiken, Minister for the Co-ordination of Defensive Measures, in December 1944:

> My husband is a Breton, a Celt and a Catholic like ourselves; he feels toward his native country as patriotic Irishmen feel about Ireland, particularly when she was part of another State, as we feel in the North: he does not want his country to die under a foreign system. He came to live in Ireland in 1931, attracted by the brotherly similitudes and because he was interested in developing the export of some agricultural products to markets abroad, a highly national activity [...]
>
> He intended to apply for Irish citizenship before the war, but feared the French would use it as an excuse to prevent him going to Brittany. When war came he knew his refusal to join the French army would debar him from going to Brittany again, so applied for Irish citizenship but was refused.
>
> Now he is treated as an alien, with all the suspicions and disabilities attached to it, while on the other hand he has not the support which aliens can expect from the representatives of their own State.

While ill-treatment at the hands of Paris and London was perhaps to be expected, G2's treatment of Mill-Arden was, in Bridie's view, 'unworthy of Irish tradition and chivalry' and tantamount to betrayal.[138]

But Mill-Arden was by no means the last Breton nationalist to find sanctuary in Ireland. The years following the end of the Second World War saw some two dozen such fugitives arrive and begin new lives in 'the only free Celtic state'. The fact that these refugees were able to come in relatively large numbers and would now be discreetly welcomed by the Irish government was the result of some significant shifts in the European geopolitical landscape. Their journey from hunted collaborators to guests of the Irish state would furthermore be facilitated by 'active pan-Celticism' of rather different origin.

CHAPTER 3

'Should the interests of the nation so require': sovereignty, the Germans and the first postwar Breton arrivals, 1944–8

On an August evening in 1946, a young man emerged from a lifeboat aboard the ship *Le Penestin*. The Dublin wharves were quiet, except for the rattle of dockyard gates as they opened to receive cargo newly arrived from Le Havre. The young man assumed the inebriated air of a mariner and made his way down the gangplank. It was an easy deception to master: to friends he was known as 'Martolod' ('Sailor').[1] In a scene that would have enraged the British Passport Control Officer at Dublin, he strolled past the dock guard and into Éire without challenge nor explanation.[2]

He had first to contend with a language barrier. He pondered this in a pub, funded with his final francs exchanged '*chez* Cook'.[3] Finally, in what seemed a logical step (at least after a few pints), he hit the streets, stopping passersby with a repeated word: '*Gaélique.*'

Directed to the Conradh na Gaeilge (Gaelic League), he found the premises closed. The doorman sent him on to a German doctor. The doctor was not at home either, but a German woman was. She spoke a little French, as it happened, and took Martolod to another address where she knew Germans were residing. These took the young man to be one of their own, and promptly shut the door in his face.

Returning in time to the German woman, 'Martolod' managed to engage her in lengthier conversation. Not only did this result in his first proper meal since stowing away aboard *Le Penestin*, the woman now revealed some interesting connections. Perhaps prompted by tales of clandestinity and bold escapes,[4] she sent him to Dr Kathleen Murphy at Rathmines. Murphy's Republican sympathies were well-known; IRA Chief of Staff Charlie Kerins had sheltered at her home before his capture and execution in 1944.[5] Murphy was also involved with the Save the German Children Society, an offshoot of the Irish Friends of Germany which the *Irish Times* labelled 'a thinly veiled excuse for the dissemination of Fascist propaganda'.[6] For fear of the scrutiny her activities and 'queer international affiliations' attracted,[7] Murphy felt it prudent to pass the young man on to someone better qualified to assist him. The man in question was currently living at Cork, and was now back in the potato trade. The next day 'Martolod', *aka* Joz-Yann Gourlet – wanted collaborator and first postwar Breton political refugee in Ireland – turned up at the home of Leon Mill-Arden.

Ireland, Breton nationalist refuge

Given that Bretons had so recently been subject to suspicion and surveillance in Ireland, the postwar influx of fugitives from Brittany appears to substantiate notions of pan-Celticist or anti-Allied proclivity now that war no longer imperilled national security. Such appears to be the attitude of key historians of the wartime Breton movement and the subsequent *épuration* (purge) conducted by French authorities after the Liberation of 1944. Many, in an echo of accounts of Ronald MacDonald Douglas' flight, note without further analysis that Bretons obtained asylum in Ireland easily or even automatically.[8] As we know, there are even claims Bretons were 'furnished with passports' owing to 'interceltic solidarity'.[9]

Celtic kinship and a sense of common struggle was no doubt a prime reason why many Bretons chose to flee to Ireland, and also why many Irish individuals, families, groups and even government figures privately assisted them. But the notion that pan-Celtic or nationalistic sympathy translated into state policy and was the chief determinant of official attitudes toward Breton asylees is a very different proposition. This policy was in fact more profoundly shaped by the changing geopolitical scene in Europe.

Allied victory in the war had been the outcome hoped for by de Valera at least, but any expectation that Ireland's 'friendly neutrality' would be rewarded in the postwar world was greatly mistaken. Allied press still railed against Irish perfidy and Britain, the USA and USSR now 'demanded respect for their power' from European neutrals.[10] This context is essential to understanding how *all* postwar asylees – including some two dozen Bretons of varying political shades[11] – were granted asylum in Ireland from 1946 to 1950. The battle of wills between the Allies and 'recalcitrant' Ireland over asylum issues began even before the final shots were fired in Europe, and the principal pawns in the contest were not Breton or other nationalist fugitives, but those aliens for whom 'Martolod' had been mistaken – the Germans in Ireland.

Germans in Ireland: neutrality and sovereignty, 1944–5

On 1 May 1945, Taoiseach Eamon de Valera paid a visit to the residence of Herr Eduard Hempel, the German Minister in Dublin, in order to pay official condolences upon news of the suicide of the Führer of the German Reich, Adolf Hitler.

To press in Allied countries, the visit confirmed pro-Axis proclivity in Irish government. For the US representative in Dublin, David Gray, the visit was a 'studied affront' to the United Nations;[12] the latest in a series of efforts to prioritise Irish neutrality above the defeat of fascism and split the Allies by appealing to Irish-American sentiment regarding Partition.

But 'studied affront' had been the forté of the US representative himself. A believer that British victory was vital to American interests, Gray had been an advocate for British control of the former Treaty Ports from as early as November 1940[13] – more than a year before America entered the war. This was also the policy of Gray's boss, President Franklin D. Roosevelt.[14] Gray furthermore regarded Irish nationalism as one of the most destabilising forces of the inter-war years – one that had exercised pernicious influence upon Irish-American opinion, contributing to isolationism after 1918. This, he believed, had hamstrung the League of Nations and encouraged fascism. Despite the Pentagon regarding Ireland's discreet wartime assistance as worthy of recognition, Gray had by war's end 'become obsessed with what he saw as the need to discredit Ireland's wartime record in the eyes of his fellow Americans'.

So long as the war hung in the balance, it was necessary to tread carefully to try to regain the ports, proffering both threats and blandishments. But by late 1943 Churchill was convinced the ports were no longer needed – Northern Irish bases would suffice, and occupation of southern ports would only strain resources and oblige their defence. Gray, however, endeavoured to ensure no postwar anti-Partition campaign could damage Anglo-American relations. The most effective means of doing this was to exploit the existing mood of antipathy in Allied countries towards Irish neutrality, and ensure de Valera was on record as hindering the war effort.[15] The American therefore decided to strike at one of the most sensitive expressions of Irish sovereignty: its independent diplomatic relations.

In O'Brien's view, 'identity, legitimacy, symbolism [and] status [...] underlay all Ireland's early efforts'.[16] As leaders of the sole western European state born of nationalist armed struggle in the twentieth century, it was vitally important for Irish state figures to be received as equals in European capitals – especially London. As the British Representative in Ireland, Sir John Maffey, commented of Joseph Walshe, the Secretary of the Department of External Affairs from 1922 to 1946:[17]

> It is impossible to avoid using the hackneyed expression 'inferiority complex' in speaking of him [...] This complex is indeed an ingredient in the whole Anglo-Irish problem [...] There is the ever present query 'Does London take our Department of External Affairs seriously? Am I not the equal in stature to the top rank of their Foreign Office?'[18]

Fully aware of the reaction it would provoke, Gray handed de Valera (who doubled as Ireland's Minister of External Affairs), what became known as the 'American Note' in February 1944. It demanded the closure of Axis legations and accused Dublin of acting 'in favour of the Axis powers and against the United Nations on whom your security and the maintenance of your national economy depend'.[19] Gray drafted the note the previous year, but Washington insisted upon redrafts and consultations with intelligence services and the British, in case de Valera surprised everyone and acceded.[20] In the end, there was no need to worry; the Taoiseach, rankling at the attempt to curtail a sovereign nation's diplomatic relations, rejected the demand immediately: 'Of course our answer will be no. As long as I am here it will be no.' Gray was reportedly delighted.[21] Security concerns regarding the upcoming D-Day invasion were said to have prompted the demand,[22] but the co-operation between Irish and Allied intelligence services, and the general effectiveness of Irish counter-espionage, indicates there was no real danger of sensitive information leaking to the Germans through Ireland. The Canadians, for example, are said to have been unperturbed by the Axis presence in Dublin.[23] Gray, it appears, had not been informed of this intelligence co-operation; in fact both MI5 and OSS voiced misgivings that his strident attitude would imperil intelligence sharing.[24] The suggestion that foreign diplomats might be engaged in espionage in Ireland particularly incensed de Valera, Dwyer adds, because the Taoiseach feared Gray might reveal the fact that Irish support for the Allies had gone so far as to authorise diplomats in Berlin, Rome and Vichy to gather intelligence for the Americans. Should this be divulged, de Valera warned, he would break off co-operation.[25]

Dublin's refusal was greeted with fresh outrage in the US, which had been Gray's objective. In an opinion poll that March, thirty-five per cent of respondents – around one million Americans[26] – believed force should be used to compel the Irish to expel Axis representatives.[27] The British, knowing how badly the American Note had been received,[28] nevertheless compounded Ireland's sense of isolation with their own version, presented soon afterwards.[29]

But this was not enough for Gray, who remained determined to brand Irish perfidy in the memory of the American public. In September 1944 a fresh demand was made to the Taoiseach: no Axis war criminal was to be granted asylum in Ireland. It was, like its predecessor, aimed at the heart of Irish sovereignty – in this case by seeking to curtail its right to grant territorial asylum.[30] It also duly received the rejection it was designed to provoke. 'The Irish

Government can give no assurance which would preclude them from exercising that right should justice, charity or honour or the interest of the nation so require,' ran the reply. There was, however, no intention of altering the existing practice of denying

> admission to all aliens whose presence would be at variance with the policy of neutrality, or detrimental to the Irish people, or inconsistent with the desire of the Irish people to avoid injury to the interests of friendly states.[31]

Sean Nunan, Irish representative in Washington, later clarified the statement, saying that the 'friendly states' referred to included Britain and the USA. He did not mention France.[32] But failure to give the Allies the blanket undertaking they demanded further damaged Ireland's reputation. Professor Savory, Member for Queen's University, Belfast, raised Ireland's recalcitrance on the issue of asylum for war criminals ('even Himmler and Hitler should they land in Southern Ireland') in the House of Commons in January 1945. Contrasting its attitude with the assurances given by other European neutrals,

> even the less satisfactory but still adequate answers given by Spain and Portugal, it would appear that this [...] is the only neutral country which has not given definite pledges with regard to refusing the right of asylum to war criminals.[33]

Rumours that Nazis were obtaining sanctuary in Éire were already circulating.[34] Hitler himself was even whispered to have fled there at one stage.[35] There was also a British parliamentary question in May 1945 as to whether William Joyce, the notorious 'Lord Haw-Haw', had managed to return to the supposed land of his birth.[36] All this was a boon to the British Special Operations Executive, which had itself devised a plan to undermine German morale by suggesting the Reich's leaders were planning to abandon their people and flee to Ireland. Damage to the country's reputation would be a pleasing by-product. Owing to political difficulties with the Foreign Office, the supposed destination for fugitive Nazis was altered in January 1945, with rather uncanny prescience, to Argentina.[37] The operation itself was known by the ever-popular title of the 'Casement Plan'.

This, then, was the Irish quandary: incapable of defending its neutrality during the Emergency, Ireland could only seek to avoid antagonisation of the military powers upon which its security ultimately depended. First and foremost was the UK, and intelligence co-operation regarding Scottish nationalists and others attests to the importance Dublin placed upon being regarded as a secure quarter from which no threat could operate. Obviously, its postwar asylum policy would continue in this cautious vein, not only to 'avoid injury to the interests of friendly states', but also to avoid providing grist to the anti-Irish propaganda mill in America. Perceptions of anti-Allied sentiment in Ireland, as

Gray had calculated, would severely damage Irish standing and hamstring any anti-Partition campaign conducted in the US.

On the other hand, demands to close the Axis legations and refuse asylum were clear infringements upon Irish sovereignty. This was the very principle that led Ireland to declare its neutrality in the first place: '[O]ur first practical claim to independence', according to O'Faolain.[38] The 'friendliness' of this neutrality towards the Allies could not be publicly acknowledged, given the value assigned to the principle and the likely fallout among Republicans should the truth emerge. 'It was vital for the national psyche [...] that the extent of Irish co-operation should not receive indecent exposure,'[39] Dwyer observes. However, the waning in strategic value of Éire after 1943 that gave Gray greater liberty to attack the Irish position likewise gave de Valera greater liberty to resist. The Allies were unlikely to threaten Éire with invasion now that the German danger was abating, and the three divisions of US forces based in Northern Ireland likewise deterred any provocative German adventures on the island.[40]

De Valera's personal relationship with Gray was also strained, owing to the American's perceived arrogance and his antagonism to the Irish position. The Taoiseach reportedly considered him 'a mischief-maker, indeed a downright enemy of this country'.[41] Conversely, the British Representative, Maffey, and the German Minister, Hempel, were regarded with respect. De Valera appreciated the 'irreproachable' conduct of the latter especially – itself perhaps motivated by the strategic utility of Irish neutrality to Germany.[42] These reasons – assertion of sovereignty in the face of Allied pressure, and the nature of his personal relationships with the American and German diplomats, respectively – motivated de Valera to pay that controversial visit of condolence to Hempel in May 1945. Frank Aiken (privately considered by some to have been pro-German)[43] emphasised that the visit was in accordance with strict neutrality, no more an indication of partiality than de Valera's adjournment of the Dáil following the American President's death a month earlier. The Allies would have taunted the Irish for breaching neutrality if they *hadn't* expressed condolences to Germany, he claimed.[44]

The visit had further negative impact upon perceptions of Ireland. Churchill chose to condemn Irish 'intransigence' in an address to the Commons almost at the very moment of victory – contrasting Northern Ireland's 'loyalty and friendship' with de Valera's 'frolic[s]' with German and Japanese representatives. The 'restraint and poise' with which Britain resisted laying 'violent hand' upon Ireland was one 'to which history will find few parallels'.[45] Dublin's isolation was only deepened by similar condolences expressed by fellow neutrals Portugal and Spain. Comparison with rightist, pro-Axis regimes was not something de Valera appreciated at this juncture. That more experienced neutral,

Switzerland, evaded the issue altogether by arguing no confirmation of Hitler's death had been issued.[46] It was this diplomatic isolation that paradoxically facilitated Irish resistance to Allied demands. Postwar isolation would not differ much from wartime neutrality, anyway, as censorship had inculcated a degree of psychological insularity.[47] De Valera had also articulated his vision of an autarkic island nation aloof from global materialism in his 'dream' broadcast of St Patrick's Day 1943.[48]

Thus, when the Allies focused their charges of pro-Axis proclivity into specific demands for the surrender of all 'obnoxious' Germans in Éire[49] (those who had contributed to the German war effort, in the Allied purview), it was perhaps not surprising that de Valera chose to make another stand on this principle of sovereignty – even if it meant Ireland would continue to be 'wholly isolated from the mainstream of world events and without the means to influence them.'[50] This 'principled' stance would vary considerably in its application, however, depending upon the political utility of the subjects involved, or indeed upon the branch of government applying it.

The 'obnoxious' Germans

'Obnoxious' Germans comprised three categories. First were diplomats of the German Legation, including Herr Hempel. The German Minister burned sensitive materials before handing the Legation keys over to Irish authorities on 8 April 1945. The Allies demanded access to the Legation files, even though the end of hostilities had not yet been declared.[51] The British thought these files so potentially valuable they considered breaching Irish neutrality to seize them. The infamous condolence visit took place while de Valera was awaiting legal opinion on this question. Finally, in mid-May, the keys were surrendered. The fact that Allied interest in the Legation promptly evaporated indicates they were chiefly concerned with the leverage it presented, as well as testifying perhaps to Hempel's incendiary thoroughness.

The following month the Allies demanded Legation staff be returned to Germany.[52] Perhaps owing to his respect for Hempel, de Valera made it known he would not deport the six former diplomats.[53] Renewed press hysteria about 'Hitler's colony in Éire'[54] and the possibility of a Nazi resurgence nurtured in Dublin resulted, even though MI5 privately conceded that the danger of the latter was 'not very great'.[55] Gray made it known in October 1945 that the USA was disposed to support Irish membership of the UN, but its attitude to Hitler's officials rendered such an application unlikely to succeed. De Valera, however, had now decided to sacrifice good relations with the Allies in the short term in order to assert Irish sovereignty in this area.[56] None of the German diplomats was ever deported, although the secretaries later returned voluntarily.

Spies

German agents arrested during the Emergency were more problematic from the Irish perspective. Unlike the scrupulous Hempel, these had generally arrived surreptitiously with a view to contacting subversive organisations and fomenting anti-British activity. They had furthermore breached Irish law (particularly the Emergency Powers Act), even if their detention was relatively comfortable lest the German government regard standard imprisonment evidence of partiality toward the British.

The fact that the spies had broken only Irish law prompted de Valera to insist they remain in Irish hands. The British advised the US that demands for the handover of both diplomats and spies be eased and efforts focused on the latter, as insistence on treating both as a single issue would 'ruin our chances of success in either'.[57] Gray, however, insisted upon the surrender of all Germans.[58] Although division among the Allies on this issue facilitated Irish resistance, the government was itself riven on the question. This would have costly consequences for one man in particular.

Hermann Görtz – the German agent whose list of contacts had included the mysterious 'Mill' – had been captured in November 1941, having spent the longest at large among an otherwise spectacularly unsuccessful series of operatives. He informed the Department of Justice that, as a former resident of Potsdam (then under Soviet occupation), he was especially fearful of deportation because he had participated in the brutal suppression of the Spartacists in 1919 and dreaded the revenge of 'the Bolsheviks'.[59] Justice, responsible for such cases under the terms of the Aliens Act (1935), was especially responsive to appeals on anti-communist grounds, as later chapters will explore. The department even went so far as to advocate the release of all German agents from detention.[60] In what would become a familiar refrain, however, Justice's sympathy for Axis refugees was matched by firm opposition from the Department of External Affairs, which understood the deleterious effect on Ireland's bruised reputation such actions would bring. These differences of opinion would have profound consequences for all political refugees in Ireland. For now, the Taoiseach exercised his power to ensure the Germans remained interned ... at least for the time being.

Suddenly, in August 1946, Justice released all detained German spies, citing expiration of the Emergency Powers Act. This was done 'off its own anti-British bat', according to Duggan,[61] and is said to have taken External Affairs by surprise. Or did it? Hull argues that de Valera had decided by this time that Irish sovereignty had been sufficiently asserted, and he now had to bow to 'political realities' and surrender Görtz and associates to Allied control. Perhaps some hint of the softening British view on this question had been communicated to the Irish government. It is also true that the spies' Republican connections were of enduring suspicion, and it is unlikely they would ever have been welcomed by Irish authorities.[62] Suddenly handing over the detainees when the primacy of Irish law had been so strongly asserted would, however, expose the government to ridicule. It was therefore decided (this line of reasoning suggests) that the spies would first be released and then, with Irish legal obligations discharged, re-arrested as illegal aliens and deported. Molohan suggests further that surrendering the spies was calculated to reduce pressure on the German diplomats. It was only after Görtz undertook a hunger strike that he and other agents were released on parole that September. It is of course at the height of this general crisis that Joz-Yann Gourlet first stumbled down the gangplank at Dublin.

Whether External Affairs was genuinely surprised by Justice's action or not, it certainly had to endure renewed criticism from the Allies. The US expressed its regret that Éire 'should choose [...] to continue to shelter the paid servants and supporters of the infamous Hitler regime'.[63] The best de Valera could now do was strike a deal that no death penalty would await a repatriated spy. One of these, Walter Simon, alleviated the situation by volunteering to return in January 1947. The British detained him for only a few weeks, no doubt following G2 head Dan Bryan's suggestion that 'the treatment of any one of them after leaving our hands should be sufficiently attractive to encourage the others to follow suit.'[64] Helmut Clissmann, on the other hand, later claimed the British beat him in their efforts to uncover his Irish connections.[65]

Wilhelm Preetz, Ernst Weber-Drohl, Dieter Gärtner and Herbert Tributh were escorted aboard a plane to Frankfurt in April 1947.[66] Even now that the Allies were being accommodated, the polite fiction that foreign pressure had in no way influenced Irish policy had to be maintained. The task fell to External Affairs, which issued a statement refuting 'the malicious suggestion that the action was taken in consequence of pressure by other governments.'

But the task was only half-finished. Görtz, Günther Schütz and Werner Unland remained, the former even becoming secretary of the same Save the German Children Society with which Dr Kathleen Murphy and Dan Breen TD were associated.[67] All three Germans were advised of their imminent deportation. After exhausting his legal options, Görtz swallowed cyanide in the halls of the Alien Registration Office at Dublin Castle.[68] Both Breen and Jim O'Donovan were said to have attended his funeral.[69] Schütz was married to an

Irishwoman, but was deported all the same the following month. Only Unland (who threatened to follow Görtz's example) was allowed to remain, not least because the judge at his deportation hearing noted he and his English wife had entered Ireland legally in 1939,[70] and he had been detained only because Schütz named him as a contact.[71] Even so, the decision to allow Unland to remain was again made by the Department of Justice. Frederick Boland, Secretary of External Affairs, had been away in Paris, and was said to be 'very apologetic' to Maffey's replacement as British representative, Lord Rugby, once apprised of the news. By way of recompense, Boland undertook not to grant either of the Unlands Irish nationality.[72] As late as 1961 their applications for citizenship were still being refused, as External Affairs felt 'that to naturalise them would provide ammunition which the more sensational press in England might [...] use against us.'[73]

German military personnel

The third group of Germans comprised military personnel interned in Ireland, mostly downed airmen or those rescued by Irish vessels at sea. There were 261 such internees by the end of the war, and many enjoyed a relatively relaxed detention regime.[74] As uniformed combatants who had broken no Irish law, these men were the legal responsibility of the Allied Control Commission. The Irish did not therefore resist demands to surrender them, but did pay attention to the position taken by other neutrals on this question.[75] De Valera insisted no German be repatriated to the Soviet zone against his will, which Gray saw as another attempt to split the Allies. The British initially refused to negotiate on this point, but a subsequent deal saw a Royal Navy battleship arrive to collect German servicemen in August 1945.[76]

Perhaps fearing delivery to the Soviets (or maybe owing to the relationships many formed with Irish women), twelve of the Germans were missing from roll-call. Although eight were soon recaptured, a further four – Fleischmann, Heinz, Arndt and Klanke – were granted asylum. The latter two cases were due to ill health, but Fleischmann's and Heinz's were political. Significantly, both were Austrian Catholics who had the support of Dan Breen TD, and who feared persecution because they had supported *Anschluss*.[77] There was no effort, however, to turn these cases into public assertions of Irish sovereignty, as the British were again raising concerns the men could figure in some sort of Nazi resurgence in Éire.[78] The asylum was therefore conditional on it being kept secret from the Austrian authorities.[79]

Following the same logic of discretion, the Irish returned fifteen German POWs who landed at Kinsale in January 1946.[80] These had escaped from a

French prison camp and commandeered a vessel, sure that Ireland, 'neutral in the war', would repatriate them to Germany.[81] This was, of course, the Allies' responsibility, and their press would have paid uncomfortable attention to assistance granted German escapees who had not even spent the war years in Ireland and therefore had no claim to Irish responsibility. Interestingly, though, at least three German POWs in Britain applied to go to Éire rather than their homeland immediately after the war, taking the British off-guard. There was no real objection on principle – not least because the three had 'good anti-Nazi records'[82] – but there were questions regarding the inconsistency in allowing Germans to enter Éire at a time when Dublin was being pressured to surrender its German 'colony'. By June 1947 the applications of Theodor Priebisch and Hans Jay had been accepted, and, while the third was still being processed, it was said to have 'the strongest case of all'. This is hardly surprising: it was that of Reverend Brother Theodor Wiemler, a Catholic cleric.[83]

Unwelcome attentions: Strasser and Mosley

Dublin's anxiety about its burgeoning reputation as a refuge for fascists was manifest in its response to high-profile requests for entry and, in one case, the mere rumour of intended arrival. As early as October 1945, Otto Strasser – former leader of the left wing of the National Socialist German Workers' ('Nazi') Party, whose brother Gregor had been purged in the 'Night of the Long Knives' in 1934 – applied to come to Ireland 'until things in Germany have cleared up more'. A devout Bavarian Catholic, Strasser had set up an anti-Hitler 'Black Front' in 1930, committed to the social revolutionary aspects of national socialism Hitler had abandoned. After the Führer's appointment as Chancellor in January 1933, Strasser went into exile: first to Czechoslovakia, later to Bermuda and Canada. His Free German Movement, formed in October 1940, remained however as implacably opposed to communism as it had to Hitler's accommodation with big business. This position reduced his propaganda value after the German invasion of 1941 brought the USSR into the Allied camp. Since then he had been cooling his heels under an ambivalent Canadian eye. Now that the war was over, he was once again involving himself in politics – and as a Catholic, anti-totalitarian and anti-communist, could think of 'no country where I could find a sanctuary and livelihood but Éire'. Given the Iron Curtain that had descended across the eastern half of the Continent, and the capitalist materialism brought by US 'occupation' in the other, neutral Éire was, in Strasser's view, 'one of the last pillars of the spirit of Catholicism and European culture'. Not even Switzerland was considered free enough for him anymore.[84]

The fact that Strasser's appeals to the Irish authorities accentuate his

Catholic anti-communist credentials indicate he was much aware how profitable this approach could be, especially to the Department of Justice. External Affairs, however, deemed him too dangerous to admit: he would likely engage in controversial politics and cause international difficulties. The Taoiseach gently rejected his application in June 1946 – right at the height of the tug-of-war over the Germans.[85] This would not be the last Ireland would hear of Otto Strasser, however. Nor was it the last inter-departmental disagreement of its kind.

The following month Justice contacted External Affairs with another thorny problem concerning a champion of the Strasserite 'Third Way'.[86] A Dublin solicitor had enquired as to the Department's reaction should his client Sir Oswald Mosley, former leader of the British Union of Fascists, take up residence in Ireland.[87] It is difficult to imagine a higher profile fascist (excepting perhaps one of the Nazi elite), and External Affairs was understandably dismayed. Like Scottish nationalists of the war years, however, there was no legal basis upon which Mosley's entry could be refused. To de Valera's embarrassment, the BUF obviously regarded Ireland with approval, as the only official letter of support Dublin received after the condolence visit to Hempel in May 1945 had been from the now-clandestine fascist movement.[88] Mosley himself was also well regarded by many in Ireland who recalled his trenchant opposition to Black and Tan reprisals during the War of Independence.[89] Noting that 'Sir Oswald Mosley's entry is not welcomed by the Irish authorities,'[90] Sean Nunan could only meekly request he wait until 'international tempers were quieter'.[91] Perhaps in honour of those old Irish connections, Mosley obliged. Like Strasser, however, he did not give up on the idea of coming to Ireland.

The starkest conflict between Justice and External Affairs occurred also at the height of the 'obnoxious Germans' dispute. At its centre was the rumoured desire of one of the most notorious wartime collaborators to emigrate to Ireland.

The Léon Degrelle debate

Léon Degrelle had led the Catholic authoritarian Rex party in Belgium; had energetically assisted the German occupation; had organised francophone Belgian volunteers for service in German uniform on the Eastern Front (the Légion Wallonie); and had seen active service in that formation himself, enlisting as a private and winning swift promotion.[92] His political, military and oratorical talents had impressed the German Führer. 'If I had a son,' Hitler remarked, 'I would want him to be like Degrelle.'[93]

Degrelle escaped to Spain in the final days of the war,[94] dropping out of sight in August 1946.[95] Speculation mounted that a move to Ireland might be afoot. The prospect of a man condemned to death *in absentia* and previously sheltered by Franco turning up in the midst of hysteria about Ireland's 'pro-Axis' leanings clearly worried External Affairs. Frederick Boland immediately wrote to Duff, Assistant Secretary of Justice, to ensure his department had no further unpleasant surprises in store. 'It would be very awkward for us to have a problem of this kind at the present juncture,' he noted with some understatement.[96]

S.A. Roche, Duff's superior, assured Frederick Boland (not to be confused with Gerald Boland, who was Justice Minister), that the Garda was on the look-out for refugees on Spanish trawlers. Both must have been aware of the pervious nature of Irish ports – even if they weren't aware of specific entries like Gourlet's – so orders for increased quayside vigilance did not allay the DEA's anxiety. Specific requests for Justice to refuse asylum to Degrelle should he land were therefore issued. This evidently ran counter to Justice's inclinations:

> I am somewhat doubtful [*wrote Roche*] [...] about your suggestion that Degrelle should be refused permission to land if he arrives here. This man is a political refugee who was sentenced to death in his absence and it seems to me that it would be very difficult for us to refuse him asylum.[97]

Boland's reply was deeply significant:

> [W]e should not expose the country to [...] intense animosity [...] unless we are satisfied that the case involved *is* a proper one and that considerations of justice and humanity impel a decision to grant asylum.
>
> This is a man who led a minority movement in his own country which relied on 'strong-arm' methods rather than on the ballot [...] When his country was invaded, he donned the uniform of the invading forces [...] to make his occupation of the country effective.
>
> Asylum [...] is not a right of the individual seeking it but of the Government according it – and whatever the theorists may say, the grant of asylum by a Government inevitably carries with it the implication that the individual concerned had, in at least natural law, the moral right to do as he did.[98]

In the end, Degrelle never came to Ireland. All this time he was being sheltered by Franco's elite.[99] He lived out his days in unrepentant comfort, dying in 1994. Another Belgian, a man named Dergent who entered Ireland with false papers in the name of Claude Lambin in October 1947, was interrogated by the Garda the following month for fear he might actually be Degrelle, as a British newspaper alleged.[100] Such allegations were still being made as late as 1955, when the truth about Degrelle's Spanish sanctuary was finally revealed.[101] Dergent was not the only refugee of Belgian nationality to reach Irish shores, however, as Chapter Seven details,

This, then, was the political and diplomatic milieu into which Breton nationalist refugees first entered Ireland. Gourlet, specifically, entered in August 1946, during that brief period when German spies had been released by the Department of Justice and were at large in Dublin prior to their re-arrest. Gourlet's rejection by Germans who mistook his nationality and feared deportation themselves is therefore understandable.[102] More significantly, he arrived discreetly – indeed, entirely unannounced and unnoticed. As the various German asylum cases and the diplomatic struggles they entailed indicate, attempts to assert sovereignty without worsening Ireland's reputation as a haven for war criminals were of supreme importance to the Irish government. Assertions of sovereignty included the asylum granted Hempel and other German diplomats, who were also largely untainted by Nazism. Cases that could damage Irish interests ranged from high-profile fugitives such as Degrelle and politically suspect figures like Mosley and Strasser, through to large-scale public arrivals of low-ranking Germans, such as the POWs who arrived at Kinsale. The spies were regarded as both useful and harmful to Irish interests at different times.

Furthermore, asylum in the cases of Fleischmann and his Austrian compatriots was a discreet, even secretive, process. Thus, in those cases unlikely to attract undue international attention (at least in the English-speaking world, where most anti-Partition campaigns would take place), something of a model of Irish postwar political asylum for Axis fugitives emerges. Low-profile figures could be quietly admitted, satisfying the Department of Justice's urge to assert Ireland's right to an independent (even 'anti-British') policy, while ensuring External Affairs did not have too much uncomfortable explaining to do to Allied governments. Moreover, if any sympathies for such fugitives were held by Irish government figures (or those close enough to influence them), they could be expressed in an inconspicuous manner without exposing the country to greater opprobrium. As Boland had observed, foreign governments would inevitably view asylum for such fugitives as tacit recognition of their 'moral right' to have acted as they had under Axis rule.

One final development took place at this time. In December 1946, Justice Minister Gerald Boland signed a new order under section 5 of the Aliens Act (1935). The Aliens Order 1946 prohibited entry from non-British ports to any alien without a visa, and delineated the ports of entry at which aliens could land.[103] This was not the first ministerial order of its kind, but went further in awarding the minister discretion over all arrivals, including asylum cases. Such power had considerable negative impact upon Jewish arrivals, owing to the pronounced anti-Semitism of figures in the Justice department.[104] In fact, a feared influx of Jewish refugees was the chief reason these powers had been demanded by the 'illiberal' ministry.[105] However, the crisis regarding the

Germans and Degrelle – and the desire to avoid embarrassments in future – must also have played a role. As for Bretons like Gourlet and other low-profile refugees, it is noteworthy that the order empowered the minister to grant leave to land retrospectively 'if he thinks fit so to do'.[106]

The first Bretons in Ireland

This brings us back to Joz-Yann Gourlet, *aka* 'Martolod', arriving at the home of Breton exile Leon Mill-Arden at Cork in August 1946. As it happened, Mill-Arden had his hands full already. Independently of Gourlet, three men had just arrived from Brittany by boat. Theirs had been a rough voyage from Pornic, with a forced stopover at Concarneau. Like Gourlet's, their entry had been undetected by Irish authorities. Armed only with old identity cards, the bedraggled mariners lost no time in going straight to the one-time 'officious representative' of their party in Ireland. They were Charles Gaonac'h, Gwion Hernot and Jacques de Quelen of the now-proscribed Parti national breton.[107]

The three belonged to what had become known as the 'PNB Croupion' (Rump PNB),[108] which had maintained a neutralist *attentiste* ('wait and see') attitude towards the German occupiers under its very Catholic leader Raymond Delaporte.[109] Gourlet represented their diametric opposite within the Breton autonomist spectrum, having joined with the young extremist Guy Vissault de Coëtlogon in offering his services directly to the German Sicherheitsdienst (the intelligence service of the SS).[110] Despite their wartime differences, the four Bretons were now united by circumstance: charges of collaboration with the occupiers or 'attacks upon the territorial integrity of the state' (French legalistic code for separatism, an offence created 'in the PNB's honour' in May 1938),[111] meant any return to France would result in a lengthy jail term, or worse. Coëtlogon had been executed by firing squad in April 1945; his comrade Joseph Le Ruyet was likewise on death row, and would make that final walk to the *peloton d'exécution* only a few weeks after Gourlet's arrival in Ireland.[112] The Bretons therefore determined to journey to Dublin and explain their position to the Garda. Thus a few days later, in the company of some unlikely allies in the form of Mrs Bridie Mill-Arden, Dr Kathleen Murphy and Don Piatt of the School of Celtic Studies at the Dublin Institute of Advanced Studies, Gaonac'h, Hernot, de Quelen and Gourlet applied for political asylum in Éire.[113] Despite their unauthorized arrival, their varying degrees of involvement with the Germans, and the intense scrutiny their compatriot Mill-Arden had endured only a short time before, the Bretons were confident of their future in their new home. Ireland was, after all, *'pays frère de la Bretagne'*.[114]

Real Irish pan-Celticism

How was this supposed Irish fraternity expressed? Unlike the Basque friends of Gallastegi who arrived in similar fashion in 1940, there were no taxis sent by the Minister of Justice to convey the Bretons to a destination of their choosing. In fact there was no processing of any kind, let alone a welcome. Their entry was, as has been noted, discreet, unannounced, unnoticed – and illegal. Before attempting to normalize their situation, they had furthermore contacted a man still regarded by Irish authorities with suspicion, who had only recently regained 'the balance of his papers' from G2,[115] and who continued to engage in exile politics. Mill-Arden had recognised the changing geopolitical landscape early, pleading Brittany's case to US representative David Gray shortly after D-Day.[116] He was also now attempting to found a pan-Celticist journal to expose what he saw as French repression in Brittany, *An Aimsir Cheilteach* (The Celtic Time).

Considering their connections with Mill-Arden and Murphy, the fact that all four newly-arrived Bretons obtained asylum seems remarkable, and owes a great deal not only to the diplomatic situation regarding the Germans, but also to the assistance of a number of Irish figures. In something of a neat coincidence, the Bretons' escorts to the Garda's Aliens' Office that day in August 1946 were representative of the three main forms unofficial Irish assistance to Breton refugees would take.

Bridie Mill-Arden had developed an awareness of Breton nationalist issues through her marriage to the exile Leon. As her letter to Frank Aiken indicates, 'brotherly similitudes' between Brittany and Ireland were more prevalent in her thinking than the average Irish person's. This is perhaps also due to the fact that she was a Catholic from the Six Counties, a region similarly occupied by a foreign power, in the nationalist purview. Personal connections of this kind form one of the simplest manifestations of assistance for Breton refugees in Ireland. Once these connections were established and the host came to know the background to Breton struggle, it was natural that parallels with the Irish experience would be drawn. Bridie Mill-Arden did this herself when protesting her husband's treatment by the Irish government. Such parallels were often drawn by Breton exiles themselves, in order that their hosts could better understand their experience. It is also interesting that the shared Catholicism of the Irish and Bretons received equal emphasis in Mill-Arden's appeal to Aiken, along with appeals to the 'chivalry' and 'honour' of a former subject nation – in other words, to Ireland's revolutionary heritage as she understood it.

Dr Murphy's assistance had perhaps a different motivation. She had previously demonstrated her willingness to assist nationalist fugitives, even at significant personal risk. If charges about the pro-fascism of the Irish Friends of

Germany were correct, she also would not have objected to Bretons compromised with Nazi collaboration. Given that the IRA courted German assistance during the war, its militants are unlikely to have condemned those who seized 'Brittany's opportunity' during 'France's difficulty'. Republican militants therefore comprised the second body of Irish support for Breton refugees.

The support Republicans such as Murphy could provide was limited to material comfort and accommodation, given that many were politically suspect and unlikely to exercise influence with government figures. The third group to assist Bretons was therefore the most influential: an educated elite prominent in Celtic studies, linguistics or cultural organisations, who had in many cases close relationships with the Irish executive. Don Piatt was one of these, employed at the Department of Celtic Studies at DIAS and as an 'interpreter/translator' for the Dáil. DIAS had been established in 1940 as an academic flagship. Its establishment was not without controversy, owing to the enormous costs to the state. Its Celtic Studies department was, however, evidence of de Valera's commitment to the Irish language. The personal interest the Taoiseach took in this subject, in addition to Piatt's parliamentary role, ensured a close contact between the two men which was of considerable help to Breton refugees. Piatt could call upon a network of Celticists to provide comfort to the Breton arrivals – Gourlet was accommodated in Dublin by Piatt's neighbours Seamus O'Tuama and his wife Roísín, who undertook to teach him English in exchange for Breton lessons.

Irish pan-Celticists had links with the Breton movement extending back many years. These included cultural nationalists such as Thomas de Bhaldraithe, who made his Dublin home available to Bretons while he was in Galway;[117] and Eibhlin Ní Chathailriabhaigh, secretary of the International Celtic Congress.[118] One of the most influential individuals was Oscar Mac Uilis,[119] an accomplished linguist and Congress member who had attended the first conference of the PNB's forerunner, the Parti autonomiste breton, at Rosporden in 1927.[120] French security services noted him as an Irish contact for Breton autonomists from at least 1939.[121] Connections with Breton nationalists were maintained through the Congress, which is held in one of the six Celtic countries on a rotating, annual basis. Mac Uilis – a 'patriotic Irish Protestant'[122] – accommodated Charles Gaonac'h in Dublin, and was evidently close enough to de Valera to organise an unofficial meeting between the Taoiseach and former PNB leader Raymond Delaporte following the latter's arrival in mid-1947. At this meeting de Valera is said to have assured Delaporte that no Breton asylee would be surrendered to the French. Like the asylum granted the Austrians, however, discretion was paramount. In fact, the Taoiseach is said to have privately advised the Breton to continue using the pseudonym with which he entered Ireland. Then, if the French ambassador were to speak of 'M.

Delaporte', de Valera could reply he didn't know any person of that name.[123] As naked as such deception appears, it is known that from March 1946 the French government had lent its voice to demands that German spies be surrendered.[124] Further antagonisation of Paris at this time would worsen an already delicate diplomatic situation. This is not to depreciate the significance of the interview, however, which testifies not only to Mac Uilis's connections, but also to the evident interest (albeit discreet and deniable) the Taoiseach took in these new arrivals.

Reports like these, testifying as they do to a high level of access enjoyed by Breton refugees, have contributed to interpretations that pan-Celtic sympathy determined postwar asylum policy. And there is certainly evidence that attests to de Valera's personal sympathy for Celtic activists. Among official Irish papers is a handwritten note to a member of the SNP, stating that the Taoiseach 'understands so well how the Scottish and Welsh nationalists feel'.[125] His department, and that of External Affairs, maintained files on nationalist movements in Celtic regions of Britain, including Cornwall.[126] These files were usually opened after Dublin received requests for assistance, however. It is also significant that de Valera's expression of sympathy with British Celts was dated November 1948 – nine months after Fianna Fáil's electoral loss to the Interparty coalition, when the party was in Opposition for the first time in sixteen years.

While in government, Fianna Fáil figures restricted themselves to discreet assistance to Bretons. Given that the asylum accorded Austrian internees was similarly handled, it seems difficult to assign such sympathy to purely pan-Celticist motives. Importantly, the Irish government lodged no official protest against the purge of Breton nationalists following the Liberation of France that caused many to flee in the first place.[127] So are there any manifestations of a public, unambiguous and (most importantly) officially-sponsored pan-Celticism exercised by the Irish government?

The fact is that expressions of this kind were almost entirely limited to the cultural sphere, particularly the linguistic. These were not unimportant, however. Radio Éireann broadcast the first programmes in Welsh from 1927 – eight years before the BBC.[128] De Valera ordered the Irish Folklore Commission to record native Manx speakers after his one-day visit to the Isle of Man in July 1947.[129] This was the Taoiseach's first trip abroad since 1939. The day after his return, the first postwar Celtic Congress began in Dublin.

This was the first to be held in Ireland since 1934, and the government gave it unprecedented support. Education Minister Tomás Ó Deirg opened the event at University College, Dublin, and President Seán T. Ó Ceallaigh threw a garden party for delegates. Ellis, however, argues that support for pan-Celticism in this period was part of a strategy to win adherents to the anti-Partition campaign.[130] This effort, including trips to countries significant in the Irish diaspora like the US and Australia, intensified after Fianna Fáil's electoral loss in February 1948, as de Valera sought to outflank the Interparty government on Republican issues – especially the second party in the coalition, Clann na Poblachta.[131] A trip to Wales in October 1948, for example, sought to attract support for the Anti-Partition League, but 'Dev' was careful to avoid condemnations of England (much to the disappointment of some Welsh nationalists) and spent much of his address praising Welsh language conservation.[132] After Fianna Fáil was returned to office in 1951, de Valera dropped even these tours and 'no longer appeared interested in pan-Celticism as part of a practical policy'.[133]

Sovereignty versus solidarity

The Irish government was isolated both by the legacy of wartime neutrality and its stance on Partition. Its 'Sore Thumb' approach of raising the latter issue in the Council of Europe at every opportunity began to exasperate even the most experienced foreign diplomats.[134] Appeals to pan-Celtic sentiment were therefore a means of levering Irish issues back onto the world stage and attracting an audience for them. Such appeals could not be seen to encourage separatism in Britain or France, and thus were restricted to the cultural sphere in general, or to the specific question of Northern Ireland. Although de Valera expressed private sympathy with nationalists in Celtic regions, policy was inevitably formulated with an eye towards the reaction of foreign powers, particularly the US and UK. In such a climate, pan-Celtic solidarity was subordinated to *raisons d'état.*

This is not to suggest that pan-Celticism did not motivate many figures – some with powerful connections – to assist Breton refugees. But while the Irish pan-Celticists who assisted them broadly fell into one or more of the categories described, there was in reality a far more profound expression of Celtic solidarity for fugitive Bretons in the postwar years. In expressing this solidarity Celts sheltered, assisted and defended Breton nationalists and their interests, even to the extent of sending a delegation to Brittany to investigate charges of French repression. In a challenge to conceptions of Ireland as the axiomatic and principal Celtic refuge, this help was provided not by the Irish government nor even Irish Republicans, but by activists of Brittany's oldest political ally – the Welsh nationalist movement.

CHAPTER 4

Real pan-Celticism: Welsh support for Breton nationalists, 1946–8

A GUEST OF THE WELSH DELEGATION at the Dublin Celtic Congress was a French national known, at least to those perusing his passport, as Dr Mauger. Although currently residing in Wales, the doctor had not accompanied Plaid Cymru president Gwynfor Evans from Cardiff via Fishguard and Rosslare, but had taken a circuitous route via Liverpool and Belfast so as to enter Éire across the virtually unguarded land border.[1] This precaution was probably unnecessary given the state of immigration control at Irish seaports, but does testify to the caution Dr Mauger had grown used to exercising when crossing international frontiers.

The doctor was welcomed to Dublin by former PNB officials Gwion Hernot, Charles Gaonac'h and their wartime leader Raymond Delaporte. Later the group met with Leon Mill-Arden and former head of the PNB's Nantes section, Germain Breton. There were important plans afoot: Mill-Arden planned to launch *An Aimsir Cheilteach* at the Congress, and with this the Bretons aimed to publicise claims of cultural repression in Brittany. There was also talk of creating a Council of Bretons Abroad.

But Dr Mauger's sojourn was cut short by bad news from Wales. His son Jean-François had damaged his eye in an accident. He left the work of publicising the plight of Bretons under French *épuration* to his exiled compatriots and made for Rosslare and the first ferry back to Wales. The urgency required meant the precaution of transiting through Belfast was abandoned, but Dr Mauger's passport went unexamined at both port of departure and arrival. This was a relief to him, because of course the passport was false. 'Mauger' was his wife's maiden name.[2] Had this been discovered the repercussions could have been serious, but more serious than deportation from Ireland was the possibility that the French embassy in Britain would learn his real identity and demand his return to France. This is because Dr Mauger was in fact Yann Fouéré, a Breton activist who fled trial in March 1946, and who had been sentenced *in absentia* to a life term in prison.[3] For the last year he and his family had been living in Wales, sheltered by their Celtic cousins in Plaid Cymru.

The Welsh connection

For many Breton exiles the route to ultimate sanctuary in Ireland lay through Wales, and in great measure the assistance provided by the Welsh movement to fugitive Bretons – and to the Breton nationalist cause in general – far exceeded that provided by the Irish. If pan-Celticism determined the attitude of any political agent in the postwar years, that agent was arguably Plaid Cymru. In a further challenge to Ireland's supposed axiomatic character as a refuge for Celtic fugitives, asylum in that country was for many Bretons actually a secondary choice, forced upon them by French pressure on London, and by Ireland's more secure status as a sovereign state with the control over immigration that had been so jealously defended by Eamon de Valera. These contrasts had profound impact upon the flight of Breton refugees, and none more so than the first and ultimately most significant to flee to Wales.

Yann Fouéré and Breton regionalism under Vichy

By the time Yann Fouéré (*aka* 'Dr Mauger') crossed to Britain in the summer of 1946, he had been associated with Breton regionalist campaigns for more than fifteen years, including the pre-war language education movement Ar Brezoneg er Skol (Breton in Schools). He was not a separatist, however, and at the time of the German invasion was even sub-prefect of Morlaix.[4] After the establishment of the Vichy regime in 1940, Fouéré determined to win concessions for Brittany by supporting Marshal Pétain's vision for the re-establishment of France's historic provinces – a vision that, some historians argue, was partly designed to defuse autonomism.[5]

Fouéré's support for Pétain's regionalism took two forms. He established the newspaper *La Bretagne* (Brittany), which appeared from March 1941 and received support both from Breton industrialists and the monarchist/proto-fascist Action française (French Action). In its first editorial, Fouéré outlined his vision of a loyal Brittany occupying the 'place of honour' among reconstituted provinces. In le Boterf's view, *La Bretagne* sought to defend Breton liberties without contesting Vichy's legitimacy – a position which weighed heavily against Fouéré come Liberation.[6]

As president of the URB,[7] Fouéré was well placed to become secretary-general of Pétain's new Comité consultatif de la Bretagne (Consultative Committee of Brittany) in October 1942. Its members were selected by regional prefect Jean Quénette.[8] Regional groupings were watered-down versions of the 'historic province' that had been promised. Each region remained centrally controlled, with economic considerations paramount.[9] Under this system the department of Loire-Inférieure,[10] containing the historic ducal capital of Nantes, was detached from Brittany in June 1941 and attached to a new 'region' centred on Angers. The CCB was thereby limited in its remit to the remaining four Breton departments of Ille-et-Vilaine, Côtes-du-Nord,[11] Morbihan and Finistère. The administrative detachment of *Bro Naoned* (the Nantes region) was decried by many Bretons as the '*décret inique*'[12] (iniquitous decree) and its return to Brittany proper remains an autonomist issue.[13]

Dismissed by the PNB as a 'new decoy',[14] the CCB achieved more in two years than the entire thirty-five years of postwar nationalist struggle put together, according to Fouéré.[15] The fact that these gains were confined to minor advances in the teaching of Breton language and history indicates not only the largely cosmetic nature of the CCB (evidence of what Déniel calls the 'pseudo-regionalism' of Vichy),[16] but also how profoundly Breton regionalism was stymied in the postwar era. Another CCB recommendation was the Projet de Statut pour la Bretagne (Statute for Brittany Project), which proposed Dominion status within France similar to that of Canada in the British Empire. By the beginning of 1944, more than 200 Breton communes (the lowest French administrative division) had voted in favour of the Statute.[17] The Allied landings in Normandy in June put paid to this scheme, along with all others under Vichy aegis.

Fouéré and épuration

As editor of a collaborationist newspaper and secretary-general of the Vichy-tainted CCB, Fouéré was arrested after the Liberation. The months leading up to the Liberation had been bloody indeed in Brittany,[18] but Fouéré and his colleagues refused to '*prendre le maquis*' (take to the hills) like the PNB leadership, believing that to do so would admit wrongdoing.[19] Many nationalists were arrested late in 1944 and interned. Collaboration, defined as 'favouring the enterprises of the enemy', was a broad offence which allowed local courts significant room for interpretation.[20] The law had been enacted by the fugitive French government at Bordeaux on the eve of defeat in 1940, but was now deemed to have been in effect throughout the Occupation – Vichy's armistice with Berlin notwithstanding.[21]

Fouéré was interned in the Margueritte *centrale* at Rennes for a year from August 1944.[22] This is described either as a 'concentration camp' or simple detention facility, depending upon competing historiographies of the *épuration*.

This is not the only point of contention. Around one thousand Bretons suspected of autonomist leanings were arrested in November 1944, Fouéré claims, with Finistère the site of such numerous arrests that authorities shipped internees from that department to Rennes.[23] Baudot contends, however, that only 148 PNB members were detained at Margueritte.[24] Nationalists believe Paris' zeal to punish the Breton movement resulted in a dragnet so widely cast that warrants were issued for simple pre-war Breton language students,[25] as well as so-called Breton separatists who were actually members of the Resistance and, in at least one case, had already been executed by the Germans as such. The fact that many of those interned were later released without charge proves to Fouéré the excessiveness of the initial arrests.[26] For his opponents, this demonstrates 'a great moderation in repression' compared to other regions.[27] Cadiou, for instance, claims one person was sentenced for 'autonomism' in all of Ille-et-Vilaine. For him, postwar repression of the Breton movement is 'a legend of Emsav' which pales beside the repression of the Resistance that took place under German occupation.[28] Not counting summary executions, for example, some sixty *Maquisards* were condemned to death by the German military court at Faouët between 23 June and 2 August 1944.[29] In contrast (again excluding summary executions and deaths from rough treatment after arrest), only nine Breton nationalists were so executed after the Liberation.[30] Hamon estimates that autonomists made up only ten to fifteen per cent of all collaborators tried in Brittany,[31] out of a grand total Novick calculates at 1,586 cases.[32]

Some fugitive Bretons were sentenced to death *par contumace* (*in absentia*). These judgements were binding, but could be retried if the accused established they had been kept from the original proceedings by *force majeure*.[33] The thirteen members of various nationalist organisations sentenced in this manner were by war's end already on the path to exile,[34] and the executions of Coëtlogon and others demonstrated the real risks of capture. A policy of death for 'extremists' of the movement and imprisonment with hard labour for the 'moderates' appeared, to Fouéré at least, to be evolving on the orders of Paris.

In his own case, a dossier sixty centimetres high detailing his regionalist 'crimes' was produced by the prosecution, and he was convinced Paris demanded a conviction from the outset. Moreover, he believed his interests in the publishing sector were coveted by members of government.[35] It is for these reasons that Yann Fouéré broke his parole in February 1946. Writing a letter for his lawyers to read in court, Fouéré promised to return and contest the charges when conditions were more equitable. Even then, such a drastic step as flight from justice evidently gave him pause: Per Denez encountered him the day before his court appearance, and he was reportedly still undecided as to whether he shouldn't attend and fight the charges.[36] The next day, however, he fled to Paris.

The 'vrai-faux passeport' network

The Paris underworld of 1946 held many secrets. The same tactics that had allowed the Resistance to operate during the Occupation now allowed collaborators, black marketeers and other fugitives to disappear into the maze of streets, cellars and alleys, there to form networks of shelter, assistance and escape.

Into this milieu fled Yann Fouéré. Breton communities were well established in the city, especially around the Gare Montparnasse, terminus for rail lines from Nantes and Rennes. Crêperies such as Ti Jos (Jos' Place) and the community centre Kêr Vreiz (Brittany House) were centres of émigré life, and the strongly nationalist Café Bel-Air had nurtured young separatists like Guy Vissault de Coëtlogon, adding weight to the remark that Breton autonomism was 'an adventure that began around a café table and ended in front of a firing squad'.[37] The PNB's section for émigré Bretons was located here until the Liberation; the party's wartime organ *L'Heure bretonne* claiming 500 attended its meeting in April 1942.[38] Kêr Vreiz had been temporarily closed in October 1939 as the French government clamped down on the Breton movement after the declaration of war with Germany.[39]

In concert with other fugitives, Fouéré established a network for the acquisition and distribution of falsified passports, or *'vrai-faux passeports'*. At least thirty were procured by Fouéré and Gildas Jaffrennou,[40] son of Taldir the 'Grand Druid', a CCB member and cultural activist who was now serving a prison term for his embrace of Marshal Pétain.[41]

Taldir Jaffrennou: the Celtic world takes notice

Taldir's trial in May 1945 first brought the alleged repression of the Breton movement to the attention of Welsh nationalists. A co-founder of the URB, Taldir (born François; the 'neo-druidical' name translates as 'brow of steel') was a respected figure on the Celtic scene. He travelled to Ireland in 1901 to connect with the elite of Irish pan-Celticism,[42] and produced publications dedicated to Breton cultural matters from his printery at Carhaix.[43] His secretary at the journal *Ar Bobl* (The People) had been Louis Le Roux.[44] Most memorably, he adapted the Welsh anthem *Mae Hen Wlad Fy Nhadau* into Breton. *Bro Gozh Ma Zadoù* (Ancient Land of My Fathers) remains the Breton national hymn, based on the same tune as its Welsh counterpart.

As a result of his Celtic contacts, particularly his role as President of the College of Bards, Taldir's trial excited Welsh attention once communications between Britain and the Continent were restored.[45] The sense that the aging druid was being persecuted on the basis of his regionalist beliefs was especially acute given he had not been a member of the PNB and had often clashed with nationalists in his editorials.[46] British newspapers began to report on the 'Breton affair', and criticised the severity of the *épuration* in Brittany. British Celts wrote submissions on Taldir's behalf. His pro-Vichy position, however, was enough to see him sentenced to five years' imprisonment, the confiscation of his goods, and *dégradation nationale* (national degradation, curtailing civic rights such as voting, access to pensions and public service jobs).[47] The assistant Information Officer at the British consulate at Nantes was nonetheless convinced he got off lightly, as he was also alleged to have 'reported two resistance groups to the Authorities' during the Occupation.[48]

Taldir's sentence spurred Fouéré's flight. If France was willing to ignore press clamour in Britain and jail an anti-separatist, regionalist member of the CCB like Taldir, it was more than likely to impose a stiffer penalty upon the CCB's chairman and a pro-Vichy newspaper proprietor of such wartime prominence as Fouéré. Moreover, Breton activists believed that juries in the Cour de Justice (Court of Justice), set up to try serious charges of collaboration, were instructed to 'judge with hate' and were dominated by communists.[49] Juries in these courts were drawn only from those with Resistance credentials,[50] and were less impartial, Fouéré claims, than the regular tribunal correctionnel (correctional tribunal) which had previously adjudged many accused not guilty.[51] Another body, the Chambre civique (Civic Chamber), was set up to hear less serious charges, including those of *indignité nationale* (national indignity). All members of Vichy and collaborationist units were charged with *indignité nationale*, as were the authors of written works advocating 'collaboration with the enemy, racism or totalitarian doctrines'.[52] Presumably this latter excluded Maurice Thorez, head of the Parti communiste français, who had fled to the USSR after deserting the army in the wake of the Nazi-Soviet Non-Aggression Pact of 1939, but had now returned to become Deputy Prime Minister in the government. Fouéré's fears about the severity of his penalty were realised when he was sentenced *par contumace* to life imprisonment in March 1946.

To Wales

Furnished with his '*vrai-faux passeport*' in the name of Dr Mauger, Fouéré arrived at Dover in summer 1946. To satisfy visa requirements, he claimed his purpose was to study the metals market in the UK with a view to re-establishing commercial links with France. Travelling to London, he visited George Palthey, an old study mate from his student days in Paris, who worked for the French embassy. Palthey was well placed to advise Fouéré not to waste his time applying for asylum in the UK; the ties between Paris and London were too close, and he would almost certainly be sent back across the Channel.

Fouéré's family was still in France, awaiting the signal to join him. The numbers of demobilised soldiers in London, who competed for scarce employment, plus the longstanding links with Plaid Cymru soon drew him to Wales. Welsh activists had also developed systems of mutual assistance away from the prying eyes of the British government. Within days Fouéré was on a train to Abergavenny to stay with Dr D.J. Davies, a prominent Welsh nationalist, and his Irish wife, Dr Noëlle. Meirion Dyffnallt Owen, a nationalist and language teacher, hurried to Brittany soon after Fouéré's arrival with the stated aim of 'keeping up her French'. Secretly she intended to deliver news of her husband to Marie-Madeleine Fouéré, and assist her and her children's passage in his wake.[53]

Dyffnallt Owen was well known to Breton nationalists. In 1927 she was the visiting Welsh delegate to the conference at Quimper of the Minorités nationales de France (National Minorities of France). Welsh and Breton nationalists had been collaborating since earlier that decade. *Breiz Atao* printed an English and Welsh edition of its supplement *Panceltia* between 1923 and 1925, edited by Ambrose Bebb, a Welshman who had studied at Rennes. Olier Mordrel claimed it was in this publication that 'the idea of a Welsh party comparable to ours' was first launched[54] – although not, it must be noted, to great acclaim: 'The French and the Breton put many people off,' observed G.J. Williams.[55]

When Saunders Lewis, the Reverend Lewis Valentine and D.J. Williams set fire to an RAF bombing school at Penyberth in 1936, many Bretons considered this 'direct action' inspired by Gwenn-ha-Du's destruction of the *Honte nationale* four years earlier. Both events occurred on the 400th anniversaries of Franco-Breton and Anglo-Welsh union, respectively. The arsonists of the bombing school (collectively known as Y Tri, or 'The Three') were however motivated as much by pacifist as nationalist concerns, and readily surrendered themselves to police. By contrast, Célestin Lainé and Gwenn-ha-Du remained underground to carry out repeated attacks on the symbols of French power in Brittany. For Fouéré, this was because such acts in France were regarded as 'attack[s] upon the integrity of the state',[56] with concomitantly severe legal consequences. For their part, however, Y Tri were angered when their symbolic protest action was likened to bombings carried out by groups like the IRA.[57]

Now in 1946, despite the wartime efforts of German intelligence to recruit Welsh nationalists,[58] the Welsh movement was well positioned to assist fugitive Bretons. Around thirty Welshmen had objected to military service during the war on purely nationalist grounds, with around half serving prison terms,[59] but others had objected owing to the same blend of Christian, pacifist and nationalist beliefs that motivated Y Tri in 1936. It was this committed core within Plaid Cymru, which had championed a neutralist line towards the war similar to that of the 'PNB Croupion',[60] that now sought to publicise the plight of their Breton cousins and expose what they saw as French repression of Breton culture.

Alerted by the trial of Taldir, Welsh journalists began to pay attention to the legal proceedings being brought against Bretons accused of collaboration or related crimes. One such journalist was Dewi Powell, who began attending the trial of Roparz Hemon at Rennes in March 1946.

Roparz Hemon

Hemon was born Louis Némo, son of an Italian father and a Breton mother.[61] From the 1920s he wrote novels designed to demonstrate the Breton language's suitability for modern literature. He edited the publications *Gwalarn* (Northwest) from 1925 and *Arvor* (Seacoast) from 1941, and directed both the Celtic Institute at Rennes and Radio Rennes, a service which broadcast in Breton during the Occupation. These activities marked him for *épuration*, but it was his role in the development of the 'KLTG' or *peurunvan* orthography that was to invite considerable condemnation.[62] Efforts to standardise Breton were inherently treasonous, as *La Voix de l'Ouest* (The Voice of the West) outlined in January 1946:

> A philologist, [Hemon] put all his skill into unifying the diverse Breton dialects in order to constitute [...] a more solid base for separatist demands.[63]

The link between linguistic conformity and national unity was well established in France. Minister of Education Anatole de Monzie declared in 1925 that the Breton language would have to disappear in the name of French unity,[64] and from 1902 the state had sought to eradicate the language from its strongholds in Lower Brittany by withdrawing financial subsidy (the *indemnité concordataire*) to priests who delivered catechism in Breton.[65] Nationalists, decrying the vulnerability of a language 'divided' into various dialects, reacted by developing a standardised form purged of French influences. Debates over the desirability and efficacy of this approach have raged ever since, but for Hemon the objective was simple:

> We can do without French. Now I will go further: as Bretons we must do without it ... Breton is our liberty, French our enslavement ... Breton must be, henceforth, a single language. Let us kill French, or French will kill us.[66]

Hemon's trial was for many the highwater mark of *épuration* against purely cultural figures. The presence of the Welsh journalist Powell ensured, in Fouéré's view, that the 'anti-Breton conspirators' task' was made more complicated. No longer could the French state conduct its 'flagrant denial[s] of justice' in secret.[67] In addition to Welsh press attention, the former Irish President, Douglas Hyde, lent his voice in support of Hemon.[68] This international support was to bring about what Fouéré calls 'the first victory of Celtic solidarity'.

Adjourning the trial until May – a move attributed by Fouéré to the presence of Powell – the reconvened proceedings began with a 'completely changed' atmosphere.[69] The capital charge of 'attacks against the integrity of the state' was dropped, although that of *indignité nationale* was upheld. The penalty: ten years' *dégradation nationale,* including prohibitions upon teaching and founding a journal or association.[70] It was this work ban that forced Hemon abroad to Ireland in July 1947. His exile was therefore not of the same nature as his compatriots in that country – he was fleeing no custodial or capital sentence – but at the same time is difficult to characterise as entirely voluntary. While Hemon's trial meant no other cultural or linguistic activists would be prosecuted for crimes against French unity,[71] it is also arguable that Paris' objectives had by then been realised: to eliminate the elite of Breton autonomism, either by legal repression or through the encouragement of emigration and exile. *Dégradation nationale* and bans prohibiting activists from residing in any of the Breton departments were but two methods of achieving this aim.[72]

Welsh support takes shape

The day after his arrival in Wales, Fouéré was taken to the PC folk school at Pantybeiliau to brief activists on the situation in Brittany. These schools were modelled upon the *folkehøjskole* system in Denmark,[73] a model that influenced Fouéré's own Ar Brezoneg er Skol.[74] In fact, all but the radical fringe of Welsh nationalism preferred Scandinavian parallels to Irish, owing to the strength of Nonconformist Protestantism in Wales. The poverty of the Irish Free State also reduced its appeal.[75]

Addressing Welsh activists in French, Fouéré's comments were translated by Don Piatt, the Irish linguist and interpreter. Piatt undertook to arrange for families to accommodate Bretons who turned up in Ireland, while the PC general secretary J.E. Jones did likewise for Wales. PC also established a committee tasked with aiding Bretons. To educate party members and the wider public,

Fouéré was encouraged to write a booklet detailing the PNB's wartime position and the situation in Brittany after the Liberation.[76] This he set about drafting in his native French.

It is significant that no official protest regarding the alleged repression of Breton particularism was lodged at this time by the Irish government. Douglas Hyde's message of support for Roparz Hemon was the most explicit statement of its kind, but even this was expressed in a private capacity (no doubt inspired by Hyde's renowned concern for Celtic language revival), and was in no way a statement of official Irish policy. Moreover, the Welsh-Breton Committee set up to aid Breton refugees had no official Irish analogue; instead, Bretons arriving in Ireland were aided by informal networks such as those involving Dr Kathleen Murphy, Bridie Mill-Arden, Don Piatt and Oscar Mac Uilis. By contrast, two Scottish mayors made official visits to Rennes in August 1946,[77] and there was even a 'Friends of Brittany' association of Cornish nationalists by January 1948.[78] Embroiled as it was in the tug-of-war over the 'obnoxious' Germans, the Irish government sought to minimise the damage to its tarnished reputation that would inevitably follow declarations of support for Bretons charged with collaboration. And while the earliest Breton arrivals in Ireland arrived independently of Irish contacts, those coming to Wales were actively assisted by Plaid Cymru.

Fouéré obtained work teaching French at Swansea. This was made possible by both the Welsh-Breton Committee and Pol Le Diverrès, a Breton member of the College of Bards who had married a Welsh woman and with whom Fouéré had campaigned in Ar Brezoneg er Skol.[79] Now established, Fouéré made contact with Breton fugitives in Paris eager to follow his lead. The first of these was Gildas Jaffrennou, Fouéré's erstwhile partner in the *'vrai-faux passeport'* network.

Secretary of the Welsh-Breton Committee was Delwyn Philips, a tailor based in Birmingham whose shop had been a centre for Welsh émigrés since 1936.[80] To circumvent visa restrictions, Philips invited Gildas to take up a local position as designer of textiles.[81] In this way, Gildas Jaffrennou became the first Breton refugee to join Fouéré in Britain, with the direct assistance of Welsh nationalists. Gildas soon moved to Wales proper, working in agriculture and teaching art at a college in Harlech. Throughout this period he maintained the false identity with which he had entered the country, being known even to close associates as 'Claude'.[82]

Assuming control of the *vrai-faux passeport* network in Paris was a fugitive who subsequently entered Britain under the name of 'Albert Horel'. Like Jaffrennou he came first to Birmingham before working odd jobs in Wales; first as an agricultural labourer at Cenarth, then as a wine waiter at a hotel in

Aberystwyth – a position for which he was completely unqualified other than by dint of his Gallic accent.[83] The irony of this is that the unassuming Frenchman Horel was in reality one of the most implacable Breton separatists to escape French justice. He was Hervé Helloco,[84] better known as 'Bob', and was fleeing a sentence of death imposed *in absentia* in June 1946 for 'attacks upon the integrity of the French state'.[85]

Helloco and the (first) Breton flight to Germany

Helloco was born at Pontivy and, like so many promising youths from Brittany, moved to Paris to pursue his studies – in his case, in law. It was in the French capital in 1930 that he, Célestin Lainé, Fant Rozec 'Meavenn' and Armand Girard formed the nucleus of a secretive nationalist group, dedicated to direct action 'in the Irish manner'.[86] This was Gwenn-ha-Du.

Helloco was chief of operations for the group, which announced its arrival with that stunning destruction of the *Honte nationale* in 1932. As Lainé's right-hand man, Helloco was at the forefront of the group's principal actions, including 'Operation Casement' – the landing of a load of arms from Germany transferred to 'Bob's yacht, the *Gwalarn,* and landed on a beach near Locquirec in August 1939.[87]

Although the arms were not found by police, Helloco spent the end of 1939 in prison. He was released for lack of evidence in January 1940.[88] By this time general mobilisation of the French army was in effect, and it appears Helloco followed the orders of his leader, joining his reserve regiment with a view to deserting to the Germans at the earliest opportunity.[89] Unlike Lainé, who was imprisoned for defeatism, Helloco got close enough to the front to do exactly this, although whether he was first captured before defecting is unclear. As they had previously attempted with Roger Casement and the Irish Legion a generation before, the Germans separated Bretons from other French POWs.[90] After the German offensive in the Low Countries in May 1940, these 'triage' camps swelled to around 60,000 Bretons.[91] Here nationalists made themselves known to their captors, and Olier Mordrel (who had also fled France) made Casement-style appeals. All responding positively were sent to the designated Breton nationalist camp at Luckenwalde, which they shared with Ukrainian nationalists from Galicia similarly separated from Polish POWs.[92] Here was created 'the first Breton community of the modern epoch,' in Mordrel's phrase, the 600-odd POWs transforming Luckenwalde into a 'Breton popular university' of nationalist agitation and language classes.[93] Joining the PNB leaders, Helloco was promoted to the staff of their unofficial 'government-in-exile' in Berlin.[94] Other nationalist POWs to assist in these efforts included Charles Gaonac'h, Roparz

Hemon, and a certain accomplished player of the *biniou* (Breton bagpipes) named Yann Goulet.[95]

The Germans hoped to recruit Bretons to act as a covert advance column in their invasion of France. Despite some reports of Bretons in French uniform performing in this capacity, the collapse of the French army before the *Blitzkrieg* was so rapid this 'Fifth Column' proved unnecessary. On 18 June the German army entered Rennes, and there were reports they were greeted as liberators by some in the town of Fougères, where nationalist sentiment was traditionally strong.[96] Conversely, many loyalist Bretons fled ahead of the German advance and sailed to England, including the entire adult male population of the Île de Sein. In London, Bretons were so disproportionately represented in General Charles de Gaulle's Free French forces he was moved to observe in a 1941 Christmas address that 'among the good and pure French [...] one in three is Breton.'[97]

Helloco during the Occupation

Between the Franco-German armistice in July and the Montoire agreement in October there were signs the Germans might make good on the ambitions of certain Wehrmacht officers and create a Breton state. Debauvais was officially referred to as *'chef des Bretons'* at this stage, and there was even talk the banks were designing a Breton currency.[98] Mordrel, 'Deb', Lainé and Marcel Guieysse declared a Conseil national breton (Breton National Council) at Pontivy in July, which many took as precursor of a Breton government. Nationalists were not alone in regarding the CNB as a threat to French unity: a crowd of loyalist Pontiviens who staged a counter-demonstration had to be separated from the nationalists by German troops.[99]

Once Pétain decided to collaborate with the occupiers, however, schemes that undermined co-operation became liabilities, and those in Berlin favouring a strong France that could assist in the war against Britain gained the upper hand. As has been noted, these included Foreign Minister von Ribbentrop and ambassador to Vichy (although he spent most of his time in Paris), Otto Abetz.[100] The separatists Debauvais and Mordrel were ousted from the PNB leadership in December and replaced with the moderate Raymond Delaporte, who expounded a federalist line less antagonistic to Pétain. Even so, the Germans continued to tolerate the PNB and financially support its journal *L'Heure bretonne*,[101] largely as a hedge against Vichy treachery. Ironically, one of the arguments now put forward by the Germans for abandoning Breton separation was the belief that the very Celtic commonalities long championed by *Breiz Atao* would draw an independent Brittany into British orbit and turn it into 'a continental annexe of England'.[102] German support for Breton nationalists would henceforth be limited to the recruitment of 'agents suitable for the struggle against England and for action in Ireland'.[103] The ultimate decision for this policy, wrote Abwehr Second Department chief Erwin Lahousen, was made by von Ribbentrop himself.[104]

The PNB was one of few parties allowed to operate in the Occupied Zone.[105] Officials grew concerned, however, about the infiltration of Vichy agents tasked with undermining the movement and discrediting it in the eyes of the occupiers.[106] Needing someone with experience of covert action to root out the Vichyites, they turned to 'Bob' Helloco.

This secretive police role within the PNB has caused confusion regarding Helloco's wartime activities. Aside from editing the low-circulation journal *Galv* (Call) from 1941, Fouéré claims Helloco and his comrade Jacques Bruchet led an 'idle existence', in which politics assumed 'secondary importance'.[107] Fouéré knew of Helloco's continuing role in the Kuzul Meur, the secret Grand Council of Breton nationalism, mostly because Fouéré himself was inducted into it late in 1940, along with Roparz Hemon.[108] It seems surprising, therefore, that Fouéré would be unaware of the security role Helloco played within the PNB. 'Bob' deputised the young Patrick Guérin with the task of neutralising Vichy intrigues in the party,[109] and continued to co-ordinate secret police efforts. According to Hamon, these included compiling lists of Jews, Freemasons and listeners of British radio.[110]

Both Helloco and Bruchet fled to Paris after the Liberation in 1944, but neither seems to have been troubled by their fugitive status. The latter felt secure enough to marry under his own name,[111] and when Helloco was sentenced to death *par contumace* he is said to have carried the sentence 'gaily'.[112] Finally he crossed the Channel to safety, leaving the *vrai-faux passeport* network to his old friend. Bruchet himself later undertook 'many voyages' to Wales without attracting attention.

Welsh assistance increases

One of Helloco's few political ventures once in Wales was to translate Fouéré's booklet on repression in Brittany into English. Helloco had previously translated Dan Breen's *My fight for Irish freedom* into French, under the pseudonym Robert Kadig. The booklet was published by Plaid Cymru under the title *Breton nationalism*. Another project with the aim of publicising the *épuration* was the monthly bulletin *Breton National News Service,* which appeared from December 1946. Created by the Welsh-Breton Committee and written by Fouéré and others, the roneographed bulletins were written in English and translated into

Welsh, Breton, Spanish and French.[113] As well as expounding upon familiar pan-Celtic and *épuration* themes, *BNNS* sought to contextualise the Breton experience within a framework of anti-colonialism, particularly in the French colonies. French attitudes towards Syria and Italian-speaking communities in the French Alps were compared to the situation in Brittany, alongside some of the earliest declarations of solidarity with Vietnamese nationalists.[114] Comparisons were also made with the repression of Ukrainian nationalism. 'Are national minorities to be found only among defeated powers?' *BNNS* asked.[115]

The appearance of both *BNNS* and *Breton nationalism* were to have serious unintended consequences for Fouéré and the Breton presence in Wales. These began to manifest soon after publication of the latter in April 1947. For in that month a very public demonstration of Welsh solidarity took place, increasing alarm in French diplomatic circles about the influence Breton nationalists were exercising over British public opinion, and leading many in Paris to wonder whether Bretons weren't indeed being sheltered by their cousins in Wales. This was the visit of a delegation of the Welsh National Eisteddfod to Brittany to investigate allegations of cultural repression.

The Welsh delegation visits Brittany

Remarkably, the idea that a Welsh delegation should visit Brittany had first been proposed by the French ambassador at London, M. Massigli.[116] In this way it was hoped media attention enflamed by the cases of Roparz Hemon and Taldir Jaffrennou could be defused. Certainly by this time the purge of cultural nationalists had begun to wane, and it was no doubt felt Welsh acknowledgement of this fact would ease ill-feeling toward Paris. Opponents of nationalism in Brittany such as Fañch Gourvil also felt the Welsh would surely cease agitation on behalf of '*collabos*' once they saw how proud most Bretons were of the Resistance during German occupation.

> One cannot say [...] that the French government have been carrying out a policy of oppression in Brittany. If one bears in mind how intense the hatred is which the treason committed by the autonomists has aroused among the Breton population, one can only say that the French Government have, on the contrary, given a very remarkable example of forbearance and moderation.

Rumours to the contrary were the work of 'Breton traitors who fled from France' and evidence that, although Germany was defeated, 'German propaganda has not stopped its baneful work yet.'[117]

The Executive Committee of the Eisteddfod accepted the invitation in March, provided they could make unrestricted enquiries concerning language and cultural instruction in Brittany, and contact Breton activists without the 'surveillance' of French authorities.[118] These included Taldir Jaffrennou, who had been released from prison after serving fewer than two years of his sentence, but was prohibited from residing in Brittany and now lived at Le Mans.[119]

Arriving in April, the delegation acknowledged the French right to prosecute those who had collaborated with the Germans, but demanded answers to a key question: had there been, and were there still, persecutions of purely cultural activists? For the delegates, accusations of collaboration with Vichy were not sufficient grounds for repression, as a cultural nationalist would logically collaborate with any French government that made linguistic and cultural concessions. And, they claimed, only Bretons had been accused of 'attacks on the integrity of the state' – a fact that undermined the French claim that Breton collaborators were being treated no differently from those in other regions of France.[120] The delegation therefore concluded that 'The simple fact of having partaken in Breton activity of whatever nature was for the French government sufficient motive for persecution.'[121] Their report called for a general amnesty of Bretons sentenced for such offences, and promised to continue Welsh support in order to keep the Breton movement alive.[122]

The Welsh report went off 'like a bomb' in France, according to Fouéré.[123] The delegation had evidently been influenced by 'persons who quit Brittany at the same time as the Germans', said M. Loyen of Rennes University.[124] Cadiou dismisses the delegation as 'militant nationalists' who reached predictable conclusions.[125] This conception is not unique to French commentators. For Gosling of the British consulate at Nantes, the Welsh arrived with preconceptions of repression that no amount of refutation nor displays of cultural freedom could shift – even if his report reveals something of his own ignorance on the subject of Breton particularism:

> The Welsh were convinced that there was still a great deal of persecution in Brittany [...] They actually claimed to have been informed that anyone organising or performing Breton dances is liable to imprisonment, and that it is forbidden to speak Gaelic [*sic*] on the telephone. It says worlds for the ruggedness of their opinion that some of them still appeared to think this after [...] 1 1/2 hours solid of Breton dances.[126]

French counter-measures in Wales

French efforts to counteract Welsh agitation on behalf of Bretons now gathered force. Missions in Celtic countries were instructed how to respond to letters expressing pan-Celticist solidarity, but by October 1947 it was felt a delegation of their own should visit Wales and set the record straight. This included Paul Hutin Desgrée, deputy for Morbihan and director of the newspaper *Ouest-France* (West France). While the delegation was welcomed at official functions (including one hosted by the lord mayor of Cardiff), Fouéré claims the visit had an ulterior purpose: to pressure the British government into deporting Bretons hiding in the UK, and have it refuse entry to future arrivals.[127]

French diplomats in London had been concerned about the assistance provided by Welsh nationalists to fugitive Bretons since the end of the war. Lacking hard evidence, let alone the names of those helped in this manner, they experienced difficulty convincing their British counterparts in the Foreign Office to take the matter seriously. '[W]e really do think that all this is moonshine', Wilson of the FO noted in May 1947 before a meeting to discuss Bretons in Wales.[128] In June the notion of 'hypothetical Breton exiles' was similarly dismissed by FO mandarins.[129]

Pressure upon the British to act increased that October and November – the very time Desgrée's delegation was visiting Wales and, according to French reports at least, was enduring heckles from rowdy Welsh nationalists.[130] This increased pressure wasn't solely due to damaged Gallic pride, however. French diplomats had now uncovered evidence linking actual identities to the anti-French agitation in Wales. Specifically, they were onto the trail of Yann Fouéré.

'Armaud Robert Jean'

Fouéré had become anxious that French authorities would learn of his presence in Wales, particularly since the appearance of *BNNS* and *Breton nationalism*. The unease had grown since his family joined him at the end of March, as they had entered the country on tourist visas under their real names. It seemed his cover was finally blown when his employers sought to have his contract renewed and encountered sudden opposition from the French embassy.

As a lecturer in French, 'Dr Mauger' had been unable to avoid interaction with the French consulate at Swansea. At one stage he and the consul even reviewed a report from Paris that featured his own real name. In what must have been a surreal conversation, 'Mauger' was informed by the consul that the exact whereabouts of this Fouéré were unknown, but he was thought to be sheltering among Welsh nationalists 'in the north of the country'.

Fouéré now departed for the Celtic Congress in Dublin. His unease concerning anonymity explains his care in transiting via Liverpool and Belfast, in addition to the fact that his own visa – fraudulently obtained though it was – was soon to expire. Legal advice from sympathetic Welsh lawyers and 'parliamentarians of Irish origin' indicated again that it would be pointless to pursue political asylum in the UK.[131] His best option was a visa extension, but this would be difficult now his employment was terminated. As Fouéré suspected, the author of this present difficulty was indeed the French diplomatic service, specifically its First Counsellor at London, M. Roché:

> For some time the Embassy have [*sic*] believed that the man behind [the agitation in Wales] is a Frenchman who calls himself Armaud Robert JEAN, who was lecturer in French at Swansea University [...] This man is certainly not the real Armaud Robert JEAN, who is in Paris. It is believed he is J.A. Fouéré, a leader of the Autonomous [*sic*] Movement under the German occupation ...[132]

Roché and Crosthwaite of the FO met on 27 October, at the height of Desgrée's visit to Wales. Although still disposed to dismiss the entire question as a 'ridiculous hare', Wilson of the FO begrudgingly acknowledged that the Home Office might now have to investigate the fraudulent entry of this alien.[133] This seemed more urgent after MI5 confirmed the substance of Roché's allegations.[134] Even then, Wilson was unwilling to act without a formal French request ... something they seemed to want to avoid, in order not to create 'a martyr of him in Celtic eyes'. The Welsh press campaign had obviously made them nervous about such matters.

The Anglo-French exchange regarding Fouéré is significant for a number of reasons – aside from the pseudonym 'Armaud Robert Jean', which indicates that either the embassy mistook another teacher of French at Swansea for Fouéré, or that 'Dr Mauger' was only one of a number of aliases Fouéré employed.

First of these is the solution proposed by Roché to avoid unpleasant attention from Celtic quarters: that, rather than be extradited in a messy legal process, Fouéré be quietly deported to France on the grounds of his fraudulent entry. It was hoped this could be an entirely British matter, without the formal French request Wilson considered necessary. As has been shown, such action would first have to overcome the scepticism of mandarins in both the Home and Foreign Offices.

More importantly, the French expressed their anxiety that Fouéré 'not be allowed to go to Ireland (for obvious reasons)'.[135] As there is no evidence that the small number of Breton nationalists in Ireland had come to the attention of foreign governments, it is arguable that these 'obvious reasons' were the familiar pan-Celticist sympathies foreigners naturally expected from the Irish state. If Breton refugees could stir up harmful propaganda from Wales, they probably reasoned, the damage they could inflict from Ireland could be worse.

And although no hard evidence had yet been obtained of Bretons arriving in Ireland, there was an amount of circumstantial evidence beyond the expectation of pan-Celticist solidarity. In July, two men had been imprisoned in Brittany for their role in planning the abortive escape of a number of Breton nationalists by fishing boat, most likely to Ireland.[136] The British likewise had been alerted to this possible escape route, their embassy in Paris being advised that certain Breton 'regionalists' in France had 'gone to ground since the liberation and [...] were anxious to seek asylum in Éire'. Such an escape would be 'easily arranged' owing to the large Breton fishing fleet operating off the Irish coast.[137] Finally, French consulates in Celtic countries had been issued copies of a leaflet circulated in Brittany by the clandestine group Stourm Evit Ar Brezhoneg (Combat for the Breton Language) which, as well as advising readers how to publicise the Breton plight by writing to Welsh publications, also assured them 'The Irish are looking for ways to help us'. Sympathetic Irish figures and institutions, according to this tract, included the '*Faoiseach*' [*sic*] himself.[138] Attempting to convince the British of the dangers of pan-Celtic co-operation, Roché also mentioned a recent publication that had appeared in Wales, the cover of which featured a 'map which showed various places such as Wales, Ireland and Brittany in colour as if they all belonged to the same country.' To the French Embassy, the FO reported, it looked 'suspiciously like some of the maps put out before the war by the German Geopolitik experts'.[139] The publication was Fouéré's *Breton nationalism.*

Fouéré's first flight to Ireland

It was this combination of French pressure upon the British government and his increasingly tenuous existence brought about by his expiring visa that prompted Fouéré to move to Ireland early in 1948. All efforts on his behalf by PC lawyers and Liberal parliamentarians came to nought, and he was advised that if he did not leave the UK voluntarily, he would be deported. He was aware that other refugees had been granted asylum in Ireland – including Jacques de Quelen, whose family had followed him in the first half of 1947. As Fouéré also had a family to consider, Ireland now seemed the best option. At Fishguard he boarded the ferry to Rosslare, giving the British authorities a destination address: the ever-reliable Leon Mill-Arden at Cork.[140]

Why did the British government allow Fouéré to decamp to Ireland, against the express wishes of their French allies? While it may have seemed to Fouéré that the campaign by Welsh nationalists (and indeed many liberals, both in Wales and England) was having no impact, the fact is the Eisteddfod's report and similar activism on behalf of Bretons had impressed London with the power of co-ordinated Celtic protest as much as it had outraged Paris. Needless antagonism of Welsh national feeling on this matter would be counter-productive. Perhaps, in an echo of their attitude towards Ronald MacDonald Douglas some years before, they determined it was better to let such a troublemaker slip away to Ireland than risk the embarrassing campaign that would eventuate were he to be surrendered to the French. The French themselves had certainly been keen to avoid such an outcry, hence their unwillingness to make a formal extradition request.

A hint that this indeed was the British attitude is to be found in the official correspondence of the period. 'If we are harbouring a condemned man we must try to get rid of him,' Hogg of the FO wrote of Fouéré at the end of October 1947, significantly avoiding the terms 'extradite' or 'deport'. More significantly, he observed that 'if we did so perhaps the fuss about the Celtic nationalists would die down.'[141] The final decision of course rested with the Home Office, which allowed Fouéré to board that ferry for Rosslare some two months later with no greater surety than an Irish forwarding address.

Before his departure, Fouéré was warned by Welsh friends to be on guard against 'Irish duplicity'; that the Irish would promise much but deliver little.[142] Pan-Celticist feeling obviously had its limitations. One thing that could not be disputed, however, was the Irish state's ability to grant asylum.

Remarkably, despite his move to Ireland, Fouéré did not immediately seek to obtain that status, and would within a few months have cause to thank the Welsh movement again. The loneliness of exile would soon force him to return to Wales to see his family, prompting the activists of PC once again to intervene to save him from deportation and a French prison cell.

An Irish interlude, a Welsh return, and a final deportation

Living again as Dr Mauger, and deciding not to apply for asylum while his family remained in Wales, Fouéré eked out a marginal existence sleeping on lounge furniture at Daisy Bank, the house on the esplanade at Bray that was rapidly becoming a centre of the Breton presence in Ireland. The family of Yann Goulet, former nationalist POW at Luckenwalde and wartime chief of the PNB's uniformed youth wing, the Bagadoù Stourm (Combat Detachments), was sharing the house with the de Quelens. Thrust together by fate and in frustrating economic straits, the families were no longer on speaking terms. Occasionally Fouéré escaped this frosty atmosphere and met other exiled friends at the General Post Office on Dublin's O'Connell Street – a location both central and symbolic.

The presence of the Goulet and de Quelen wives and children exacerbated Fouéré's loneliness. His falsified French passport was now expired, but such had his anxiety become that he determined to travel back to the UK regardless. He did take the precaution of attempting to extend his passport through the consulate at Belfast rather than the embassy at Dublin. In something of a poisoned chalice, the consul instead arranged to inform British authorities that a Dr Mauger was returning to the country. There was now no chance of travelling to the UK clandestinely.

The British government had extended a beneficial deal to Fouéré some months earlier in allowing him to slip over to Ireland. Now that he had taken advantage of their goodwill by so brazenly returning, via Belfast, Liverpool and Birmingham, they moved swiftly to detain him and carry out the wishes of their allies in Paris. There would be no further leniency towards this Celtic renegade ... or so they imagined.

Two days after the Breton's departure from the residence of Delwyn Philips, the Welsh tailor at Birmingham received additional visitors: two police officers bearing a warrant for Fouéré's deportation. Philips promptly informed Fouéré, who had by that stage joined his family at Llandeilo. Fouéré had no choice, he says, other than to telephone the police chief at Birmingham and arrange to surrender himself. Officers were despatched the following day to conduct him to the frontier ... 'the French frontier'.

Welsh pressure had forced the mandarins of the Home and Foreign Offices to quietly defy the French before, but there had been no official deportation order issued. Now Fouéré was properly served with such a writ, and later learned that the French embassy had asked he be handed over forthwith. He was promptly conducted to London, there to await transfer across the Channel.

It is at this juncture that the power of Welsh activism on behalf of their Breton cousins becomes fully apparent. PC president Gwynfor Evans immediately reignited the press campaign on the Breton's behalf. Geraint Dyffnallt Owen, nationalist husband of Meirion (she of the longstanding Breton contacts), worked for the BBC and ensured the press took up the story. Students from the Swansea campus organised a petition on behalf of their former French teacher, demanding he be given asylum in Britain or be allowed to return unmolested to Ireland. Newspaper, government and French consular letterboxes were deluged with expressions of support for Fouéré. Welsh parliamentarians began to pressure the Home Secretary, James Chuter Ede, and threaten awkward questions in the House – an occurrence made more remarkable by the fact that PC had no parliamentary representation of its own at this time, and could rely only upon the goodwill of Liberal members of the Opposition. PC also was doing its utmost to turn the issue to nationalist advantage: Gwynfor Evans remarked in a radio interview that Wales didn't even possess the right to admit whoever it wanted. In short, the 'Celtic martyr' both Paris and London feared had now been created, even before he had been surrendered to French control.

Finally, as the campaign peaked, Fouéré claims deliberations within the Home Office took place at the 'highest level'. This had certainly been the case late in 1947 when the issue had first come to the government's attention, as HO records attest. After some deliberation, in which the impact of the case upon Anglo-French relations was no doubt weighed against the cost in Welsh, Scottish and ethnic Irish support, Fouéré was visited in his cell by the chief of police from Birmingham. He was to be deported after all, and would not be allowed to return to the UK. The police chief was therefore to conduct Fouéré to a port of departure. Their destination would not be Dover, however, but Holyhead. Within days he was escorted aboard the ferry to Dún Laoghaire, and even given half a crown expenses courtesy of His Majesty's Government.

England, Breton nationalist refuge

Other Breton nationalists in Wales viewed the furore engulfing Fouéré with alarm. But not all of them were to move on to Ireland. Gildas Jaffrennou continued to live 'unnoticed' in Wales.[143] Remarkably, 'Claude' went on to become mayor of a British town. In something of a disappointment to champions of a purely pan-Celticist interpretation of Breton refuge, that town was not in Wales nor even Cornwall, but Deal in the very English county of Kent.

Likewise, 'Bob' Helloco continued to live in Britain. The once-notorious Breton nationalist chose Wales over Ireland, but also later took up residence in England – first to undertake an art course at Corsham near Bath, and then as an art teacher at Dartington School in Devon. He never sought to obtain British citizenship, retaining his *'vrai-faux'* French passport until later amnesties finally enabled him to abandon the name of 'Albert Horel'.[144]

Real pan-Celticism

Welsh nationalist assistance to fugitive Bretons after the Second World War lends considerable substance to assertions of pan-Celticist solidarity. The long-standing cultural and political links between the Welsh and Breton movements facilitated networks of accommodation and assistance; personal friendships forged through earlier cultural contacts could be called upon in times of flight. Moreover, Welsh journalists first brought the British public's attention to the *épuration* taking place in Brittany, a campaign that is acknowledged on both sides of the Channel to have brought its more repressive elements to a halt. The visit of the Eisteddfod delegation publicised such charges even further, and provoked a strenuous French counter-campaign. Finally, Fouéré himself, as the unmasked 'face' of Breton refugees in Wales, was to owe his continued freedom to the organisational skills of the Welsh movement on two separate occasions: the first, exercised through discreet political channels, resulted in an equally-discreet exit to Ireland; the second a more desperate and public campaign following his ill-conceived return to Britain.

However, this Welsh solidarity also challenges much of the historiography on Irish asylum. If a stateless Celtic movement such as the Welsh could so publicly and tenaciously defend the interests of Breton nationalists both at home and abroad, it would seem logical that a sovereign Celtic state such as Ireland would be even more vociferous. Certainly, the Irish state could grant asylum, whereas the Welsh movement could not. An observer schooled in pan-Celticist historiography *à la* Lebesque might therefore anticipate vigorous defence by Dublin of Breton *cultural* nationalism at least, whether in the form of an official protest to the French government, a general appeal to international opinion, or perhaps discreet diplomatic pressure upon Paris. Yet no evidence that the Irish government took any such action exists. Cautious of how such actions would be viewed in the context of its reputation as a haven for 'war criminals', Dublin's only support was discreet asylum to those Bretons who gained entry to the country by their own means. As the next chapter illustrates, Irish nervousness in this area meant even this would have its limitations.

Ireland was not, furthermore, an axiomatic refuge for Breton nationalists. Many Breton refugees in Wales – Fouéré included – moved on to Ireland only after French pressure on the British government made their continued presence untenable. Employment was difficult for fugitives to obtain after the exposure of 'Armaud Robert Jean', and it was feared pressure would increase once the real number of Breton refugees in the country became known. Once in Ireland, the material and moral support of the Welsh movement would be sorely missed, and many would have remained in Wales had it been possible. In the cases of Helloco and Gildas Jaffrennou, this is precisely what happened, and in time even residence in England was, for these two former Celtic activists at least, a preferred alternative to Ireland.

Caerléon is one of the few Breton historians to give any consideration to Irish motivations in the granting of asylum, albeit briefly. As a consequence he acknowledges this reality, remarking that, compared to the Welsh movement,

> The sympathy of Ireland manifested itself in a less spectacular fashion, but its position as an independent state permitted it, conforming to international law, to accord the right of asylum to very numerous European refugees of all nationalities, among whom were the Bretons.[145]

Fouéré himself, having experienced exile in both Wales and Ireland, likewise acknowledges that the admission of Breton refugees was more 'in accordance with Irish neutrality in the previous war' than 'any sentiment of Celtic fraternity'.[146] This is not to denigrate the value of the political asylum offered, nor to suggest the sympathies of influential Irish individuals did not exercise considerable moral suasion in certain Breton asylum cases. It is, however, a challenge to assertions that pan-Celticist concepts were the prime motivation for both fugitive and host, both Breton refugee and Irish state. For Helloco and Jaffrennou at least, material concerns such as financial stability exercised an obviously greater influence upon choice of refuge. Even continued clandestinity was evidently not too great a hardship in the pursuit of these ends. And, as the following chapter also explores, Breton nationalist fugitives would end up in a variety of other, non-Celtic countries, and not always as a result of the exigencies of luck and international politics.

Such then was the assistance granted by the Welsh movement to the many Breton fugitives who arrived in the immediate postwar years. But in addition to the support of PC activists, Fouéré himself had offered his residence at Swansea as a staging post for fellow exiles. One Breton who enjoyed Fouéré's hospitality was Yann L'Haridon. Former second-in-command of the Bagadoù Stourm, L'Haridon had remained loyal to the PNB throughout the Occupation. At Fouéré's lodgings he was forced to share a small bed with a younger man, similarly condemned to death *par contumace*. In one of the ironies of exile, the younger fugitive with whom L'Haridon competed for the blankets had belonged to quite an opposite nationalist tendency.

In the aftermath of Fouéré's exposure, the Bagadoù Stourm lieutenant decided to proceed to Ireland only after first returning secretly to Paris.[147] The younger Breton soon followed. Unlike many Breton exiles in Wales at that time, however, his intended destination had always been Éire, ever since beginning his journey from the Continent around a year earlier. And whereas many had fled from Brittany, Paris or other French centres, this young Breton had begun his postwar flight in Germany. Moreover, unlike L'Haridon's Bagadoù Stourm, the uniform he had worn during his wartime service had been without Breton insignia – rather it had sported the death's head device of the SS. He, too, appreciated the practical aspects of Welsh assistance and, despite going on to asylum in Ireland, came to contrast it favourably with the *laissez-faire* attitude of the Irish. The young man's name was Louis Feutren, and he was the first to reach Ireland from the Bezen Perrot.

CHAPTER 5

Bezen Perrot: Breton fugitives and the limitations of Irish asylum, 1947–54

IN DECEMBER 1947, two Bretons stepped from a Welsh ferry onto Irish soil. One was that former guest at Fouéré's spartan flat in Swansea: born in 1922 at Pleubihan, Côtes-du-Nord, to brittophone parents; currently under sentence of death for 'attacks upon the integrity of the French state'.[1] His associate was older: a tall thirty-nine-year-old also fleeing capital punishment, and long familiar to French police. Despite this, the pair's journey from Paris had been without incident, owing perhaps to the convincing *'vrai-faux passeports'* they carried. To anyone examining his documents, for example, the younger man was not Louis Feutren, *aka* 'Maître', but a simple French traveller by the name of 'Michel Kelleg'.[2]

In Dublin, the two sought out the home of Frank Gallagher, a confidant of Eamon de Valera, former editor of the *Irish Press* and assistant director of Radio Éireann, and current head of the Government Information Bureau.[3] In this latter capacity Gallagher had been responsible for wartime censorship.[4] The men knew they were expected, their imminent arrival communicated by associates in Wales. As the door opened, 'Michel Kelleg' saw no further need for subterfuge.

'We are the Bretons,' he announced, introducing himself and his companion: the architect of Breton 'physical force' nationalism since 1930, 'Neven Henaff', otherwise known as Célestin Lainé.

The pair was welcomed by Gallagher, but not sheltered. The Irishman instead directed the new arrivals to a local hostel. For the first time in months both slept easily, knowing they faced no peril of arrest, deportation or execution. The following morning Gallagher contacted their compatriot Jacques de Quelen, and arranged for them to make their way to the house he shared at Bray with his family and that of Yann Goulet: Daisy Bank, on Strand Road. 'It shows you how they were supporting us,' Feutren would comment of the Irish establishment almost sixty years later.[5]

The final wave of Breton fugitives

The flight to Ireland of veterans of the Bezen Perrot (Perrot Unit), the military formation that donned German uniform in the name of Breton independence, has hitherto remained almost completely unexplored. As a result of their alliance with the occupiers, most of these militants found themselves in Germany at war's end. As a consequence (not least because their notoriety placed a premium upon their capture), reaching Ireland was a more difficult proposition than for those who commenced their exodus in France.

As Gallagher's welcome indicates, figures in the Irish elite were aware that Breton fugitives were on their soil. But to what extent were they aided in their flight? What in particular was the attitude toward Bretons seeking help from Irish missions abroad? Determining the limitations of support for fugitive Bretons is of paramount importance in assessing the influence both of 'inter-Celtic solidarity' and 'pro-Axis proclivity' upon Irish asylum policy.

As we know, Ireland features in Breton historiography as an axiomatic sanctuary. Yet many Bretons were granted asylum in – or first attempted to flee to – other, non-Celtic countries, and not always owing to circumstances beyond their control. And, although Welsh nationalists were once again central to a number of these escapes, it is significant that in many cases agents of assistance were not Celts at all.

The attitude of the Irish state toward these refugees after asylum was granted is also of significance. Many Bretons were obliged to live a semi-clandestine existence at odds with perceptions of a welcoming sanctuary, and inter-departmental disputes between Justice and External Affairs recurred when exiles sought naturalisation. In particular, changing political circumstances obliged the last Breton postwar refugee to adopt a surprising false identity. His story in particular demonstrates that the Breton expectation was not necessarily the Irish reality.

The flight of virtually all Breton fugitives at this time stemmed from the activities of a particular military unit: 'a purely Breton force' that aimed to combat France 'in the ranks of its enemies'.[6] Although source of a significant proportion of Bretons who found asylum in Ireland, the history of this formation has commonly been misrepresented, even in recent Irish historiography.[7] This was the unit listed in the German order of battle as the Bretonische Waffenverbande der SS 'Bezen Perrot'.[8]

Bezen Perrot

Although this formation hunted the Resistance on the orders of the German Sicherheitsdienst, its members did not view themselves as collaborators. Indeed, they regarded the 'Jacobin' forces of Vichy or French fascist parties as inimical to Breton interests as the Gaullist and communist fighters of the Resistance. 'All the French political class were the same for us', Bezen veteran Alan Heusaff wrote in *Argoad*, an exile newsletter that appeared in the 1950s.[9] 'We are Breton soldiers', Célestin Lainé insisted early in 1945. 'We have therefore always rejected the idea of enlisting in French formations.'[10]

Inspired by foreign-sponsored forces in Breton history,[11] and more recent examples such as the Czech and Polish legions of the First World War, militants steeped in tales of Irish rebellion found their most powerful inspiration in the struggle of their Celtic cousins to the northwest. MacBride's Brigade, which fought for the Boers in South Africa, was a potent example.[12] Roger Casement's Irish Brigade of former POWs, although never seeing combat, was likewise intertwined in the Breton nationalist imagination with the glories of the Easter Rising in 1916. Pearse, Breen and other Irish heroes were of course familiar to Breton militants, thanks to the efforts of Louis Le Roux and 'Robert Kadig'.

The Bezen Perrot was also the child of the uncompromising 'physical force' nationalism Lainé had instigated with Gwenn-ha-Du in 1930.[13] Owing to the popularity of the destruction of the *Honte nationale* in 1932, Lainé had been inducted into the Kuzul Meur or Grand Council of the Breton movement. Although this secret group sought to rein in the extremist by granting Mordrel and Debauvais a veto over his actions,[14] it also allowed Lainé to cultivate his image as the movement's designated military chief. From 1937 he trained a small cadre of militants in the Kadervenn (roughly 'nursery of combat'), and also created an intelligence and special operations group – a 'secret within a secret' – called the Service Spécial.[15] Links with the Abwehr were developed as Lainé became convinced only defeat by Germany could force Paris to relinquish its grip on Brittany. 'I started to observe with attention all that happened in Germany,' Lainé writes in his unpublished memoirs, 'as one examines a viper likely to bite one's enemy.'[16]

Lainé orchestrated 'Operation Casement' in 1939 and was imprisoned during the Phoney War for defeatism. He was liberated in time to attend the CNB proclamation at Pontivy in July 1940, by which time he had renamed the Kadervenn the Lu Brezon (Breton Army) in anticipation of independence under German aegis. German accommodations with Vichy and the ouster of Mordrel and Debauvais from the PNB leadership marginalised Lainé, however. With the neutralist Raymond Delaporte at the helm of the nationalist party and the average Breton resenting occupation, Lainé and his cohort of extremists were regarded with antipathy not only by the burgeoning Resistance, but also by Vichy authorities and the majority of German officers anxious to maintain Pétain's support. Only a small group of German Celticists who doubled as

Abwehr operatives – among them Dr Gerhard von Tevenar, who was by now a 'very, very close friend' of Lainé's – were supportive.[17]

Frustrated by the PNB's neutralism, Lainé drilled the Lu Brezon and awaited an opportunity to demonstrate to the Germans that it was in their interests to create a Breton state. Although resistance had grown since the Armistice, it was not until the invasion of the USSR in June 1941 that the PCF abandoned opposition to the 'imperialist' war and threw its experienced clandestine operatives into the struggle. These efforts increased further after the Axis defeat at Stalingrad. The communist fighters of the Maquis, the Francs-tireurs et partisans français, thereafter posed a serious threat to the occupiers and their supporters. As 1943 progressed, many Bretons began to regard nationalists as no different to fascists of the Parti populaire français, or the Vichy Milice. According to some historians, the FTP began targeting PNB members in an effort to drive them into direct collaboration.[18] PNB chief at Quimper, Yann Bricler, was shot dead by Resistance gunmen in September, but it was in December at Scrignac that a prominent Breton cultural figure was assassinated, provoking fury among nationalists and setting the entire movement on a fateful path. That figure was Abbé Yann-Vari Perrot.

Perrot was director of the Catholic regionalist association Bleun Brug; member, alongside Yann Fouéré, of the CCB; and editor of the journal *Feiz ha Breiz* (Faith and Brittany). In this latter capacity he had written favourably of the clerical-fascist regime of Msgr. Tiso in Slovakia and of the Axis campaign against 'Bolshevik hordes' in the East.[19] His commitment to Breton nationalism was well known, a position that put him at odds with the Church hierarchy, whose bishops supported Pétain and his État français (French State). Perrot's nationalist convictions may have prompted the Church to post him to Scrignac, a town noted for its leftism and hostility to autonomism, where the inevitable occurred.[20]

Shock at Perrot's death shook even many non-nationalists. Mordrel claims the communist press regarded it a 'tragic error'. For Lainé, however, this was an opportunity to 'step from the shadows' and offer militant Bretons an instrument of vengeance:

> When all the means of discussion are exhausted [...] when offers, promises and seductions remain ineffective [...] Then [...] the cause has no further need of sloganeers *[phraseurs]*, but of soldiers. Victory will decide the issue.[21]

Although the appeal moved some younger extremists, Lainé's displays of neo-paganism at Perrot's funeral shocked conservative Catholics.[22] Lainé had been strongly influenced in his spirituality by the German Celticists von Tevenar and Friedrich Hielscher who were, in addition to their secret service work in the Abwehr, 'pagans' who carried out research for the Ahnenerbe, the Germanic ancestral research office of the SS.[23]

But Lainé had determined to throw in his lot with the Germans before Perrot's death. He had renamed his Lu Brezon the Bezen Kadoudal a month earlier, sensing that the targeting of nationalists by the Resistance presented an opportunity to prove his worth to the Germans. Evocation of the Chouan leader Georges Cadoudal, who had resisted Republican forces in and around Upper Brittany in the 1790s, likewise asserted the enduring Breton military heritage with which Lainé was fixated. He 'tried to have us as a unit protecting trains,' says Feutren. 'Anything at all that would have given us a uniform.' Mindful perhaps of how its enemies would portray it, however, Lainé was reportedly concerned the unit should not operate on behalf of the SD.[24]

By this time, however, the occupiers were desperate to recruit collaborators for counter-insurgency work. They were also loath to jeopardise Vichy co-operation. They therefore had very different plans for the Breton unit, and the result was a curious compromise: Bezen Kadoudal members would be classed as agents of the Sicherheitspolizei (Security police of the SD, or Sipo), but men of the unit could consider themselves Breton soldiers of an independent military formation. 'All precautions were taken that the German quality of the formation would remain unknown in Brittany,' Mordrel explains, 'and that the Breton character imprinted on the troop by its animators would not be known outside.'[25] The terms of enlistment specified engagement only against 'French' power within Brittany.[26] It is testament to Lainé's obsessive desire to combat France in whatever form that he accepted this role of German police auxiliaries for his unit, at a time when it was clear the Nazi leadership would never reward his efforts with Breton independence and an increasing number of Bretons were rejecting the occupiers and all who supported them. Instead of a clear battle between nationalists and loyalists – 'Bretons' versus 'French' – the struggle was now between the great majority of Bretons who were, in Mordrel's words, allied to 'international communism, Anglo-Saxon capitalism and Gaullist revanchism' on the one hand, and 'the German people, allied to international fascism, a minority of Bretons and the collaborationist fraction of the French people' on the other.[27]

Bezen Kadoudal members voted to rename their unit in December 1943, this time in honour of the new Breton martyr in priest's robes.[28] The division between these thirty militants and the rest of the Breton movement thereby became blurred. The 'peaceful regionalist' Perrot – and, by extension, all moderate streams of Breton autonomism – was now forever associated with direct collaboration.[29] The Bezen Perrot's very existence, let alone its wartime conduct, would soon 'allow Brittany's enemies [...] to crucify the Movement with the assent of the Breton people.'[30]

The Bezen in operation

Gour (a Breton term for 'men')[31] of the Bezen began operations early in 1944. In order 'not to offend the French!' they served first in mufti and then in SS *Feldgrau* devoid of Breton insignia.[32] To many in Brittany they therefore resembled civilian informers or German Sipo. Members were known by *noms de guerre,* often carried over from previous clandestine organisations, designed to confound French authorities and limit Resistance reprisals.[33] Beginning with an initial core of around thirty militants, the unit more than doubled at its peak.

At first *gour* were armed only with pistols. In addition to assisting in attacks on Resistants, they mounted guard at the SD interrogation centre at Rennes. By spring the elite groups were armed with sub-machineguns. They carried out raids on evaders of Service du Travail obligatoire (a compulsory labour draft), intercepted arms drops intended for the Maquis, and participated in arrests. More than one Resistance fighter in Brittany is said to have been unpleasantly surprised when their 'German' captors conversed in fluent Breton.[34]

Sharp engagements with the Maquis became common. Alan Heusaff 'Rouat'/'Professeur' was gravely wounded in a skirmish with Free French commandos shortly after D-Day, in which two of his comrades perished. Peasants who came to his assistance were stunned by his explanation that his wounds were the result of a firefight 'between Bretons and French'.[35] One fighter was killed by a captured Resistant; another summarily executed by the Maquis.

Some *gour* were known for excessive violence. Gilles Foix 'Eskob' was said to have struck prisoners during interrogation. Ange Luec 'Forster' was renowned for his 'bestiality'. André Geffroy 'Ferrand' is said to have bragged of his role in the execution of fifty captives of the Forces françaises de l'Intérieur (the amalgamated forces of the Resistance after March 1944). After the unsuccessful attempt upon Hitler's life in July, the SD was ordered to take no prisoners in its counter-insurgency operations. The Bezen Perrot were thereafter accused of participating in massacres of Resistance suspects, although veterans of the unit maintain they simply stood guard while the SD and other auxiliaries carried out the atrocities.[36]

All of this fueled division between radicals and the PNB. Lainé and his political affairs chief Marcel Guieysse broke with the 'PNB-Croupion' of Raymond Delaporte, and revived the defunct journal *Breiz Atao*. This managed only a single issue.[37] In August, American forces broke out of Normandy and advanced on Rennes. The Germans ordered the Bezen to join their retreat to the east. Most *gour* piled into trucks and fled, pausing to collect other nationalists who were likely to fare badly under Gaullist rule such as Fant Rozec 'Meavenn', Roparz Hemon, Guieysse and his daughter Denise.

Flight from Rennes

The Bezen's flight alongside the retreating invaders sealed its image as a force serving purely German interests. Some came to question the wisdom of this precipitate departure. Celtic militants schooled in the romantic heroism of the Easter Rising, they asked how different the outcome might have been if Breton militants had seized a public building at Rennes, run up the Gwenn-ha-Du and defended it against all challenges.

Lainé's unstinting belief in German victory was perhaps the major reason why an uprising *à l'Irlandaise* was not attempted. What would be the value in sacrificing the best fighters of the movement in a heroic but futile gesture if the Germans were to hurl the Allies back with devastating 'miracle weapons' soon afterwards?[38] Having attached his fortunes so closely to the Reich, German surrender was obviously beyond Lainé's imagining. His immersion in Celto-Nordic mysticism could not have assisted an appreciation of military realities, either. So, in August 1944 just as in June 1940, the opportunity for nationalists to fill a brief power vacuum in Brittany evaporated without result. All that was left now was flight toward the east, and a hope that Breton nationalists would eventually return in the van of a reconquering German army.

At Troyes, 'Eskob', Yann Guyomarc'h 'Pipo'[39] and 'Bleiz' were accused of assisting the SD in the mass execution of prisoners.[40] 'Eskob' maintains the arrival of the Bezen simply 'coincided' with this German atrocity, and that his unit was 'wrongly accused' of taking part.[41] Whatever the truth, the unit was now associated with the worst kind of collaboration.

Arriving at Tübingen in southern Germany, Feutren was surprised the Germans did not pressure them to serve in further capacities.[42] As for Lainé, he remained with his inner circle of *'celticards'*,[43] increasingly turning in upon himself while still exhorting others to maintain the struggle.[44] After several desertions, the original core of around thirty militants was now all that remained.

In December 1944, the 'smallest fighting army in the world' celebrated its first anniversary with a formal photograph. 'Pipo' predicted to 'Eskob' that this would be their 'first and last' photo as a unit.[45] Some among them, Maurice Lemoine 'Manac'h' told 'Eskob', were already planning to flee abroad. The destination was decided: Ireland, the country that had haunted their dreams since that biography of Pearse by Louis Le Roux.

Endgame 1945

Rumours circulated that separatist guerrillas were fighting in the forests of Brittany. These diehard 'Breiz Atao' were said to be co-operating with German stragglers, Vichyites and fascists,[46] and operating with support from besieged German pockets at Lorient, St-Nazaire and Brest, as well as airdrops from mysterious aeroplanes said to be sighted at night by nervous FFI sentries.[47]

While there were some autonomist partisans operating after the Liberation, most such units trained by the Germans for 'stay-behind' duties belonged to the Milice or PPF.[48] Members of the Bezen in Germany were ignorant of this fact. As veterans of Yann Goulet's Bagadoù Stourm, many were thrilled to hear he was leading this organisation in defence of the St-Nazaire pocket. They asked if they could be dropped into that area to again serve their heroic drillmaster.[49] Unknown to them, this was but another wild rumour: Goulet was not at St-Nazaire, nor even in Brittany, and the Bagadoù Stourm had ceased to exist. At this time he was, as shall be seen, living clandestinely with his family at Angers.[50]

Finally, at the behest of the Germans, the Bezen divided into groups. Two of these went on to train in sabotage and radio operation, respectively, for reinsertion into Brittany. Another went to the Waffen-SS. A fourth was to become, according to 'Eskob', a 'propaganda' unit,[51] but Feutren insists this was a title they awarded themselves.[52] Whatever their selection, the dream of a unified Breton force in action against France was over. The 'propaganda' and staff sections remained at Tübingen as the others departed for missions around Germany.

Quiet Götterdämmerung

In April 1945, as the Führer prepared to commit suicide in his bunker at Berlin, the staff section of the Bezen Perrot retired to a 'little hideaway' in Marburg. The hiding place was arranged by Professor Leo Weisgerber, whose German Society of Celtic Studies was based in this university town on the Lahn.[53] Weisgerber's society had provided cover for researchers like von Tevenar to establish links with Celtic movements on behalf of the Abwehr.

Finally recognising no miracle weapons would turn the Allied tide, Lainé and his inner circle resolved to preserve their movement. Bezen veterans were instructed, according to Hamon, to get back to Brittany and lie low in regions where they were not well known, there to await further instructions.[54] Mordrel, however, contends that those who had not joined the Waffen-SS or were outside Lainé's clique were abandoned to their own devices.[55] Many spent the war's final weeks wandering between southern Germany and northern Italy, searching for some way to escape the French armies fording the Rhine and their vengeful intelligence service, the Deuxième Bureau.

Weisgerber sheltered Lainé and his associates first as Marburg fell, and then as the Reich finally surrendered early in May. Soon they were joined by Friedrich Hielscher. This 'left Nazi' had been liberated from a concentration camp, where he had been incarcerated for his involvement in the plot to assassinate the Führer. He had first put Lainé in touch with the Abwehr in the 1930s.[56] Still a passionate defender of Breton culture and a close friend to both Lainé and Feutren,[57] with Weisgerber's help he obtained false documents that testified to the Bretons' anti-Nazi credentials. With these, Lainé and his associates were placed in neighbouring farms, 'where they never had anything to fear'.[58]

Whether these false documents testified to Resistance service in France, or as liberated German political prisoners, is unclear. It is also possible they declared their bearers to be STO workers released from labour service. This was an artifice used by *gour* abandoned in the Tübingen area, who managed to track down Olier Mordrel at Innsbruck in the war's final days.[59] It was especially popular to claim residence in one of the German-occupied Breton ports, as these were the last areas of occupied Europe to fall to the Allies and French *gendarmes* could not easily discount such claims.[60] As for Tübingen, it was now in the French Zone of Occupation, meaning many Bezen veterans were forced onto the road and eventual capture.

After some months, most of Lainé's circle moved north to the British Zone. Here they engaged in woodcutting work into the winter of 1945–6.[61] Although safer than the French Zone, the Anglo-Saxon Allies were aware of the Bezen Perrot and the fact that many were still at large. Guy Vissault de Coëtlogon, captured by the Americans in Normandy and handed to the British, identified Lainé as one of the principal Breton collaborators in his interrogation by MI5. The British in turn confirmed that documents captured at Rennes identified the Bezen leader as Sipo agent no.794.[62]

Peril of exposure, in addition to a severe winter labouring in the forest, led one of Lainé's former staff members to dream of 'other skies'. This was Louis Feutren 'Maître', and the skies he dreamt of were Irish.

Louis Feutren and 'the only free Celtic country'

'Manac'h' disclosed his intention of escaping to Ireland at the Bezen's first anniversary. Now, in early 1946, Feutren was confident that he would be welcomed there should he make the journey. Neither he nor any of his comrades in Germany knew of any precedent of asylum for Bretons, however:

> We were too small and closed a group to think of what the others were doing. We didn't know what happened in Brittany, and so on. We hadn't had any news because very few people knew where we were.

Lainé had visited Ireland before the war, but his efforts had been directed at contacting the IRA – hardly a recommendation to the Irish government. When Feutren proposed that he make an attempt to get to Ireland himself, he was therefore acting solely upon his faith in the solidarity of his ethnic cousins in that 'free Celtic country':

> It was the only one! There had always been contact between the Irish and Breton movements [...] I had no doubt whatever [that they would accept me]. It was logical.[63]

Fulfilling secretarial and internal security roles within the Bezen, Feutren had earlier been earmarked for a trip to Germany to research comparisons between Celtic and Germanic religions – a subject of obsession for Lainé.[64] Feutren was visited at Pleubihan in 1943 by Hielscher, who was ostensibly researching Celtic artifacts on behalf of the Ahnenerbe. In reality, this was an Abwehr mission to assess the strength of the Breton movement.[65] Such missions had to take place in secret once the Reich officially opposed Breton separatism.

Lainé and Feutren were on close terms. 'Cadoudal' later complained to interrogators of the latter's 'servility' towards the Bezen leader,[66] which attests to the divisions within the unit and the resentment felt towards its inner circle. But it was this trust that recommended Feutren as the man best suited to go to Ireland. 'Neven chose me to go. He felt he could rely upon me not to be troublesome, not to be taking risks.'[67] Feutren would be accompanied by two comrades, one of whom was Ange Luec 'Forster',[68] the other probably Job Hirgair 'Skav' or Alphonse Le Boulc'h 'Jan'.

The first goal was Paris. To get there, they would travel on foot across Belgium, posing as French students returning from vacation.[69] This required two separate border crossings and the requisite documentation. Here assistance from the Bretons' Celtic cousins was again crucial. Once again, this came not from the Irish state nor its representatives, but from a surprising Welsh quarter.

Welsh assistance in Germany

Owing to their liaison with the Abwehr and SD, some members of Lainé's Service Spécial spoke German. Owing to contacts with Irish Republicans and British Celts, some also were proficient in English. One such polyglot member of the Service and veteran of the Bezen Perrot found employment as a translator for occupation forces in the British Zone early in 1946. It so happened that the regiment to which he was attached was Welsh, and that one of its officers was a committed nationalist.[70]

Many Welsh nationalists were repelled by Nazism and fought it as steadfastly as their Unionist countrymen. Ambrose Bebb, for one, had been horrified to learn that the PNB was leaning toward supporting the Nazis.[71] And, while some went to prison rather than enlist in the British army, many took up arms against the German regime that had so brutally crushed the independence of small states like Denmark. But, now that Hitler was defeated, some felt that minority nationalists swept up in the maelstrom of war on the Axis side, from Brittany to the Ukraine, could not always be tarred with the same brush as the architects of the Holocaust. In addition, the media attention now focused upon French *épuration* in Brittany was already exciting passions in nationalistic sectors of Welsh opinion.

Whether aware of the plight of the nationalist movement in Brittany or not, this Welsh nationalist officer of the British army in Germany was told of the plan to filter veterans of the Bezen back to France, and thence to Ireland. Whether he condoned their wartime choices is unknown. But within a few weeks he had taken the enormous risk of procuring false French identity cards for Feutren and his two comrades, which would see them safely past military police checkpoints.[72] It was an extraordinary act of solidarity which, had it been exposed at that time, would have had severely negative consequences not only for the officer involved but for the entire Welsh movement both at home and abroad.

Feutren and his associates were handed these false documents the day they were to leave. Thus equipped, and with the connivance of at least one member of the Allied military authorities, Feutren and his comrades crossed into Belgium early in May 1946.

To Paris

Gambling that security might be relaxed, the Breton trio made the Franco-Belgian border crossing on the evening of the first anniversary of VE Day. Entering a village on the French side of the border, Feutren was accosted by two MPs. He showed them his false ID, indicated his briefcase and told them he and his companions were French students returning from Belgium with tobacco. The MPs waved them on without inspection. This was fortunate for the Bretons: among other papers in Feutren's briefcase were 'the political testament of Guieysse; a note from Gwenn-ha-Du to be published; [and] a letter of contact with Welsh nationalists.'[73] It is interesting that Lainé had decided to resurrect his clandestine 'physical force' movement at this time – even if the 'note' referred to was directed against a fellow Breton who was jeopardising others with risky conduct.[74]

In Paris, the trio dispersed. Despite the size of the capital Feutren still managed to encounter familiar faces during his stay of many months –

including a Resistance veteran from Brittany who reacted with hostility and almost brought about his arrest. Feutren soon contacted the Breton underground with a view to organising his journey to Ireland. He was aware that Yann Fouéré was planning to travel to Wales, but claims his own *'vrai-faux passeport'* was organised independently of Fouéré's network,[75] which would soon devolve upon Helloco and Bruchet. Assisting them was Paul Perrin, *aka* 'Gwirieg' of the Bezen, who had not fled to Germany and would later make it to Wales. Many others led a clandestine existence in the city: 'Bretons fraternised with escaped Flemings from Belgium, Basques fleeing Spain and Alsatians who didn't know where to hide anymore', writes Mordrel.[76] Underscoring the perils of capture, in July 1946 Bezen veterans Léon Jasson 'Gouez' and André Geffroy 'Ferrand' were executed by French firing squad.

To Britain

Once Fouéré was in Wales, Feutren prepared his own crossing. He set about obtaining a false passport, the details of which he reveals for the first time:

> two v[ery] close personal friends gave me their passports, identity cards and military papers. Their photos were lifted and replaced by mine with the help of an expert in our Service Spécial. Denise Guieysse contacted Fouéré in Wales to let him know a parcel was coming.[77]

The Guieysses, *père et fille,* had accompanied the Bezen on its retreat to Germany. Marcel Guieysse later faced court in Rennes – the only defendant present in a trial that sentenced Olier Mordrel, Célestin Lainé and Yann Goulet to death *par contumace*. Guieysse himself received a five-year sentence, despite his unrepentance: 'For a Breton,' he declared, 'a uniform, whether it be French, English, American or German, is always a foreign uniform.'[78]

Fouéré's 'parcel' made his way from Paris to Dieppe, then by ferry to Newhaven. Once in Wales, and after those restless nights wrestling over the blankets with Yann L'Haridon, Feutren was sent to a Dr Jones at Swansea, then to the Daniel family at Bangor.[79] J.E. Daniel had been Plaid Cymru president the year before, succeeded by Gwynfor Evans.[80] While staying with the Daniels, Feutren made the acquaintance of an Irishwoman who was a close friend of Frank Gallagher.[81] It is probable this was Dr Noëlle Davies, who is known to have spoken good French and been well-connected in Ireland. It was via this connection that Feutren was assured of shelter should he manage to cross the Irish Sea.

Given that Feutren arrived in Wales some months after Fouéré, and that he stayed with the Daniels for 'six to eight months',[82] it was early to mid-1947 when he received this assurance. By this time several Bretons, including

Gourlet, Gaonac'h et al., had been granted asylum. These precedents acted as a 'green light' for later arrivals. There was no offer, however, of any assistance to get to Ireland. This fugitives would have to do on their own.

At this time the French were conducting their counter-propaganda campaign in Wales, and were uncovering Fouéré as the source of much of their troubles in that country. Pressure thereafter mounted on Bretons there, and many were forced underground or abroad. L'Haridon was so unnerved he found it prudent to return to Paris for a few years before relocating to Ireland.[83]

Feutren, too, returned to Paris, but with different intentions. Every leg of the escape route from Germany to Wales had been scouted, and he had confirmation that other Bretons were sheltering in Ireland. He also had it on good authority that men from the Bezen would be welcome. Consequently, his return to Paris was not to evade exposure in Wales, but to 'prepare further crossings Germany–Paris–Wales–Ireland'.[84]

The first to join him in the French capital was his close friend Célestin Lainé, now known by his 'Breton' name, Neven Henaff.[85] Henaff had just come from Belgium. He crossed the German frontier in the company of Youenn Le Noac'h 'Ruzik' and Anton Leroy 'Collet', in response to Feutren's 'green light' from Paris. At Verviers the trio hid in a cemetery, whereupon Henaff departed to rendezvous with Denise Guieysse.[86] When he returned neither Le Noac'h nor Leroy could be found. Eventually, Henaff continued to Paris by himself, from whence he and Feutren departed for Ireland in December 1947.

They were joined in subsequent months by Bezen comrades travelling the same route, often in pairs as had Feutren and Lainé. These included Maurice Lemoine 'Manac'h', who had stated his desire to reach Ireland in December 1944; and Job Hirgair 'Skav', who was subsequently known by his 'Irish business name' of Christian.[87] Only later were the errant Le Noac'h and Leroy able to follow – the former arriving on a passport in the name of 'Yann Colas'.[88] The delay had been beyond their control: both were imprisoned for six months in Belgium after being arrested in that cemetery at Verviers for 'suspicious conduct'. Posing as Germans who were seeking work in France, both were fortunate to have been convicted only of illegally crossing the border. Their masquerade was assisted by the fact that the proceedings, although dutifully translated into German for their benefit, were initially conducted in French. Deported back to Germany at the termination of their sentences, Le Noac'h and Leroy set about planning another crossing into France, which was ultimately successful.[89]

Establishment in Ireland

In addition to Oscar Mac Uilis and the discreet assistance of Gallagher and de Valera, Bretons in Ireland assisted each other with accommodation and employment. Most remained in the Dublin area, but Henaff departed for Galway, where he put his chemical engineering skills (honed by bomb-making for Gwenn-ha-Du) to work at the Hygea chemical plant, owned by Danny Coyle. Coyle was related to the Andrews family, whose scion 'Todd' Andrews, head of Bord na Móna (the Peat Board) from 1946, also assisted Bretons. Youenn Le Noac'h worked for Coyle, making toys. Feutren enrolled at University College, Galway. To pay for his studies he set up a photographic studio in the town, taking on Yann Guyomarc'h as a partner after the latter's arrival. It survives to this day as 'Yann Studios'.

On the east coast, Fouéré was visited by Cearbhall Ó Dalaigh, attorney-general in the de Valera government. After Fianna Fáil's electoral loss in February 1948, Ó Dalaigh returned to the legal profession. He became chief justice of Ireland in 1953 and president in 1974. At this time, however, he visited the Bretons in a charitable role on behalf of the Society of St Vincent de Paul, and in accordance with his personal 'sentiments on Celtic fraternity'.

Ó Dalaigh was a native of Bray, where several refugee Bretons passed through Daisy Bank. Alphonse Le Boulc'h 'Jan', the Bezen's driver, spent some time here, as did Henaff and Feutren, mostly to visit Jacques de Quelen. Although a 'PNB Croupion' member to the end, de Quelen had not shared his faction's opposition to the Bezen Perrot. He had been instrumental in putting the young Feutren in touch with Lainé some years earlier. De Quelen, his wife and children now shared Daisy Bank in icy silence with the family of Yann Goulet.[90]

The 'Renards' of Bray

Former head of the Bagadoù Stourm, Goulet was the only Breton to travel to Ireland accompanied by his family.[91] Their journey was therefore unusual. They did not transit through Wales, nor did they travel directly from Brittany.

When Goulet read of his death sentence *par contumace* in March 1947, he was, as has been noted, residing clandestinely at Angers. Born at St-Nazaire in 1914, his parents were natives of the Breton-speaking Kernev (Cornouaille) region. Their influence was profound: he became an accomplished player of the *binioù*, the Breton bagpipes, and his artistic flair expressed itself in sculpture and drawing. He founded the Breton artistic group Nevezadur (Renaissance)[92] and was a member of the Seiz Breur (Seven Brothers), an artists' circle that favoured nationalistic themes.[93] While a student at the École des Beaux-Arts at

Paris, Goulet fell in with the Breton émigré crowd, including Olier Mordrel.[94] His interest in traditional Breton dancing led him to the young Yvonne Picquet, *aka* 'Vonig', whom he later married.[95] His interest in cultural nationalism soon broadened to the political, and his adherence to the PNB section at Paris resulted in police searches and interrogations.[96] These peaked as French nerves frayed in 1939, but his alleged German connections caused most anxiety. Although much German interest in Breton culture had been a front for intelligence activities – as had been the case with von Tevenar of the Abwehr – Goulet came to rue some perfectly innocuous dealings with the regime in Berlin. In 1936 he was photographed shaking hands with top Nazis Dr Josef Goebbels and Robert Ley. Testifying as it did to collusion between the German regime and Breton nationalism, the photo was produced to devastating effect at Goulet's trial. What was not disclosed to the court was the fact that Goulet had been in Berlin not as clandestine liaison for the PNB, but as lead *biniou̇* player and one of many cultural attachés to the French Olympic team.[97]

Goulet was captured in 1940 and sent to the segregated POW camp at Luckenwalde.[98] Upon his return to Brittany, he assumed command of the Bagadoù, although he claimed not to have participated in its creation.[99] Initially working in concert with Lainé, the two fell out over the creation of the Bezen Perrot, to which Goulet was implacably opposed. Some felt Goulet resisted the formation of a real fighting unit because he would be 'left with no army' of his own,[100] but Goulet insisted only the Bagadoù could claim to be a purely Breton force in both appearance and conduct. As he and his lieutenant L'Haridon had been arrested by Vichy's gendarmes in 1943, the Bagadoù were, he claimed, 'the only ones who were thrown in prison for the crime of Breton nationalism' from 1941 to the Liberation.[101]

Goulet hoped to lie low and avoid the *épuration*. This desire was especially acute because he had two young children. Owing, perhaps, to the fact that it lies beyond the borders of Brittany, Angers proved a suitable place to hide – until March 1947, when news of his death sentence convinced Goulet to flee the country.

This course of action presented new difficulties. Although son Hervé was too young to be vocal, daughter Armelle (baptised by Abbé Perrot only days before his assassination) had to be schooled not to reveal their true names or other details.[102] Obtaining false documents courtesy of Fouéré's network,[103] the Goulets entrained for Paris. Their cover story was that they were attending an art exhibition in Britain. The family went to Calais after some anxious days in Paris, then to London.

Unlike most Breton fugitives, the Goulets did not go to Wales. Instead they went to Liverpool with a view to entering Éire across the land border via

Belfast, just as Fouéré would a few months later. This appeared a safer option because the upcoming Celtic Congress might cause British authorities to increase surveillance of traffic to Ireland. Once safely across the border, the Goulets were put up by Oscar Mac Uilis at Dalkey before moving on to rent Daisy Bank at Bray. They lived under the name 'Renard': the maiden name of Goulet's mother.[104]

The limitations of Irish assistance

Again, there was no assistance from the Irish government for the Goulets to reach Éire. The networks the family employed were entirely Breton – although it is possible they passed through the Welshman Delwyn Philips' residence at Birmingham. The Goulets and other Bretons were discreetly assisted by the Irish elite only after arrival, or more openly welcomed by figures such as Mac Uilis. Even so, Irish welcome did not translate into support, and for many Bretons life was difficult. For those who had transited through Wales, there was a stark contrast between the hospitality of Plaid Cymru and the aloof attitude of the Irish. Louis Feutren notes that the Welsh were generous, but the Irish generally ignored them after arrival. Fouéré ascribes this attitude to 'propaganda' that rendered the Irish incapable of understanding why refugees would flee 'liberated' countries,[105] but for Feutren the cause lies in the differing fortunes of the two countries, and the separate planes upon which they conducted their international relations. Put simply, 'The Irish had arrived; the Welsh had not.'[106]

Of course, Welsh who assisted Bretons were an activist minority. The average Welsh person did not have any more awareness of Brittany than the average Irish person. But it is true that, regarding Breton fugitives at least, a conflicting set of forces were at play upon Welsh nationalists and the Irish government. The former clearly believed that, without their assistance, a fraternal movement would be persecuted, perhaps even destroyed. 'Stateless nations' had no forum in which to air such grievances – particularly if they were accused of aiding the defeated Axis. In addition, many Welsh saw an opportunity to further their own objectives in publicising the Breton case. The two countries had much in common, and increased awareness of one could assist the other.

The Irish government, on the contrary, could not be seen to help fugitive Axis collaborators, regardless of the nuances of their political platforms. Unlike the Welsh movement, it dealt with other states that had only just emerged from a major international conflict, and which had the power to take stern action against minor powers they regarded as resistant to the new international order. And while de Valera jealously defended Ireland's national sovereignty, there was simply no value in antagonising British and American public opinion when it was already so critical of Irish policy.

Irish missions abroad

As the branch of government most sensitive to Ireland's burgeoning reputation as a haven for 'war criminals', the Department of External Affairs had argued against asylum for German spies, or any public ambivalence on similar issues. Dwelling in foreign capitals, reading foreign press and letters from outraged citizens, its overseas representatives were keenly aware of how Ireland's reputation had been tarnished by wartime neutrality, the rejection of demands to refuse asylum to 'war criminals', and the furore over 'Hitler's colony in Éire'. When Léon Degrelle was rumoured to be coming to Ireland, this department argued compellingly against granting him asylum. It is therefore clear that External Affairs, unlike Justice, was the department most opposed to sheltering Axis fugitives – or, at the very least, to asylum being granted in any fashion other than with utmost discretion. It must be remembered that in 1947 the department was headed by de Valera himself – the man who privately advised Raymond Delaporte to continue using his pseudonym in case the French asked awkward questions.

It should not be surprising therefore to learn that there is no real evidence of Irish missions abroad assisting Breton fugitives. One Bezen veteran (*nom de guerre* 'Braz') was arrested under a false identity at Rennes in August 1946 and found to be carrying (according to Hamon) a letter in English written 'by an Irish personality of Paris recommending him to MacDonald, consul of Ireland, so as to procure him a means of gaining that island.'[107] For Capdevila, the Irish consulate was therefore 'the centre of an escape network for militant Bretons to get to the British Isles in 1945 and 1946'.[108] The French police may have been equally convinced, as he claims.

A personal letter of recommendation from a private Irish citizen is not evidence of an escape network centred on the consulate, however. It must also be noted that no Breton actually granted asylum in Ireland is known to have employed such a network. This is not to insist that no Irish diplomat could have been involved in secret capacities, but greater evidence is obviously required. Significantly, the only credible allegation of Irish consular assistance for an Axis fugitive occurred not in France, but Switzerland and, as the next chapter explores, the beneficiary was no Celt.

Whatever their origin, Ireland did not shelter fugitives within its overseas missions. This is known as diplomatic asylum, and such cases can draw considerable adverse attention in the host country. Ireland therefore granted only territorial asylum in this period; that is, to those arriving discreetly on Irish soil who requested the protection of the government, away from international attention.

Olier Mordrel doesn't come to Ireland

Olier Mordrel learned this lesson in Irish *realpolitik* the hard way. Head of Breton affairs in Jacques Doriot's French fascist 'government-in-exile' in Germany near war's end, the PNB co-founder and his family drifted thereafter to Innsbruck. Here they encountered a wandering party of Bezen Perrot men led by 'Eskob'. Mordrel assisted them with false documents attesting to their STO service, then crossed to northern Italy.[109]

After unsuccessfully attempting to enter Switzerland, Mordrel ended up at Rome. Here he and his family lived a marginal existence until the death of Mme. Mordrel at the end of 1947. Shortly afterwards, Olier contacted Fouéré in Wales, who put him onto the '*vrai-faux passeport*' network.

Mordrel and sons Malo and Tanguy were waiting to emigrate to Argentina, hence the need for false documents. This was not their first preference, however. Mordrel had already contacted the Irish consulate at Rome. It was a natural choice for this pan-Celticist, who had edited *Breiz Atao* when it commemorated the Easter Rising in 1935 and had even visited Dublin on a 'pilgrimage' ten years earlier.

The Irish consul at Rome, Michael MacWhite, did not share this sense of Celtic solidarity. Mordrel's enquiries were immediately refused by this decorated veteran of the French Foreign Legion, and he was discouraged from any further pursuit of Irish asylum.[110] The consulate was under surveillance by British MPs, and British intelligence had been routinely intercepting Irish transmissions from Italy since 1941.[111] If Irish representatives were at all aware of this surveillance, it would only increase their nervousness about approaches from erstwhile fascists. There would be no assistance for fugitive Bretons, even if they were pan-Celticists with a history of adulation for Irish heroes. This stance was not MacWhite's own, either, nor confined to Mordrel: Youenn Le Noac'h was told the same as he waited at Paris to head to Ireland via Wales. The advice came from an Irish woman said to be well connected with de Valera's government – most likely Feutren's friend in Wales, Dr Noëlle Davies.[112]

So thwarted, the Mordrels emigrated to Argentina. They lived at Cordoba in the interior, isolated from the many Axis fugitives who thronged to Buenos Aires in the postwar years. Amnestied in 1968, the family spent time in Spain before returning to France in 1971. Assessing his father's South American exile, Malo observes, 'He would have felt better in Ireland.'[113]

Other Breton destinations

Although Mordrel's experience with the consular service demonstrates the unwillingness of the Irish state to assist Breton fugitives, it is indicative of the allure Ireland exercised upon their imagination. As Feutren says, the 'only free Celtic state' was for Breton nationalists a 'logical' place of refuge.

It is surprising then to learn that not every Breton who gained sanctuary abroad did so in Ireland, and not always after first being rebuffed by Irish authorities. Some sought to enter Éire but, for a variety of reasons, could not. Others, however, sought sanctuary in third countries and remained there even when opportunities to relocate to Ireland arose. We have seen how Wales featured prominently as a Breton refuge, and how some were uprooted from there only by French pressure upon the British government. If pan-Celticism was the primary motive for both the seeking and granting of Irish asylum, it is significant that some Bretons first attempted to flee to non-Celtic countries. Among these were Fouéré himself and the first postwar Breton refugee in Ireland, Joz-Yann Gourlet.

Spain

Gourlet fled Brittany late in 1944. He turned against his German bosses and headed south, attempting to cross the Pyrenees into Spain.[114] The FFI anticipated such an exodus, and detailed units to guard the border crossings. This increased patrolling forced 'Martolod' to Marseille and eventual arrest. Only his escape after transfer to Paris set him on the path to Ireland.

Three Bretons who made it to Spain included Gourlet's comrade from Coëtlogon's group, Auguste Ménard; and, from the Bezen Perrot, Goulven Jacq 'Maout' and Ronan Guyomarc'h 'Morin'. Ménard hid in the St-Malo area before making for Paris, where he found Helloco and Bruchet and the '*vrai-faux passeport*' network. While other Bretons were heading to Wales, he requested assistance to go in the opposite direction, across the Pyrenees. Directed to a Breton who lived at Bidart in the Basque Country, he there encountered Guyomarc'h, who had trekked back from Germany, swimming the Rhine by himself.[115] They crossed the mountains guided by Basque smugglers. Once in Spain, they found Jacq at a detention camp, along with a PNB official named Le Toiser. Guyomarc'h and Le Toiser established themselves at Barcelona.[116] Jacq and Ménard eventually departed for Brazil. Another Bezen veteran, Julien Le Boëdec 'Poher', ended up with Mordrel in Argentina after a similar stint in Spain.[117]

Most remarkably, Fouéré himself first considered fleeing to Spain, at the invitation of Basque nationalists. His connections with the Basques had been forged providing legal assistance to refugees. He even began to learn Spanish, before changing plan and fleeing to Wales.[118] Franco's hostility to regionalism was possibly a factor in this decision, although other Breton nationalists seemed unperturbed by it. Franco's regime was entirely suitable for Catholic anti-communists, however; nor was it unique in this regard.

Escape to Ireland when sea lanes were patrolled by warships was of course a difficult undertaking, and this no doubt made Spain more attractive in 1944. Caerléon notes that, once the war was over and international communications were restored, Ireland rapidly exceeded Spain as a preferred destination for Breton militants.[119]

France, Germany and Switzerland

Many wanted Bretons were captured in Brittany or other parts of France, especially Paris.[120] In some cases sojourns in the capital were temporary expediences before moving to Ireland, such as in L'Haridon's case. Others still attempted to get to Ireland directly from Brittany, such as Yann Guyomarc'h 'Pipo' and Yann Bourc'hiz 'Guével' of the Bezen, who made it from Douarnenez to Castletownbere on a small fishing boat by way of Penzance early in 1948. This pair crossed France from Germany, bypassing Belgium and making the Franco-German border crossing without any documentation, false or otherwise.[121] Why they chose to return to Brittany instead of employing the false passport network at Paris is unknown, but theirs was the only successful direct crossing by members of the Bezen.

Eskob's group of *gour* – which initially included Ronan Guyomarc'h – wandered from Austria north to the Danish border in search of a vessel that might carry them to Ireland. Encountering setbacks at every stage, they eventually separated near Baden-Baden. Guyomarc'h, as noted, ended up in Spain. Others eventually found themselves in French prisons.[122]

There were others, however, who had no intention of fleeing to Ireland. Ange Luec 'Forster', who accompanied Louis Feutren to Paris, chose to remain in the French capital. He eventually married Denise Guieysse, living in penury under a false name until his death in the 1990s.[123] Why he and Guieysse opted for such a difficult lifestyle when others were crossing to Ireland is again unknown.

Ange Péresse 'Cocal', field commander of the Bezen, remained in Germany, living under an assumed name at Münster. He died in 1984.[124] Paul 'Fred' Moyse, the redoubtable Abwehr–IRA liaison at Brussels, is likewise said to have obtained German citizenship, living at Frankfurt.[125]

Reaching that archetypal neutral, Switzerland, was a more difficult proposition, and not one that featured highly in the preferences of fugitive Bretons. One who did manage to cross the Swiss border and apply for asylum was promptly deported to France. He, too, first attempted to get to Spain.[126] Another, Ernest Lelandais 'Nenesse', arrived in Ireland by air from Zurich, but soon decamped for Tangiers.[127]

It is evident, therefore, that in several cases even Bretons who had the opportunity preferred not to take sanctuary in Ireland. There are of course myriad reasons why this would be the case, not all of them relating to views on pan-Celticism. But the fact that Breton nationalists chose asylum in non-Celtic countries does make the argument for pan-Celticism as the prime motive in both the seeking and granting of Irish asylum more difficult to sustain. In addition, the lack of assistance for these fugitives while abroad only strengthens the argument that such abstractions did not shape Dublin's policy.

For there was one other Breton nationalist who stayed in Germany after the departure of his comrades. He was the last to arrive in Ireland from the Bezen Perrot – indeed from any proscribed wartime Breton organisation. And while the discreet assistance of the Irish elite had been important to those who preceded him, this, too, had its limitations. These were most evident following the election of the Interparty government in February 1948, and in particular the accession of Seán MacBride as Minister of External Affairs. The Breton nationalist in question was Alan Heusaff,[128] formerly 'Rouat' or 'Professeur' of the Bezen Perrot – or, as he would be known for his first five years in Ireland, 'Bernhard Heubacher'.

Alan Heusaff at war

One of Lainé's *'celticards'* who went to ground at Marburg, Heusaff was from Finistère. A Breton-speaker who had not learned French until school, *'mab Ivi'* (son of St-Yvi) joined the PNB in 1938.[129] Gravitating to the 'direct action' wing of the movement, he joined the Kadervenn and Service Spécial.[130] Heusaff's work as a primary school teacher, which brought him into contact with a system that punished children for speaking their mother tongue,[131] inculcated a fervent desire to preserve his native language:

> For me the compelling motivation in co-operating with a foreign power [...] was to arrest the decline in the Breton language, which risked becoming so weak that only the establishment of a Breton state could ensure its survival; to this problem we had to devote all our strength.[132]

Heusaff remained a clandestine militant until joining the Bezen Kadoudal in 1943, becoming *kerrenour* (lieutenant) of its second section, commanding four sub-groups.[133] Contrary to certain claims, there is no evidence that Heusaff spent the year 1942–3 on the Eastern Front with the Légion des volontaires français contre le Bolchevisme. Heusaff's Bezen comrade Yves Le Négaret 'Le Floc'h'/'Lizidour' was a veteran of this French unit of the Wehrmacht, and both were reportedly linked to an 'Amis de la LVF' association. For Broderick, this means the two must have seen active service together in Russia. Pursuing this logic, one must note that the association also included Taldir Jaffrennou,[134] yet there is no suggestion the illustrious bard served on the Eastern Front. Le Négaret later deserted the Bezen with the intention of joining the Resistance,[135] yet Broderick mysteriously stops short of insisting Heusaff must have done likewise.

The only 'evidence' proffered of Heusaff's supposed LVF service is the testimony of a third party (presented as Heusaff's 'own'), who alleges the Breton spoke in 1966 of his Eastern Front service with the 'Charlemagne Brigade'.[136] This was actually a successor unit to the LVF not formed until September 1944.[137] Broderick further claims service against the Soviets would have 'brought [Heusaff] into prominence with Bezen Perrot as an officer in late 1943',[138] which ignores the fact that no other 'officer' of the Breton nationalist unit – neither Lainé, Feutren nor Péresse – had served with the Germans on the Eastern Front or elsewhere. Lainé in fact resisted appeals for individual Bretons to enlist with the Germans, 'always insist[ing] on the need […] to treated [*sic*] collectively' with them.[139] Heusaff's late widow, Bríd, further emphasised in interview that her husband would never have joined a 'French' organisation like the LVF.[140]

Regarding 'all the French political class' as the same enemy, Heusaff's combat service was in fact confined to Brittany. Wounded in the shoulder and lung in that firefight with Free French commandos in 1944, Heusaff was hospitalised then evacuated to Germany.[141] Rejoining his comrades at Tübingen, he was awarded the German wound medal at the Bezen's anniversary celebration.[142] Even after the disbandment of the Bezen he did not join the Waffen-SS, and only one former *gour* is known to have subsequently fought the Soviets: Marcel Bibé 'Targaz'.[143]

At Marburg, Heusaff was given the German identity of 'Bernhard Heubacher' by Friedrich Hielscher.[144] He, too, spent that first postwar winter in forestry work, reduced to eating nettle soup with his comrades.[145]

An Aotrou Heusaff to Herr Heubacher

It is easy to become confused as to the timing of Heusaff's journey from Germany and the actual means of entry into Ireland. This is not helped by statements by Heusaff himself on Welsh television in 1989, in which he conflated the stories of other Bezen fugitives with his own:

> There were twelve of us who received German names. We crossed the borders of Belgium and France by night without papers. We went to Paris and got false papers to go to Wales – two of us. The rest went from Brittany to Ireland.[146]

Perhaps Heusaff felt he would in this way protect his German and Irish contacts, but the facts of his journey to Ireland are quite different.

First, not all fugitive *gour* received German names. Many had French aliases, or even Breton-sounding ones such as 'Yann Colas' and 'Michel Kelleg'. Yann Bourc'hiz adopted the name 'François Ellies', perhaps a secret nod to Fañch Eliès 'Abeozen', a Breton translator of Welsh epics.[147] Heusaff could be referring here to the false identities used in Germany, rather than those for the journey to Paris. In addition, Lainé's circle was indeed furnished with IDs for the Franco-Belgian border crossing at least, although it is said there were not enough for everyone, as the document-free crossing of Bourc'hiz and Yann Guyomarc'h attests.[148]

Most importantly, Heusaff never traversed this route at all. He enrolled at the University of Marburg in 1947, and did not depart Germany until May 1950. Throughout this period he lived as 'Bernhard Heubacher', supported by Hielscher and his group of Celticists, and also by former comrades who sent money from Ireland. Heusaff had been encouraged by Henaff to study mathematics and physics in Germany because this might be 'helpful for further action', in Feutren's words.[149] Exactly what kind of 'action' was envisaged is uncertain, but it may have been the kind Gwenn-ha-Du practised.

When 'Heubacher' finally travelled to Ireland, he did not follow the trail blazed earlier by Feutren. Perhaps the *'vrai-faux passeport'* racket had ceased operation, but Heusaff went first to Aachen by rail, then on to Ostend.[150] He had not completed his degree at Marburg, and it is uncertain as to why he should now leave the country. Certainly, arrests of fugitive *gour* were still taking place at this time: 'Eskob' was arrested at Karlsrühe as late as 1952.[151] It is more likely that Heusaff was summoned by Henaff and his associates, now established at Galway.

Heusaff did not 'escape to Ireland on a coal boat from somewhere in the Low Countries'.[152] Instead he simply caught the ferry to Dover, then to Holyhead by rail. It does not appear that he tarried in Wales, nor had any dealings with the Welsh nationalists who had assisted his compatriots. He caught the ferry to Dún Laoghaire that same evening, then on to Galway via Dublin.[153]

Heubacher in Ireland

The most remarkable element of Heusaff's tale unfolds in Galway. Breton exiles lived under pseudonyms at this time: Raymond Delaporte had been advised to do this by de Valera himself, if Fouéré (or 'Dr Mauger') is to be believed. In all cases, however, the Irish authorities had been apprised of both the arrival and identities of these Bretons, and had discreetly approved their presence. In addition, high-profile Republicans, cultural nationalists and Fianna Fáil identities lent their support, often on a personal level. Frank Gallagher attended Louis Feutren's wedding, signing the guestbook under his alias 'David Hogan'. He also later sponsored Henaff's application for citizenship.[154] The Ceann Comhairle Frank Fahy similarly sponsored Leon Mill-Arden.[155] Others were helped by the novelist Máirtín Ó Cadhain.[156]

'Bernhard Heubacher', however, did not inform authorities that he was in fact Alan Heusaff, fugitive Breton nationalist. He maintained his false German identity throughout the early 1950s as he completed his studies at UCG, the truth known only to a select band of confidants. Jacques de Quelen, long a friend of the Bezen Perrot men, wasn't even aware Heusaff was in the country until he recognised him among mourners at the funeral of Yann Bourc'hiz, who died of a brain haemorrhage in July 1953.[157]

Heusaff had an aptitude for languages, and conducted German classes after hours. It was here he met his future wife Bríd Ní Dhochartaigh, whom he informed of his real identity.[158] Despite his fluency in German he lived in fear of exposure, particularly when obliged on occasion to explain his curious accent to 'other' Germans.[159]

Changed circumstances: MacBride and the Interparty government

What made such deception necessary? What changed between the arrival of Feutren in December 1947 and Heusaff in May 1950? The Irish government in previous years had been very supportive, provided the Bretons entered discreetly. But in February 1948 that government lost power and, for the first time since 1932, Fianna Fáil was on the opposition benches.

Taking over de Valera's portfolio of External Affairs was Seán MacBride, a former IRA leader who had been raised in Paris. As well as his family's experience of exile, his father had led the Irish Commando which fought the British in South Africa – an inspiration Henaff had acknowledged. He was, moreover, an implacable foe of communism,[160] whose militants had been the Bezen's chief opponents during the war in Brittany. Although in coalition with the conservative Fine Gael and other parties, MacBride's Clann na Poblachta appealed to Republicans dissatisfied with Fianna Fáil, especially concerning Partition. Although he broke with the IRA in 1937, MacBride nevertheless continued to be considered (at least by *The Times* in its 1988 obituary) a 'high priest' of 'physical force' Republicanism.[161] Ellis furthermore considers him a 'committed pan-Celt'.[162]

A Republican champion of pan-Celticism with personal experience of exile might be expected to be even more accommodating to Breton asylees. Yet, within months of taking over External Affairs, Louis Feutren received dismaying news:

> MacBride said he wanted nothing to do with the Bretons [...] There were others in the government who were more supportive, but he certainly was not.[163]

This was of course no official pronouncement, but communicated through personal connections in both Clann na Poblachta and Fianna Fáil.[164] At a time when most were living under aliases, this made the Bretons 'even more careful' about anonymity. Heusaff's subsequent arrival would therefore have to be even more anonymous – to the extent of hiding his identity altogether from a minister who had made his hostility plain.

Why was MacBride so hostile to the Bretons? The view to which Feutren subscribes is that MacBride's Parisian upbringing had instilled within him strongly 'francophile' attitudes.[165] His supposed 'pan-Celticism', then, if it existed at all, was entirely focused upon the British Isles, and did not (or would not) include Celts under French rule. For a native French-speaker no doubt raised on stories of the Wild Geese and the rebellion of 1798, fugitives from Republican France were unlikely to attract his sympathy. The External Affairs minister's francophilism was not uncommon among Irish Republicans, anyway, as the annual Wolfe Tone commemorations at Bodenstown, Co. Kildare, attested. Yann Goulet, a great admirer of Irish Republicanism, was moved to deliver a 'long verbal protest' during the singing of *La Marseillaise* at one such commemoration,[166] much to the chagrin of the French ambassador and Republicans less schooled in the broader implications of Celtic solidarity.

Francophilism was probably a factor in MacBride's hostility. Taking on the portfolio most attuned to foreign perceptions of Ireland, whose civil servants had been opposing asylum for 'war criminals' for some years, was probably another. It is claimed, for example, that the French ambassador, Count Ostrorog, pestered MacBride to refuse citizenship to Breton asylees, but MacBride always changed the subject. This is one of the few indications that the French were actually aware of the Bretons' presence at this time, and was reportedly related to Yann Fouéré by MacBride himself some time after the Interparty government lost power.[167] Although not on the same level of support as Dev's private meeting with Delaporte, it does suggest MacBride's francophilism had its limits and he was not prepared to bend to all French demands. It was, after all, an internal Irish matter, albeit one for which he had not been responsible. However, it was also known at the time that the Deuxième Bureau was active in Breton nationalist networks, both in Brittany and abroad, and any support for Breton refugees might come to Paris' attention.[168]

It must be noted also that MacBride was a shrewd politician whose rhetoric regarding Partition, pan-Celticism and Republicanism was pitched to a certain constituency and was not non-negotiable. 'Dev' exploited pan-Celticist sentiment as a means of outflanking MacBride while in Opposition. Likewise, Lord Rugby, the British representative, wrote to his superiors of a meeting he had with MacBride soon after his election. Despite gaining ten seats in the Dáil by campaigning on the left, the new External Affairs minister now assured the British government he was 'committed to a move to the Right'. He also assured Rugby he wanted improved Anglo-Irish relations. This wouldn't necessarily preclude criticism of Partition, of course, but might have dismayed Clann na Poblachta members all the same. Indeed, many were already resigning over the party's coalition deal with Fine Gael. Nevertheless, MacBride declared he was determined to keep his party program 'in abeyance' now he had attained office.[169] All this might have been designed to assuage nervous onlookers in Britain, but it does suggest the pragmatism of political office in general, and the culture of External Affairs in particular, had something of an instant impact upon MacBride. He was unlikely to jeopardise this for the sake of a few Breton exiles.

MacBride's hostility, which did little more than bring External Affairs' long-standing opposition to embarrassing refugees to the Bretons' notice, probably accounts for Heusaff's conflicting tales of entry. He would not want to draw attention to the fact that, for the first years of his new life in the country, he deceived the government that had been so welcoming to his comrades. That government had, of course, been de Valera's Fianna Fáil, and it was with that party that the Bretons had forged close links, facilitated by prominent locals. No such favours were owed to MacBride, and the feeling was evidently mutual.

Towards naturalization

De Valera's party was re-elected in May 1951. Sympathetic figures were therefore back in power. Frank Aiken, a former IRA fighter who had been forced into hiding himself during the Civil War, took over External Affairs. Feutren, for one, describes Aiken's attitude towards Breton refugees as 'marvellous'[170] – a stark contrast to MacBride's. Gerald Boland resumed control of Justice. Despite this, Heusaff had already established a life as Bernhard Heubacher, and could not easily discard it. Close friends were aware of his true identity, but it was not until he became acquainted with Senator Liam Ó Buachalla that he was able to explain his situation to someone in government.[171] Ó Buachalla was a resident of Galway and had been a member of Seanad Éireann since 1939. He was interested in Irish language issues, and had supported DIAS and its Celtic

Studies department.[172] The Senator's influence was crucial in normalising Heusaff's situation – even though he remained 'Herr Heubacher' until naturalised.[173] After graduating he entered the Irish Meteorological Service, and was secretary-general of the Celtic League from its inception in 1961.

Even though External Affairs was now under Aiken's leadership, the anxiety of its civil servants regarding the attitude of foreign governments to high-profile asylum cases remained. By the mid-1950s Breton exiles were eligible for citizenship, having been resident for five years or more. Anxiety therefore extended to the issue of naturalisation, and the possible international entanglements this might bring. These were demonstrated by an unlikely occurrence: the reaction to the death sentence passed upon Andrev Geffroy 'Le Grand Geff' in France.

The case of Andrev Geffroy

Geffroy had been a Gwenn-ha-Du militant, and had hunted Resistants not with the Bezen Perrot, but with a smaller Britto-German SD unit called the Kommando de Landerneau. He retreated eastwards with the Bezen, but decided not to cross to Germany. Imprisoned in 1945, in 1949 he was further accused of having betrayed two British officers to the Germans. For this he was sentenced to death. In 1951 facts were made public that appeared to exonerate him, but he was refused a retrial. He then went on hunger strike.[174]

Welsh nationalists began a campaign in Geffroy's favour. They were promptly joined by Irish bodies: a Coiste Cosanta André Geoffroy (Andrev Geffroy Defence Committee) was set up, and South Tipperary County Council wrote letters of protest to the French ambassador. Traditional Irish francophilism qualified sympathy for this Breton too, however; the *Evening Mail* reminding his supporters that 'The one and only nation on the Continent of Europe which gave any practical proof of her sympathy with our downtrodden country was "la belle France"'.[175]

In Britain, Welsh and Scottish nationalists – as well as Dr Noëlle Davies – brought the case to the attention of parliament.[176] The Foreign Office opined that the French President (who held the power to reprieve Geffroy) was unlikely to be 'influenced by the fact that the verdict has aroused indignation among Irish and Welsh national groups', but in 1953, after 618 days on death row, Geffroy was released.[177] 'But for an intense campaign in his favour in the other Celtic countries, particularly in Ireland and Wales, the sentence would have been carried out,' wrote Alan Heusaff in *Breton News*, a newsletter which appeared from 1960. 'It was a great victory for inter-Celtic solidarity.'[178]

The official Irish reaction was less ebullient. Sean Nunan, now chief civil servant in External Affairs, wrote to T.J. Coyne of Justice soon after Geffroy's pardon. The issue was whether to naturalise political asylees, as the Geffroy case 'has enabled us to form a better opinion than we might have given earlier'. That opinion was that 'as a general rule, we ought not to grant naturalisation to political refugees to whom we have given asylum in this country'. While this was a natural extension of his department's attitude, it is surprising to learn this was also the initial view of Justice. The Geffroy case, mobilising as it did so many sectors of public opinion, promised particular difficulties for the future. Nunan explained:

> [W]e should suffer considerable embarrassment if a political refugee, e.g. A Breton nationalist [...] were to return to France [...] and there claim Irish protection on the basis of his Irish passport [...] If the police were after him, we might even find him seeking asylum in the local Irish mission.

This was precisely what the DEA had hoped to avoid by deterring diplomatic asylum several years earlier. Nunan concluded:

> We have only to think of the multiplicity of resolutions from County Councils in the case of Geoffroy, who is not even an Irish citizen, to see how impossible it would be for the Government not to intervene in such a case; and, at the same time, to see how impossible it would be for them to intervene effectively or appropriately.[179]

Another consideration that militated against the naturalisation of political asylees was the probability that, even if they never left Ireland, they would likely engage in 'furthering their particular nationalist policies'. 'While he remains an alien, a political refugee can be restricted in his political activities; but as a naturalised citizen, no such restriction could be imposed,' noted Nunan.[180] It is significant in this context that publications in Ireland publicising the Breton cause do not appear in English until *Breton News*, some twelve years after the last issue of *BNNS* appeared in Wales.[181] Before gaining citizenship, most exiles avoided political action that could jeopardise their security. Neven Henaff published a few clandestine issues of *Breiz Atao*, but these were distributed secretly in Brittany, and may not have come to the attention of Irish authorities.[182] Heusaff's *Argoad* was similarly in French and Breton only, and appeared in the 1950s as a single-sheet newsletter.[183]

Despite opposition to their naturalisation, the Bretons had some influential sponsors, particularly within Fianna Fáil. Most fulfilled their five-year residency requirement during Dev's government of 1951–4, and evidently succeeded in allaying concerns they might embroil Ireland in international incidents. Nunan himself recognised final determinations were out of his hands, and were properly the remit of Gerald Boland, Minister for Justice, who was free to make exceptions to the general principle he outlined. 'I am thinking in particular of a case,' he wrote to Coyne, 'where your Minister was satisfied that the person in question had ceased all foreign political activities and had decided to become a good citizen of Ireland, having his principal and overriding loyalty here.'[184] The identity of this person is not revealed, but Youenn Le Noac'h, for one, became a naturalised Irish citizen on 10 June 1954.[185] Louis Feutren had to wait a little longer than his comrades, as he learned too late that, constitutional claim on Northern Ireland notwithstanding, the few years he spent teaching in Belfast did not count.[186]

The limitations of Irish asylum

Far from being immediately 'furnished with passports', Bretons in Ireland were regarded (at least by senior civil servants) as potential embarrassments who could embroil Dublin in diplomatic incidents. Asylees were expected to arrive discreetly, live under assumed names and do nothing to draw attention to the fact that Ireland was sheltering them. The Irish government gave no assistance to these fugitives to reach the country, in contrast to the activists of the Welsh movement who helped them escape French justice. In this way, Dublin hoped, media in Britain and the US would not be given ammunition for their portrayal of Ireland as an Axis refuge only marginally less objectionable than Spain. At the same time, sticklers on the principle of sovereignty – including de Valera himself – could feel Ireland's status as a nation-state equal to any European power had been asserted.

For the Bretons themselves, Ireland was for many a 'logical' refuge, and the asylum gained by some was then communicated to others. But, although the impact of the 'Irish example' upon the Breton nationalist imagination was profound, it must be remembered that Ireland was not always the first choice of refuge. Many fugitives evinced a preference for Wales. Others chose Spain or South America, or opted to live clandestinely in Germany or even France. Many, it is true, first attempted to reach Ireland or approached Irish missions. Equally, others who ended up in Ireland first attempted to reach Spain. Whatever difficulties existed owing to severed communications, this fact challenges the assumption that Breton nationalists opted invariably for Irish exile, and that the Irish government accepted them simply because they were Celts, and for no other reason related to contemporary political concerns.

There is no evidence of Breton nationalists being refused asylum after arriving in Ireland. There is evidence, however, of Bretons being turned away from Irish missions. There is ample evidence of influential Irish figures assisting, advising and sponsoring Breton exiles. But again, there is no evidence of this being done publicly. This was no demonstration to the world of the strength of pan-Celtic solidarity. It was, perhaps, all that a small, impoverished nation could do, castigated as it was by powerful states for its neutrality in the recent war. Its 'revolutionary heritage' perhaps demanded it extend assistance to these Celtic exiles from the Continent, these Wild Geese in reverse. Postwar political constraints meant that assistance could only be discreet, deniable and limited. External Affairs, the international 'face' of the Irish government, insisted upon that much. Even within that department fortunes fluctuated, from the discreet 'Dev' to the francophile MacBride, and finally the old Republican soldier Aiken.

But once in the country, the final determination belonged to that most 'anti-British' and 'illiberal' department, Justice. As Seán Nunan acknowledged, this had the greatest say over who was permitted to remain and who was naturalised. The last Breton arrival posed as a German rather than allow MacBride and Fine Gael Justice Minister, General Seán Mac Eoin, to learn his real identity, but for most Bretons it was Fianna Fáil's Gerald Boland who authorised applications. And, perhaps for Boland, their Celtic identity influenced these determinations.

But Justice had argued for the admission of non-Celtic fugitives, too, not least the Walloon fascist Léon Degrelle. And, despite the neo-paganism of their leader, many veterans of the Bezen Perrot were Catholic conservatives dedicated to the 'Faith and Brittany' vision of their beloved *Abbé*. PNB activists, particularly Perrot's erstwhile secretary in Bleun Brug Raymond Delaporte, were Catholic traditionalists, also. Most importantly, all Breton exiles had opposed the forces of communism in the form of the French Resistance, dominated as it was by the FTP. In the early years of the Cold War, when an 'Iron Curtain' descended across Europe and the Church and Western powers feared both France and Italy could go 'Red' from within, 'proven anti-communists' became preferred entrants in many countries, including Ireland. It was therefore not pan-Celticism but Catholic anti-communism that commanded real solidarity in postwar Ireland – and Bretons were not the only nationalist refugees to arrive.

CHAPTER 6

A solidarity more powerful: Ireland, asylum and the Church's struggle against communism, 1945–56

IN JULY 1947, a man bearing Swiss documents in the name of 'Alois Anitch'[1] arrived in Ireland accompanied by his wife and two children. Established at Zion Road, Rathgar, Alois obtained work teaching history, and when Mrs Anitch gave birth to a son the following June her only visitor apart from her husband was a Franciscan friar, Brother Luji Ivandić.[2]

Locals who became acquainted with the Anitches and the friar Ivandić also learned something of their circumstances. They were, it was understood, unfortunate Catholics forced to flee Tito's godless tyranny in Yugoslavia, which was particularly vindictive in its treatment of the Franciscan order. Ivandić himself was 'hysterical' about the 'Reds', 'always listening to the ups and downs of Communism on the wireless'.[3] But few asked questions of Anitch, according to Hubert Butler, who later unravelled the story. 'In general he was befriended as a foreign refugee from Communism, and [...] I have found no trace of sinister international intrigue among those who gave him hospitality.'

The higher echelons of the Catholic Church and (in all probability) successive Irish governments between 1947 and 1948 were not ignorant of the wartime conduct of these foreign guests, however. Because the man known as Alois Anitch was in fact Andrija Artuković, former Interior Minister of an Axis client state, the Nezavisna Država Hrvatska (Independent State of Croatia). Assisted at every stage by the Catholic Church, Artuković had fled via an Irish consulate, and when they left for the USA the following year the 'Anitches' travelled bearing Irish documentation.[4]

A solidarity more powerful

Both Fianna Fáil and Interparty governments sheltered fugitives from Croatia, the Ukraine, and (as the next chapter explores) Flanders, in total numbers greater than the Bretons. Obviously, the impulse to provide sanctuary in these cases cannot be ascribed to pan-Celticism. Equally, although most of these fugitives had been members of German armed forces, their allies, or of local collaborationist movements, their admittance cannot be entirely ascribed to pro-Axis sentiment, either. Such sentiment had not influenced Irish policy during the war itself, and if fugitive Axis detritus could now count on Irish succour it was not because they promised a Nazi resurgence, but rather because they had acted in the interests of an institution dear to the conception of 'Irishness' itself, and against an ideology long regarded by it as antithetical and immoral.

Comparisons between 'oppressed' foreigners and domestic heroes such as Pearse and Casement were indeed voiced by the Irish mainstream at this time.[5] James Dillon TD, Minister for Agriculture in two Interparty governments,[6] further exhorted Irish students to model themselves upon these foreigners, who had 'so gallantly defended freedom of thought and freedom of conscience'.[7] Like Artuković, however, the figures to whom Dillon referred did not belong to a Celtic, or even an ethnic minority movement. Singled out instead were Alojzije Stepinac, Catholic archbishop of Zagreb, imprisoned by Tito's regime in 1946; and József Cardinal Mindszenty of Hungary, arrested for treason in December 1948. Outrage over their treatment would in time mobilise more Dubliners in a demonstration of solidarity than any pan-Celticist organisation could hope to muster in the whole of Ireland – religious persecution being, de Valera told the Dáil, 'particularly hateful to the people of this country, whose forebears had to endure such persecution for centuries'.[8] More remarkably, Dillon, like many Catholic voices in Ireland, also directed Irish sympathy to the plight of one Ante Pavelić.[9]

That an Irish TD should consider Pavelić, Stepinac and Mindszenty equal victims of communist oppression is extraordinary, given that the first was not a clergyman but Poglavnik (Führer) of a Croatian fascist terrorist organisation installed in power by the Nazis in 1941, which then presided over some of the worst atrocities of the Second World War. But such was the fear of communism among Catholics at the time that many unrepentant fascists like Pavelić – and their supporters in the Church – were not reviled as war criminals, but instead began to 'shape-shift' into 'martyr[s] of the struggle between Christianity and Communism'.[10]

Pavelić, however, was not languishing in a communist prison like the two churchmen. Instead, the former leader of the Ustaše ('Insurgents') was safely ensconced in Buenos Aires. His escape from Tito's vengeance goes to the heart of an astonishing tale of collusion between the Western Allies and the Vatican to assist Axis fugitives, in preparation for an anticipated showdown with Moscow. In this tale staunchly Catholic Ireland had its own part to play, and its role was not confined to abstract sympathy. 'Proven anti-communists' from Catholic regions would find ultimate sanctuary either in or via Ireland, and in this endeavour Dublin acted in secret accord with the Western Allies – much as it had in the intelligence field during the recent war. In contrast to Breton cases, the entry of these fugitives was facilitated by the Catholic Church – with the probable collusion of Irish government.[11] The highest-ranking of these fugitives to find shelter in Ireland was Andrija Artuković ... a man later dubbed the 'Yugoslav Himmler'.[12]

Artuković and the 'bulwark of the Christian West'

Artuković was born to a Croat peasant family in Ljubuški, Herzegovina, in 1899. Educated at the Franciscan monastery of Široki Brijeg, he joined the Ustaše soon after its formation.[13] This organisation was created by Ante Pavelić and others in 1929, after ethnic parties were banned by the Yugoslav monarch. It was committed to the destruction of Yugoslavia and to the establishment of an independent Catholic Croatia. Like all recruits, Artuković swore allegiance to the exiled Poglavnik before a crucifix framed by a dagger and revolver.[14] Such extreme Catholic nationalism developed in reaction to the repression of Croat particularism, culminating in the killing of a moderate parliamentarian by a radical Serb deputy on the very floor of the national parliament.[15] These tensions originated in the division of the Balkans between Orthodox and Catholic Christianity, and the aftermath of the Great War of 1914–18.

Like pan-Celticism in Ireland, pan-Slavism exercised little influence upon Croatian nationalists. Ustaše identified with their co-religionists in Hungary and Austria more than with their Orthodox cousins, the Serbs. Many had fought Serbs in the Great War, and saw the Hapsburg empire as a fortress of Catholic civilisation. Owing to its frontline status in this struggle, Pope Leo XIII had dubbed Croatia 'bulwark of the Christian West'. That the post-1918 Kingdom of the Serbs, Croats and Slovenes (Yugoslavia from 1929) incorporated the Empire's south-eastern marches and came under the domination of Orthodox Serbs was to Catholic conservatives a major affront.

The collapse of Austria-Hungary left Catholic Europe vulnerable, in the Vatican's view, but the rise of fascism presented opportunities.[16] Irredentist goals in Dalmatia disposed Italian fascists toward antipathy to Yugoslavia, and Mussolini supported Croat separatists. Church and Italian state attitudes harmonised further after the Lateran Treaty in 1929. The exiled Ustaše thereafter found willing hosts in Italy, as well as other neighbours eager to dismember the new South Slavic kingdom.

The Ustaše to 1941

The Ustaše engaged in terrorist operations both within Yugoslavia and abroad. In regions like the Velebit Mountains their actions received some support, but rebellions fomented by the nationalists failed. Involved in an unsuccessful uprising in this area in 1932 was none other than Andrija Artuković, who subsequently fled into exile.[17]

Pavelić's fighters became understudies of an older South Slavic extremist movement, the Internal Macedonian Revolutionary Organisation. An IMRO hitman assassinated King Alexander I of Yugoslavia at Marseille in 1934, in an operation supported by the Ustaše.[18] Part of that support network had been Artuković. Based in London (next stop on the king's itinerary), Artuković was to succeed should the Marseille attempt fail.[19] He was arrested in connection with the plot and extradited to France. Although no link was proven, he was deported to Yugoslavia, whereupon he escaped to Berlin. McAdams claims he was arrested by the Gestapo as Hitler tried to woo Belgrade, but escaped again to Belgium.[20] Butler, however, claims he made his way to Czechoslovakia and Hungary.[21] Even Pavelić was detained in Italy after Alexander's assassination.[22] This was a charade to allay Yugoslav anger, however, as bands of Ustaše continued to train in secret camps financed by their hosts.[23]

Their opportunity came in April 1941. Hitler wanted Belgrade bound to the Axis under the Tripartite Pact,[24] but Serb officers staged a *coup d'état.* Although they quickly reversed their position, the die had been cast. Hitler resolved to postpone his invasion of the USSR and assist his hapless Italian ally, whose forces were floundering after a disastrous invasion of Greece, and that plan was expanded to include Yugoslavia.[25] After eleven days of resistance – in which most Croats deserted to the invaders – Yugoslavia capitulated to a combined force of Germans, Italians and Hungarians. Accompanying the invaders, and simultaneously rising up from within, were units of the Ustaše.

The NDH

Ustaše leader in Zagreb was Slavko Kvaternik, who declared Croatian independence in the name of the Poglavnik. The declaration was made, according to Hoare, 'on the orders of SS Colonel Edmund Veesenmeyer', the Reich's specialist in *coups d'état.*[26] Veesenmeyer is believed to have drawn up similar schemes for Éire.[27] Right from its inception the NDH was an Axis creation: Rome and Berlin installing the Ustaše and sidelining moderates. Despite awarding Bosnia-Herzegovina to the new state, the Axis powers also established zones of occupation that divided the NDH between them.

Of a population of 6.3 million, only 3.3 million were Catholic Croats. Around 1.9 million were Orthodox Serbs, and 700,000 were Bosniak Muslims.[28] There were also various minorities, including ethnic Germans (Volksdeutsche). Indicative of its weakness and indebtedness to Axis sponsors, the NDH ceded much of Dalmatia to Italy, and Berlin bypassed Zagreb and illegally conscripted Volksdeutsche into Waffen-SS units.[29]

It was this political weakness that guaranteed the savagery of the warfare that raged in the NDH between 1941 and 1945. Anti-Serbian hostility was unleashed in horrific violence, which also consumed minorities and dissident Croats. While violence against Jews, Roma and political enemies followed Nazi practice, the effort to eliminate Serbs was an entirely domestic matter. Its brutality, Hoare argues, was guaranteed by:

> the abnormality of an extreme-nationalist but militarily weak regime attempting to establish its rule over a disparate collection of territories populated by a nationally mixed and generally hostile population.[30]

The Church and Nazism

The Catholic Church had supported anti-communist regimes since the Lateran Treaty,[31] if not since the spectre of revolution first arose in 1917. Pope Pius XII narrowly escaped a Spartacist mob in 1919 when papal nuncio at Munich, thereafter nurturing a passionate hatred of 'Bolshevism'.[32] The Church forged relationships with Catholic authoritarian states from Austria under Dollfuss to Portugal under Salazar.[33] It was recognised in the new constitution of Éire in 1937,[34] but de Valera was still criticised for his opposition to the Italian invasion of Abyssinia in 1935 and his refusal to recognise Franco in Spain until early 1939.[35] Both had been endorsed as Christian crusades by conservative Catholics – the indigenous Christianity of most Abyssinians notwithstanding.

The Church's relationship with Nazism was more complex. Hitler originated from Catholic Austria and the party's powerbase was in Bavaria, but Nazi efforts in the religious sphere were initially directed at winning over the Lutheran clergy of northern Germany, especially Prussia. The Catholic Centre party remained aloof and the Church prohibited the faithful joining the Nazis, partly because of racial notions and other 'paganistic' concepts. These prompted Pius XI to publish *Mit brennender Sorge* ('With Burning Concern') in March 1937. Braham argues this did not condemn the Nazis' anti-Semitic policies, but protested at them being applied along racial lines which did not recognise Jewish conversion to Christianity. And while the Church fought 'successfully' against the Nazi euthanasia program, most bishops ignored violations of Jewish civil rights after Hitler's rise to power in January 1933.

Hitler needed an accommodation with the Catholic Church to consolidate power. A conference of bishops at Fulda dropped the prohibition on Nazi party membership, and a Concordat between Berlin and the Vatican, modelled on the treaty with Mussolini, was signed in July. Anti-Semitic legislation was then enacted in concert with drives against leftists. For many in both Church and state, Jews and communists had long been synonymous: Archbishop Conrad Gröber of Freiburg describing Bolshevism as 'Asiatic despotism ... in the service of a group of terrorists led by Jews'.[36]

Not all in the Church supported such views. But, while the Church found elements of national socialism objectionable, it generally found the ideology less offensive than atheistic Bolshevism,[37] which was pledged in its view to the destruction of the 'Christian West'. And while the Church wielded influence in Portugal, Francoist Spain, Italy and the État français of Marshal Pétain (not to mention Ireland), it was actually Nazi Germany that furthered the Vatican's geopolitical objectives by creating 'semi-independent clerical fascist states' in Central Europe.[38] The first, Slovakia, was actually ruled by a priest, Monsignor Jozef Tiso. And although the second was ruled by Pavelić and his Ustaše, Catholic clergy were involved not only in its administration and every aspect of its ideology, but also some of its worst atrocities.

The Church and the NDH

> [A]s confused as today's fateful events may be [...] one can nonetheless see the working of the divine hand.[39]

So wrote archbishop of Zagreb Alojzije Stepinac soon after the foundation of the NDH in 1941. On 27 April, His Grace met with Pavelić and received the impression that the new ruler of Croatia was 'an upright Catholic and that the Church would have freedom in its actions'. This is because the Poglavnik had promised 'not to be tolerant' of Orthodoxy.[40] In time, the state instituted the death penalty for abortion and a month's jail for swearing – all of which met with approval from the Church's prelate in the Croatian capital.

But the Ustaše program went much further. Minister for Education and Culture, Mile Budak, explained:

> The basis for the Ustaše movement is religion. For minorities such as the Serbs, Jews, and Gypsies, we have three million bullets. We will kill a part of the Serbs. Others we will deport, and the rest we will force to accept the Roman Catholic religion. Thus the new Croatia will be rid of all Serbs in its midst in order to be 100 per cent Catholic within ten years.[41]

Although Stepinac criticised some excesses of the regime, he also criticised Italian occupiers in the south, who were allowing what he felt was excessive religious freedom for Orthodox believers, partly owing to their disgust at Ustaše atrocities. In Stouffer's view, any criticism Stepinac levelled at NDH authorities was confined to 'a general pattern of private protest and public support, of lauding the goals but baulking at the means'.[42]

More vocal in his support for ethnic cleansing was Archbishop Ivan Šarić of Sarajevo, who had been a secret member of the Ustaše from 1934.[43] Dedicating an 'Ode to Pavelić' in December 1941, Šarić beseeched the Poglavnik to rescue Croats from 'the greedy Jews with all their money' and the 'hell' of Marxism.[44] It was 'stupid and unworthy of Christ's disciples to think that the struggle against evil could be waged in a noble way,' he declared. The NDH's Central Propaganda Office was likewise headed by a priest, Fr Grga Peinović. The Church was therefore at the centre of efforts to articulate the ideology of Ustaše hatred to the Croatian people;[45] Church and state both aiming to make 'Croat' and 'Catholic' inseparable concepts. This relationship was manifest even in field operations. '[I]t is almost impossible to imagine an Ustaše punitive expedition without a priest at its head spurring it on, and usually a Franciscan,' notes Falconi.[46]

Artukovic and the Croatian death camps

While most of the killings perpetrated by the Ustaše took place in a wild and 'disorganised' manner,[47] the regime also established death camps along the Nazi model. Chief of these was Jasenovac,[48] and its commandant was, for a time, the Franciscan friar-cum-Ustaša Miroslav Filipović.[49] Almost 60,000 people – Serbs, Jews, Gypsies and dissidents – perished here between 1941 and 1945. Total Serbian deaths from Ustaše terror throughout the NDH (not including combat fatalities) total almost 300,000.[50]

Andrija Artuković, Minister of the Interior during much of the NDH's existence, has borne much responsibility for this genocide.[51] In particular, he stands accused of approving the construction of the camp system, and its subsequent administration. It is for this reason he was labelled the 'Yugoslav Himmler' – although this epithet, like 'Butcher of the Balkans', appeared only after the war.[52] According to Lituchy, for example, Director for Public Security Eugen 'Dido' Kvaternik (son of Slavko) 'was ordered by Interior Minister Andrija Artuković to create a series of concentration camps throughout Croatia'.[53] For many commentators, Artuković was therefore the 'most implicated' in Ustaše terror.[54] He was found guilty of war crimes and sentenced to death in 1986, but died while awaiting execution.

There is no doubt that Artuković was an enthusiastic Ustaša, willing to assume a senior role in the NDH and thereby become part of what Hoare terms a 'joint criminal enterprise'.[55] Like Education Minister Budak, Artuković incited hatred towards minorities. These were all working towards a common and nefarious purpose, he told the NDH rubber-stamp parliament, the Sabor, in February 1942:

> Immediately after the founding of Yugoslavia, all the enemies of the Croatian people – the Jews, the Communists, and the Freemasons – united with those of the so-called 'Piedmont of the Balkans' [Serbia] in order to destroy the Croatian people and suppress all national aspirations [...] The Independent State of Croatia, led by the Ustaše, finding itself in a state of siege and self-defence against these insatiable and poisonous parasites, has indeed settled the so-called Jewish Question through resolute and sound actions.[56]

Artuković's moral and political culpability in the Ustaše genocide is therefore beyond question. According to the historical record as it stands, however, specific *organisational* responsibility for camps like Jasenovac was more complex.

Artuković served as Minister of Internal Affairs from 16 April 1941 to 10 October 1942, and again from 30 April to 11 October 1943. In the interim, he was Minister of Justice and Religion. In October 1943 he became Ministar-Prabiljeznik or Keeper of the State Seal, a largely ceremonial office in which he co-signed legislation. He maintained this role up until his flight from Croatia in May 1945.[57] Interior Ministries commonly handle internal security forces – the very forces responsible for political repression. The camp system might be presumed to have fallen under this ministry's remit. But the NDH was no ordinary state in this regard. State functions were frequently subordinated to party organisations, and most reliable of these, from the Poglavnik's view, was the feared secret intelligence service, the Ustaška Nadzorna Služba (Ustaše Surveillance Service).

The UNS acted on the orders of 'Dido' Kvaternik, Director of Public Security. Its role was to 'investigate persons believed to be politically objectionable and dangerous to the state, and to determine which of these persons were to be forcibly interned'. Department XIII of its counter-intelligence branch was, significantly, 'directed against enemies advocating a split in the close relationship between the Croatian state and the Roman Catholic Church and clergy'.[58]

Section III of the UNS was responsible for the camps. This was created by Mijo Babić, 'acting on direct orders from Pavelić, specifically for the purpose of setting up concentration camps in Croatia to be used for killing Serbs, Jews and Gypsies'. When Babić was killed in July 1941, Vjekoslav 'Maks' Luburić took his place. He and the Poglavnik set out the structure of the camps,[59] and the legal decree for the detention of undesirables was signed by Pavelić and the then Justice and Religion Minister, Mirko Puk, in November 1941.[60] 'It is important to emphasise that the sole authority [...] for authorising liquidations was the director of UNS Section III,' notes de Zeng.[61] For the Goldsteins, 'Pavelić,

Kvaternik and Luburić comprised the three levels of genocidal crimes in NDH: Pavelić as the prime instigator, Kvaternik as planner and organiser, Luburić as the chief and most severe enforcer.'[62]

Only in January 1943 was UNS (now RAVSIGUR)[63] placed under Interior Ministry control. Artuković was minister of this department between April and October. De Zeng, however, argues that while RAVSIGUR was now formally under Artuković's command, its chief, 'Dido' Kvaternik, continued to act 'exclusively at the orders of the Poglavnik'. The regular police likewise were subordinated to RAVSIGUR, and the Gendarmerie's command was independent 'through legal decree'.[64] Informal patronage exercised greater influence than such legal niceties, though, argues Hoare: '[I]t would have mattered very little if the gendarmerie were formally "independent" of the Interior Ministry, according to the letter of the law which Ustaše leaders themselves did not respect.'[65] Although in no way excusing Artuković for the crimes of the regime in which he participated, accusations concerning the direct *administrative* responsibility for the Croatian death camps should be more accurately levelled at Luburić, Kvaternik and, above all, the Poglavnik Ante Pavelić.

The Vatican and the triumph of communism

Tito's Partisans ruined Ustaše plans for an ethnically 'cleansed' Croatia. This movement swelled with recruits of all ethnicities, including Croats disgusted by Ustaše excesses. At the same time, the Red Army beat Axis forces back from Stalingrad, and eventually to Berlin.

Communist gains like these alarmed the Church. The Vatican facilitated efforts to negotiate a compromise peace, or a separate agreement between Berlin and the West that would leave Germany free to fight the USSR alone.[66] SS Major Albert Hartl, a former priest and Nazi specialist in Catholic affairs, was dispatched to Rome in 1944 with orders to begin negotiations through the offices of the Church.

But the Vatican didn't stop at peace overtures. From March 1944, US military intelligence became aware of clandestine efforts to fund and co-ordinate anti-communist guerrillas in Soviet-occupied Europe. Operating under the name of the Christian Front,[67] these were centred in Lithuania and the western regions of Byelorussia and the Ukraine, but later expanded to include virtually all regions behind the Red Army as it rolled westward. As the Third Reich crumbled and the Western Allies faced the new threat of Soviet preponderance in Europe, these networks rapidly increased in perceived value ... despite the reality that many within them had committed atrocities in their zeal to expel the forces of 'Judeo-Bolshevism' from their homelands.

The sense of impending conflict between the West and Bolshevism shaped attitudes towards fugitive 'proven anti-communists' – particularly those with combat or intelligence experience of regions overrun by Moscow. General Reinhard Gehlen, German intelligence chief in the East, surrendered to the Americans and was later brought back to Germany to re-establish his networks under their control. Former Nazi protégés brought into the US fold included Byelorussian nationalists, who fled Minsk before the Soviet liberation in June 1944. 'The SS made a list of those to be evacuated,' remarks Loftus of these collaborators, 'and nearly every person on it ended up in the United States.'[68]

Yalta and Axis collaborators

The Yalta agreement of February 1945 divided Europe into spheres of influence. Consolidation of these led to duplicity by both East and West. The Red Army waited outside Warsaw as the Germans destroyed the Polish Home Army's uprising in 1944. The British army fought the communist faction of the local Resistance after landing in Greece the same year.[69] There were even rumours of a scheme called 'Technica' within the French Resistance, in which communists were secretly betrayed to the Nazis by their non-communist countrymen.[70] The jostling for advantage in the postwar world began long before the defeat of the Nazis.

Under the Yalta agreement, the Western Allies undertook to repatriate Soviet citizens in German uniform. Some had entered German service only because Stalin regarded all POWs as traitors,[71] and were not regarded by the Western Allies as being of operational worth. Moreover, no Western power had the military muscle nor the political will to antagonise the Soviets by sheltering large numbers of former collaborators from Eastern Europe. To do so would leave them open to charges that they were sympathetic to fascism themselves, at a time when they were pressuring neutrals like Ireland on this score. In 'Operation Keelhaul' many thousands of Soviet turncoats captured in Austria were handed back to Moscow – many to face death in the GULAG.

But not all were handed over. Like hardcore Byelorussian nationalists, the Allies sheltered and assisted those they believed had the skills and experience to destabilise communist rule. Just as the Irish government did with Breton refugees, the assistance provided these individuals would have to be discreet and deniable. The networks operating in support of fugitives were therefore considered perfect for the task.

The Argentine connection

Many fugitives caught in the Reich as it collapsed fled first to Denmark or Norway, which remained under German control until the surrender. One who did this was Walloon fascist and later bugbear of External Affairs Léon Degrelle, who abandoned his Waffen-SS soldiers in Berlin and made his way to Oslo. Commandeering an aeroplane, he and five others made an incredible non-stop flight across Europe before crash-landing in Spain.[72]

Most escapes by the 'Nordic Route' weren't so spectacular.[73] After the German surrender, many fugitives obtained false papers and visas from the Argentine consul in Copenhagen. The consul, José Bessone, was alleged by the British in 1947 to have been 'involved [...] in organising the illegal movement of Germans from the British Zone of Germany via Denmark to the Argentine'.[74] Danish police were also alleged to have allowed embarrassing collaborators to escape.[75] Most fugitives crossed to Sweden, flying from Stockholm to Geneva and on to Buenos Aires.

The Argentine and German leaderships had been colluding for years, Juan Perón being disposed to 'Nazify' Argentina and dominate Latin America. He also sought the Vatican's assistance to establish a 'Catholic bloc' as a counterweight to the US. By Perón's own admission, war was declared upon Germany in March 1945 solely to ensure Argentine representatives would be present in liberated Europe to assist Axis fugitives. An anti-communist bastion would be created in Argentina utilising their skills. In addition to the Nordic Route, from late 1944 fugitives could seek out the network in Madrid of Charles Lesca, formerly of the French *collabo* newspaper *Je Suis Partout*. In March 1945 this was supplemented by a route run by Argentine-German SS Captain Carlos Fuldner, sent to Madrid to facilitate escape for top Nazis. These networks operated with the connivance of the Spanish government. From early 1946 the Spanish end of a conduit to Argentina was in operation, with large-scale shipping of fugitives beginning that September.[76] The Argentines had assured the British in September 1944, at the same time Gray demanded similar assurances from Dublin, that 'in no event would persons accused of war crimes be allowed in Argentine territory' – a position they reaffirmed in the Act of Chapultepec of March 1945.[77]

Both the Nordic and Spanish routes began to close, however, owing to a combination of Swedish police action and Franco's efforts to placate the Allies. Like the Argentines, both Swedish and Spanish authorities had previously undertaken – in less equivocal manners than the Irish – not to admit war criminals. Anthony Eden, the British Foreign Secretary, reported to the House of Commons in October 1944 that Spain had assured him 'that it will forbid asylum to any Fascist or Nazi war criminals whom the Allies desire to bring to judgment'.[78] It was still considered a possibility that the Allies might seek to topple Franco's regime. This, in addition to the sense that it might become a valuable partner in the struggle against communism, obliged Spain to tone down its pro-fascist image. One means of doing this was to put pressure on high-profile Axis asylees to 'disappear'. This is what obliged Degrelle's benefactors to send him into hiding in 1946, prompting rumours of his flight to Ireland. The same pressure forced Pierre Daye to Argentina in 1947.[79] Numbers of Axis exiles remained in Spain, but for a Catholic Church eager to assist fugitives, and for an Argentine government eager to accept them, a new route had to be opened once the Nordic/Spanish one ground to a complete halt in November 1947.

Beginnings of 'The Ratline'

The Church sheltered Axis fugitives who found themselves in southern Germany, northern Italy or Austria at war's end. Marcel Déat, Jacques Doriot's rival for leadership of French fascism, ended up at a monastery near Turin.[80] Once the Nordic Route closed, Otto Skorzeny, Hitler's commando chief, organised an escape route from northern Germany to Italy and Switzerland known as Die Spinne (The Spider), which complemented a 'Monastery Route' from Austria to Italy.[81]

Fugitives were funnelled to Rome, where camps for displaced persons were established. Those considered most useful to a future 'anti-communist crusade' were sheltered in superior Church accommodation, away from the prying eyes of Allied (especially Titoist or Soviet) intelligence. Central to this mission was Austrian bishop Alois Hudal, one of the most enthusiastic pro-Nazis in the Vatican.[82] Hudal instructed Italian police to direct fugitives to churches and monasteries, and organised false papers – chiefly Nansen 'stateless' passports or Red Cross certificates – which allowed them to shelter incognito while awaiting transfer overseas.[83] At the Vatican's Collegium San Girolamo and Collegium Illyricum, however, Croatian friars sheltered fugitives with more immediate anti-communist interests.[84]

The Križari

Axis soldiers from Yugoslavia poured into Austria in May 1945. At Bleiburg, the British received the surrender of up to 116,000 Croats and others. The British turned them back, whereupon up to 50,000 were massacred.[85]

This forced repatriation was not uncompromising, however. Certain persons were allowed to slip through the British cordon – a move facilitated, it has been claimed, by truckloads of loot plundered from the NDH's victims.[86]

Accompanying this booty were the Poglavnik Ante Pavelić and the former Keeper of the State Seal, Andrija Artuković. The bulk was not spent on local bribes, but made its way to Rome where, according to a 1999 lawsuit filed on behalf of NDH victims, the Vatican bank laundered it to pay for another of its anti-communist guerrilla operations, this time in its former 'bulwark' of Croatia.[87]

When the British intercepted Pavelić and Artuković, they recognised them as important pawns in the postwar game of advantage that began with Yalta.[88] Washington had stolen a march by snaring Gehlen and his intelligence networks,[89] but Ustaše leaders could destabilise communist rule in Yugoslavia, then known as 'Soviet satellite number one'.[90] The fact that Tito's Partisans had won power largely through their own efforts meant Belgrade was viewed as the most dangerous partner in Moscow's march westward. No one predicted the schism between Tito and Stalin that would develop shortly afterwards.

In addition to their experience fighting the Partisans and the plentiful loot with which they fled, the Ustaše leadership had another card to play: not all of them had evacuated Croatia. A number had taken up guerrilla operations like the Ustaše of old.[91] These guerrillas, known as Križari (Crusaders), continued the fight against the Partisans. And, owing to the close relationship between them and the Catholic Church, the Vatican's 'Christian Front' networks were central to their operations.

British and Vatican interests thereby intersected. The top Ustaše, including Archbishop Šarić, soon made their way from British-occupied Austria to Rome with their truckloads of loot.[92] Both Pavelić and Artuković made the journey disguised, perhaps unsurprisingly, as priests. Initially, the Americans were unaware of this collusion between London and the Vatican. Soon after Pavelić was installed in Rome, however, American intelligence bugged the City State's code room.[93] Before long, officers of the Counter-Intelligence Corps had their suspicions confirmed: the Church was indeed assisting individuals on the run from the communists – individuals whose wartime conduct had, in many cases, earned them the title of 'war criminals'. In July 1946, the CIC decided to learn how these networks operated and who was running them. 'Operation Circle' was put into action.[94]

Anti-communism had now become a stronger motivation than the Church's hatred of 'schism', and the Americans learned that the Vatican was sheltering other 'Quislings' from the Balkans, some Orthodox or Muslim.[95] A Croatian friar named Krunoslav Draganović – decorated for his services to the NDH, and a wartime member of its Committee of Five for the conversion of the Orthodox[96] – was in charge of their care.[97] More significantly, the Americans learned that the Poglavnik himself was being sheltered. But as the Nazi hunters of the CIC made ready to arrest Pavelić, a curt counter-order came through: 'Hands off'.[98] Destabilising communism now took precedence over bringing the Ustaše leaders to justice – unlike the high-profile leaders of the Reich who were tried at Nuremberg.

Despite their support from British intelligence and the Vatican, Križari operations were a failure. Croatian exile organisations were riddled with informants, and British intelligence's knowledge of this campaign, as well as similar efforts in Albania and the Baltic states, was regularly betrayed to Moscow courtesy of a certain Kim Philby.[99] As Križari came to trial in Yugoslavia, they revealed embarrassing details of the collusion between the Ustaše, the Western Allies and the Church. To forestall exposure, Pavelić was sent down the new 'Southern Route' to Argentina early in 1948, where he would join at least 5,000 Croats given shelter by Perón.[100] This route came to be known as the 'Ratline'.

'The Ratline'

Draganović had been assisting Axis fugitives reach Latin America since 1946. Only in mid-1947, however (at the same time the CIC had been ordered to stay the arrest of Pavelić), did the Americans begin to employ his network. As Paul E. Lyon of the 430th CIC detachment explained in a classified report in 1948:

> The agreement consists of simply mutual assistance, i.e., [CIC] agents assist persons of interest to Father Draganovic to leave Germany and, in turn, Father Draganovic will assist these agents in obtaining the necessary visas to Argentina [...] for persons of interest to this Command [...] This operation cannot receive any official approval and must be handled [...] with a minimum amount of general knowledge.[101]

Escorted from Austria to Rome, 'persons of interest' were handed to Draganović, who, with the illegal assistance of an American at the International Refugee Organisation, obtained documents to facilitate travel to South America.[102] Argentine officials fast-tracked the process, on one occasion issuing landing permits to 2,000 fugitive Croats at a stroke.[103] Once furnished with documents, fugitives were escorted to safehouses in Genoa, there to take ship across the Atlantic or, in some cases, the Middle East.[104] Draganović asked no questions about the wartime conduct of his charges – which, in addition to Pavelić, included the 'Butcher of Lyon' Klaus Barbie and the architect of mass Jewish deportation Adolf Eichmann – but did insist that any mixed couples be married and any children baptised.[105] Even then, Christian charity alone could not pay the bills: Draganović charged $1,000 per head, $1,400 for VIP treatment.[106] Nazi hunter Simon Wiesenthal alleged the Catholic aid agency Caritas paid Eichmann's expenses.[107] The total number of fugitives assisted is unknown, but may total tens of thousands.

The Swiss connection

Artuković, however, did not follow his Poglavnik to Buenos Aires. Instead he was sent north to Switzerland, and eventually to Ireland. What prompted him and his family to take this alternative route?

One probable explanation is to be found in the administration of Ustaše plunder used to fund Križari operations. In addition to the loot driven across the Austrian border in 1945, there were also secret Swiss bank accounts set up by the Poglavnik as early as 1944.[108] Archbishop Šarić and Archbishop of Ljubljana, Gregorij Rožman, were sent to the Swiss capital to launder these funds in 1947. According to Loftus, CIC officers noted that:

> Rožman is going to Berne to take care of these finances. The money is in a Swiss bank, and he plans to have most of it sent through to Italy and from there to the Ustaše in [the] Argentine.[109]

The Argentines had established an 'Emigration Centre' in Berne – a centre which, Goñi alleges, facilitated the escape of known war criminals.[110] This functioned as part of the Argentine network for postwar immigration, the Sociedad Argentina Recepción Europeos (Argentine European Reception Society).[111]

It seems unlikely that Artuković and his family travelled to Switzerland by coincidence when safe shelter was available in Rome and 'The Ratline' would soon be in operation. It is probable that Artuković was part of this mission to launder funds in Swiss accounts. Fr Luji Ivandić accompanied Artuković, in a role Butler believes was escort, bodyguard, and protector of the Croatian state seals.

Once in Switzerland, it appears the police – like their Swedish counterparts – came under pressure to act against Axis fugitives. Artuković himself claimed he was given two weeks to leave by Swiss authorities, but also that the Swiss Ministry of Justice helped him obtain identity documents.[112] Like their Irish counterparts, many in this ministry were renowned for their anti-Semitism, and were said to be complicit in Perón's schemes to recruit ex-Nazis. The anti-Semite Rothmund, chief of Swiss police, was that country's delegate to the IRO from April 1945 to September 1947.[113] Butler, however, believes the Swiss police acted in good faith, forcing Artuković to seek assistance to quit the country. That assistance was provided by friars of the Franciscan order, who directed him to the Irish legation at Berne.[114] If indeed the Swiss authorities were complicit, as Artuković claimed, both state and Church may have acted in collusion.

The Irish *chargé d'affaires* at the legation, Frank Cremins, was aware of the presence of Axis fugitives in Switzerland, and had been sending reports to Dublin regarding the Swiss attitude to these refugees.[115] Why at this sensitive time, when Breton fugitives had been warned they could expect no assistance from Irish diplomats, would Croatian fugitives in Switzerland be so assisted?

First, it is not possible to determine from the available evidence whether Artuković's entry was even known to Irish authorities, let alone facilitated. It is entirely possible that Cremins and other legation staff were unaware of the real identities of 'Alois Anitch' and his family, who did, after all, present themselves bearing seemingly authentic Swiss documents. If indeed Swiss authorities and the Franciscan order were conspiring to conceal the truth, it would have been safer not to reveal this to the Irish.

Given, however, that the Artuković family later left Ireland for America bearing *Irish* documentation, it does appear likely there was some measure of complicity on Dublin's part, at least subsequent to their arrival. The Americans, for one, were well aware of the background of the fugitives they assisted: Archbishop Rožman, after successfully laundering the Ustaše's Swiss funds, went to the US consulate in Zurich early in 1948 and obtained a visa, apparently under his real name.[116] If the flight of the 'Anitches' operated in any way similarly, it is probable figures in Irish administration were aware of their real identities. Irrespective of the details of entry, however, a national identity closely associated with Catholicism, in addition to strong domestic anti-communism, predisposed Irish governments toward assisting 'persecuted' co-religionists from behind the 'Iron Curtain'.

Catholic anti-communism in Ireland

Nine months prior to the arrival of 'Alois Anitch', Fine Gael leader General Richard Mulcahy rose in the Dáil to question Eamon de Valera:

> Is the Taoiseach aware that it has been prominently stated that the struggle that has begun between the Soviet [*sic*] and the Catholic Church in Europe is at the bottom of the unrest and disturbance that exists in the world, and no country, no party and no class of people can afford to ignore it?[117]

Mulcahy did not specify who had 'prominently stated' this view, but his question indicates the depth of concern that existed in Ireland regarding the march of communism – particularly its persecution of Catholics. Those Catholics to whom Mulcahy was referring were Croats, in a debate occasioned by the conviction in Zagreb, on a charge of high treason, of the Church's prelate in that city, Archbishop Alojzije Stepinac.

In positing a Manichaean struggle between communism and Christianity, Mulcahy was appealing to longstanding Irish fears. Spurred on by the anti-Red

Cardinal Joseph MacRory, a mob had attacked Connolly House and the Workers' College in Dublin in March 1933.[118] A St Patrick's Anti-Communist League soon appeared in the Irish capital, 'pledg[ing] themselves to resist Communism and "No God Blasphemy" to the end of their lives'. [119] Irish attitudes towards the civil war in Spain also predominantly favoured Franco. In his trenchant criticism of de Valera for not declaring support for the *caudillo*, Paddy Belton TD had declared the Spanish struggle a battle of 'Christ versus anti-Christ', and had likened the Taoiseach's neutral stance to that of 'Communist France under its Jewish Freemason Premier'.[120] As in many other countries, the equation of Jewish elements with Bolshevism and other 'anti-national' forces led to pronounced anti-Semitism in many sections of administration, especially the Department of Justice. Its secretary, Peter Berry, described Jews as 'political undesirables' and a 'social problem' in departmental memoranda as late as 1953.[121]

Although External Affairs was more liberal in this regard, some of its high-ranking civil servants had themselves been seduced by the Catholic anti-communism of Axis regimes. Joseph Walshe, Secretary from 1922 to 1946, was an admirer of the French Right and a champion of Marshal Pétain. He was, however, repelled by Nazism, unlike the Irish representative to Berlin, Charles Bewley, whose increasing fondness for Hitler obliged de Valera to order his replacement in 1939.[122] Walshe, a former Jesuit, was deeply honoured to become the first Irish ambassador to the Holy See from 1946. Once established in the Vatican, he urged his country not to remain aloof from the new global struggle as it had from the recent war: 'In this topsy turvy world of Communism and Atheism the Church requires the help of Catholic states, especially of Ireland'.[123]

Censorship had also concealed Nazi wartime conduct from the Irish public. One legacy of this was scepticism towards reports of Nazi death camps, especially as the Allies themselves comprised 'godless communists' and the heirs of Cromwell and the Black and Tans. One newspaper alleged the British faked footage of liberated camps, peopling them with 'starving Indians'. Even when the Nuremberg trials were underway, the notion that the Axis alone was guilty of war crimes was vigorously rejected by sections of the Irish press.[124]

This combination of factors focused Irish attention upon the plight of Catholics under communist rule – in particular the prelates tried for treason. While wartime neutrality encouraged isolationism, now the focus was on international Catholic solidarity. In defence of Stepinac, Mindszenty and the Church, around 150,000 people rallied in Dublin in May 1949.[125] Even the declaration of the Republic the previous month had been subdued by comparison.[126]

The Interparty government, Partition and NATO

It was the Interparty coalition, governing from February 1948 to June 1951, that transformed Éire into the Republic of Ireland. While this was a seemingly unlikely alliance of radical Republicans, conservatives and others, most of its members were united by two major factors: a mutual loathing of Fianna Fáil; and, especially in the cases of Clann na Poblachta leader Seán MacBride and Fine Gael, strong anti-communism. MacBride wanted Ireland 'to play a major role in the international politics of the Cold War', and assured the US plenipotentiary that 'if any country is attacked by the Communists, we're in it'.[127]

As it had in 1939, the Partition of the island precluded Irish membership of the new anti-Soviet alliance, the North Atlantic Treaty Organisation, signed in April 1949. To many observers, Ireland was once again playing the spoiler – and endangering Western civilisation in the process. An English nun wrote in this vein to Taoiseach John Costello soon after the Republic was declared:

> Xtain [*sic*] civilisation is threatened by Marxist communism, a worse personification of anti-Christ than Nazism [...] Éire [...] does her best to inflame fanatical Irish nationalism [...], which may [...] cause division in the Western Camp, where unity is so necessary, if the march of the enemies of God is to be stopped![128]

As MacBride made clear, however, Ireland's neutrality in any third world war would not be automatic. A bilateral treaty with the US was contemplated, and MacBride made the point publicly on 20 July 1948 when he told the Dáil that Irish sympathies 'lay with Western Europe'.[129] Significantly, Artuković and family departed for the US with Irish papers only five days previously. Ivandić departed for Canada around the same time, reportedly on the orders of Rome.[130]

This de facto alignment with the West was inextricably linked to a greater involvement of the Church in domestic issues. The IP cabinet declared its 'filial loyalty' to the Pope after its first meeting, and thereafter there was significant clerical penetration of what had been 'civil space' under de Valera.[131] The influence of the Church eventually provoked Dr Noël Browne's resignation over the 'Mother and Child' health scheme.[132] But for the moment Church and government were united in opposition to communism both at home and abroad. Keogh observes that Irish embrace of the 'Red Menace' concept, while undoubtedly faithful to Interparty proclivities, also went a considerable way towards rehabilitating the Irish in American eyes after the 'intransigence' of the de Valera years.[133]

Ireland and the threat of communism in Italy

One of the foreign policy focuses of the Interparty government was the threat of communist electoral victory in Western Europe. In 1948 communist-inspired strikes paralysed Italy and France, and there were fears that both could 'go Red' from within – especially as the first Italian election under universal suffrage was scheduled.[134] There was therefore a convergence of interests between the Church, the Catholic right and the Americans, who had already determined to use covert means to stymie a leftist takeover in Italy.[135] American intelligence services and the Vatican set up 'Catholic Action' committees, and the Irish government, Church and people poured funds into their coffers.[136] MacBride himself donated 'generously' to this cause, and was central to galvanising Dublin's support. Ireland received the Vatican's thanks when the Christian Democrats emerged as the largest parliamentary party in April.[137] The idea had even been mooted during the campaign that the Pope might have to retreat to Ireland if Italy went 'Red' – a concept that incensed Unionists in the North and was, to them, the real reason why Dublin later cleared the constitutional decks and declared a republic.[138]

The Ukrainian connection

Artuković was not the only fugitive from the 'Eastern Bloc' to be given shelter in Ireland. While the elite of Byelorussian collaboration found its way to the US, Ukrainians who joined the Germans in the hope of winning independence from Moscow were scattered to many countries ... provided they evaded repatriation. The majority of Ukrainians in German service hailed from western Ukraine, a region that was under Austro-Hungarian rule until 1918. After the Treaties of Brest-Litovsk and Versailles, these Ukrainians found themselves under Polish rule, or in the various Ukrainian republics that rose and fell during the Russian Civil War. A third Ukrainian population known as Ruthenians inhabited areas of Central Europe. Their greatest concentration was in eastern Czechoslovakia, where an independent state of Carpatho-Ukraine flowered briefly in 1939.[139]

Like Byelorussia, the Ukraine was culturally and religiously divided between an Orthodox east and a west that looked to Rome. Although there were many regular Catholics (especially among Ruthenians), others belonged to the Uniate or 'Greek Catholic' Church, which practised Orthodox ritual but recognised the Pope. As such, they were viewed – like the Croats – as defenders of Catholic Europe from both 'schism' and communism. They also represented Catholic reconciliation with the East, and were a valuable propaganda tool in campaigns to recapture leadership of all Christendom.

Ukrainians in exile were among the earliest foreign volunteers in the German armed forces. The 600-strong 'Sushko Legion' accompanied the Wehrmacht in its invasion of Poland, and the 'Nachtigall' and 'Roland' units sowed chaos behind Red Army lines after the German attack in 1941.[140] The Germans never countenanced the idea of Ukrainian independence, however, and many nationalists took up arms against all 'foreign occupiers', be they Soviets, Germans or even the Polish Home Army, fighting a complex four-way struggle of ever-shifting alliances in the forces of the Ukraiinska Povstanska Armiia (Ukrainian Insurgent Army). Some units continued the fight long after Soviet re-occupation, one battling its way westward to surrender to US forces in Germany as late as September 1947.[141] Others, however, remained within German forces in a largely notional Ukraiinska Vyzvolne Viysko (Ukrainian Liberation Army) from 1943, finally and desperately reorganised as a Ukraiinska Natsionalna Armiia (Ukrainian National Army) in the war's final weeks.[142]

Committed Catholic opponents of communism hailing from regions within the USSR were highly valued as the Cold War began, and many Ukrainians featured in the 'Christian Front', or in the various anti-communist armies known to US intelligence by the codename 'Integral'.[143] Many escaped through Church networks to Britain, Spain and Argentina, or to émigré communities in the US, Australia and Canada.

The Irish role in the shelter of fugitive Ukrainians was modest. There was however a level of sympathy for these exiles, and not solely along broad anti-communist lines: a branch of the Redemptorists, a religious order that worked among Uniate communities, existed in Ireland. Ukrainian Redemptorist Bishop Nicholas Charnetskyj of Volhynia had also forged close ties with Irish supporters when he attended the Eucharistic Congress in Dublin in 1932. He was arrested following Moscow's proscription of the Uniate Church in 1944, charged with being 'an agent of the Vatican'.[144] Such persecution, reminiscent of Mindszenty and Stepinac, guaranteed Uniate Ukrainians both Church assistance and favourable reception in Ireland. Louis Feutren, the Breton veteran of the Bezen Perrot, shared student lodgings in Galway with a number of such Ukrainians in the late 1940s – men who had, like himself, donned German *Feldgrau* in the hope of winning national independence. These men arrived through Church networks, transiting through Italy. One, Josef Turko, became a teacher like Feutren; the others studied medicine. All made the time-honoured Ukrainian emigration to Canada in the late 1950s.[145]

A few other Eastern refugees used Ireland as a staging post. In one instance, Mikhail Vasiliyev, a Kuban Cossack resident at Portarlington, Co. Laois, turned up hopefully at Holyhead late in 1951, only to be promptly deported back to Ireland – his anti-communist record (presumably in German service) and a 'political testimonial of the Russian anti-Communist centre in the USA' notwithstanding. '[O]ne is moved to ask oneself,' he complained to the British

Foreign Office, 'whether there is not here some influence of a Soviet Union 5th Column in your country?' [146] Many Cossacks joined the Germans during the war, some performing anti-Partisan duties in Yugoslavia. From here they too fled across the border to Italy and Austria. Many were handed back to the Soviets during 'Operation Keelhaul'.[147] How this presumably Orthodox anti-communist evaded this round-up and entered Ireland is unknown, but, as is evidenced by Draganović's willingness to shelter non-Catholic anti-communists, it is entirely possible he escaped employing Church networks.

The contrast of large-scale arrivals

As witnessed when the fifteen German POWs landed at Kinsale in January 1946, entries on a large scale were treated differently to discreet, small-scale arrivals. As a net exporter of people, Ireland had never been a popular refugee destination. Its government signalled as early as the 1938 Evian Conference that it would not be able to contribute significantly to refugee resettlement.[148] In the view of government departments responsible for refugee policy, large-scale entries either threatened the Irish labour market or presented 'social problems'. There was also the danger that press in Britain or America would exploit large-scale arrivals to cement Ireland's image as a reactionary haven – an image that was already contributing to the Soviet refusal to allow it to join the UN.[149]

In September 1949, a vessel called the *Victory* put in at Cobh. On board were 385 mostly Estonian refugees, en route from Stockholm to Canada. Despite Ottawa's objections, Cabinet refused to admit them permanently for fear more would be encouraged to leave Sweden, itself deluged with Baltic refugees. The regular refugee programme (as distinct from discreet entries) had been devised to cope with an orderly 'queue'. Although they differed on the final numbers that should be admitted, such had been the consensus when the Departments of Justice and External Affairs had first conferred on this question in September 1945.[150]

Ireland finally joined the UN ten years later, but its first major intake as a signatory to the 1951 Convention on the Status of Refugees was a disaster. Eager to be seen as a 'paid up member of the international community' after years in the diplomatic wilderness, Ireland in 1956 registered its willingness to accept 1,000 refugees.[151] That these were Catholics fleeing repression of an anti-communist uprising in Hungary makes their subsequent treatment all the more noteworthy.

For, by the following year, most of the 517 who had by then arrived left for Canada – and some even preferred to return to Hungary.[152] Irish enthusiasm had disintegrated as the refugees had not 'conformed to Irish customs without placing burdens on Irish institutions' as expected. Rancour over employment and freedom of movement led to hunger strikes and clashes with the Garda, and many Irish felt there had been a lack of gratitude and deference on the part of these fellow Catholic anti-communists.[153]

What had changed? As has been noted, control over immigration is a fundamental expression of sovereignty. By 1956, however, Ireland was a republic, a member of the international forums that safeguarded such status, and the dispute over NATO membership had eased. The need to assert sovereignty was fading, and other concerns, such as protecting Irish society from 'social problems', were coming to the fore. It is also noteworthy that other nationalist exiles in Ireland arrived singly, in pairs or discreet small groups. Their 'gratitude and deference' to the state would also become well documented. By contrast, the Hungarians appear to have arrived too late and in too great numbers, thereby outweighing – and outstaying – their political utility. For Ward, Ireland's overall attitude was shaped by 'an instrumental interest in appearing to participate in the international effort rather than any interest in the Hungarians themselves'.[154]

Conclusion

Although Croats and Ukrainians granted asylum in Ireland were numerically fewer than the Bretons, there was a much greater mobilisation of sympathy for oppressed Catholics behind the Iron Curtain than was ever expressed for pan-Celticist or autonomist questions. Outside of Republican and linguistic circles where pan-Celticism held sway, appeals drawing parallels with Irish history were furthermore almost entirely confined to Catholic figures under communist rule. Irish sympathy for these figures, coupled with the determined anti-communism of the Church, added up to a general willingness to elide the wartime record of 'proven anti-communists' and 'shape-shift' them into 'martyrs'.

In the effort to assist the Church spirit these Eastern European 'crusaders' to safety, Ireland played a relatively minor role. Virtually all former neutral states in Europe – not to mention former Allied belligerents – had a hand in facilitating the escape of these fugitives, allowing them to make their 'expertise' available for the expected clash with Moscow. As the following chapter explores, neither Church involvement nor Allied collusion in this effort was confined to fugitives from the East, nor was the anti-communist struggle seen as entirely focused there.

There also remains the question of how much official assistance was granted to Artuković – the highest-ranking Axis fugitive to enter Ireland – either by the Irish legation at Berne, or by Dublin in providing him papers to continue to the US. The circumstantial evidence suggests complicity, but the precise attitude of Irish governments toward their Croatian 'guest' remains secret. Whether he entered through Church or Irish channels or some co-operative effort between the two, Artuković's inward and outward journeys must be contrasted with the Irish attitude toward Breton fugitives, who were forced to travel entirely through their own or Welsh nationalist networks. And while Seán MacBride is said to have wanted 'nothing to do' with exiled Bretons, the zeitgeist of Cold War anti-communism guaranteed figures like Artuković a more welcome reception.

Was this pro-Axis sympathy at play in Irish asylum policy? If so, it appears a curious one that waited until Nazi defeat before swinging into action, and even then was in secret accord with the objectives of Allied intelligence. It also seems to have assisted certain Axis fugitives (those who presented a subversive threat to communist regimes, for example) more than others.

But there was one other group of foreign nationalists who entered Ireland at this time, in numbers roughly equal to the Bretons. Like their Celtic counterparts, they too were inspired by the 'Irish example'. Unlike most Bretons, however, the majority arrived not during de Valera's premiership, but under the Interparty government, and once again it was not Irish inspiration nor nationalism that guaranteed them welcome. It was instead their Catholicism and 'proven anti-communism' that impressed official Ireland about Flemish fugitives, and ensured the sympathy of the Catholic clergy who assisted them at every stage of their flight.

CHAPTER 7

'All for Flanders – Flanders for Christ': Flemish exiles and Irish asylum, 1947–8

ON 15 OCTOBER 1948, two Dutch-speakers arrived in Dublin by air from Amsterdam.[1] For one, it was the first flight of his twenty-seven years. Although requiring no visa, the two were obliged to back up their passports with identity cards. This is because the twenty-seven-year-old's passport bore a Spanish entry stamp with no corresponding exit authorization,[2] and was marred by an inkblot where the birthdate was recorded.[3] Had the document not been damaged in this way, the bearer – Meneer 'Peeters' – would have been presenting himself as an improbable sixty-year-old.

Dublin Airport was not like the waterfront or some small southern harbour. The immigration official demanded to know what financial support these aliens had to ensure they would not become social burdens, and would enable them to return to the Netherlands. Neither had anything of the kind. 'Peeters' had in fact only five pounds to his name. The two were not tourists as they claimed, concluded the official, but illegal immigrants.

The two 'aliens' had to think fast. Thankfully they had been briefed on what to say in this situation. 'We are going to Glenstal Priory', 'Peeters' said. 'They will help us, and pay the return trip.'[4]

With the approval of the Catholic Church so implied, both men were soon at liberty in Éire, save a simple undertaking to report to the Aliens' Office at Dublin Castle. In this way, Alexander Colen (*aka* 'Peeters') and Staf van Velthoven (*aka* 'Michel van Houhe') began their 'new life in free Ireland'.[5] Despite arriving from the Netherlands, neither was actually Dutch. They were in fact Flemish. More importantly, both were also Oostfronters – veterans of the Waffen-SS and its fight against communism on the Eastern Front.

Flemings in Ireland

Flemish nationalists were granted asylum in postwar Ireland in numbers roughly equal to the Bretons. Although impossible to ascribe Irish motivations in these cases to pan-Celticism, it is true that Flemish intellectuals drew inspiration from the Irish struggle for independence. It might then be presumed that Flemish nationalism was perceived as a fraternal movement, and that asylum functioned as an expression of solidarity on this basis.

Most in the Flemish movement were motivated however by a conservative Catholicism that championed the war in the East as a crusade in defence of Christian civilization. In contrast to the majority of their nationalist counterparts in Brittany, many Flemings volunteered to defend 'Christian' interests not just in local service against the Resistance, but in German uniform on the Eastern Front. As a consequence, most who later fled Brussels' vengeance did so not through their own or kindred channels as did the Bretons, but through Church networks similar to those that assisted Artuković, Eichmann and other 'persons of interest' in the anticipated final war with Bolshevism. This Catholic, anti-communist solidarity guaranteed them asylum in Ireland, and significantly not all Dutch-speaking Catholic asylees were Flemings.

While acknowledging the impact of Irish independence upon Flemish nationalist thought, it will again be seen that Catholic anti-communism was both the prime motivator of Flemish action during the war and the determinant of Irish asylum policy after it; a force more powerful than pan-Celticism or nationalistic sympathy. Those who helped Flemish nationalists escape Belgian vengeance – whether Catholic clergy or foreign governments, including the Irish – viewed them as persecuted co-religionists and 'proven anti-communists'. Importantly, Irish attitudes in this regard were not as incompatible with the objectives of Western governments as they may have at first seemed. To understand what brought Flemings to Ireland, we must first understand the interaction of Catholic conservatism and nationalism in Flanders.

'Il n'y a pas des Belges'

France occupied the area that is now Belgium from 1795 to 1815, during which time the upper strata of Flemish society became gallicized.[6] The Dutch were awarded these territories after Napoleon's defeat, absorbing Dutch-speaking Flanders and French-speaking Wallonia into a United Kingdom of the Netherlands. In 1830, however, Flemings joined their Walloon co-religionists in rebellion against the Calvinist ruling class, and in agitation for a Catholic state.[7] Two Dutch provinces bordering Flanders remained majority Catholic, however.

The new Kingdom of Belgium was cast in the centralist mold of France.[8] The elites and the hierarchy of the Catholic Church sought to cement French as the language of state. This would not only instil unity, they believed, but also prevent Protestant ideas infiltrating from the Netherlands.[9] The Catholic solidarity that bound Walloons and Flemings thereby quickly unravelled, supplanted by linguistic discrimination. At the same time, industrialisation in Wallonia led to the rise of liberal ideas that challenged the Catholic order. Flanders, by contrast, remained predominantly rural and conservative, dominated by Dutch-speaking lower clergy that, as in Brittany, saw French as a conduit of immoral ideas pushed by a materialist state.[10] From these tensions, a Flemish autonomist movement arose.

Flemish priests created a student movement at the turn of the twentieth century which – similar to the Ustaše – 'emphasised the unbreakable bond between Flemish and Catholic struggles'.[11] The movement won some linguistic concessions, not least because, unlike other 'minorities' in Europe, the Flemings actually comprise a majority in their governing state.[12] By 1883 Dutch was in limited use in courts and secondary schools.[13] Many complained that francophones undermined reforms, however, and even if these checked the gallicization of Flanders they did little to reform state administration.[14] Flemings also became alienated from bishops who championed French, yet remained devoted to their local clergy.

In many respects it was Walloon opposition that heightened a sense of Flemishness and promoted separatism. A Walloon Movement formed which resisted bilingualism and other 'favours' to Flemings.[15] It was however a socialist Walloon, Jules Destrée, who outlined the ethnic fissures in the country in an open letter to King Albert I in 1912: '*Sire, il y a en Belgique des Wallons et des Flamands. Il n'y a pas des Belges.*' (Sire, there are in Belgium Walloons and Flemings. There are no Belgians.) Destrée argued that a federation of two 'independent and free peoples' would be 'infinitely more robust than a Belgium where one half believes itself to be oppressed by the other half'.[16] His warning went unheeded, and the unity of the Belgian state was soon tested from an external quarter.

AVV-VVK

The German invasion of 1914 left only a small corner of Flanders under Belgian control. Conscription from this region soon swelled the Flemish majority in the army to eighty per cent. The officer corps had long been predominantly francophone, and resentment of this imbalance was heightened by press characterisations of the war as a racial conflict between Latin civilization and Germanic *Kultur*.[17] The French newspaper *Le Figaro* made known in 1916 how it regarded Flanders in this context:

> Flanders is a march where [...] Gallic tribes became intermingled with the blood of Germanic invaders [...] Germanic idioms became the popular tongue, but [...] all manifestations of superior civilisation there were French.[18]

Few Flemish soldiers mutinied, however.[19] A 'Front Movement' formed among the troops,[20] but even this hoped that sacrifice in battle would be rewarded by a grateful state. The headstones of fallen soldiers of the Movement did not read *Vive la Belgique* or *Vive le Roi*, however, but were inscribed with six letters in a cruciform pattern:

A
VVK
V

Alles voor Vlaanderen–Vlaanderen voor Kristus ('All for Flanders–Flanders for Christ').[21]

There were two instances of frontline desertion by Flemish troops, involving a total of four soldiers. These were delegates of the Front Movement tasked with contacting Flemings behind German lines who were turning to the occupiers to realise dreams of autonomy.[22] These collaborators were 'Activists', and the repercussions of their accommodation with the forces of the Kaiser bear remarkable similarities with that of the subsequent generation under the Nazis.

First round of Flemish collaboration

While some advocated absorption of Flanders as a lost Germanic province, level-headed German military and political bosses were unwilling to incense francophone opinion any more than was necessary – especially as the bulk of Belgian industry was in Wallonia. As the war ground on, however, racialist characterisations of the conflict presented Germany with an opportunity to prise the formerly loyal (if unenthusiastic) Flemings away from the Entente camp. The result was *Flamenpolitik* – the courting of Flemish opinion by extending vague assurances of German support. This double-game was in Hossay's analysis an attempt 'to divide the Belgian polity in an effort to weaken resistance while simultaneously promoting the continuation of the prewar administration as much as possible'.

The decision to work with the Germans split Activists from those who rejected collaboration, or 'Passivists'.[23] Even then, many Activists insisted no purely German objectives would be served. Cyriel Verschaeve, a Catholic priest, expanded upon this theme in a tract he distributed secretly to Flemish troops:

> *Q: So the Flemings could accept German help?*
> A: Yes, on one condition – that they use it only to further their own Flemish interests, and in no way those of the Germans.[24]

By 1917, the Germans abandoned hopes of exploiting Belgian industry without social disruption, and *Flamenpolitik* became more pronounced. Language laws were enacted, and the University of Ghent became unilingually Dutch.[25] Finally, in December, the Raad van Vlaanderen (Council of Flanders) declared Flemish

12 à vis Mai 1935 LE N° 0 fr. 50 12 Mai 1935

17 ANNÉE – N° 223

breiz atao

ORGANE BI-MENSUEL DU PARTI NATIONAL BRETON

Direction - Administration : 4, Rue des Francs-Bourgeois – RENNES

ABONNEMENTS :

"Mais où pourrons-nous tirer de l'eau,
Dit Pearse à Connolly,
Quand tous les puits sont desséchés ?
Oh ! il est évident
Qu'il n'y a rien que notre propre sang rouge
Qui puisse rendre la vie au Rosier."

W. B. YEATS

THE LIBRARY
TRINITY COLLEGE
DUBLIN

LUN FASK

1916 !

IL Y A DIX-NEUF ANS

les Irlandais ont sauvé leur pays en versant leur sang pour lui

1 Easter Rising commemorative issue of *Breiz Atao* (Brittany Forever), 12 May 1935. 'Easter Monday 1916! Nineteen years ago, the Irish saved their country by shedding their blood for it.' (Trinity College, Dublin)

2 'Bretons see a new sun shining over the land of Brittany', *Breiz Atao,* 12 May 1935. (Trinity College, Dublin)

3 DSSO anti-conscription poster, 1934. (National Archives, Kew)

4 Ronald MacDonald Douglas, from *The Irish book*. (Dublin, 1936).

L'IRLANDE MILITANTE

LA VIE
DE
Patrice PEARSE

avec une Introduction historique
et 15 Photographies

par

Louis N. LE ROUX

RENNES
IMPRIMERIE COMMERCIALE DE BRETAGNE
1932

5 *La vie de Patrice Pearse* (The life of Patrick Pearse) by Louis Napoléon Le Roux.
(Bibliothèque nationale, Paris)

6 Célestin Lainé (l) and Dr Gerhard von Tevenar on a Breton beach, 1938. (Trystan Mordrel)

7 *La Bretagne* (Brittany), 13 May 1941. (Bibliothèque nationale, Paris)

bretagne

[...]TIDIEN DU SOIR – le n° 1 franc

MARDI 13 MAI. — N° 45.

N ACCORD SECRET AURAIT ÉTÉ CONCLU

LONDRES et WASHINGTON avec TCHOUNG-KING, l'AUSTRALIE [...]es INDES-NÉERLANDAISES

[...]KIO, 12 MAI. — LE CORRESPONDANT A SHANGHAI [...]CHI-NICHI SE FAIT L'ECHO DES RUMEURS SENSA[...]ELLES SELON LESQUELLES IL RESULTERAIT QU'UN [...]D SECRET MILITAIRE ET NAVAL AURAIT ETE CONCLU [...] LA GRANDE-BRETAGNE, LES ETATS-UNIS, LE GOU[...]MENT DE TCHOUNG-KING, L'AUSTRALIE ET LES [...]NEERLANDAISES, AFIN D'ASSURER LEUR DEFENSE [...]NE.

[...] conférence anglo-américaine-chinoise serait tenue aujour[...] à Singapour. Le programme de la conférence, suivant [...] correspondant, comprendrait les six points suivants :

[...]'établissement d'un plan d'opérations des forces combinées [...] signataires,

[...]'examen de l'aide que peut apporter l'aviation des Etats[...] gouvernement de Tchoung-King.

[...]a mobilisation sur pied de guerre de toute la population [...] libre, aussi bien en Chine même que dans les colonies [...] de l'Extrême-Orient,

[...] système d'échange d'informations entre les puissances [...],

[...] de l'attitude du gouvernement de Tchoung-King [...] de l'Italie et du Reich,

[...] des nationaux anglais et américains de l'Ex[...] ainsi que les mesures à prendre à l'égard des [...] et allemands en Chine [...] américaines de l'Extrême-Orient,

Yann FOUERE

l'un des animateurs du mouvement breton d'aujourd'hui

expose à la radio LES LEGITIMES ASPIRATIONS de la BRETAGNE

Poursuivant le cycle de ses conférences sur le Folklore des provinces françaises, Radio-Paris consacrait son émission de samedi dernier à la Bretagne.

Un hasard particulièrement heureux — hasard qui, en réalité, n'en est pas un — a voulu que, pour la circonstance, le micro soit confié à notre directeur, Yann Fouéré, que le speaker présenta aux auditeurs, comme l'un des animateurs du mouvement breton d'aujourd'hui.

Tous ceux qui connaissent [...]

8 *Breton nationalism* by Yann Fouéré, written while in Welsh exile. (National Archives, Kew)

9 Bagadoù Stourm preparing for a route march, from the PNB internal newsletter *Triskell,* April 1943. (National Library of Wales, Aberystwyth)

10 Reserve lieutenant of artillery and clandestine head of Gwenn-ha-Du, Célestin Lainé, 1931. (Bezen Perrot archives)

11 (l–r) Louis Feutren 'Maître', Yann Guyomarc'h 'Pipo' and Ange Luec 'Forster' in the SS uniform of the Bezen Perrot, Tübingen, early 1945. (Bezen Perrot archives)

12 SS-Oberscharführer Louis Feutren 'Maître' of the Bezen Perrot. The plain black collar patch indicates membership of the SD. (Bezen Perrot archives) **13** SS-Untersturmführer Célestin Lainé 'Neven Henaff' of the Bezen Perrot. (Bezen Perrot archives) **14** Ronan Guyomarc'h 'Morin' (l) and his brother Yann 'Pipo' of the Bezen Perrot, Germany, early 1945. Ronan fled to Spain, Yann to Ireland. (Bezen Perrot archives) **15** ID photo for Louis Feutren *aka* 'Michel Kelleg', used while a fugitive in Paris, 1946–7. (Bezen Perrot archives)

NOTRE ENGAGEMENT

J. DE QUELEN

CHACUN de nous, dans le tout qu'est le monde n'est qu'une fraction. C'est un fait. Nous participons nécessairement à la vie collective de la société dont nous sommes. Mais nous pouvons y participer de deux manières : la mauvaise et la bonne.

1) *La mauvaise* : c'est l'embrigadement. N'ayant pas été capable faute de connaître ou faute de vouloir, de prendre place parmi ses pairs pour marcher avec eux vers le commun destin, « l'embrigadé » a été emmené par la première troupe qui a passé. La seule déterminante ? Le besoin d'être avec d'autres, de faire comme d'autres. Il est « un de plus », il fait nombre.... ou poids, mais il ne coefficie pas avec ces autres.

2) *La bonne* : c'est l'engagement. Sachant ce que je suis (un être individuel et collectif tout à la fois), sachant ce que je veux (me réaliser moi-même, et porter ma mission sociale de qui je la tiens à qui je la dois), je choisis ma place parmi ceux qui montent vers ce même but qu'ils connaissent et qu'ils veulent eux aussi. J'apporte ma personnalité active à l'organisme constitué par d'autres personnalités actives avec lesquelles ma propre personnalité coefficiera.

Il n'y a pas d'autre voie : ou bien s'engager ou bien subir l'embrigadement, c'est-à-dire : marcher ou suivre.

⁂

Quelle voie avons-nous choisie, nous, nationalistes bretons ? Evidemment, la question posée comme elle l'est plus haut, chacun répondra : « la bonne, celle de l'engagement ». Oui, mais l'engagement de la personne humaine n'est pas si simple ; il ne suffit pas que je dise : « J'engage ma personne » pour que ma personne soit réellement engagée. L'engagement ne se décide pas dans un instant; il se pratique dans la série de tous les instants qui sont, en somme, toute notre vie ; il se pratique dans la série des actes accordés entre eux et avec notre vocation, actes qui, par le fait qu'ils ont été tels, établissent notre caractère, déterminent notre direction, notre axe, et produisent en nous la connaissance de « nos valeurs ».

Vivre dans la fidélité d'un tel engagement n'est pas chose aisée. Cela suppose un effort presque constant, car il existe toujours une certaine tension entre notre personnalité engagée et la collectivité dans laquelle elle s'est engagée, ou plus exactement entre le moi individuel et le moi collectif qui co-existent en chacun de nous.

⁂

Cet état de chose qui, à première vue, semble présenter des inconvénients, dans ce sens qu'il est de nature à amener une lassitude et le désir de s'isoler, de se retirer du jeu, de se mettre à l'écart des événements en spectateur écarté, présente en fait surtout des avantages : il permet le perfectionnement de nous-même et de l'organisation du groupe dans lequel nous sommes engagés. En effet, l'effort de chacun tendra à chaque instant à diminuer cette tension et à rapprocher la cause collective de l'élan individuel et aussi l'élan individuel de la cause collective. Ainsi le groupe et l'individu agissant réciproquement l'un sur l'autre, et partant, sans cependant qu'elle soit jamais atteinte — nous ne sommes que des hommes — la perfection deviendra plus proche. En outre, la conscience constante que nous avons de l'imperfection de la cause (par le fait de cette tension) nous gardera de ces grands enthousiasmes qui peuvent nous conduire à commettre de grandes erreurs et nous entraîner irrémédiablement hors de notre véritable vocation.

Fidélité à notre engagement, à notre cause, mais aussi respect de notre vie individuelle dans l'intérêt même de notre cause d'ailleurs. Dans cette marche aux flambeaux qui nous mène vers notre destinée, chacun doit veiller à ce que *son* flambeau reste allumé, car chaque flambeau est la condition de cette grande lumière qui nous donne à tous la certitude et la confiance.

Ceux qui s'échappent *complètement* de leur vie individuelle pour s'identifier à n'importe quelle puissance, pourvu qu'elle soit forte, ou même à une puissance choisie, trahissent leur fonction d'homme, et parmi les autres hommes ne sont jamais que des émasculés.

⁂

A la lumière de ces quelques principes trop brièvement énoncés, nationalistes bretons, membres du P. N. B., examinons notre conscience:

Pouvons-nous nous considérer comme « engagés » véritablement ?

Vivons-nous chacune de nos journées dans la fidélité à notre engagement ?

Avons-nous vraiment réalisé l'équilibre entre le moi « réservé » et le moi « engagé » ? Ne nous est-il pas arrivé trop souvent de paver de moi son dû à celui-ci et de garder pour celui-là toute notre réelle activité ?

Avons-nous été chaque jour, de notre parti, de notre pays, autant que de notre métier, autant que de notre famille, autant que de nous-même ?

Avons-nous considéré les conditions matérielles d'existence de notre organisation nationaliste avec autant de souci et de sérieux que les conditions matérielles d'existence pour nous-même et pour notre famille ?

⁂

Ces questions — et beaucoup d'autres — il faut que nous nous les posions... et que nous y répondions. La droiture et la sincérité doivent être la marque distinctive des hommes de notre groupe. C'est la condition de l'authenticité de notre vie. Nous nous sommes décidés pour une cause qui est devenue *notre* cause, nous avons assumé la responsabilité d'une œuvre à réaliser, en même temps que nous nous réalisons nous-même. Si nous ne réalisions pas cette œuvre, nous ne nous réaliserions pas nous-même non plus; et dans ce cas nous serions un mensonge vivant, un mensonge que notre habileté pourrait peut-être cacher à nos contemporains mais qui ne saurait nous tromper nous-même.

J. DE QUELEN,

Chef Départemental des Côtes-du-Nord.

16 Jacques de Quelen, departmental head of the PNB for Côtes-du-Nord, in *Triskell*, July 1943. (National Library of Wales, Aberystwyth)

17 Louis Feutren (l) welcomes Youenn Le Noac'h and Anton Leroy (r) to Ireland, early 1948. (Bezen Perrot archives)

18 Louis Feutren (centre), Maurice Lemoine and companions enjoy the summer weather beside an old bus which doubled as Feutren's first abode in Ireland, Galway, 1948. (Bezen Perrot archives)

19 Maurice Lemoine, formerly 'Manac'h' of the Bezen Perrot, Ireland, 1948. Lemoine first suggested fleeing to Ireland at the unit's anniversary celebration in Germany four years earlier. (Bezen Perrot archives)
20 (below) Yann Goulet, head of the Bagadoù Stourm, in *Triskell*, September 1943. (National Library of Wales, Aberystwyth)

SEPTEMBRE 1943

Lizer miziek
STROLLAD BROADEL BREIZ

TRISKELL

LETTRE-CIRCULAIRE MENSUELLE DU PARTI NATIONAL BRETON

Yann GOULET

« SOYEZ sûr qu'en Allemagne nous, Bretons, saurons toujours nous montrer, parmi les étrangers avec lesquels nous vivons, des modèles de tenue et de moralité. Je crois, d'ailleurs, que ces sentiments sont innés chez les vrais Bretons, et le peu que nous sommes ici, malgré que certains ne partagent pas toutes nos opinions, saura se montrer digne de notre Patrie. »

Cette ferme certitude, je l'ai trouvée dans une lettre que je viens de recevoir d'un de nos camarades, qui travaille depuis près d'un an en Allemagne, et qui fut, avant son départ, l'un des meilleurs parmi nos jeunes militants nantais.

Cet attachement à la Patrie, cette foi en son destin, qui n'ont pas faibli au cours de longs mois de séparation, et souvent de solitude et de silence, sont, pour les jeunes des Bagadou Stourm qui n'ont pas eu à quitter la Bretagne, un exemple viril d'énergie morale.

Ils sont aussi, pour nous qui, depuis trois ans, assumons la charge de diriger le Parti, un puissant réconfort.

Et ce sera une joie pour le Chef des Bagadou Stourm d'apprendre que ses jeunes sont capables d'une telle force de caractère.

□

Il verra ainsi que, durant ces trois années, il n'a pas gaspillé son temps en se consacrant à la Jeunesse Bretonne et en renonçant à ce qui avait été jusque là le but de sa vie.

Il en est peut-être, parmi les jeunes auxquels il donne la meilleure part de lui-même, qui ignorent quel sacrifice a dû faire Yann Goulet pour répondre à mon appel, en janvier 1941, et accepter les fonctions de Chef de la Jeunesse du Parti. Pour ceux-là, il est bon que je le dise dans ces semaines où Yann Goulet leur donne, une fois de plus, une leçon de courage.

□

Avant la guerre, il comptait au nombre de ces jeunes qui faisaient espérer à la Bretagne, à la suite de la première équipe des « Seiz Breur », un riche épanouissement de son Art national. Avec ses camarades, Yann Goulet avait travaillé avec cœur au magnifique Pavillon de Bretagne à l'Exposition Internationale de 1937, qui fut, pour ses visiteurs, la révélation d'un « Manifeste de la Jeunesse artistique bretonne ».

Dès cette époque, il était aussi un homme d'action et fut, avec les frères Le Voyer, l'âme du Groupe « Nevezadur », dont le nom, à lui seul, était un programme de vie pour les jeunes Bretons émigrés qui en faisaient partie.

Sous son impulsion, « Nevezadur » ne fut pas seulement une société folklorique de chants et de danses bretonnes. Par ses cours d'histoire, de langue et de musique, par les conférences qu'elle suscita, elle effectua un incomparable travail de formation bretonne. Elle fut aussi, dans ces années d'avant-guerre, la cheville ouvrière de « Ker-Vreiz », la Maison Bretonne de Paris.

□

En janvier 1941, à son retour de captivité, pendant laquelle il avait consacré tous ses instants à la Bretagne et à ses camarades bretons, Yann Goulet aurait voulu retourner à son atelier de sculpteur et à la direction de « Nevezadur », qui n'attendait que lui pour renaître d'une vie nouvelle.

Il donna alors la plus grande preuve de dévouement qu'un homme puisse apporter à son Pays. Cédant à ma demande, qu'appuyait celle de tous les Chefs départementaux du Parti, il sacrifia tout ce que, pendant sa vie de prisonnier, il avait espéré retrouver à sa libération et accepta de créer, là où il n'y avait rien, une organisation de la Jeunesse bretonne.

□

Ce qu'a été son travail depuis janvier 1941, je n'ai pas à le retracer. Le Parti tout entier l'a suivi avec espoir au cours de ces mois et de ces années d'efforts patients, souvent ardus, pénibles, mais toujours poursuivis avec la volonté inébranlable de parvenir au but.

Depuis trois ans, Yann Goulet s'est dépensé sans compter, parcourant le pays en tous sens, sans cesse en tournées d'inspections, visitant ses centres, en créant de nouveaux, réveillant ceux qui s'abandonnaient, toujours à la tête de ses hommes à travers les campagnes bretonnes, vivant exemple de dévouement pour tous les jeunes des Bagadou Stourm.

Car il ne leur a jamais demandé ce qu'il n'exigeait pas d'abord de lui-même.

Et c'est là ce qui donne la mesure d'un chef.

Depuis quatre semaines, Yann Goulet donne à ses jeunes un nouvel exemple de sa force de caractère et de son indomptable énergie.

Je suis sûr que tous sauront le comprendre et que bientôt il les retrouvera aussi fièrement Bretons que dans ce château du Rusquec où voici deux mois il les a quittés.

R. DELAPORTE.

21 Alan Heusaff, *aka* 'Bernhard Heubacher', soon after his arrival in Ireland, 1950. (Bríd Heussaff)

22 Material in support of Andrev Geffroy authored by Dr Noëlle Davies, early 1950s. (National Archives, Kew)

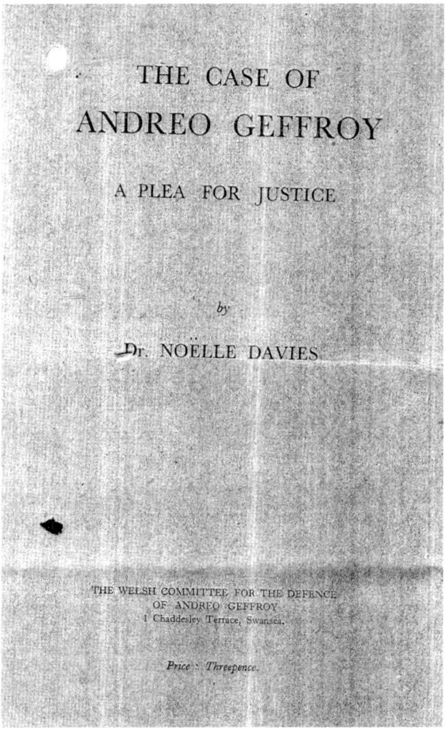

THE CASE OF

ANDREO GEFFROY

A PLEA FOR JUSTICE

by

Dr. NOËLLE DAVIES

THE WELSH COMMITTEE FOR THE DEFENCE
OF ANDREO GEFFROY
1 Chaddesley Terrace, Swansea.

Price : Threepence.

BRETON NEWS

A Bulletin issued by

The Breton Information Bureau

Articles from the bulletin may be republished freely. We will appreciate however if cuttings or copies of the issues in which any of the material appears are communicated to us.

No. 1. Dublin, Eire. January, 1960.

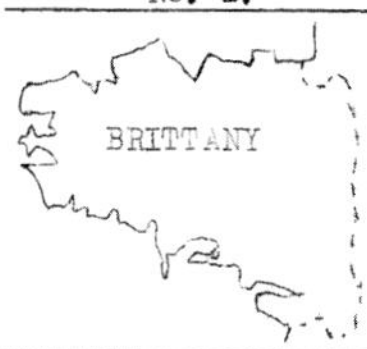

CONTENTS.

WHY WE PUBLISH THIS BULLETIN. Between 1944 and 1947 the Breton movement as a whole was suppressed by the French government. Its foremost leaders were eliminated. Its publications, cultural as well as political, were banned, their equipment being confiscated and handed over to French press concerns.

It has not been possible ever since to redress this situation. Whereas in 1944 the Breton movement controlled two dailies, two weeklies and many monthlies, since the setback of the Purge it has only succeeded in putting up again a few monthlies and quarterlies.

Nowadays news and information from Brittany can come only through the channels of the Agence France Presse (A.F.P.). But for the last twenty years information in France has been strictly controlled by the State. In fact the French government possess a monopoly in the diffusion and distribution of news to the press and broadcasting system, and A.F.P. is hardly more independent from the State than an ordinary ministerial department.

Consequently, news and information concerning Brittany are nearly always subject to an official screening, interpretation and distortion before reaching the public of foreign countries. More than often especially when relating to the Breton movement, they are not conveyed at all. The French papers and press agencies in Brittany apply the same policy of silence. When the news cannot entirely be concealed, they are biased and aim at throwing doubt about the sincerity of Breton leaders.

We deem it necessary therefore to provide the foreign press with information from genuine Breton sources, free from the French official prejudice. We hope it will be of interest to many journalists now unaware of the Breton problems. We also hope it will be of some assistance to the legitimate aspirations and interests of Brittany by throwing light on the efforts our small Celtic nation is making in defence of her social, cultural and political rights, too often neglected and denied to her by the long standing imperialism of the French State.

BRETON FARMERS THREATEN ILLEGAL ACTION On October 19th last, the main roads of the Finistere departemement were barricaded at 18 different places to protest against the incomprehension of the Government towards agricultural problems. 25 participants were wounded at Roc'h Trevezel, near Morlaix, when police charged them.

On Nov. 13th. delegates of the Federations of Farmers syndicates for all 5 Breton departements met in Gwened (Vannes). They requested the Government through its Préfect in Vannes, to revise its antiagricultural policy and to stop dis-organizing agricultural markets by "shock" importations. They demanded the return of indexation of farm products, guaranteeing the vital minimum prices in terms of an index, as well as social benefits and security comparable to those enjoyed by

23 *Breton News* No.1, January 1960, edited by Alan Heusaff in Dublin. (National Library of Ireland, Dublin)

24 Staf van Velthoven in SS uniform with his wife and daughter, Antwerp, 1944. (Staf van Velthoven)

25 *Aiséirí Flóndrais* (Resurrection of Flanders) by Albert Folens, 1958. (An Chéad Chló: An tÚdar a Fhoilsigh)

26 Flemings in Ireland, late 1940s. Staf van Velthoven front centre; Alex Colen behind him. (Alex Colen)

27 Flemings in Ireland, early 1950s: Staf van Velthoven (second from right) with Ward Op de Beeck (r). (Staf van Velthoven)

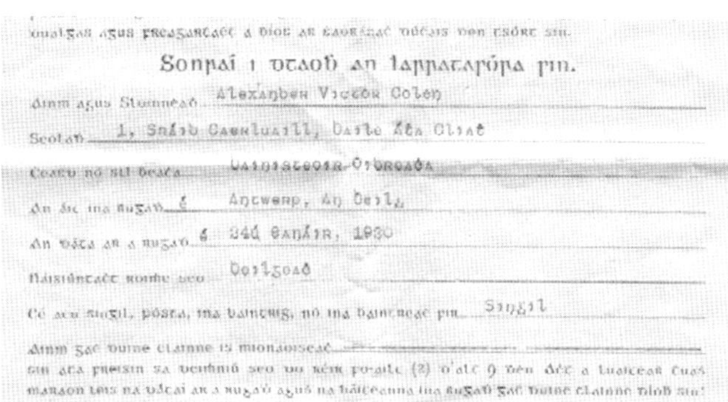

[illegible]

Sonraí i dtaobh an Iarratasóra sin.

Ainm agus Sloinneadh: Alexander Victor Colen

Seoladh: 1, Sráid [illegible], Baile Átha Cliath

Ceird nó slí beatha: [illegible]

An áit ina rugadh é: Antwerp, An Beilg

An dáta ar a rugadh é: 24ú Eanáir, 1930

Náisiúntacht roimhe seo: Beilgeach

Cé acu singil, pósta, ina baintreach, nó ina baintreach fir: Singil

[illegible]

28 Alex Colen's certificate of Irish naturalisation, 1954. Note 'Nationality: Belgian'. (Alex Colen)

29 Yann Goulet's memorial at the Custom House, Dublin. (Photo by author)

30 Neven Henaff in Japan, early 1960s. Henaff developed a 'Celtic' version of Japanese 'Yin/Yang' philosophy he called 'Giam/Sam', courtesy of an association with George Ohsawa. (Bríd Heussaff)

31 Neven Henaff *aka* Célestin Lainé, Ireland, late 1960s. (Bríd Heussaff)

32 Breton exiles bear a wreath for Roger Casement, March 1965. (l–r) Louis Feutren, Neven Henaff, Alan Heusaff, Yann Goulet. (Bríd Heussaff)

33 Bretons at Arbour Hill cemetery, Dublin, for Easter 1966. At right, Alan Heusaff (l) confers with Yann Fouéré and Plaid Cymru president Gwynfor Evans (r). At centre, an Irish detective takes the names of participants. (Bríd Heussaff)

34 'Local beatniks'. Protest led by Yann Goulet (l) outside the French embassy in Dublin, 1967. Staf van Velthoven is at right with the sign concerning French Flanders. (Bríd Heussaff)

35 Sign hung outside Staf van Velthoven's flat to welcome the King and Queen of Belgium during their Dublin visit, May 1968. (Staf van Velthoven)

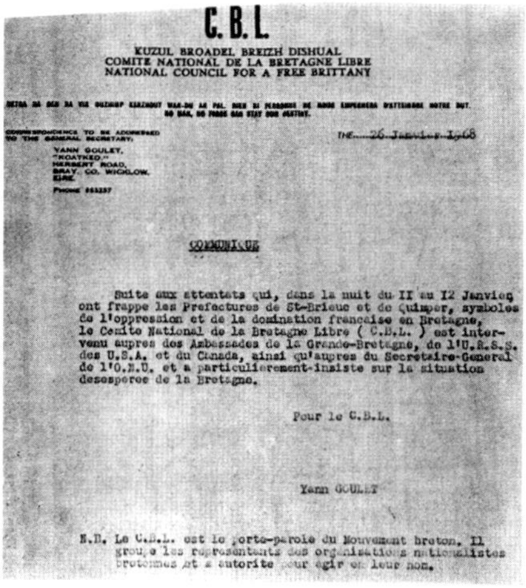

C.B.L.

KUZUL BROADEL BREIZH DISHUAL
COMITE NATIONAL DE LA BRETAGNE LIBRE
NATIONAL COUNCIL FOR A FREE BRITTANY

YANN GOULET,
"KOATKEO,"
HERBERT ROAD,
BRAY, CO. WICKLOW,
EIRE.

THE 26 Janvier 1968

COMMUNIQUE

Suite aux attentats qui, dans la nuit du II au I2 Janvieq ont frappe les Prefectures de St-Brieuc et de Quimper, symboles de l'oppression et de la domination francaise en Bretagne, le Comite National de la Bretagne Libre (C.B.L.) est intervenu aupres des Ambassades de la Grande-Bretagne, de l'U.R.S.S. des U.S.A. et du Canada, ainsi qu'aupres du Secretaire-General de l'O.N.U. et a particulierement-insiste sur la situation desesperee de la Bretagne.

Pour le C.B.L.

Yann GOULET

N.B. Le C.B.L. est le porte-parole du Mouvement breton. Il groupe les representants des organisations nationalistes bretonnes et a autorite pour agir en leur nom.

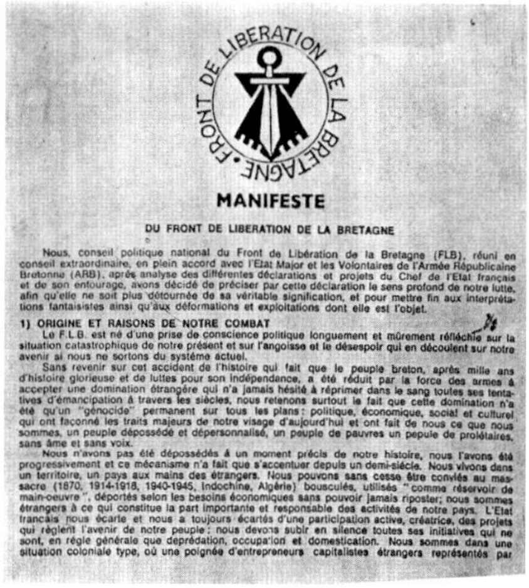

FRONT DE LIBERATION DE LA BRETAGNE

MANIFESTE

DU FRONT DE LIBERATION DE LA BRETAGNE

Nous, conseil politique national du Front de Libération de la Bretagne (FLB), réuni en conseil extraordinaire, en plein accord avec l'Etat Major et les Volontaires de l'Armée Républicaine Bretonne (ARB), après analyse des différentes déclarations et projets du Chef de l'Etat français et de son entourage, avons décidé de préciser par cette déclaration le sens profond de notre lutte, afin qu'elle ne soit plus détournée de sa véritable signification, et pour mettre fin aux interprétations fantaisistes ainsi qu'aux déformations et exploitations dont elle est l'objet.

1) ORIGINE ET RAISONS DE NOTRE COMBAT

Le F.L.B. est né d'une prise de conscience politique longuement et mûrement réfléchie sur la situation catastrophique de notre présent et sur l'angoisse et le désespoir qui en découlent sur notre avenir si nous ne sortons du système actuel.

Sans revenir sur cet accident de l'histoire qui fait que le peuple breton, après mille ans d'histoire glorieuse et de luttes pour son indépendance, a été réduit par la force des armes à accepter une domination étrangère qui n'a jamais hésité à réprimer dans le sang toutes ses tentatives d'émancipation à travers les siècles, nous retenons surtout le fait que cette domination n'a été qu'un "génocide" permanent sur tous les plans : politique, économique, social et culturel qui ont façonné les traits majeurs de notre visage d'aujourd'hui et ont fait de nous ce que nous sommes, un peuple dépossédé et dépersonnalisé, un peuple de pauvres un pepule de prolétaires, sans âme et sans voix.

Nous n'avons pas été dépossédés à un moment précis de notre histoire, nous l'avons été progressivement et ce mécanisme n'a fait que s'accentuer depuis un demi-siècle. Nous vivons dans un territoire, un pays aux mains des étrangers. Nous pouvons sans cesse être conviés au massacre (1870, 1914-1918, 1940-1945, Indochine, Algérie) bousculés, utilisés "comme réservoir de main-oeuvre", déportés selon les besoins économiques sans pouvoir jamais riposter; nous sommes étrangers à ce qui constitue la part importante et responsable des activités de notre pays. L'Etat francais nous écarte et nous a toujours écartés d'une participation active, créatrice, des projets qui règlent l'avenir de notre peuple ; nous devons subir en silence toutes ses initiatives qui ne sont, en règle générale que déprédation, occupation et domestication. Nous sommes dans une situation coloniale type, où une poignée d'entrepreneurs capitalistes étrangers représentés par

36 Communiqué and FLB manifesto issued by Yann Goulet's CBL at Bray, County Wicklow, 1968. (Archives du Ministère des Affaires étrangères, Paris)

37 Alan Heusaff (second from left) and Yann Goulet (standing) at a Celtic League meeting, Dublin, *c.*1964. (Bríd Heussaff)

38 Alan Heusaff teaching Breton to a class at Conradh na Gaeilge, Dublin, *c.*1967. (Bríd Heussaff)

39 Alan Heusaff (l), with Breton folk singer Alan Stivell, *c.*1972. (Bríd Heussaff)

40 Alex Colen, 2006. (Alex Colen)

41 Yann Fouéré in his study at St.-Brieuc, June 2005. (Photo by author)

Judge rules Scot's crime was 'political'

Irish Press 17 October 1984

THE High Court in Dublin yesterday ordered the release of a Scottish nationalist wanted by British police for causing malicious damage to British Ministry of Defence vehicles.

The court was told that Adam Busby (35) of Seedhill Road, Paisley, had daubed such slogans as "Brits Out" on vehicles at Berwick-on-Tweed. But Mr Justice Barrington found that the offence was political or connected with a political offence, and granted him an order under Section 50 of the Extradition Act, 1965.

In an affidavit, Busby said that on August 25, 1982, he went to Berwick-on-Tweed to protest at celebrations to mark the 500th anniversary of the capture of that town by the British in 1482.

A model of the aircraft carrier Hermes was on exhibition. When the exhibition closed for lunch, [illegible]

Adam Busby after his release from the High Court.

Meanwhile, at the same court, a warrant was issued for the arrest of another Scot, who failed to turn up for a hearing of his action challenging an extradition order to Scotland, on a charge of sending an incendiary device through the post to the Earl of Mansfield.

42 Adam Busby after being granted relief from extradition to the UK, October 1984. (*Irish Press*)

43 Issue of Leon Mill-Arden's *An Aimsir Cheilteach* (The Celtic Time), 1952. (National Archives, Kew)

An Aimsir Ceilteac
THE CELTIC TIME

MONTHLY PAPER OF THE CELTIC PEOPLES

THE ORGAN OF INFORMATION WITHIN THE CELTIC PEOPLES AND ABROAD. THE INSTRUMENT OF INTERCELTIC OUTLOOK & CO-OPERATION

PRINTED PAPER RATE. YEARLY SUBSCRIPTION 5/. SEND TO "AN AIMSIR CHEILTEACH", SRAID AN DÚIN, CORCAIGH. (FORT STREET, CORK)

IUIL–LUNASA (JULY–AUGUST) 1952

"AN AIMSIR CHEILTEACH"
Is Now Published By:
"Na Nuachtain Cheilteacha" ("The Celtic Press"), Portlairge,
Grouping Irish, Welsh and Scottish Members.

Letters are still to be posted to the usual address until further notice.

"A HATCHET STILL UNBUIRED"

"The Irish Question" was a phrase much used in England before 1922 to summarise the conflict between Irish nationalism and English imperialism. English people commonly believe that it was settled by a treaty in 1922 and that the question of Partition is a living proof that the Irish can soon think up some new grievance when an old one is settled.

The fact is that the old quarrel has never been settled. The insistence on a so-called free state three decades ago, instead of the external relationship that was accepted (albeit grudgingly and with reservations) in 1937, [illegible] the partitioned area in peacetime, grew higher than ever. Proportional representation was abolished to be replaced by gerrymandering in all those areas (about ⅔ of the whole region) where Nationalists predominated. A classic case is the city of Derry, where a large stretch of the countryside has been included in the so-called City Division to prevent the Nationalists, who form 60% of the civic population, from obtaining a majority in the Corporation.

Riots broke out in the 'twenties and 'thirties, as a result of which many people (mainly National- [illegible]

Expert Cynicism and Hypocrisy at the Service of Oppression

Hereunder is a page out of the history of the Breton life-saving effort (as one might call the Nationalist movement) during the last war, now being compiled.

It contains many *facts*. Facts are not subject to opinions: they are either true or untrue. If they are true they are binding, even if at variance with any reader's previous beliefs.

In challenging here any contradiction of these facts, we meet the desire of the author across the water.—(Editor).

"An Aimsir," the only newspaper which at present regularly keep its columns open for the defence of the Breton national cause, has been recently described as "Communist" by the French weekly issued in Brittany, "Le Petit Bleu des Cotes du Nord". The fact is important, as this weekly is owned by M. Pleven, former Prime Minister. It is also sympotmatic. It just means that before long Breton Nationalists, after having been persecuted as Nazis, will be persecuted as Communists! French hypocrisy never changes [illegible] of death) because she put L'Heure Bret. on sale in the district. In August, M. Angeli, prefet of Finistere and his comrade, the prefet of Morbihan, forbade the sale of the Heure Bretonne in their districts and seized the copies of the newspaper in the bookshops. On August 27, 15 young nationalists, who had come to Quimper to sell the newspaper in open defiance of Angeli's order were taken to the police-station, where they barricaded themselves and held a 30-hours siege, without any food, against the police and gendar- [illegible]

CUNNINGHAM-GRAHAM CENTENARY

On the 24th May, 1952, a gathering of Scots assembled on Inchmahone Island in the Lake of Menteith, where Cunninghame-Graham lies buried, to honour the memory of a great and remarkable man who was one of the chief founders of modern Scottish Nationalism. Other gatherings paid homage to him elsewhere.

Born in London on the 24th May, 1852, Robert Bontine Cunninghame-Graham was a member of an aristocratic Scottish family who owned the lands of Gartmore and Menteith. He finished his education at the English public school of Harrow, thereafter emigrating to Argentina in 1868, where he made his name as a cattle-rancher. In fact he got to know the Pampas better than the natives themselves, and could ride like a Gaucho. He won the respect of the Argen- [illegible]

44 Parade in Bilbao celebrating the first Aberri Eguna (Fatherland Day), Easter 1932. Eli Gallastegi is indicated by the arrow. (Iker Gallastegi)

45 Eli Gallestegi (r), with wife Margarita and son Lander, UCD, Dublin, *c.*1952. (Iker Gallastegi)

46 The Gallestegis at the 'Big House', Gibbstown, Co. Meath, *c.*1942. (l–r) Iker, Lander, Ninbe, Margarita, Unai, Eli and Argiñe. (Iker Gallastegi)

47 Basque refugees – including some of those who fled St Jean de Luz in 1940 – with Eli Gallestegi and family at Gibbstown, 1941. At right is Eli's Irish secretary Eileen Mulrennan. (Iker Gallastegi)

independence. In a parallel with Brittany in 1940, this 'went further than the [...] Chancellor and Foreign Ministry desired at that moment'.[26] The term 'autonomy' was therefore substituted prior to publication.

Most Flemings still rejected collaboration. Others embraced the Activist position as the war progressed, partly because the Belgian press now equated all Flemings with collaboration regardless of their actual conduct. More ominously, some newspapers were appealing for French assistance to turn postwar Belgium into a fully francophone state.[27]

Épuration and exile: 1919

In November 1918 many Activists slipped across the border to the Netherlands. Here they formed a Flemish Committee which contacted US President Woodrow Wilson at the Versailles Peace Conference. Drawing parallels with subject nations in Austria-Hungary, the Committee detailed Flanders' wartime sacrifice and the history of francophone dominance in Belgium. Gains were made under the Germans which any right-minded Fleming would support, they argued, but now that Belgium was again under Walloon control, 'veritable terror [has] set in against the Flemish movement. Prisons in Belgium are filled with Flemish who had dared demand a better future for their people.'[28]

Even many Passivists were targeted during the postwar repression.[29] Nationalists remaining in Belgium received lengthy jail terms or worse. Dr August Borms, a leading Activist, was condemned to death, although the sentence was later commuted to life in prison.[30]

For the Front Movement, the repression proved that no sacrifice for Belgium would result in reform. As hundreds of thousands of veterans did across Europe, they came to believe only force and militaristic organisation could achieve the objectives democracy had failed to provide. These veterans formed the Frontpartij (Front Party) in 1919– the first step towards Flemish fascism.[31]

Moderate Flemings were also aghast at the repression that followed the war. Frans van Cauwelaert, leading figure among those who rejected collaboration,[32] who is known (at least to his Irish grandson Paul) as 'Belgium's Daniel O'Connell',[33] upbraided the government for its vengefulness. 'The Flemish people now knows that it cannot obtain justice, not even as a reward for the shedding of its finest blood.' Van Cauwelaert further challenged the government in the national parliament:

> has the repression of Activism [...] resulted in any improvement in the authority and security of the state [...]? [... T]he authorities have [...] create[d] universal bitterness and resentment, so that even people who had resisted all temptations during the war have been [...] shaken in their attachment to Belgian national unity.[34]

For Activists, the lesson of the war was that collaboration could realise objectives impossible under the existing system. Wartime advances were now being wound back, which only served to mark the occupation more starkly as a period of Flemish renaissance. The Activists, like their Breton nationalist counterparts, began to hope that a 'new German war of revenge would eventually destroy Belgium'.[35]

Meanwhile, another devoutly Catholic people was fighting for its independence from an Entente power, and its struggle exercised significant influence upon the Flemish movement.

'If I weren't Flemish, I wish I were Irish'

Like Louis Le Roux, Father Jules Callewaert fled to the UK during the First World War – in his case following condemnation of his pacifist and autonomist views in the francophone press.[36] Two factors drew this Dominican friar to the Irish, as he later explained in his study *Ierland en het Iersche volk* (Ireland and the Irish people): first, 'Every priest will naturally [...] pay eager attention to the expression of religion of all Catholic people'; and second, 'By nature, a Flemish person has sympathetic feelings for every people under oppression'.[37]

Working among Irish communities in England, this blend of Catholic and nationalistic sympathy brought Callewaert to Irish shores on several occasions.[38] Folens claims he was even present during the Easter Rising.[39] In 1922 the friar determined to take up permanent residence 'to study [...] the organisation of the Irish Free State'. In the year that followed, 'the Irish people [...] bewitched my eyes, and I have become more Irish than the Irish themselves.'

For Callewaert, Catholic piety and national self-realisation were inseparable. Writing from Tallaght soon after the Free State's establishment, he felt the religious devotion and self-sacrifice of the Irish could be transposed to Flanders with similar outcomes. 'There is nothing left than to celebrate Ireland as a civilisational model of self-sacrifice, and as an ideal Catholicism', he instructed his Flemish audience. As for Sinn Féin, 'they are all good Catholics and heroes without equal.' Flemings would do well to follow their example, and trust that their own hour would come. 'God is honest and God can wait,' he wrote.[40]

This inspiration the Flemish movement shared with many movements around the globe but, as has been noted, was especially pronounced in Catholic regions such as Brittany and Euskadi. Just as the Basques acknowledged the dual Irish-Catholic influence in adopting Easter Sunday as Aberri Eguna, so too the Flemish adopted a famous Irish Catholic symbol, through an unlikely connection. Albert Folens explains in *Aiséirí Flóndrais* (Resurrection of Flanders), an Irish-language booklet that appeared in 1958:

> In 1949, when my wife and I [...] were [...] in Dublin, she came to a sudden halt: 'Look over there, Albert,' she said, 'a Flemish cross!' This surprised us greatly [... T]his is the explanation [...]: the artist who first designed the Flemish crosses was known by the name Joe English. He was called by that nickname because English was his native language. But he was Irish, and [...] when he was asked to design a memorial to the dead soldiers, he thought of the old Celtic cross [... T]hat cross became the fashion for Catholic graves in Flanders [...] On the four faces of the cross, these letters were engraved: AVV-VVK.[41]

Whither Flanders?

By the mid-1920s there were indications of a Dutch-Flemish rapprochement, not least the willingness of Dutch government ministers to fête exiled Activists who were advocating a radical political creed – Groot Nederland, or Greater Netherlands,[42] otherwise known as Dietschland.[43]

This owed much to 'pillarisation' within Dutch society.[44] Catholics now formed their own separate 'pillar' in the Netherlands, complete with schools and press, and this *'apartheid'* eased sectarian frictions. For Flemings, Dutch accommodations with their Catholic minority removed the greatest obstacle to interaction with their Protestant co-linguists.[45]

Chief advocate of Dietschland was Joris van Severen, who established in 1931 a League of Netherlandish National Solidarists, better known as Verdinaso. This organisation praised Hitler and the Dutch national socialist, Anton Mussert. A smaller organisation committed to unification of Dutch-speakers was the Dietse Opvoedkundige Beweging (Netherlandish Educational Movement) which became in the months prior to the German invasion the Dietse Arbeiders Partij (Netherlandish Workers' Party) – an echo of the German Nazi party. Among its founders was one Staf van Velthoven.[46]

Most nationalists, however, wanted Flemish independence. This tendency commanded most support in the Vlaamsch Nationaal Verbond (Flemish National League). Adopting the far-right trappings of Verdinaso, it praised Nazi ideas of race, anti-Semitism and anti-Marxism under leader Staf de Clercq. Ideas of Flemish independence ('Minimalism') or union with the Netherlands ('Maximalism') also generated suspicion in Berlin, which disdained the idea of a potentially rival Dietschland.[47] These tensions within the Flemish movement – coupled with German desire to enlist Walloon support – militated against absolute Nazi backing for Flemish objectives after the invasion of 1940; not least because Germany's plan was to incorporate both Flanders and the Netherlands into the Greater German Reich.[48]

Finally, there were Flemings who opposed nationalism in any form. Even if many wanted reform of the Belgian state, they could not countenance collaboration. Likewise in Wallonia, although Léon Degrelle's Rexists advocated their own Catholic authoritarian 'Third Way' and received funds from Berlin and

Rome, the majority of Walloons were committed to keeping out of any European conflict. To this end Belgium renounced its security pact with France in 1936 and hoped that a renewed declaration of neutrality would be respected.[49] In May 1940, as in August 1914, that hope was shattered.

Occupation

Blitzkrieg forced Belgian surrender in eighteen days. Many Flemish soldiers – like the twenty-year-old Alexander Colen – deserted rather than fight the invaders.[50] The government fled to England, where some forces regrouped under British aegis. Suggestive of a beneficent attitude, the Germans segregated Flemish POWs and attached French Flanders to the Military Administration at Brussels.[51] From October, Flemish prisoners – Colen among them – were released. In a revival of *Flamenpolitik*, this was designed to discover 'who can be guaranteed to stand by Germany unconditionally in a future political New Order', according to General Falkenhausen. Other expressions of Flemish autonomism were encouraged, but separatism was not. In these early months, the Germans could not afford to antagonise Walloons. Heinrich Himmler did, however, obtain Hitler's approval to recruit Flemings into the Waffen-SS. These were intended to smooth the way for eventual *Anschluss* with Germany.[52]

De Clercq met with German authorities as early as June and some VNV officials were placed in the administration, but full collaboration was not yet envisaged. Many in the party nursed bad memories of the last round of collaboration under German rule. As for ideas of Dietschland, Verdinaso leader van Severen had been arrested and transferred to France shortly after the invasion, where he was hauled before an impromptu firing squad.

Degrelle had also been arrested and transferred to France, but was soon rescued by Pierre Daye and other Rexists. He went on to curry favour with Otto Abetz, German chief at Paris, in hope of gaining access to Hitler and establishing Rexism as the chief political movement in Belgium. One of the proposals Degrelle put forward to Abetz was the creation of a Greater Burgundy as a counterweight to Dietschland.[53] At this time, however, Walloons were considered racially unsuitable to serve in German uniform.[54]

Collaboration was therefore in operation on both sides of the Belgian linguistic divide from the earliest days of Occupation. It required a dramatic external development to galvanize the enthusiasm of Catholic Belgians for armed collaboration, however. That development occurred on the morning of 22 June 1941.

'Holy War'

The invasion of the USSR was portrayed in both communities of Belgium as a European crusade against atheistic Bolshevism. Cyriel Verschaeve, the priest who had advocated limited collaboration during the Great War, now went further. The war in the East was a 'holy war that Germany has declared,' he said, 'and the youth of Flanders has a moral duty to take part.' De Clercq encouraged Flemings to join the Waffen-SS and combat 'the Jewish Empire, Freemasonry, plutocracy and Bolshevism'.[55] Both Rex and the VNV flocked to the German colours. Although they were handled differently by the Germans, anti-communism was the prime motive in all recruitments.[56]

Flemings formed the SS Volunteer Legion 'Flandern' on the Eastern Front. Degrelle's Walloons were excluded from the 'Aryan' SS, and so formed a volunteer brigade of the Wehrmacht, the 'Légion Wallonie'. Degrelle himself enlisted as a private, earning swift promotion.[57]

Appeals to anti-communist sentiment not only supplied manpower, but ensured troublesome ideas like Flemish nationalism were diverted towards German objectives. For Flemings, military service against the USSR also asserted independence. The 'crusade' against the communists was one in which all European nations were equal under German aegis, and service in the Waffen-SS, as 'the first pan-European army',[58] indicated equal Flemish membership of the New Order.

But, although Flanders contributed the highest proportion of collaborators in Western Europe, there were still many in the region who resisted the occupiers – particularly communists. And while the Resistance was never strong enough to mount an uprising,[59] it was capable of sabotage, assassination and disruption of the Axis war effort. Collaborators were therefore sought throughout Belgium for police and guard duties, freeing German personnel for frontline service. The VNV sought to keep favour with the occupiers by providing such personnel, which also protected the party from Resistance attack and could perhaps serve as nuclei of future armed forces.[60] To this end the VNV's uniformed Dietsche Militie was employed. A division of this organisation was the Zwarte ('Black') Brigade, which fulfilled an auxiliary police role.[61]

Dissent within the VNV, and the rise of Degrelle

Succeeding de Clercq as leader of the VNV after his death in 1942 was a moderate who sought to distance the party from close collaboration.[62] Dr Hendrik Elias was viewed with suspicion by the occupiers, especially by Gottlob Berger, the SS chief tasked with incorporating Flanders into the

Reich.[63] Elias is even said to have predicted German defeat, but could not bring his party to abandon collaboration as the feared alternative – a communist takeover – was even more unpalatable.[64] The VNV did more forcefully assert its vision of an independent Flanders as the war progressed, however, fuelled by the disillusionment of many who realised Germany had imperialist designs upon their country. Shared anti-communism could also not disguise neo-pagan elements of Nazism, which distressed devout Catholics.

As in Brittany, the Church hierarchy in Belgium was critical of separatism, regardless of the piety of its adherents. Nationalists were frequently excommunicated – a punishment some priests in Flanders enforced.[65] Even nationalistic lower clergy began to have doubts about the German alliance, and Fr Callewaert himself, who had written so movingly about the Irish struggle twenty years earlier, wrote an open letter to Elias in March 1943 critical of aspects of collaboration. Even so, he and most other nationalists realised only a German victory could bring about the independence they craved.[66]

As the VNV asserted its independence, so the Germans began to search for more compliant partners. Sensing an opportunity, Léon Degrelle courted the SS. Pan-European, anti-communist solidarity – assisted by the grave outlook after Stalingrad – was relaxing the Nazis' insistence upon the 'Aryan' character of SS foreign legions. Slavs, Balts and even Central Asian Turkics were donning *Feldgrau* in the fight against Bolshevism, Degrelle reasoned, so like-minded Latins from Wallonia should provoke no objection. This effort was assisted by revisionism that accentuated the Germanic Burgundian ancestry of Walloons.[67] This sounded good enough to the increasingly-desperate SS, and Degrelle became the favoured Belgian collaborator in the war's latter stages.

Épuration 1944–9

When Brussels fell to Allied forces in September 1944, thousands of Flemish and Walloon collaborators fled with their German sponsors. Jef van der Wiele, head of the pan-Germanist group DeVlag, set up a Flemish government-in-exile in Germany;[68] and Degrelle waited in Luxembourg in December, hoping to declare a Rexist government on 'liberated' Belgian soil during the Ardennes offensive.[69] When the offensive ground down, there was no alternative but retreat to Berlin.

2,940 Belgians were sentenced to death after the Liberation, of which 242 were executed: 'Twice as many […] as in the whole of the Netherlands, Denmark and Norway combined,' according to Folens.[70] Dr August Borms was one of these – his second (and final) death sentence in two separate *épurations*. In the five years from 1944, moreover, Belgian authorities investigated 346,283 acts of *incivisme*[71] (lack of patriotism), compared to approximately 310,000 in France – a population more than five times greater.[72] Flemings, perhaps unsurprisingly, insisted that the *épuration* was less severe in its application to Walloons.[73] 'From 1945–49,' wrote Folens, 'it was enough to be Flemish to draw the wrath of the Communists throngs upon you. If you were spirited enough to oppose them you had to stand trial as a collaborator.'[74] This came down hardest on minor figures such as himself, the exile further complained: '[D]*e kleine* lampisten *moesten boeten voor de groten*.' (The small fry had to pay for the bigwigs.)[75]

The severity of the repression appears to have had an additional, extra-legal motivation: thousands of *incivikien* (Flemings charged with *incivisme*) could be so curtailed in their professional lives that emigration would become an attractive alternative. Then, as Scottish police had intimated regarding the irksome Ronald MacDonald Douglas in 1939, 'political undesirables' could be forced abroad. A senator of the non-nationalist Christian Democratic Party articulated this view late in 1945.[76] Migrations such as these had an impact upon the Flemish presence in Ireland.

Flight into exile

Many collaborators facing more severe sentences spent the postwar years on the run. Some like Robert Verbelen of DeVlag and the priest Cyriel Verschaeve went to ground in Austria, assisted by the Church's escape networks in that country. The latter died in a monastery in 1949.[77] Others went into hiding again in the Netherlands.[78] Some others, as did the Bretons of the Bezen Perrot, hid in Germany – Jef van der Wiele and Hendrik Elias were captured in that country and served lengthy prison terms.[79]

Although Flemings ended up in Allied countries as far afield as South Africa and Canada,[80] it was Spain and Argentina that saw the greatest influxes. Spain, as has been noted, was also selected by Léon Degrelle, Pierre Daye and other Walloons, although Daye later unwillingly decamped to Buenos Aires. Spain was reached through the 'Nordic Route' and the assistance of the Argentine consul in Copenhagen, José Bessone. This was convenient for those who found themselves in Berlin and surrounds in the war's closing weeks. Others came by alternative routes: Leo Poppe, propaganda chief of DeVlag, fled to Paris. He eventually escaped across the Pyrenees with 'the complicity of a Catholic organisation'.[81]

Fugitives in France such as Poppe sheltered at Benedictine and Dominican monasteries, from whence they were smuggled to brother institutions across the Spanish border. Although Breton nationalist networks operated with the help of the Welsh movement and their own sympathisers, there were instances of monastic assistance in their cases, too. Yann Fouéré was sheltered by Dominican friars in France before he made the crossing to England.[82] Republican authorities launched a drive against this 'Cassock's Plot', raiding places of sanctuary. Roger Wybot of the French Directorate of Territorial Surveillance suspected a 'veritable convent International of evasion of which the French network was only a link'.[83] Crackdowns like these led to howls of protest by clergy and supporters of fugitives alike, such as the Breton National News Service:

> Searches of monasteries have been made on a nation-wide scale, and many monks have been arrested on charge of having given refuge to political offenders – a right which the Church had been exercising since her early days. It must be said out *[sic]* that the Germans [...] never transgressed this Christian practice.[84]

Some Flemings ended up in Paraguay,[85] but by far the largest exile community developed in Argentina,[86] assisted first by consuls such as Bessone and later by SARE. Poppe made the move from Spain, whereupon he set up the support network Vlamingen in Argentinië (Flemings in Argentina).[87] Large numbers entered via Spain, although others later employed the 'Ratline' from Genoa. Still others employed their own resources to travel, like the VNV's Vital Elewaut, who flew with twenty-five others by seaplane across the Atlantic over five dramatic days.[88]

Why Ireland?

What then drew some two dozen Flemish fugitives to Ireland? As noted, Franco no longer threw out the welcome mat for Axis fugitives once relations with Washington thawed. Pierre Daye was pressured to move on to Argentina, while Degrelle went into hiding. José Bessone was even transferred away from Denmark, effectively closing the 'Nordic Route'.

Cold War battlelines were also becoming more entrenched. Many former Axis identities now served Western governments in the struggle against the Soviets and their satellites. Flemings, too, served in these capacities: employed by American intelligence in Austria was Robert Verbelen, convicted in Belgium of war crimes.[89]

As fears of communist electoral victory or invasion increased, so too did the utility of 'proven anti-communists' with military or intelligence experience. Those who had fled to safe havens were at the service of Franco, Perón or other staunch anti-Reds. Those who were still in hiding were mostly known to the Church, even if it wasn't sheltering all of them directly. Those in prison, however – especially Flemings in Belgian jails – were too far from escape networks in Austria and Italy. A closer Catholic sanctuary would have to be found ... provided they could manage the seemingly impossible and escape. For many *collabos,* however, incarceration proved less of an obstacle than might have at first appeared.

Escapees

It is astonishing how many fugitives who later found asylum in Ireland escaped Allied detention between 1945 and 1948. The historian is, however, too often reliant upon the accounts of the escapees themselves, who are seldom willing to explain how escape was effected. It is possible some were genuine plots hatched by inmates without external assistance, but in many cases the suggestion is otherwise.

Alex Colen, for example, was sentenced to twenty years' hard labour in the coal mines of Zwartberg for his service as an Oostfronter. An early volunteer for SS Legion 'Flandern', he was rejected on the grounds his 'luxuriant black hair' and 'Jew nose' didn't meet 'Aryan' entry requirements. Determined to shake his resulting 'inferiority complex', he joined the Organisation Todt (the Nazi construction group) and was sent to Pskov in Russia. Flemish elements of the OT were incorporated into the Waffen-SS at the end of 1943, and the former racial reject Colen went on to earn the Iron Cross Second Class in action in Hungary.

According to his account, Colen and others escaped from the claustrophobic labour at Zwartberg and made for Germany. It seems there was a measure of external assistance for this operation, as Colen's associate Bert Rits had a list of 'contact addresses', and a guide was detailed to take them to Eupen. Whether these were Church or collaborationist networks, or just friends or paid assistants, is unspecified. Only when his companions refused to cross the border did Colen double back to Antwerp.[90]

Staf van Velthoven was likewise sentenced to twenty years' hard labour, but managed to escape before the term commenced. Also enlisting in 'Flandern', in 1943 his unit was visited by an illustrious soldier of the Reich – Colonel Otto Skorzeny. The Fleming volunteered for the Austrian's elite commando unit, Jägdverbande (Hunting Group) 502, in which he specialised in demolitions. He took part in 'scorched earth' operations around Arnhem at the time of 'Operation Market Garden', and around Berlin in the war's final weeks.[91] Wounded in an air attack, van Velthoven was arrested in hospital by American forces.[92] Condemned to death *in absentia,* the sentence was later commuted, and he was put aboard a train under British guard bound for Belgian prison. The train arrived somewhat lighter than intended, however; mid-journey, and under the noses of his British guards, former SS commando van Velthoven leapt from the moving carriage to freedom.[93]

Another tale of escape comes from Albert Luykx.[94] Scion of a 'very Flemish-minded' family from Limburg which built barracks for the German army,[95] Luykx served in the Zwarte Brigade, which he later disingenuously described as the 'militant Civil Rights wing' of the VNV.[96] For this and his economic collaboration Luykx was sentenced to death, also subsequently commuted to twenty years.[97] According to one allegation, he had also denounced a man in 1942 for making derogatory comments against the VNV, which saw the unfortunate sent to a concentration camp.[98] In 1971 Luykx admitted to the *Irish Times* that he had been charged with informing, but disputed the circumstances of the case.[99]

Unlike van Velthoven, Luykx served time behind bars. Here thoughts revolved around liberty of various sorts: '[B]y day we talked concerning the freedom of our people, yet at night we dreamed of our personal freedom.'[100] Exactly how long Luykx served is unclear, although he later wrote of 'years' in a prison cell. By 1948, however, he was in Ireland. 'Exile is the nearest neighbour to the prison,' he wrote in the publication for former VNV members, *Broederband* (Band of Brothers), in 1966, 'and [...] it is from the prison that we walked away.' How precisely this was achieved is left unsaid, although it supposedly took 'long months of planning'.[101]

Albert Folens

Another sentence cut short by escape was that of Albert Folens. A native of Bissegem, Folens also joined 'Flandern'.[102] Unlike Colen and van Velthoven he was denied an opportunity to 'prove' his anti-communism in combat, succumbing to a stomach ulcer upon completion of his training.[103] Invalided back to Brussels, he endeavoured to further Flemish aspirations in other, less heroic ways.

According to his 2003 obituary in the *Irish Times,* Folens was unable to find work, and scraped a living 'by private translating and newspaper book reviewing'. His postwar sentence of ten years' jail was thereby presented to Irish readers as punishment for his enlistment with the Flemish Legion alone – another example, perhaps, of excessive Belgian *épuration.*[104]

The reality, which Folens admitted in a 1985 interview unpublished until 2007, is that the 'translating and newspaper reviewing' Folens undertook was on behalf of more reliable paymasters. Installed at its Belgian headquarters on the Avenue Louise in Brussels, Folens monitored the Flemish press on behalf of the SD, the security service of the SS.[105]

> So then in the SD I was ... Department 3CB ... that was *'Lektoraal'*. The whole *Abteilung* 3 consisted of no police work whatsoever, it was only keeping an eye on the future development of Flanders and Belgium [...] Gathering information on people who might be useful for this and that and for everything.[106]

This section of the SD advised the censor on which publications should be permitted to appear.[107] Whether Folens' duties in this bureau were limited to the translation of texts, or included interpretation during interrogations of suspects as his listing in the *Central registry of war criminals and security suspects* (CROWCASS) implies, remains uncertain.[108] His description as 'interpreter' in that lengthy directory could be shorthand for a range of deskbound duties. It is known, however, that Folens was a gifted linguist who later produced a French primer in Irish, in addition to his native Dutch and acquired English, German, Russian and Italian.[109] Whether these linguistic skills were employed verbally or only literally is again unclear. Folens however later described himself in a Flemish publication as a 'war criminal *honoris causa*'.[110] Of all the Axis exiles in Ireland, none – not even Artuković – is on record describing himself in anything approaching such terms.

In a statement rejecting the claims of the *Ireland's Nazis* programme in January 2007, Folens' widow Juliette declared that Albert 'was never sentenced to death, as has been alleged'.[111] Yet this allegation was fostered by Folens himself. According to his *Aiséirí Flóndrais*, Folens declared at his postwar trial that his ardour for Flemish nationalism began with a childhood love for *De leeuw van Vlaanderen* (The Lion of Flanders), the seminal nationalist text by Hendrik Conscience. Perhaps Folens imagined Irish-speakers were better disposed to tales of patriots defying the courts of their oppressors, but in this account his ten-year prison sentence becomes heroically inflated:

> [I]n 1947, half an hour before a sentence of death was passed on me, the judge asked me what had brought me to commit such political 'crimes' against Belgium. If it had been of any use to answer, one way or the other, I would have answered: '*The lion of Flanders* was the cause of it, my Lord.'[112]

The timing also appears inaccurate. Most accounts claim Folens spent no more than thirty-two months in prison,[113] arriving in Ireland in October 1948.[114] His sentencing would therefore have occurred around February 1946, not sometime in 1947. Whatever the length of his incarceration, Folens too mysteriously escaped. The details of how this was effected, or who assisted him, remain undisclosed.[115]

Allied complicity

Flemings were not the only 'war criminals' to escape detention. Otto Skorzeny, van Velthoven's erstwhile commanding officer and 'the most dangerous man in Europe',[116] also managed to escape from prison, although he was more open about how this was effected.

Skorzeny was tried in 1947 for 'Operation Greif', in which his men donned

American uniforms and infiltrated Allied lines during the Ardennes Offensive. Testimony from a British officer that the Allies had also used such tactics led to his acquittal. Both the Soviets and Czechs then demanded his extradition for the alleged massacre of partisans in 1945. The Americans, already employing General Gehlen, contemplated the loss of such a skilled anti-communist with alarm. Consequently, although MPs turned up at Skorzeny's prison to 'extradite' him in July 1948, he later surfaced not in Prague, but Madrid. The MPs had not been Americans at all, but ex-SS men repeating the ruse of 'Greif'.[117] Skorzeny himself later rejected the allegation that he organised this bold escape through his own resources. '[The uniforms] weren't stolen,' he laughed. 'They were provided by the Americans.' He later headed to Berlin to recruit former comrades for US intelligence, and was exposed in Paris in 1950 conducting surveillance on the PCF.[118] Skorzeny even turned up much later in Ireland, although his circumstances were different to political asylees.

A similar tale unfolds around Willem Sassen, a Dutchman from Geertruidenberg. Like Folens and Luykx, Sassen was imprisoned after the war – in his case at Fort Blauwkapel in Utrecht.[119] Here in late 1945 the former war correspondent for SS-Division 'Wiking' staged a self-penned play for the amusement of inmates and Canadian guards.[120] The play, provocatively titled *De Ontsnapping* (The Escape), culminated in Sassen leaping from the stage and disappearing into a cell from which the window bars had been removed. Ducking out into the night, Sassen made for Antwerp where he assumed the name of 'Albert Desmedt' – a Belgian Jew whose family had perished at Auschwitz.[121] Under this name he recrossed the Dutch border and holed up in Amsterdam in December 1946.[122] According to one source at least – and bolstered by its daring circumstances – Sassen's escape was arranged with the complicity of his Canadian captors.[123]

However their escapes were effected, most Dutch-speaking fugitives relied upon the Church and its networks to reach the safety of Ireland. Set free perhaps with Allied complicity, wholly reliant upon clerical networks and often accompanied by wives and families, the flight of these fugitives differs starkly from those of Breton nationalists. In this way, one might perceive the operation of a 'Northern Ratline' running from the Low Countries to Ireland. When assessing the impact of nationalistic sympathy as a motive for the granting of Irish asylum, it is particularly significant that the first among this particular set of fugitives to reach Irish shores was not Flemish, but rather the Dutchman Willem Sassen. For those aiding his flight, and for his Irish hosts, solidarity was assured not by minority nationalism, but rather Sassen's status as a former 'Oostfronter', a writer of anti-communist articles for Church publications, and a devout Catholic from the province of North Brabant.

Meeting in Amsterdam

According to Lauryssens, a meeting of similar 'devout Catholics' took place in Amsterdam in December 1946. Sassen was present, as was Leo van Overveldt, a Flemish Nazi who had supplied bicycles for the Wehrmacht.[124] Also in attendance was Willem Smekens, a former *collabo* journalist and member of the Vlaamse Wachtbrigade,[125] part of the Dietsche Militie.[126] The purpose of the meeting was to select a destination for Sassen and decide how to effect his escape. Like many fugitives, the Dutchman expressed a preference for South America. Far from the agencies of SARE and the Ratline, however, he lacked the requisite papers. Among those present at the meeting was the group's 'undisputed leader', whom Lauryssens has expound upon an alternative:

> Ireland seems a good idea to me [...] The Irish are Catholics, like ourselves, they're fierce nationalists *and* they are decidedly anti-British. The Irish will welcome you with open arms.

Ward Op de Beeck had been tipped, according to Lauryssens, as a 'future fascist prime minister' for Flanders.[127] His postwar prison sentence *in absentia* of ten years seems rather lenient for such an important figure, however. That sentence was actually for the crime of informing upon the Resistance.[128] Op de Beeck, a lawyer, had been defending a Resistance man detained by the Germans, but in the course of conversations with his clients overheard a plan to assassinate a personal friend. Op de Beeck slipped that friend a warning note, which was found when the latter was arrested after Liberation.[129]

Most accounts of Op de Beeck paint a portrait of a committed Catholic nationalist whose pre-war affiliations were with Flemish student associations rather than fascist parties. His wartime activities appear confined to heading the aid organisation Winterhulp (Winter Aid) in East Flanders, and working for the publication *Nederland Eén* (One Netherlands) which published Fr Callewaert's open letter to Hendrik Elias. Houthaeve claims Op de Beeck went to ground at his brother's residence in Ostend before fleeing to Ireland with his family.[130] Lauryssens, however, has him working at a book importer in Amsterdam at this time.[131] Both Lauryssens and Colen are agreed that Op de Beeck and Sassen were old friends, having studied together at the University of Ghent.[132] This personal connection may have had as much influence upon the Fleming's efforts to assist Sassen as any shared Catholic anti-communism, although this was doubtless a factor.

His destination chosen, 'Albert Desmedt' lay low in Amsterdam until mid-1947, writing anti-communist articles and waiting for a Dutch passport to be procured. Finally, one belonging to a Jacobus Jansen was purloined for him. Supplanting his own photo, Sassen was ready to travel.[133] Not for him, however, a long journey *à la Bretonne* with potential exposure a constant companion; he and most other fugitives escaping the Netherlands would fly courtesy of the newly-opened air route between Amsterdam and Dublin. This was an extravagance in the late 1940s, and an indication of the financial backing this network enjoyed courtesy of its Church and ex-Nazi sponsors. Remarkably, the very first flight from Amsterdam to Dublin some weeks before had borne the first Flemish fugitive into Irish exile: a former VNV member named Nic Stassen.[134] With his one-way ticket paid, 'Jansen' followed Stassen on 27 May.

If Amsterdam was the hub of the 'Northern Ratline', how did Flemish fugitives cross the border and assemble there? Sassen himself reportedly crossed the Belgian-Dutch frontier twice between 1945 and 1946. Colen, on the other hand, struck out for Germany in 1948 only to double back. Once in Antwerp, however, he was put onto a more reliable route, courtesy of the Catholic Church in general and the network of Trappist monasteries throughout the Low Countries in particular.

'Northern Ratline'

OT and SS contacts in Antwerp provided Colen with a false ID in the name of 'Albert Pauwels'. With this, he made his way to the monastery at Steenbrugge to meet with Dom Dumont, former secretary of the abbot Dom van Assche[135] – a champion of Flemish interests who died following ill-treatment after the Liberation.[136] Here Colen outlined his intention to flee to Spain. Dom Dumont, however, proposed an alternative. By this time, Colen was told, other fugitives – Stassen and Sassen among them – had fled to Ireland, 'and the reports were favourable'. Assisted by the Spekpater ('Bacon Priest') Wierenfried van Straaten[137] – a Dutch cleric at the Belgian abbey of Tongerlo who assisted German Catholics expelled from the East[138] – it was determined that Colen should be smuggled over the border for the flight to Ireland. It was the Spekpater who informed Colen about Glenstal Priory.[139] It was also decided Colen would be accompanied by another fugitive: Staf van Velthoven.

Following his daring escape, van Velthoven sheltered in a safehouse variously described as a 'place of recuperation'[140] and a 'vegetarian house'.[141] Here he met Albert Folens, also awaiting the signal to cross to Ireland via Amsterdam. Folens' obituary even suggests the house's residents were 'vegetarian hippies living a Franciscan lifestyle'.[142] Its connection to the Church was more significant than any Bohemian orientation, however. Folens was here for around four to six months,[143] and when van Velthoven was teamed with Colen to make the crossing, Folens was told he and his wife would soon follow.

Colen obtained a passport from a Dr Peeters, who had previously lent it to another Fleming to reach Spain. The passport now returned by post (hence its lack of exit stamp), Peeters arranged for Colen to 'steal' it from his house. Replacing Peeters' photo with his own, Colen blotted the paper trying to change the birthdate. Equipped with this imperfect document, Colen and van Velthoven were ready to travel. Trappist monks rented a taxi to convey them to the monastery at Achtel, near the Dutch border.[144]

The area around Achtel (especially Baarle) was not properly delineated by the Treaty of Maastricht in 1843, and remains a patchwork of enclaves and exclaves of variously Dutch and Belgian territory. In many cases the frontier divides buildings and even rooms.[145] The monastery was a 'huge complex', says Colen, with more than 500 Trappist monks. What was most interesting about the establishment was that its front entrance was in Belgium while its rear stables were in the Netherlands.[146] No perilous crossing of the Pyrenees or swimming of the Rhine for these fugitives, then; Colen and van Velthoven's flight to foreign soil involved a simple stroll across a courtyard.

From here, the former secretary to the abbot of Achtel took them in a jeep to a Dutch MP post some way inside the Netherlands. He ducked inside with Colen's clumsily doctored passport, yet all were soon allowed to proceed – the MP even personally returning Colen's document. Colen later learned the same Trappist regularly assisted fugitives across this border – both collaborators fleeing postwar justice and refugees fleeing the Eastern bloc.[147] At no time does it appear the Dutch or Belgian police put a stop to his activities.

Deposited at Eindhoven, van Velthoven and Colen entrained for Amsterdam. The following day they flew to Dublin via Manchester. Albert Folens and his wife Juliette followed a week later.[148] The assistance granted Folens may have been more generous, as until the declaration of war he had studied for the priesthood. Colen says Folens' family was so dismayed by the abandonment of his vocation that they refused further contact with him.[149] Whether the brother Trappists knew of Folens' vocational choices or were bothered by them is uncertain. They are unlikely to have voiced opinion either way.

Another ex-seminarian assisted to get to Ireland was Leo Schotsaert. Fourth of four brothers – the others all priests – Schotsaert also opted for secular vocations. By 1944 he was propaganda chief for the VNV at Aalst, south-east of Ghent. Living some distance from the town, he was obliged to choose a different route home each day in hopes of avoiding assassination by the Resistance.[150] One fellow VNV member was perhaps not so careful and was killed at nearby Zottegem that August – an event that provoked a cruel reprisal, which would itself have important repercussions for Schotsaert ... and, perhaps surprisingly, eventually for all political asylees in Ireland. That lay in the future, however. In 1948, Schotsaert was simply one of a growing number of Flemish and (Sassen included) Dutch Catholic fugitives flying to discreet asylum in Ireland.

Céad míle fáilte

How were these new arrivals perceived by their hosts, and who assisted them? As Op de Beeck supposedly opined in December 1946, shared Catholicism headed the list of reasons why Flemish refugees would be welcomed in Ireland.

We know of the political context of the late 1940s, in which Irish governments sided with the Church and West. In the Church's purview, Axis fugitives faced persecution from godless Reds of one stripe or another. Many Flemings had furthermore fought in Russia against the forces of Stalin himself.

Such had been the strength of Catholic vocationalism in Ireland that refugee determinations were devolved in 1938 to the non-government Irish Co-ordinating Committee for the Relief of Christian Refugees from Central Europe. Only late in 1945 did government departments confer on their attitude to an expected influx of refugees. In general it was decided to discourage unskilled arrivals – and of course of Jews, skilled or otherwise. De Valera's insistence that a more liberal policy be adopted ultimately prevailed, although conservatives strove to delay its implementation.[151] These policy attitudes applied to orderly arrivals through established channels. For more discreet arrivals, different rules applied.

Importantly, Flemish arrivals span both Fianna Fáil and Interparty governments. Most Bretons – L'Haridon and Heusaff excepted – arrived between August 1946 and February 1948. Heusaff in 1950 kept his identity secret from the Interparty External Affairs Minister MacBride, who allegedly 'wanted nothing to do' with him and his compatriots. Beginning with Stassen and Sassen, however, arrivals from the Low Countries entered from around July 1947 to as late as October 1948. The entry of many thereby coincided with the Vatican's campaigns in favour of prelates such as Mindszenty, and the IP government's efforts to forestall communism in Italy.

Ireland's place in the operation of these escape networks must therefore be viewed as part of a Catholic International; a global solidarity cemented by fear of communism. Catholic orders and Allied governments co-operated against this mutual threat, and orders in Ireland, as they had apparently done with Artuković, also assisted Flemings. The implied sanction of the Catholic Church enabled Colen and van Velthoven to allay the suspicions of Irish immigration officials. Similarly, Lauryssens has Sassen approached in Dublin by Fr John Senan, a Capuchin friar who commissioned the Dutchman to write anti-communist articles for the *Capuchin Annual* – including accounts of his Eastern

Front service which Senan reportedly described as a 'crusade against Communism'.[152] Senan was, furthermore, a friend of de Valera's.[153] These payments enabled Sassen to establish himself in the Irish capital, although Lauryssens admits none of the pieces was published.[154]

Flemings already in Ireland

Part of the support network for incoming Flemings was itself Flemish. Early arrivals like Nic Stassen supported those who followed,[155] but Stassen and others could themselves rely upon compatriots established in the country for some years. Most arrived via Church connections before the war. Karel Seeldrayers, a Church organist, was in Ireland as early as 1931.[156] Others remained following the Eucharistic Congress of 1932. Colen and van Velthoven were assisted by one Jan Hol, who went on to teach in the UK.[157] It must be emphasised that these individuals – and various other Flemings in Ireland – were not escapee *collabos,* but legal immigrants. Autonomist views may occasionally have prompted their relocation, however. Seeldrayers, established at Carlow, was for example reportedly relieved to obtain Irish citizenship before the war, as he could then avoid Belgian military service.[158]

Herman van Cauwelaert's was a different case again. Son of Frans, the Flemish constitutionalist, Herman took up residence in Dublin in 1936 as representative of a Belgian firm. He married an Irishwoman in 1939, prior to being reposted to The Hague. When war came the couple and their infant son Paul managed to escape back to Ireland.[159]

Herman, like his father, remained a Belgian loyalist. The Belgian government-in-exile considered employing him in a propaganda role in Ireland, but it was determined the utility of that mission was not 'sufficiently demonstrated'.[160] Herman was then ordered to join Belgian military forces at Tenby in Wales, which he did without objection. The van Cauwelaerts, therefore, were not exiled nationalists ... indeed, until amnesties restored exile Flemings their civic rights, the loyalist family would 'cross the street' whenever encountering them.[161]

Finally, some were forced to emigrate because of wartime *incivisme*. The Dehaenes of Oostvleteren were one such family. Omer Dehaene was wartime mayor of this village in West Flanders, but a visit by the VNV's Hendrik Elias 'made enemies'. Although detained at the end of the war, it was not until 1955 that Dehaene emigrated. Shortages of arable land in Flanders, plus restrictions on *incivikien,* sent him searching as far afield as Canada, but finally Ireland was settled upon. Not only was land cheap, Dehaene was also acquainted with Ward Op de Beeck, who had followed Sassen to Dublin in July 1947 and set up an import/export firm, EXIMORG.[162] Many Flemings like the Dehaenes prospered in Irish agriculture – Nic Stassen, for example, established an oyster farm near Galway.[163] Others, however, bought land known to locals as inferior,[164] and in some cases returned to Belgium at the earliest opportunity after considerable hardship.[165]

'Fierce nationalists'

The second most compelling motive for the Irish to grant asylum, according to Lauryssens, is that they were 'fierce nationalists'. As Chapter Three explored, assertion of Irish sovereignty was indeed an important motive in the asylum granted not only to Bretons, but also Austrians and Germans. This context was key regarding Flemish entries as well. In this sense, interpreting the notion of 'nationalism' broadly to imply staunch defence of national rights – as well as rejection of internationalist notions like communism – then indeed the 'nationalism' of the Irish state in the late 1940s contributed to its asylum posture. Such had also been significant in the policy of wartime neutrality.

The presence of the Dutchman Sassen, however, suggests that nationalistic sympathy, on the basis of shared concepts of self-determination, was not the prime motive either for the Irish state to admit fugitives, nor for Dutch-speaking Catholics to flee there. Isolation from more popular hubs of postwar flight like Genoa, Madrid or Copenhagen exerted greater influence over the decision to come to Ireland. Most of these centres had also ceased operation by the time these fugitives were free to travel. Ireland, moreover, seems only rarely to have been a first preference. Of all the Flemings who arrived, only Staf van Velthoven is on record as considering Ireland's revolutionary reputation influential in his decision. Even then, the idea had first to be suggested to him:

> I was told that some of our people had gone to Ireland and that they had been given asylum, and what did I think about that? Now, very early on in our movement we had discussed sooner or later we might have to take up weapons to get our aims fulfilled. So my first idea was 'Ireland: IRA. I can learn something there.' So that's how I decided […] I'll go to Ireland.[166]

For others, Ireland was simply part of a wider Catholic network. Colen, it will be recalled, initially expressed a preference for Spain. Another source suggests Panama.[167] Once in Ireland he was content to remain, but others viewed the country as a mere stop-over.

Sassen the Dutchman was joined by the Flemings Smekens and Achiel Hollants, another former Nazi journalist. All three lived with their families at Normanby House, Rathgar Road, Dublin. Leo van Overveldt, who also attended that meeting in Amsterdam in December 1946, was now in Dublin as well. Eventually, a vessel named *De Adelaar* (The Eagle) appeared offshore. Skippered by a German former U-boat captain and financed by van Overveldt, its goal was South America.[168] In September 1948, *De Adelaar* departed Irish shores with Sassen, Smekens, Hollants and their families on board.[169]

One family that made an unusual journey from Belgium to catch *De Adelaar* was Renaat Verbruggen's. A veteran of the German National Socialist Motor Corps (NSKK),[170] which had absorbed its VNV analogue the Dietse Militie Motor Brigade in 1943,[171] Verbruggen and his family could not afford to fly to Ireland, which suggests they were not considered important enough to travel by Church networks. Applying instead to emigrate to Paraguay, they were eventually able to buy passage on a freighter from Antwerp to Dublin. Here they hoped to catch *De Adelaar* and continue to South America. The delay was costly, however – the boat had left. The Verbruggens then had no choice but to remain in Ireland.[172]

Even including Artuković and various Ukrainians, the small number of fugitives who used Ireland as a staging post suggests it did not play a major role in international escape networks. Most arrivals were happy to remain, given that they could live in freedom and be close to their homelands should political fortunes change. It is worth noting that Fr Senan was reportedly behind the commissioning of *De Adelaar* to take on Sassen et al. at Dublin,[173] but whether he acted out of anything other than personal motives is uncertain.

There was, however, a noteworthy diplomatic posting in Ireland just a few months prior to the voyage of *De Adelaar.* In April 1948 the Argentines announced their intention to open a legation in Éire. 'Extraordinary Envoy and Minister Plenipotentiary' at Dublin would be none other than José Bessone, fresh from his previously busy post at the centre of the 'Nordic Route' in Copenhagen.[174]

Whether or not it was thought Bessone would engage in similar activities in Dublin, evidence did come to G2's attention of an escape network using Ireland as a staging post. What tipped off military intelligence was not the flight of Flemings to Argentina, but the capture of a former German POW by the name of Dorendahl. Details of his case, and accounts provided by the Flemish fugitive Alex Colen, suggest that G2, the Garda and the Department of Justice were aware of Axis escape networks operating in their country.

Fugitives and Irish police

Dorendahl was apprehended in June 1948 in possession of a false travel permit. During the war the German handled agents along the Brazilian coast, so he was considered qualified to run an escape network to South America. According to

Dan Bryan, G2's redoubtable chief, Dorendahl was just the tip of the iceberg, however:

> I understand from the Garda that there are now 34 of those aliens in the country and the Department of Justice is considering the whole problem of their registration and future.[175]

Whether this accounts for all Breton and Flemish asylees as well as Germans is impossible to determine. Many of the Flemings were yet to arrive. Bryan did seem to acknowledge, however, that nationalities other than Germans were involved, and that relocation to a third country might not necessarily be on their agenda. 'It would seem at any rate [...] that there is some kind of concerted effort on the part of the Germans and others to at least escape to this country.'[176] While determinations of asylum were made by bureaucrats and elected officials, it is significant that the existence of such networks was known to Irish security agencies. Whether they acted to stymie these networks remains unclear.

It was to the Aliens' Office of the Garda that Colen, van Velthoven and other arrivals were obliged to report, just as Joz-Yann Gourlet and other Bretons had in August 1946. Save for those like Alan Heusaff who kept their identities secret, all asylees landing in Ireland sooner or later reported to their local Garda.

After a weekend spent at Nic Stassen's residence – and not before posting their borrowed passports back to Belgium – Colen and van Velthoven reported to Dublin Castle as directed. Here the two Flemings got a 'good reception', the detectives listening with interest to their tales of Eastern Front service and escape. There was even mirth regarding the Glenstal Priory ruse. Finally obtaining their alien's notebooks, both Flemings were congratulated by the detectives and free to begin new lives in Ireland. Until they obtained citizenship, they would need to report back only once a year.[177]

According to Colen, considerable knowledge of the real identities of fugitives was displayed by these officers. Nic Stassen discovered this firsthand. Arriving in mid-1947 and apparently unaware of the legalities of asylum, Stassen maintained to detectives that his false identity of 'van den Brande' was legitimate. A few days later he was called back to the Castle. 'Would it surprise you to learn,' one of the detectives challenged him, 'that Mr van den Brande is comfortably at home [...] in Antwerp?' Stassen could only stammer a full confession. Having entered the country under false pretences, he could expect immediate deportation. He needn't have worried; he was simply told never to lie to the Garda again and sent on his way.[178]

Irish extradition law

One reason cited for the selection of Ireland as a refuge was its lack of extradition arrangements with other countries, or the fact that extradition was prohibited for political offences.[179] Dirk Folens, son of Albert, claims this influenced his parents' decision to come to Ireland in 1948,[180] and Broderick likewise maintains this determined the choices of Breton refugees like Heusaff.[181]

De Valera acknowledged to the Dáil in March 1946 that, outside of the warrants procedure with Britain detailed in Chapter One, Éire at that time had concluded 'no extradition treaties or arrangements [...] with other states'.[182] External Affairs had argued for Irish legislation in this area since 1933, and a draft bill made it to the floor of the Dáil the following year. Questions about how this legislation would regard Republicans fleeing the North caused delays, and the entire issue was shelved in 1939 over concerns about the IRA's bombing campaign in England. As one of the central tenets of sovereignty that de Valera held dear, the issue of political asylum was one upon which the Taoiseach could be expected to be 'firm to the point of obtuseness', in Farrell's phrase.[183] This attitude, if they were aware of it, may indeed have influenced fugitives' decisions.

This is not to say, however, that there was no framework for the extradition of offenders. In December 1949, eight months after the declaration of the Republic, the government received its first request for extradition of an alleged foreign war criminal. The charges related to the murder, in August 1944, of a civilian mayor by the German SS, acting in concert with a Continental collaborationist organisation. Of the eight members of that organisation believed responsible for the killing, two had managed to escape post-Liberation justice. These were now believed to be sheltering in Ireland.[184] The requesting country was Belgium, and the two men sought were Flemish nationalists.

The harsh *épuration* in Belgium was perhaps one reason why this request came first from Brussels. The fact that the murdered mayor had been a nobleman – Baron Idesbald della Faille d'Huysse of the village of Elene south-east of Ghent – was perhaps another.[185] What is most significant about this request is what it revealed both about Irish extradition law, and the extent of Dublin's knowledge of the wartime activities of its asylees.

Baron d'Huysse had been murdered allegedly by members of the VNV's Zwarte Brigade in reprisal for a killing by the Resistance. The Irish government undertook to investigate the request, yet remarkably, for all the detective powers of the Aliens' Branch and G2's awareness of foreign escape networks, it took almost three years to report back. Even then, the Belgians were not happy with the outcome: one of the men named in the warrant could not be found.[186]

As for the other, he had at least been located. Leo Schotsaert, the former official of the Aalst section of the VNV who had so striven to avoid Resistance hit squads on his way home each evening, was now living at Blackrock, Co. Dublin.[187] The bad news was that the Irish government, under Article Seven of the pre-independence Anglo-Belgian Extradition Treaty of 1901, refused to extradite him on the grounds that his alleged offences were political.[188]

Dublin thereby acknowledged this treaty was still in force and, by extension, other pre-1922 treaties forged under the terms of the Extradition Act (1870) still applied.[189] Even the Aliens Order 1946 makes specific reference to this legislation.[190] Belgium thereafter considered Ireland to have acceded to all pre-independence extradition treaties, complete with political exceptions.[191] In 1960, Ireland itself requested an extradition from Switzerland under the terms of a similar treaty. Therefore, although there was no expressly Irish extradition legislation until 1965, there clearly was an extradition mechanism in force between Dublin and other countries. Whether the 1952 determination concerning Schotsaert had been properly tested before a magistrate is unclear. But the endurance of political exception clauses of British-era treaties may explain why no further extradition requests were made by the home states of asylees in Ireland. Ironically, until 1965 the extradition mechanism between Ireland and Great Britain continued to be the Petty Sessions (Ireland) Act (1851), which allowed for no political exception at all.[192]

'Decidedly anti-British': the legacy of Ireland's asylum stance

Years of media outrage that Ireland was a haven of 'anti-Allied sentiment' had lasting impact upon its reputation. Standing aloof from NATO, waving the 'sore thumb' of Partition in the exasperated faces of European diplomats, castigated as reactionary by Moscow and sticking to the protocols of neutrality even when it meant expressing condolences on the death of Hitler, Ireland limped into the late 1940s 'wholly isolated from the mainstream of world events and without the means to influence them'.[193] Alive to the deleterious effects these perceptions were having upon Ireland's standing, External Affairs sought to deter notorious Nazis like Léon Degrelle even from attempting entry.

Word that Ireland refused to extradite fugitives wanted for crimes committed during German occupation was guaranteed to worsen its reputation. Its ultramontane social climate and obstinacy regarding 'obnoxious Germans' – combined with the anti-Semitism of its Justice department – led many to believe the country was at least regretful that the Allies had emerged victorious from the war. To others, Ireland was now a beacon of the 'Third Way' between capitalism and communism. Although none applied for asylum, the interest in postwar Ireland shown by former Nazis and neo-fascists only deepened this perception.

One of these was 'one of the worst citizens that any country has ever produced', according to his trial judge. Norman Baillie-Stewart, the Briton dubbed 'Lord Haw-Haw' for his Nazi broadcasts (a tag later affixed to William Joyce),[194] entered Ireland with false papers in October 1949 after release from prison. Unusually, these papers were not provided by Catholic orders, but by Quakers.[195]

Another former Allied officer authored an influential neo-fascist text in Ireland. In 1948, at Brittas Bay, Co. Wicklow, a former prosecutor at the Nuremberg war crime trials named Francis Parker Yockey wrote *Imperium*, a work influenced by the ideas of Oswald Spengler. Yockey had been sacked from the US 7708 War Crimes group for sympathising with national socialism.[196] He had also been influenced by the Catholic fascism of Fr Francis Coughlin and the 'Third Way' of Otto Strasser.[197]

Strasser, the 'left Nazi' and Bavarian Catholic, had pestered the Irish government from October 1945 to grant him refuge. Almost ten years later he again applied, although by now the idea of residency had lapsed and he expressed a desire only to visit the Order of the Divine Word at Donamon Castle, Co. Roscommon.[198] Even then, the DEA hoped his entry would be denied as harmful to Irish-German relations.[199] Justice, once again, had no objection to the visit.[200] The DEA's disquiet on the issue appeared vindicated when A.K. Chesterton, former editor of the BUF's *Action* newspaper, accompanied Strasser. The superior of the Order denied the visit had any political significance, however.[201]

Oswald Mosley's BUF had been the sole (and unwanted) voice of support when de Valera expressed condolences on the death of Hitler. Mosley had, however, obliged an anxious DEA in 1946 by rethinking a decision to relocate to Ireland. Four years later, enticed by an abundance of food and 'the desire to win the freedom to become a European', Mosley at last made the move across the Irish Sea.[202] As with Scots exiles of the 1940s, 'there was really nothing much we could do to prevent Mosley coming here' complained External Affairs.[203] G2 undertook to watch him at his residence at Clonfert Palace, Co. Galway, but there was no evidence Mosley was engaged in subversion. Having lost an important tax case in Britain, the real attraction was, it is said, the tax-free provisions which encouraged foreigners to settle and generate exchange. Even then, Mosley is said to have preferred France, and visited Ireland infrequently after a few years.[204]

Another notorious figure taking advantage of these provisions was Otto Skorzeny. From 1957, the Austrian bought estates in Ireland for his former comrades – up to seventy in total.[205] In 1963, Dr Noël Browne questioned Minister for Justice Charles Haughey as to whether Skorzeny had applied for citizenship. Not only had the Austrian 'no right' to reside in the country, Haughey replied, he 'never [having] done so, the question of his naturalisation does not arise'.[206] While Skorzeny may not have been officially resident in Ireland, he was certainly known to frequent social evenings with Dublin's elite – including Haughey himself.[207] For some, Skorzeny aimed to establish a 'beach-head' close to Britain for his secret neo-Nazi network, the Organisation of Former SS Members (ODESSA). This purportedly had as its Irish front the Amsterdam Coffee Bar in Dublin.[208] Perhaps Britain proved more resistant to Nazi penetration than he had hoped, or maybe the attention of TDs like Browne was a little too close for comfort. Whatever the reason, Skorzeny abandoned Ireland in 1964.

Lauryssens levels similar allegations at Op de Beeck's EXIMORG: that it transferred funds to fugitives, and never actually owned assets nor even registered at Company House. Sassen was supposedly selected as agent for this organisation in Dublin, replaced by Op de Beeck after the former's departure.[209] Colen for one insists this was never the case and that Op de Beeck was an 'anti-Nazi'.[210] And EXIMORG was indeed a legitimate trader in later years, importing electrical cabling (among other items) to the value of more than eighty million Belgian francs annually by 1989.[211] It is significant, however, that EXIMORG's 'paper' offices were located not only in Dublin and Amsterdam, but also (according to Lauryssens) Antwerp, Rome, Barcelona and Buenos Aires – each a centre in the Flemish fugitive network.[212]

Similar to rumours regarding Hitler's presence in 1945, speculation fuelled by real entries grew to include war criminals who never set foot on Irish soil. Perhaps, it was said, Adolf Eichmann was snatched by Israeli agents not from Argentina, but Ireland. This question was put to an Israeli representative at Harvard University in June 1960. Demurring on the details of the operation carried out by Mossad, the representative limited himself to what must have been for Dublin a tiresomely frequent observation: 'All I know is that our government people are worried about the situation in Ireland and the screening of ex-Nazis entering the country.'[213] This seemed justified in 1976 when Pieter Menten, a Dutch millionaire who had divided his time between the Netherlands and Co. Waterford from 1963, was exposed as the perpetrator of a wartime massacre in Poland. Captured in Switzerland, he spent ten years in Dutch prison. He was later barred from returning to Ireland.[214]

A 'typically Irish' gesture declined

Cases like Menten's indicated that Dublin could refuse entry (or re-entry) if adverse publicity threatened its interests. This was so even if there was precedent for admission of persons of similar background.

In April 1959, a Catholic rightist made known his desire to seek asylum in Ireland, this time from an unusual quarter. Like Artuković, his country had fallen to communism, while he himself had led a regime that could hardly be described as democratic. This man was Fulgencio Batista, former dictator of Cuba, recently deposed by Fidel Castro.

Currently in the Dominican Republic, Batista enquired through his lawyer as to the attitude of Dublin should he request asylum. DEA officials weighed up the pros and cons. In this way, the Republic's revolutionary heritage was invoked – a true rarity in official discussions of asylum. 'As a country which has suffered [...] from foreign oppression and many of whose patriots have had to seek refuge abroad, [...] Ireland should generally follow a liberal policy in the matter of according asylum to political refugees.'[215] They also insisted it was legally 'incontrovertible that every State has the right to admit anyone it chooses [...] even if this should arouse the displeasure of another State'.[216] Even so, it was thought prudent to enquire of the likely responses of key governments should Ireland actually shelter the ex-dictator.

All responded that they would regard refuge for Batista as harmful to Irish interests.[217] The UN, which Ireland had joined four years before, noted that his regime had been regarded even by other Latin dictatorships as especially cruel and corrupt.[218] Most compelling perhaps was the response from Canada. Asylum for Batista, replied Ottawa, would be regarded as a wrong-headed and 'typically Irish' gesture.[219] The Cuban ex-dictator was, perhaps unsurprisingly, refused asylum.

Conclusion

Like that for Croats and Ukrainians, the asylum granted fugitive Flemings was an expression of Catholic solidarity. Although many found inspiration in Irish independence, it was not their nationalism but their 'proven anti-communism' – whether in domestic collaborationist or Catholic organisations, or as Oostfronters – that guaranteed the sympathy of Irish Church and state. The presence of Dutch Catholics like Willem Sassen is significant in this context, not just in assessing the motives of Irish actors, but in determining why these fugitives selected Ireland as a refuge. More often than the Bretons, Flemings in Ireland originally hoped to flee to other countries, and came to Dublin only because other routes were unavailable and their Church helpers suggested it as an alternative. Of these, some always intended to move on to third countries, and at least two Flemish families did so within a year of arrival. Even Paraguay, a country far removed, eventually hosted a Flemish exile population some six times greater than Ireland's. Argentina's was much larger again.

The Flemish influx into Ireland did, however, force the government to declare its legal position regarding extradition – something that earlier entries from Brittany and Croatia had not. By invoking the political exception clauses of British-era treaties, Ireland was asserting its right to grant asylum – a right it had jealously defended since Gray's ultimatum on 'war criminals' in 1944. But something more significant had also occurred: it was now suggesting, just as Frederick Boland had warned in 1946, that acts committed by its asylees during the Nazi occupation were justifiable on political grounds. This stance attracted unsavoury rightist characters over subsequent years who, regardless of the Irish government's attitude towards them, served to deepen the perception that the country was a haven of anti-British, fascistic or extremist sentiments. It is a perception of postwar Ireland that persists in some quarters to this day, fuelled further by the bizarre actions of certain exiles over subsequent decades.

CHAPTER 8

'Bombing Bray?': Ireland, foreign struggles and asylum, 1951–2008

EARLY IN 2002, Cherie Blair, wife of British Prime Minister Tony, was sent a surprise package. The 'complimentary sample of eucalyptus oil', reported *The Observer*, 'in fact contained sodium hydroxide, a substance which can cause serious injury and even blindness if rubbed on the face'.[1] This was the latest in a series of bizarre 'attacks' ranging from a supposedly ricin-laced Christmas card sent to Prince William,[2] to threats to contaminate the English water supply with weed killer if there was not a 'total, permanent and unconditional' British withdrawal from Northern Ireland.[3]

An arrest in connection with the Blair incident soon took place in Dublin. It was not, however, found to be the work of a dissident Irish Republican group. In fact, the attacks had not been carried out by an Irish group at all. The suspect was fifty-four-year-old Adam Busby, a Scotsman living in exile in Ireland since 1983. Although he was later released without charge, the attacks, claimed by the 'Scottish National Liberation Army',[4] were allegedly co-ordinated from what the rival Scots group Siol nan Gaidheal calls Busby's 'dingy little Dublin flat'.[5]

Perceptions of Ireland as a haven for such activities were already fixed in the popular mind, influenced by Republican campaigns to eject British rule from Northern Ireland. As organisations like the Provisional IRA grew in power, so other, more marginal militants from other countries attempted to exaggerate their significance by claiming links with them that were beyond the mere inspirational. In several cases, Ireland was reported as a site of training, finance, or even base of operations. Such claims were readily reproduced in the press, suitably sensationalised for a scandalised readership.

Claims of foreign involvement in Irish militancy were not unique to the era of 'The Troubles', either. Similar rumours had followed Otto Skorzeny – that he involved himself not only in secretive political machinations while in Ireland, but had revived something of the old Abwehr assistance of the 1940s and 'advised the leaders' of the IRA in the military tactics he had perfected during the war.[6] Lauryssens, too, claims the Flemings Hollants and Smekens instructed the IRA in 'the noble art of sabotage' to make ends meet before departing for Argentina,[7] and the former SS commando Staf van Velthoven would also become associated with the Official IRA.

How did Dublin react to claims that foreign militants operated on its territory, and did these claims have any basis in fact? By the mid-1950s, it appeared Ireland would be able to relax its double-game of asserting sovereignty while seeking to deter embarrassing arrivals. The Republic was from 1955 a member of the UN, and when External Affairs minister Frank Aiken later told the General Assembly that Ireland knew 'what imperialism is and what resistance to it involves', it appeared its revolutionary heritage was finally exerting a determinative influence upon its foreign policy.[8]

But what of relations with autonomist movements close to home, whose militants drew most inspiration from Irish independence and still looked to Dublin for moral and political support? Would this anti-colonialist stance in the assembly of nation-states translate into support for those 'stateless nations' whose fugitives found asylum in Ireland? Like so much in this story, the reality of Irish *raisons d'état* weigh heavily against the image projected by foreign nationalists themselves, eagerly devoured by international media – and even foreign diplomats.

Exiles helped create this image, and few did more than two who bookend Ireland's asylum policy after 1945. The first represents that older generation so inspired by Easter Week. Issuing communiqués from his 'headquarters' at Bray, the Breton stalwart Yann Goulet came to personify militant pan-Celticism, exacerbating the image of Ireland as a haven from which foreign movements could act to subvert neighbouring governments. Adam Busby is the more recent arrival, garbed in the rhetoric of Maoist 'national liberation' and exerting an equally powerful influence in the media owing to his bizarre activities and a general misapprehension of the 'political exception' in extradition law.

Along this timeline – from the 'Emergency' to the 'Global War on Terror' – Ireland evolved from international pariah to enthusiastic champion of the EU; from putative agrarian autarky to the 'Celtic Tiger' of the Eurozone. Along the way it joined the UN, commemorated fifty years since Easter 1916, and signed the Treaty of Amsterdam that essentially abolished political asylum between EU states. At almost every stage foreign nationalists and attitudes to their struggles have served to sharpen Irish conceptions of identity and the national interest.

Ireland and foreign movements in the 1950s

It was the second Interparty government of 1954–7 that first attended the UN General Assembly. Here External Affairs minister Liam Cosgrave (Fine Gael) offered lip service to the principles of self-determination in colonies such as Algeria, yet ultimately supported European colonial powers for fear of communist influence upon Third World liberation movements. As Skelly observes, 'the Inter-Party government's pro-Western, anti-communist predilections overrode its compassion for colonised peoples' whenever there was conflict between the two impulses.[9]

In the latter part of that government's term, however, a singular request to bring the case of a 'stateless people' before international bodies was put to Dublin. This came not from colonies in Asia or Africa, but from Ireland's Gaelic neighbour of Scotland.

In May 1956, Irish officials received a letter from the Scottish National Congress, an offshoot of the Scottish National Party led by Roland Muirhead – he who had assisted 'nationalist objectors' escape to Ireland in 1941. Now in his eighties, Muirhead was still doggedly pursuing legal avenues for the re-establishment of Scottish statehood thrown up by England's purported abrogation of the Treaty of Union, and thought that Ireland might be willing to help bring this issue before the UN. He also hoped Ireland could facilitate separate Scottish representation at the upcoming Commonwealth Conference in London. Evidently he had not been following developments in the Celtic world as closely as he should: '[A]s this country is an independent republic it is not represented at the Commonwealth Conference,' Dublin curtly replied.[10]

The SNC's request presented problems all the same. Peoples were not a subject of international law; only states. Scottish nationalists had discovered this themselves when they first put a 'claim of right' before the UN in 1947, only to have it dismissed as an 'internal British matter'.[11]

But strict adherence to international law problematised Ireland's own historic transition to independence. Clearly there would have to be acknowledgement of the striving for statehood of other 'peoples', but, equally, articulated in a way that did not meddle in Britain's internal affairs.

The formula devised after much internal discussion was communicated to Muirhead. Although 'the traditional sympathy of the Irish people with the national aspirations of other peoples' could be expected, support could only be extended to 'representatives authorised to give expression to those aspirations'.[12] This meant simply that Scots nationalists would have to gain an electoral mandate, just as Sinn Féin had done in December 1918.

Regaining power in March 1957, Fianna Fáil's attitude was anticipated to be more generous. Frank Aiken championed the Afro-Asian bloc in the UN, and the lockstep support of Western interests evolved into a more independent posture. When the External Affairs minister spoke in October 1960 of Ireland's 'historical memory [...] which makes it impossible for any representative of Ireland to withhold support' for minority rights, many in neighbouring regions began to hope that Irish assistance in their struggles was at hand.[13] Condemning Chinese aggression in Tibet was consistent with this posture (as well as an expression of anti-communism),[14] but would Fianna Fáil's reaction to overtures from Celtic nationalists differ from its predeccesors?

The first request of this kind the new government received sounded familiar. Would Dublin assist the tireless Roland Muirhead in hauling London before an international body – this time the International Court of Justice? 'The fact that many Scots are citizens of Éire is a particular reason why [it] might be willing to give Scotland assistance,' Muirhead reasoned, perhaps sensing that pan-Celtic appeals were potentially less profitable than those courting Irish self-interest. Even then there was to be no reversal of the policy developed by the previous government. Until the Scottish people demonstrated at the ballot box their willingness to authorise such endeavours, de Valera reiterated, Ireland could not become involved.[15]

There was one deviation from this posture in 1958, however, concerning not the Scots but another nationalist movement in Britain. Far from setting a new foreign policy course, the negative assessment by Dublin of this exception guaranteed it would not be repeated.

Gwynfor Evans at the UN

Perhaps emboldened by its new influence at the UN, the Irish delegation received in November 1958 a British political leader currently on tour in North America. Ireland was at this time sponsoring 'surprising initiatives' such as the withdrawal of all troops from Central Europe,[16] so Plaid Cymru president Gwynfor Evans scheduled a meeting with Irish delegates to discuss the presentation of his own party's proposal to place all colonies under UN control – including, presumably, the 'colony' of Wales. Evans also scheduled a meeting with the Afro-Asian bloc that was at the forefront of decolonisation efforts. Given the sequence of the meetings, the Irish probably facilitated the latter – evidence of a 'brotherly arm about the Welsh movement', according to the *New York Times*.[17]

This assistance was not remembered fondly, however. Despite its stance on anti-colonialism, this first real effort to accord a Celtic movement support in international forums was regarded with regret. 'We were embarrassed' a DEA official recalled, 'by the presence of and publicity given to [PC's] President when he visited the UN with our help'.[18]

This did not mean that Celtic requests for assistance were ignored, but support would henceforth, throughout the remaining de Valera years and into the premiership of Seán Lemass from 1959, adhere strictly to unofficial contacts on personal bases. Secretary Cremin of the DEA, for one, is known to have spent an evening in September 1962 with William Wolfe, president of the SNP, in which the Irishman shared 'much advice'.[19] But, like asylum admissions in the postwar years, the watchword was discretion. 'Our representatives do not, of course, identity [*sic*] themselves publicly with these causes,' DEA noted of the Scottish and Welsh movements – a position that Wolfe politely understood.[20] Even then, when Lemass was asked to contribute an article for PC in 1965, his advisers did not scupper the proposal outright. It was made clear, however, that the piece could appear only if it 'will not be used in any way by [PC] to indicate or imply that their policies have the support of the Irish Government'.[21]

Meanwhile, foreign nationalists granted asylum in Ireland had not only obtained citizenship, but had in some cases established themselves in influential circles. The most prominent of these was an artist living in a seaside community south of Dublin.

'M. Renard' of Bray

> Artists in exile are decidedly unpleasant, and their stubbornness insinuates itself into even their exalted works.[22]
>
> *Edward Said*

By the time the attitude to British Celts had been formulated, Yann Goulet had become a well-known character in Bray, conducting art classes in a garage he constructed himself. Among 'M. Renard's pupils was Terry de Valera, son of Eamon. 'Renard, although a Breton, also spoke French,' de Valera junior seems surprised to learn.[23]

Ignorance of Breton culture was not confined to the Irish elite. French being the household language at 'Koatkeo'[24] (as it is in most Breton homes), locals naturally assumed the 'Renards' embraced French identity. Beholding Goulet's beret and hearing his accent, the sculptor Imogen Stuart is said to have directed him to admire her red, white and blue skirt as a national compliment. He curtly informed her that, as a Breton, his colours were black and white.[25] 'We could have been two-headed ducks, for all [the Irish] knew about us,' observes Yann's daughter Armelle.

Life for the 'Renards' had been difficult. For some years they shared Daisy Bank with the de Quelens, and Yann's wife Vonig led a lonely existence, obliged to carry drawings of desired groceries with her to the local shops.[26]

Money was short, and, until 1952 when he obtained Irish citizenship, Goulet kept a low profile and disengaged from politics. Such self-effacement did not agree with this former soldier and youth squad leader. According to Gwion Hernot, killed in 1950 in a riding accident, Goulet adored heroism and practised it 'even in the simplest acts of life'. Raymond Delaporte believed Yann 'was always dramatic'. He led his family as he had the Bagadoù Stourm, says Fouéré: 'with authority and firmness'. For these, Goulet was a stubborn but strong figure for whom they held great affection, and who evidently rankled under the enforced anonymity of exile. Positive views of Goulet were not shared by all Breton nationalists, however, neither in Ireland nor Brittany.

Goulet's famed stubbornness was manifest in his attitude toward a French amnesty of August 1953, which encompassed all those convicted of *indignité nationale* as well as those aged under eighteen at the time of their offences.[27] Job 'Christian' Hirgair, who employed skills acquired with the Bezen Perrot in Germany to run a radio repair shop in Dalkey, took advantage of this latter provision and returned to Brittany.[28] Also amnestied were all those sentenced to five years' prison or less, while those with longer sentences could seek review without fear of sterner penalty. Yann Fouéré, Charles Gaonac'h and Jacques de Quelen took advantage of this provision and were acquitted by French military tribunals in retrials of their cases between 1954 and 1955. Raymond Delaporte had his sentence for 'attacks on the integrity of the state' reduced from twenty to five years at his own retrial, and was immediately amnestied as a result.[29] Only those sentenced to death *par contumace* remained aloof – the implied admission of wrongdoing in the amnesty application process striking Goulet for one as offensive. 'I haven't done anything wrong. I'm not looking to be pardoned for something I haven't done.'[30]

Family fortunes began to turn in 1957, when Yann won a competition to design a memorial at the Custom House, Dublin.[31] Not only did this improve finances, but Goulet became acquainted with figures in the Irish establishment.[32] A memorial to Republicans massacred at Ballyseedy followed, which brought Goulet into contact with the IRA.[33] For Fouéré, Goulet became 'more Irish than the Irish themselves', castigating concessions to 'the English' and opposing Dublin's entry into the European Common Market on nationalist grounds.[34] He identified as a 'Breton nationalist and an Irish Republican'– the epitome of pan-Celticism.[35] As for his art, it did not appeal to all tastes. Commissioned to paint a portrait of Mrs Sinéad de Valera, neither the subject nor a number of others were satisfied with the bold technique employed.[36] Eulogising at his funeral in 1999, Tom Ryan of the Royal Hibernian Academy chose his words diplomatically: Goulet 'never pretended to be a genius but he was competent – a rare quality'.[37]

Concerns that foreign nationalists could embroil Ireland in embarrassing incidents prompted External Affairs to oppose their naturalisation back in 1953. Exiles like Goulet may have been apprised of these concerns through their connections, and even after they acquired Irish passports many continued to use pseudonyms.[38] It is ironic, therefore, that the scenario the DEA had feared when opposing naturalisation materialised not with an embarrassing former *collabo*, nor indeed with one who had previously engaged with the domestic politics of his home region at all.

Homecomings

Although some never went home, several exiles in Ireland did return for varying periods. Some like Job Hirgair seized upon amnesties to return for good. Raymond Delaporte returned to his native Châteauneuf-du-Faou with the intention of retiring, only to move back to Ireland when he saw how far the Breton language had retreated from the area while he had been in exile.[39] He later became reader of Breton at University College, Cork.[40]

In addition to these legitimate homecomings there were some clandestine returns. Joz-Yann Gourlet returned to Paris in the mid-1950s, where he lived rough for a time before surrendering to face a prison term.[41] Louis Feutren claims he too made secret returns to Brittany. Although these supposedly took place after acquiring Irish citizenship, Feutren, sentenced to death *par contumace,* claims he returned 'two or three times' before the amnesty. He thus faced execution if arrested by French authorities – precisely the kind of diplomatic nightmare the DEA dreaded. Having arranged the flight of Bezen veterans in 1947, Feutren knew when not to be foolish: the precaution was taken of transiting through Belgium, and, once in Brittany, 'As soon as I saw that within twenty-four hours six persons had come to say hello ... Finished.'[42] Yann Goulet had to travel to Italy around the time of the Custom House memorial and, concerned this might require a stopover in France, took the precaution of having his passport made out in Irish. Fortunately for him, the travel documents of Mr 'Ó Goblaigh' were not subjected to the scrutiny of French officials on that journey.[43]

But it was the Basque Iker Gallastegi who led the most daring existence of returning exiles. Naturalised by Dublin in 1949, his father Eli subsequently returned to his beloved mountains of Euskadi. He resided at St Jean de Luz, from whence his friends had set out for Ireland back in 1940.[44] Son Iker, however, boldly set out for Bilbao by secretly crossing the Pyrenees in 1952. Irish passport notwithstanding, a Basque of Gallastegi's pedigree would have faced an uncomfortable time at the hands of Franco's Guardia Civil. Yet in

Bilbao Iker remained, until he was forced by unwelcome police attention to flee back to the French side of the mountains on New Year's Eve 1959.[45]

Spanish attitudes formed only part of the incident that caused headaches for the Irish a few years later. In November 1962 Iker was served with an order demanding he quit the Basque Country – the *French* Basque Country. Fearing an Irish citizen would be made 'a plaything between de Gaulle and Franco', Joseph Barron TD (Clann na Poblachta) raised the issue with Taoiseach Seán Lemass. Lemass assured the Dáil that the expulsion order had not yet been enforced, and that Irish representations had softened Paris' demands that Iker relocate to a distant part of France. Although he would not be allowed to live near the Spanish border, he would, Dublin was assured, be allowed to find a district 'acceptable to him'. It seemed as if the Irish had intervened skilfully to defuse the incident, and, in any case, 'the issues involved here are entirely within the jurisdiction of the French Government'.[46]

That government probably did not disclose the real reasons for its expulsion order: that Iker Gallastegi was one of many Basque nationalists it had decided to remove from the frontier in return for Madrid acting against terrorists of the Organisation armée sécrète (Secret Armed Organisation), which had opposed Algerian independence and operated from bases over the Spanish border.[47] The expelled Basques had not been entirely innocent, either: the young nationalist movement Euskadi Ta Askatasuna (Basque Country and Freedom) – formed as a purely political movement in 1959, but adopting 'direct action' methods two years later – held in May 1962 its first assembly at an abbey in the French Basque region. Whether Iker Gallastegi was involved is not known, but it appears Madrid regarded his presence no coincidence ... especially as ETA's posture of castigating the PNV for allying with Spanish parties firmly associated it with the radical *Aberri* and *Jagi-Jagi*, founded by Iker's father Eli more than three decades before. [48]

All this underscored the prescience of Sean Nunan back in 1953. Moreover, the inability to control the political activities of citizens (as opposed to asylees) now seemed a grave issue. If the forcible relocation of an Irish citizen within France was embarrassing, how damaging could his involvement in terrorist activities be? It could not then be imagined that allegations of foreign militant involvement in Ireland would multiply over the coming years and manifest in frequently bizarre ways. This first came to attention during the fiftieth anniversary commemorations of that seminal event in all minority nationalist militancy, the Easter Rising, and the quintessential pan-Celtic militant Yann Goulet was once again involved.

Easter 1966

We know that the Rising had especial resonance for foreign nationalists. Its veneration in various literatures installed Irish heroes in equally (sometimes more) exulted positions as indigenous figures. From Aberri Eguna to *La Vie de Patrice Pearse* and the work of Fr Jules Callewaert, the significance of that week in Dublin became firmly established in the movements of Euskadi, Brittany and Flanders. It also inspired Celtic movements in the UK, especially their militant fringes. The Easter rebels had taught kindred Celtic peoples, said PC leader Gwynfor Evans (himself a pacifist) that 'their subjection to England and France was neither inevitable nor permanent.' [49]

It is not surprising, then, that foreign nationalists desired to visit Dublin in 1966. What are perhaps surprising, given the Irish state's reticence to identify with such causes, are reports testifying to the participation of foreigners in the commemorations themselves – not only representatives of constitutionalist parties, but also members of militant organisations. Free Wales Army leaders Julian Cayo Evans and Dennis Coslett, for example, are reported to have carried 'the Red Dragon flag during the fiftieth anniversary celebrations of the Easter Rising in Dublin'.[50] According to sundry reports, their 'troops' in the city that April were numbered in the 'scores', at eighty, forty, or only 'between six or seven'.[51] Likewise, militants of the so-called Scottish Liberation Army were said to have accompanied the Welshmen, numbering up to thirty participants,[52] and these just one contingent of a mass that included 'the Breton Liberation movement [...] the Flemish, the Vec Mannin [*sic*] (Manx Independence movement),[53] Irish Americans, Cornish Republicans [... and] even a bunch of Glasgow Celtic football supporters'.[54] The 'celebration of 1966', according to excited pan-Celticist commentators like Faligot, was a fully-fledged 'grand festival of Celtic nations'.[55]

Beyond the unreliable reportage regarding the numbers of foreigners present, a more important question emerges: how did Dublin move from 'embarrassment' over the presence of Gwynfor Evans at the UN in 1958, to apparently allowing both PC and more militant Welsh organisations to participate in the official Easter events eight years later? How also could Scottish nationalists participate, when SNP president William Wolfe made clear in 1962 that he 'entirely appreciates that [Ireland] could not become officially involved in the Scottish National Movement'?[56] Just as accounts of the flight of fugitives to postwar Ireland imply their axiomatic acceptance, so the media coverage of foreigners at Easter 1966 omits discussion of official attitudes towards them. As government records demonstrate, Dublin was in fact not comfortable with its commemorations becoming a stage for others to air constitutional grievances, especially as the targets of such protests would be Ireland's European state partners. The contradiction was especially acute given the nature of the events. 'Having attained statehood through violence', Higgins observes, 'the Republic now wanted to uphold the power of sovereign states'.[57] Diversion and narrow interpretations of the Rising's significance would therefore take precedence over 'solidarity'.

Fortunately (from the Irish government's perspective), there had been ample time to prepare a response to the anticipated foreign influx that Easter, given their attendance had been proposed several months in advance. Among the earliest proponents was that familiar 'Breton nationalist and Irish Republican' resident of Bray.

Repaying a 'debt of gratitude'

> Since Easter 1965, I have created in Brittany a new association called the 'Committee Brittany-Ireland', the main purpose of this association is to group all the Breton Nationalists anxious to come to Dublin [...] to pay their respects to the Irish heroes of the 1916 rebellion.

So wrote Yann Goulet to the Bray representative of the 1916 Committee in October 1965. Goulet claimed a delegate of his committee was now in 'every [Breton] province plus Paris'. These were creating study groups in Irish revolutionary history, with certificates to be presented upon completion. 'I was hoping that these certificates would be presented to them in Dublin by survivors of the 1916 rebellion.' Rounding out the programme, Goulet asked each cultural association to produce a play entitled *Tribute of the Bretons to the 1916 Irish heroes*. The winning troupe would be brought to Ireland to perform. 'That play will have to be understood by a non-Breton speaking public,' conceded Goulet. Excitingly, it would therefore be 'more a mime than a play'.

The prospect of earnest mime troupes coming from France was enough to arrest the attention of any 1916 Committee member, but it was Goulet's evident intention to broaden the political implications of the commemorations that concerned the DEA:

> For us, Breton Nationalists [...] Easter Monday 1916 has always been a memorable date. The old generation will not fail to recall the memory of that sensational issue of BREIZ ATAO dedicated to the Irish insurrection [...] We have benefited from that example and in doing so we have contracted a debt of gratitude.

This debt could only be repaid by forming a common front of 'convinced Nationalists ready to fight'.[58] The implication, therefore, was that the Bretons Goulet proposed to bring to Ireland would be militant nationalists, likely to propagandise their grievances against Paris before the Irish – and the world's – media.

In exploiting such events, Goulet already had a track record: there were claims he had 'officially represented Brittany' when Roger Casement's remains were repatriated from England in March 1965.[59] Although this was one of the few occasions when Breton exiles acted in concert, 'official representation' from Brittany was recognised neither by Paris nor Dublin. In an indication of Goulet's personal connections, the Irish embassy in Paris advised that he be 'told verbally that political demonstrations were not desired' come Easter.[60]

The participation of cultural organisations also presented problems. Per Denez, president of the Celtic Congress, similarly proposed to bring 'quite a number' of Breton pipe bands, scouts and others to Dublin. There was more where that came from: Denez predicted 'strong delegations' from Scotland and Wales, and even from non-Celtic regions further afield:

> Only two days ago, I had also a very favourable answer from Catalonia. We are all grouped in a European Committee of the Friends of Ireland, and we think we should show our gratitude to Ireland for what she did for the cause of freedom.[61]

The cultural focus of the Celtic Congress was appreciated by the DEA,[62] but the risk that even law-abiding regionalists might claim Irish support for their platforms was enough to spark vigorous departmental discussion.

The first problem concerned the official parade. The 1916 Committee envisaged the march past the GPO on Easter Sunday as having a general public contingent, so as to involve voluntary organisations and other community bodies. It was obvious that visiting foreigners might join this section of the parade, perhaps indicating to the attendant media that they enjoyed official sanction. While the Bretons posed an especial risk owing to French sensitivity on the issue of national cohesion, other groups such as the SNP were soon asking why they too had not received invitations to the proceedings.[63] Some plausible formula for deterring these participants had to be devised quickly, warned the DEA, 'Otherwise minority groups from various countries would be given the opportunity of publicising their respective causes, to the displeasure of various governments.'[64] It was, that department noted,

> imperative that we avoid causing any embarrassment to the French or British representatives by allowing the Bretons, Scots and Welsh to avail themselves of these opportunities of making anti-French or anti-English propaganda.[65]

The solution was to fall back upon that 'insular' character Hubert Butler had identified in Irish nationalism. In November 1965 the DEA decided, 'Should the Bretons want to take part in the march past the GPO, it could be explained to them that the parade is being confined to Irish bodies'.[66] Lemass indicated his opposition to foreign Heads of Government being invited, and Aiken left his UN Afro-Asian bloc off the guest list.[67] The 1916 Committee confirmed this overall stance to the SNP in March: 'Invitations to participate in the ceremonies are not being sent to foreign Governments or organisations in other countries.'[68] Given the importance of its diaspora, however, 'Irish bodies' had a broad definition. Welcome in the GPO parade were 'persons of Irish birth or descent from abroad' and representatives of Irish societies overseas, such as the Éire Society of Boston.[69]

Restricting participation went a considerable way toward defusing the potential embarrassment come Easter. But there was no way consular officials resident in Ireland could be left out, nor could the government prevent Breton, Welsh or Scottish tourists from coming to Dublin. Were any attempt made to do so, Celtic outrage could prove as embarrassing as protest by Paris or London. The DEA knew the Bretons would still be coming 'in such strength they would not wish to go unnoticed'. Their 'psychological need' to be recognised would have to be fulfilled, 'provided that the impression is not created that the Government [...] acknowledg[es] their political claims'. Hoping that harmless cultural displays such as 'recitals, dancing, pipe-playing etc.' might do the trick, the solution was to host the Celtic Congress at the same time as the Easter commemorations.[70]

The Celtic Congress 'umbrella'

Former Chief Justice Conor Maguire suggested late in 1965 that the Celtic Congress be held in Dublin specifically to provide an 'umbrella' under which foreign Celts could arrive. As this was an anodyne cultural body, their presence would be rendered 'less provocative' as a result.[71] By November Eibhlín Ní Chathalriabhaigh, member of the Congress's Irish council and one who had assisted Breton asylees in the past, also favoured hosting the event, her decision 'influenced by the news that Breton groups were coming [...] at Easter'.[72]

The DEA could not pretend, however, that foreigners would be content with 'pipe-playing etc.' 'If the Celtic Congress is in session here then it should serve to draw the attention [...] of the Bretons but it cannot be doubted that they will wish to take part in the 1916 Ceremonies.'[73] This sense was heightened by the news that the Celtic League had also decided to assemble in Dublin during Easter Week. Formed in 1961, this organisation had as its general secretary the Bezen Perrot veteran and naturalised Irishman Alan Heusaff, and was considered more 'extreme' than the Congress.[74] Foreign participation would therefore have to be 'discreet, orderly and unprovocative', and unconnected to the official programme.[75]

Foreign Celts were therefore confined to private commemorations, or events organised by the Celtic Congress or Celtic League. A small party of Bretons was permitted to lay a wreath at Kilmainham Jail and Arbour Hill cemetery.[76] Even at these events Irish detectives were on hand. No official representation from Brittany took part in the official parade; foreign participation being confined to the general public contingent in an unofficial capacity. The journalist James Nicholson reported that an 'unofficial group of forty marchers' brought up the rear of this march. Among them was Cayo Evans of the FWA, carrying the Red Dragon and wearing his organisation's homemade green uniform. Even he was marching unofficially at this point. 'So far we have not marched as the Free Wales Army, but we shall do so in the near future.' He also alluded to more extensive co-operation between Welsh and Irish militants: 'While we are here we shall see some of our friends in the IRA. They might give us some idea about fighting for freedom.'[77]

Flemings in Dublin 1966

The potential embarrassment posed by visiting Celts was considered minor in contrast to another group. In February 1966 the 1916 Committee received a letter from the head of the 'Flemish Group in Dublin', explaining that there was great interest for a Flemish delegation to visit that Easter. Would such a delegation be welcome? Would it have a reserved place at the Easter Monday services? Could they also lay a wreath at Kilmainham Jail? The author was Ward Op de Beeck, political asylee since 1947.[78]

A Vlaamse Club Dublin (Flemish Club Dublin) had existed since 1964, but the Flemish 'community' in Ireland was never as cohesive as larger communities in South America. It had its own newsletter, *Echo,* edited by Leo Schotsaert,[79] but Flemings were still 'riven by mistrust and jealousy', according to van den Driessche.[80] Alex Colen, for one, lived at Clones, Co. Monaghan, and had few dealings with his compatriots. He and his wife, daughter of Renaat Verbruggen, returned to Belgium after an amnesty in 1967.[81] A few events did however manage to bring both exile and immigrant Flemings together. One of these was a 'Father Callewaert' day at Tallaght in November 1965, commemorating that influential champion of the 'Irish inspiration'. Unfortunately, this drew the attention of Belgian journalists, and a subsequent article in *Le Soir* listed Ireland alongside Argentina, Austria, Canada and the US as a centre of Flemish exile extremism.[82] Press attention like this dismayed External Affairs. The ambassador at Brussels especially was against recognition of a Flemish delegation if Op de Beeck was associated with it.[83] His involvement was particularly problematic given that he had not taken out Irish citizenship.[84]

Robert Verbelen had been recently unmasked in Austria, and his subsequent trial again excited passions in Belgium regarding Flemish *collabos.*[85] Any Flemish activity in Dublin would doubtless be 'commented upon unfavourably' in the Belgian press.[86] There was still resentment in that country over the 'stab in the back' Irish rebels had delivered Britain while Belgium fought for its existence in 1916.[87] The reasons for deterring Flemish participation were therefore considered 'even stronger' than for the Bretons. Following this reasoning, the 1916 Committee's decision that Flemings be shunted off to 'discreet and unprovocative' ceremonies at Kilmainham or the Garden of Remembrance was soon amended. '[I]t would not be considered appropriate that they should lay a wreath at either location,' the DEA concluded.[88] For that department,

> The character and objectives of an essentially domestic political movement in Belgium are not [...] a matter for the Irish Government even if they claim to draw inspiration from Irish nationalism.[89]

Unable to shelter under the Celtic Congress umbrella, when the Broederband of former VNV members did finally visit their 'outlaws in Ireland' it was obliged to come later in the summer. Significantly, they did not arrive until six days after the Flemish national holiday, which fell on 11 July. Flemish expatriates celebrated that event by themselves with gatherings at Howth and Blackrock,[90] but it seems that events involving visiting ex-*collabos* were pre-emptively thwarted by the DEA, or at least postponed in deference to its sensitivities. The best that could therefore be offered the visiting Broederband in the way of commemorations was an unenthusiastic 'glass of lemonade on an empty stomach' to mark the Belgian national holiday ten days later.[91]

The Republican march

What then of sightings of foreign militants – including Flemings – marching through Dublin that Easter? These were no doubt participants in the public contingent past the GPO, or confusions with the separate Republican march from the Custom House to Glasnevin Cemetery. Unconcerned with diplomatic reactions and keen to accentuate the solidarity of the occasion, the organisers of this parade allowed foreigners to participate, including the motley assortment of Cornish, Manx and so on identified by Cayo Evans. Here too there is dispute over numbers, and the existing film record seems to cast doubt upon claims that 'scores' of FWA men were involved. RTÉ's footage of Cayo Evans carrying the Red Dragon indicates he was flanked by only two such 'troopers',[92] although perhaps this was only the 'colour guard' of a larger group as, according to the FWA leader, 'The Flag parties of each contingent led, with the rank and file following the massed banners'.[93] On the other hand, the same James Nicholson who observed Cayo Evans at the rear of the official 'Free State' parade was later called as a witness when Welsh militants were tried at Swansea in April 1969. Nicholson testified then that the entire FWA contingent in Dublin three years earlier numbered no more than 'six or seven' and that Cayo Evans' green uniform had been 'badly dyed' to boot.[94]

Kudos by association

Whatever the size of the FWA contingent and its garb, its presence was orchestrated to maximise propaganda value. Welsh militants were apprised of the upcoming parades by their IRA contacts and the fact that, for the Republican one at least, 'revolutionary independence organisations from all over the world were to be invited to take part'. Even if that were the case, someone had left the FWA off the guest list – Cayo Evans had to 'get to work' on his Irish connections before Sinn Féin extended him a 'cordial invitation'. FWA men came disguised as rugby supporters to elude Irish detectives. 'Plaid Cymru was also to be represented in Dublin,' Cayo Evans believed, 'but their invitation came from official Irish Government sources.'[95] It didn't, of course – PC was there officially for the Celtic Congress and Celtic League meetings.

The cohort of Scots from the SLA was led by Major Boothby – a former British army intelligence officer. His SLA is not believed to have achieved much other than elementary weapons training, graffiti campaigns, providing the FWA with sawn-off shotguns ... and of course parading in Dublin.[96] Again, the intended effect of marching at Easter was to portray greater organisation than the group possessed. One of its members believed it 'had absolutely no security, no real ideology other than a set of vaguely romantic notions, no revolutionary creed and no politics other than a general support for the SNP'.[97] The SNP, however, regarded Boothby as an *agent provocateur.*[98] Labelled in time with a similar charge would be that SLA member so critical of the organisation – Adam Busby. He does not appear to have been in Dublin in 1966, however, as he had joined the Argyll and Sutherland Highlanders the previous year 'in order to get training and equipment, and to recruit new SLA members from the British Army's own ranks'.[99]

Per Denez knew there to be up to 1,000 foreign Celts in Dublin for Easter. As for his own contingent, there was debate over which of the marches to attend – 'Free State' or 'IRA' – but in the end Kilmainham Jail was decided upon in consultation with the government. Goulet insisted the Bretons march to Kilmainham as 'soldiers', which demonstrated to Denez at least that the exile's thinking was 'of the past' and out of step with the 'national liberation' character of contemporary Breton nationalism.[100] That disjuncture would be demonstrated repeatedly over coming years, and in often extravagant ways.

Vive la Bretagne libre!

Not long after the Easter commemorations in Dublin, an unexploded bomb was found at the tax offices at St-Brieuc, Brittany. Investigations led police to a certain Émile Lecoq, a former PNB member who had allegedly been in contact with a nationalist in exile since the *épuration*.[101] In correspondence seized from Lecoq, this exile reportedly voiced desires to regroup Breton autonomists 'on bases similar to those we had in 1943–4'.[102]

Increasing in frequency and organisation over subsequent years, symbols of French power or 'colonial exploitation' in Brittany were targeted by a new generation of militants employing the name Front de Libération de la Bretagne (Liberation Front of Brittany). The FLB's ideology – steeped in the 'national liberation' zeitgeist sweeping the globe from Algeria to Vietnam – was very different to its wartime forebears. Further linkages with the discredited '*collabo*' past soon appeared, however.

'The French only pay attention if you use violence,' remarked the exiled head of the Comité nationale de la Bretagne libre (National Council for a Free Brittany)[103] to a British journalist in March 1968. 'Now we mean serious business. A new stage is starting for Bretons.' Thinking 'constantly of his action groups' in the FLB, the CBL's head boasted of illicitly crossing to Brittany to 'visit his men in the field'.[104] It was a claim he hinted at again to German television reporters in January 1969:

> Q: All [FLB] operations are co-ordinated here, with your participation?
> A: I'd prefer not to respond to this question.
> Q: Have you recently been to Brittany?
> A: It's been a long time since I've officially been to Brittany.
> Q: And unofficially?
> A: No comment.[105]

The CBL, its head explained, was modeled on the Irish Republican Brotherhood, which 'led Ireland to victory from America'.[106] But 'leading the guerrilla fight for the freedom of his native land' from abroad was one thing; visiting Brittany clandestinely was quite another: 'Were I to be found in France at any time I am liable to execution because of my struggle for the freedom of Brittany.'[107] The capital sentence had been passed *par contumace* in 1947, but the self-styled '*Rener*'[108] (director) of the FLB from exile was not the former Gwenn-ha-Du bomber Neven Henaff, nor even a veteran of the Bezen Perrot. He was Yann Goulet, wartime head of the PNB's youth wing, the Bagadoù Stourm. His CBL – supposedly grouping all Breton autonomist organisations[109] – was headquartered in the study of his home: 'Koatkeo', Herbert Road, Bray.

The claim that Breton guerrillas were training in Ireland first appeared in 1960 in *L'Avenir de la Bretagne* (The Future of Brittany), edited by former exile

Yann Fouéré.[110] But it was not until Charles de Gaulle's controversial visit to Québec in 1967 that Goulet's CBL burst into prominence. The French president's cry of *'Vive le Québec libre!'* may have delighted Québécois separatists, but it enraged their counterparts in Brittany. The Breton language still faced official prejudice, and underdevelopment, unemployment and 'colonial exploitation' in the region remained concerns. Until 1966 it was illegal even to record a Breton given name on a child's *état civil* in preference to a French variant – a prohibition overturned only by a lengthy court battle in which Paris was hauled before the International Court of Justice.[111] It seemed to many Bretons therefore that France championed minorities only if they spoke French – those within the French 'Hexagon', on the other hand, were pressured to assimilate, and efforts by foreign bodies even to investigate these issues were resisted as interference in the country's 'internal affairs'.[112] The irony was not lost upon Canada's Justice Minister Pierre Trudeau, who wondered what the reaction would be if a Canadian Prime Minister shouted 'Brittany to the Bretons!' during a tour of France.[113]

De Gaulle's pronouncements in Québec led to spontaneous eruptions of both popular and militant anger in Brittany. But 'direct action' in the peninsula was not conducted by an organisation in the traditional sense of the term. Beginning with individual acts like Lecoq's, the idea spread to other independent actors or small groups with the ability to carry out attacks. Each attack inspired another in a different part of the country ... including Paris.[114] Targeting of persons was avoided in favour of property damage and symbolic actions – a strategy the press dubbed '*terrorisme souriante*' (smiling terrorism).[115] Whatever support the FLB enjoyed would doubtless be lost if lives were taken – a reality recognised as far back as Gwenn-ha-Du, and perhaps disastrously ignored by the Bezen Perrot.

Algeria's success in throwing off French rule in 1962 was inspirational. Many Bretons were conscripted into that conflict, and some had deserted with the alleged assistance of Algerian Front de Libération nationale (National Liberation Front) networks.[116] Veterans had also learned guerrilla tactics first-hand. Many therefore identified not as 'Breton Sinn-Feiners' as had their antecedents in the PNB, but as 'Breton *fellaghas*'.[117]

The re-emergence of nationalist violence also owed something to events in Dublin. Not only did the Rising continue to inspire, the concept of 'direct action' against symbols of colonial power had been recently driven home by the IRA's demolition of the Nelson Column in March 1966.[118] Such symbolism resonated with those who still revered Gwenn-ha-Du's destruction of the *Honte nationale* in 1932.

Goulet and the CBL

Although intending to resume nationalist struggle from the moment he reached Ireland in 1947 (or so he told historian Ronan Caerléon), Goulet actually did very little until de Gaulle's Canadian visit.[119] Owing to this initially low profile, it appears French consular staff didn't recognise the organiser of a demonstration outside their Dublin embassy in August 1967 – dismissing the placard-wielding participants as mere 'local beatniks'.[120]

In March 1968 Goulet's CBL claimed responsibility for all FLB attacks of previous years. He published the Front's manifesto that December.[121] There were inconsistencies between occurrences in Brittany and Goulet's communiqués, however. On one occasion the CBL declared a truce, only to rescind it when attacks continued regardless. It also claimed responsibility for attacks by another group calling itself the ARB, which Goulet insisted stood for 'Armée républicaine bretonne' (Breton Republican Army). This Irish-style formula was not preferred in Brittany, where the term 'Republican' connotes Jacobinism. There, the initials were said to represent the Breton *Revolutionary* Army.[122]

Obviously, if there had been a cohesive FLB/ARB commanded by Goulet, these embarrassing contradictions would not have occurred. The reality is that, as the FLB/ARB was not initially a co-ordinated operation, Goulet was not capable of commanding it from Bray even if he had been empowered to do so – which he was not.

Goulet's real role in Ireland was twofold – the first agreed with the Breton militant leadership, such as it was; the other self-awarded. Primarily, he functioned as a 'letterbox', allowing the FLB/ARB to communicate externally without fear of exposure. The PNB had run a similar letterbox from the Channel Islands in the 1930s.[123] Goulet's role in this regard was confirmed by former FLB militant Jean Bothorel. Neither he nor his recruiter 'Hervé'[124] were satisfied with linkage to the old exiles, however. In fact, Bothorel found the CBL 'bizarre and deplorable', handing the press ammunition to condemn the FLB as 'children of *collabos*'. The CBL's communiqués were, moreover, 'obsolete and pompous [...] award[ing] themselves a role and an importance they didn't have'. In Bothorel's view, exiles like Goulet had 'to understand that the best gift they could give Brittany would be to retire from combat.'[125]

Goulet also took it upon himself to publicise the Breton cause. A legitimate function for exile organisations, this melded with the 'love of heroism' (some claimed egotism) for which he was renowned.[126] There was no voice in the English-speaking media to contradict him, and the more the FLB/ARB could be presented as under his command, the greater the propaganda impact. This again reflected the old-fashioned politics Per Denez objected to in 1966, and grated upon the younger generation who embraced decentralised 'people's resistance'. Goulet's claims that he braved execution by secretly returning to Brittany were especially fictitious. Even if he *had* ever returned (Feutren claims he didn't),[127] he must have known that his sentence of death had fallen into abeyance (*peine préscrite*) from 25 March 1967.[128] While short of an amnesty, this meant the capital sentence would not have been carried out even if Goulet was captured. Renowned for exaggerating his importance in this way, Goulet was for fellow exiles not military head of the FLB but a noisy *'Maréchal de Théâtre'*.[129]

Goulet's claims did however attract media attention that FLB attacks would not otherwise have commanded beyond France. Heusaff and the Celtic League were publicising perceived iniquities in Brittany, but petitions to the UN or public lectures on language conservation could not compete with Goulet's claims of IRA training or allegations that French agents had taken potshots through his study windows.[130] Goulet took on his role as 'spoofer' in the Breton publicity effort with relish, boosted no doubt by his personality and desire for renewed relevance, but fed in turn by the sensational reportage his pronouncements received. He was even said to be involved in an 'International Celtic Army' run by one Breffni O'Rourke, an Irishman in Birmingham, which claimed 'associate' members as far afield as Nagaland and the 'Patriots of Manchu'.[131] In the reporter Julian Mounter's unbounded excitement, even Alan Heusaff was unmasked as one of 'twenty-five alleged leaders of extremist groups' connected with Goulet in the ICA. Heusaff 'admits to being a member of an underground movement,' in addition to his Celtic League activities, wrote Mounter. 'He is adamant, however, that his two activities are completely separate.' Setting a trend for others to follow, the journalist then went on to suggest Goulet and Heusaff had served together in the Bezen Perrot.[132]

France takes notice

Allegations that Breton campaigns were co-ordinated by exiles caused concern in Paris and, as a result of his media profile, there was no greater focus of that concern than Yann Goulet. There persisted also that perception that Ireland tolerated the CBL's activities owing to Celtic solidarity. The French therefore determined to learn more about Goulet and his fellow exiles than mere news clippings could provide.

It is remarkable how little intelligence on Breton exiles Paris possessed. We know that their ambassador reportedly pestered Seán MacBride about Bretons in the late 1940s, and of course others had by now returned home. But it appears personnel turnover in the foreign ministry combined with a dearth of intelligence sources in Ireland to ensure Paris had essentially to start from scratch. Diplomats failed to recognise Goulet at a protest right outside their Dublin embassy and, like Irish journalists, couldn't determine to which wartime organisation Goulet had actually belonged, nor even in what year he had fled. Their intelligence was so poor, moreover, they still felt it was possible to lean on Dublin to curtail the Bretons' political activities as being in breach of the conditions of asylum, little realising most had obtained citizenship over a dozen years beforehand.[133] It was therefore felt by May 1968 (at the height of '*Les évenements*' in Paris) that more definite information was required. A mission to Ireland was ordered 'to make contact with the local authorities regarding the renewal of activity by certain Breton autonomist refugees'.[134] It would be drawn from the Renseignements généraux, which gathered intelligence on threats to the internal security of France.

The RG mission uncovered most of the Bretons in Ireland. The reason many had fallen off the French radar, it insisted, was because they had craftily adopted Celtic names rather than the French versions recorded on their birth certificates.[135] 'Yanns' were evidently harder to locate than 'Jeans'. The mission requested the foreign ministry seek Dublin's assistance in formulating an exhaustive list of exiles, and even to issue a *démarche* demanding they be put under surveillance. This would have to be handled delicately, owing to the Irish citizenship of many concerned.[136]

French suspicion that Ireland protected Breton exiles dated from the *épuration*. This was not dispelled by the quality of co-operation received in 1968. M. Bitard of the Dublin embassy expressed his frustrations along these lines in a letter to his minister in February 1969, a few months after the RG mission's report. Although the Garda had supposedly acceded to French requests, it had provided no information Paris didn't already possess. In addition, Bitard had only now learned that 'Alain' Heusaff had adopted Irish citizenship without renouncing his French, and that Dublin 'omitted' to mention he belonged to a government service – the Civil Aviation Authority. 'This fact,' Bitard thundered,

> delivers concrete proof of the duplicity of the Irish police services who, under the aegis of the Ministry of Justice, openly protect the Breton autonomist refugees in Ireland.[137]

'Bombing Bray?'

Anxiety about Ireland sheltering Breton militants was not confined to French government. So much had appeared in the press by early 1969 that even Irish citizens had begun to worry about French warplanes darkening the skies over Co. Wicklow. As one John C. Tozer wrote to the *Irish Times* in January:

> [A] series of bombing attacks have been taking place in the French province of Brittany for some years [...] and [...] these attacks are being directed by a gentleman named Yann Goulet [...] Accordingly [...] it would seem that the French Government would be fully entitled to bomb Bray [...] owing to the fact that our government is prepared to 'harbour this terrorist' [...] It's a terrifying thought.[138]

Civilian nervousness aside, the Irish government was of course not willing to jeopardise state security by affording Goulet or any other foreign nationalist the sort of safe haven he might claim in the media. As Irish citizens, Breton exiles were entitled to involve themselves in whatever lawful political activity they chose. Goulet's contacts in both the establishment and Republican circles knew very well, however, his claims were chimerical. Had Dublin believed he was actually involved in bombing campaigns in Brittany, their reaction would have been very different.

Aside from Northern Ireland, Dublin's neighbours had little to fear regarding Irish interference in their regional disputes, anyway. Focus upon economic modernisation during the Lemass era softened the old nationalistic and autarkical concepts that characterised the de Valera years, and integration into Europe was now the goal. Those separate planes of political fortune upon which Ireland and the 'stateless nations' of the Celtic Fringe operated were never more apparent than in the aftermath of an article that appeared in June 1968, in which the Irish Minister for Education, Brian Lenihan, advised Scotland and Wales not to separate from the UK but to maintain economic links and develop regional parliaments. Ireland's recent progress, he warned, was the result of an entire generation's efforts, and came at the price of mass emigration and poverty. Intending only to remark that 'national independence is not a cure-all', Lenihan's comments were seized upon by Unionists in Britain, who crowed that an Irish politician had admitted 'Nationalism Doesn't Pay'. 'A fall in the standard of living would be the inevitable price of a declaration of independence from England,' the Labour Party trumpeted in a Caerphilly by-election it subsequently won.[139] The reaction to Dublin's perfidy in the Celtic nationalist world was intense, and Conradh na Gaeilge joined criticism of Lenihan's 'reactionary' comments.[140] Far from championing minority nationalism, Irish ministers were letting down the entire Celtic team. 'The harm done to Plaid Cymru is immense,' wrote Malcolm N. Thomas to the Taoiseach. 'I would ask [...] the Irish Government to shut up and not retard Welsh freedom by making irresponsible remarks.'[141]

As a final straw, Charles de Gaulle even visited Ireland a year later. The French president had retired after a failed regionalist referendum, and came as personal guest of Eamon de Valera. The two statesmen had 'a lot in common', according to son Terry.[142] Bretons suspected the commonalities were limited, however. 'De Valera won't be coming to Rennes to proclaim "*Vive la Bretagne libre*",' Fouéré's journal predicted.[143]

If the Irish government disappointed autonomists, the attitude of its diplomats remained consistent. As Olier Mordrel learned in 1947, no Irish mission would risk the displeasure of its host by sheltering nationalist fugitives – whether postwar *collabos* or contemporary 'smiling terrorists'. Alan Le Coq and René Kerhousse, two FLB militants on the run in December 1968, encountered this policy when they approached the Irish embassy in Paris and requested asylum. Discreetly ushered to the residence of a diplomat, they were reportedly told their requests would be denied so as not to 'irritate France'. Deflated, the two returned to Brittany, and arrest.[144]

The arrest of Yann Fouéré

When the 'First FLB' (as it came to be known) was rolled up by police in 1969, Goulet was 'inconsolable'.[145] Its clandestine successor – 'FLB-72' – repudiated him,[146] but Goulet still exercised a hypnotic effect upon the French foreign service. Many of its files concerning Breton exiles are fixated upon him, down to newsclippings of his daughter's wedding – indeed, any mention of persons bearing his surname.[147] It presents the historian with the probability that, were it not for his extravagant claims, French authorities may never have had much interest in Breton exiles at all. Although he tried to resurrect an FLB/ARB structure under his 'command', Goulet's efforts were largely abandoned by 1973.[148]

One Irish citizen was arrested for alleged involvement in attacks in Brittany, and Goulet's attempts at maintaining relevance played a role. Late in 1975, Yann Fouéré was preparing to make one of his periodic returns to Connemara when he was detained by French police. Found at his residence at St-Brieuc were documents detailing FLB structures originating from Goulet, and correspondence containing mysterious references to red and blue lobsters which the police naturally took to be code for bombmaking equipment. Found separately were detonator caps Fouéré claimed were used to clear boulders at his lobster farm at Cleggan … all of which convinced police that the former exile and naturalised Irish citizen was secretly 'Minister of War' in the FLB.

Fouéré was detained until February 1976. He was released as a result of political pressure brought to bear upon France by various elected representatives, including TDs from the west of Ireland and the SNP's Winifred Ewing. Welsh parliamentarians also came to his assistance, as they had thirty years before.[149] Irish press attention was attracted by a vigil outside the French embassy staffed by Fouéré's family, the effect upon public opinion being such that the French ambassador complained to the *Irish Times*.[150] Fianna Fáil simply urged Fouéré's case –'an internal French matter' – be dealt with expeditiously. As many noted at the time, the party was allied to France's ruling Gaullists in the European Parliament.[151]

The apparent flimsiness of the case was not helped by inflammatory pronouncements from French officials. Not only did it seem Fouéré was being punished for his political views, hostility towards his alleged collaboration still lingered. Gaullist deputy Gabriel Kaspareit declared there was little sympathy for Fouéré owing to 'bad memories' of his wartime conduct. 'If you did not take part in the war, you are in no position to judge', he concluded, dismissing not only France's contemporary Celtic critics but also the French military tribunal that acquitted Fouéré of all charges in 1955.[152]

Fouéré did acknowledge his participation in the constitutionalist 'Second' or 'Open FLB' that included many public figures.[153] It also appears he was informed of at least one FLB attack before it took place, and was supportive of its actions generally in his *L'Avenir de la Bretagne*. He maintains he was not involved in operations, however, contrary to recent claims.[154] As late as 1979 Paris attempted to connect wartime collaboration and contemporary Breton activism by including both Fouéré and the Bezen Perrot's Ange Péresse in charges against the FLB/ARB.[155]

A new generation of Breton 'exiles'

Tensions in Brittany, as well as a heightened sense of 'Celticness' created by the Interceltic Festival at Lorient, motivated young Bretons to visit the Irish Republic in the 1970s. Most were simple vacationers and, whether aware of their wartime conduct or not, naturally sought out local connections. Alphonse Le Boulc'h was known as the unofficial Breton 'consul' in Dublin,[156] and the Heussaff sisters Anna and Kintilla recall young Breton campers in their garden at Spiddal, Co. Galway.[157] Many were of military age, and came not just to explore Celtic affinities with Irish girls but to avoid national service in France. Some spoke of going into Irish 'exile' as had their antecedents in the PNB. Others recruited for the FLB/ARB,[158] and are known to have sought out an older compatriot renowned for his pre-war exploits in 'violent propaganda' – a certain 'Neven Henaff'.[159]

French police complained about these Breton draft-dodgers. The Irish were content not to stir up trouble, however, not least because extradition law generally exempts offences against military regulations.[160] In 1978, the FLB bombed a wing of the Versailles palace to protest against 'the humiliation of Breton culture', and French pressure increased.[161] Dublin was still wary of extradition, however, owing to the 'political exception' clauses of the Extradition Act (1965).

As will be recalled, Irish legislation in this area was proposed in the 1930s, but it was under pre-independence legislation that Leo Schotsaert's extradition was refused in 1952. The 1965 Act empowered the High Court to grant relief from extradition if the alleged offence was political, related to a political offence, or there were 'substantial reasons for believing that the person will be prosecuted for a political offence' if surrendered under a separate warrant.[162]

Paris made no specific extradition request, however, perhaps still nervous about creating 'Celtic martyrs'. All the same, Dublin appears to have pressured some Bretons to leave in the interests of Franco-Irish relations. In 1980, Bernard Alexandre and Yves Masson approached the Irish media ... not because they resented their hosts' unwillingness to shelter them, but because a communiqué purportedly from the FLB had threatened to attack Irish interests in France if either was deported or extradited. Such threats would never be made by the fraternal FLB, they insisted, as these could only harm the 'entire Breton community' in Ireland.[163] Whether the threat originated with the FLB or a provocative source keen to disrupt 'interceltic solidarity', it was clear that Ireland was unwilling to repeat the asylum of the postwar years. This issue was now very public, and Dublin had nothing to gain. This point was communicated to Masson and Alexandre by their lawyers, and they subsequently decamped for more welcoming refuges: Algeria and the Ivory Coast.[164]

'Revolutionary co-operation': Wales

Just as involvement in the Easter commemorations had propaganda objectives, groups like the FWA also made much of their connections with the IRA, which ensured sensational press coverage. Throughout the late 1960s, reports claimed the IRA 'advised' the FWA; that bank raids in the Republic financed it; that the IRA helped it conduct attacks in Britain; and, in a recurring favourite, that FWA men were trained in Ireland.[165] Irish newspapers even suggested the Official IRA sold its weapons to the FWA ... a report Cayo Evans later admitted 'was just not true'.[166] Finally the spectacular claim surfaced that the FWA had an escape network to Ireland 'from where sabotage and guerrilla activities would be carried out [in Wales] in the manner of the wartime Special Operations Executive'.[167] Again, the attitude of the Irish government to such schemes was apparently immaterial.

The source of most claims were FWA men themselves, fed to journalists at their 'manoeuvres': 'The open display of uniforms brought the Press and TV to us', said Cayo Evans.[168] Ironically, the grandiose claims resurfaced as evidence at their trial in 1969. 'Their own fictions,' wrote the *Guardian* of the militants, 'were turned into the facts that would convict them'.[169] The FWA was therefore in many respects the propaganda arm of the extremist wing of the Welsh movement – their struggle being 'a war of propaganda, punctuated by acts of sabotage and shows of strength'.[170] They were disavowed by Plaid Cymru, and occasionally comical in contrast to a truly clandestine 'direct action' movement, the Mudiad Amddiffyn Cymru (Movement for the Defence of Wales).

This organisation began by bombing dams constructed in Welsh valleys for the use of English cities. Shunning attacks against persons, the MAC caused considerable damage before its leader, Owain Williams, was arrested in 1963 and jailed for three years. It resurfaced in 1967, and in 1969 two of its members, Alwyn Jones and George Taylor, were killed at Abergele when a bomb they had planted to disrupt the investiture of Prince Charles as Prince of Wales exploded prematurely. As far as foreign assistance went, however, the MAC 'had no help from the Irish or anyone else, we were our own people,' according to its leader after Williams' arrest, John Jenkins. Links with other movements were maintained, but active co-operation was not, 'since this would have meant increased security problems and no actual advantages in helping us to gain our objectives'. Breton militants informed them 'that we could go across there at any time and be well taken care of', but when Owain Williams was again arrested and jumped bail early in 1968 he did not escape to Brittany but across the water to Ireland.

Although the 1965 Act enshrined the 'political exception' for UK offenders, Williams did not apply to become the first Welsh nationalist asylee in Ireland. In fact, Irish authorities were unaware of his presence until he returned to Birmingham and arrest six months later. An Interpol search had been conducted as far afield as Colombia, but all the while he'd been camping at a beach near Kinsale with his Irish girlfriend. It was therefore a brief and unofficial exile for Williams, and one which ended well for him, also: he was acquitted on all terrorism-related charges upon his return.[171]

Flemings and Irish nationalism

There was a Flemish exile renowned for his lust for adventure as much as Yann Goulet, and whose adulation for 'physical force' nationalism influenced his very decision to come to Ireland in 1948. Initially limiting himself to legal protests, Staf van Velthoven came also to embrace Republican politics – and joined the Official IRA.[172] In this latter capacity he liaised with the Vlaamse Militanten Orde (Flemish Militants' Order) with a view to staging a protest at the Irish embassy at Brussels. Directed against Irish membership of the EEC, the protest fizzled when it was discovered the embassy occupied the seventh floor of an office tower.[173]

One notorious linkage between a Flemish exile and the Northern Ireland question emerged during the controversial Arms Trial of 1970. By then a successful businessman, Albert Luykx interpreted for Captain James Kelly when a consignment of arms for the Catholic Northern Defence Committees was arranged to be shipped to Northern Ireland via Antwerp and Dublin. A firm of which Luykx was principal, Weluks Ltd, was cosignee for the shipment.[174] This role, plus his interests in the Sutton House restaurant in Co. Dublin, had Luykx commonly described as a 'Belgian businessman' rather than a Flemish nationalist asylee,[175] but two TDs were more colourful in their characterisations once details of the case emerged. Barry Desmond (Labour) demanded to know of Justice Minister Desmond O'Malley if there had been examination of Luykx's background in 1948, given that he 'had been convicted in Belgium of a very serious war crime in 1946'.[176] Dr John O'Connell (also Labour) went all out and described the man who had entered Ireland under the name of 'Franciscus Josef Faes' as a 'Nazi criminal'. These attacks were muted somewhat when it was learned that the Minister of Justice who approved Luykx's naturalisation in 1954 had been Labour's own James Everett.[177] Luykx himself went to the *Irish Times,* challenging O'Connell to repeat the allegations outside parliament.[178]

Claims regarding Luykx's 'Nazi activities' brought about a mistrial in the first of the proceedings against himself and others in September 1970. Justice Secretary Peter Berry revealed in cross-examination that he had provided Luykx with 'a letter of clearance as a person who had not come into contact [...] with any subversive groups in Ireland'.[179] The implication was, says Justin O'Brien, that Luykx might have been involved in such activities beforehand.[180] The original Belgian letter alleging Luykx's neo-Nazi connections which prompted Berry's 'clearance' was about to be read in court when defence counsel Ernest Wood objected and accused Justice Ó Caoimh of bias. The judge promptly discharged the jury and withdrew from the case.[181] A retrial acquitted all defendants, but had a 'shattering effect' on Luykx. His business interests were in disarray, and the unusual burden of having to pay costs in the original, abortive trial caused extra hardship.[182] He was found dead in his car in February 1978.[183]

Scottish militants and postwar Ireland

Co-operation between Scottish and Irish militants never entirely evaporated. Mostly this involved theft of munitions in Scotland for the use of Irish Republicans. One incident in 1951 in which the traffic was reversed was noted by G2's Dan Bryan for this aberrant reason. In that case, Irish munitions bound for Scotland were seized after a tip-off by 'Orangemen informers'.[184]

From the mid-1960s, the militant fringe of Scots nationalism sought connections with the larger Irish Republican movement, or with Irish nationalism generally. The 1320 Club, named in honour of the Declaration of Arbroath, was committed to the strategy that freed Ireland forty-five years earlier: once a majority of Scots voted nationalist (which it regarded as a near certainty for 1968), a provisional government would be formed to combat the English repression that would surely follow.[185] The Club's executive contacted the DEA for advice on how Ireland set up its armed forces after Sinn Féin's electoral win in 1918.[186] But it was the Club's foreign affairs specialist who, as a 'pan-Celt of long standing', possessed the Irish contacts to impress his comrades.[187] He was Ronald MacDonald Douglas, recently returned from exile. True to the form established in the 1930s, the SNP expelled the 1320 Club as an 'elitist, secret society' in March 1968.

The Club's military wing – the grandly-titled Army of the Provisional Government – claimed in 1974 that the Provisional IRA had offered it training facilities.[188] Its leader was Major Boothby, who had led the SLA marching contingent at Easter 1966. Trials of APG members the following year 'exposed a bizarre milieu of death oaths, assassination squads and plans for military subversion.' [189] One source of support the APG is said to have successfully courted was that of Idi Amin in Uganda, who undertook to raise the Scottish case in the UN. Although more forthcoming than Ireland had ever been, a letter of support Amin sent to the SNP was mysteriously declined.

Other 'Tartan Terrorists' aspired to Irish links. In 1980 a planned Army of the Scottish People raid on an explosives depot in Glasgow aimed to 'demonstrate to the Provisional IRA that the [ASP] was a serious terrorist group worthy of fraternal support and co-operation.' The group's leader, Peter Wardlaw, aimed to trade the explosives for training and weaponry, but a premature explosion at his flat ended these plans.

As in 1939, attempts to connect their struggle to that of Irish Republicans led to the flight of wanted Scots to Ireland. Fugitive Workers' Party of Scotland bankraider, Alex Watt, lived in Dublin in 1972, where he attempted to contact the Provos, but the most significant case is that of the alleged architect of the 2002 postal attacks, Adam Busby.[190]

The SNLA

In December 1983, Adam Busby and David Dinsmore were arrested in Dunnes Stores, Dublin, on a charge of shoplifting. Over the next eight months the two Scots were held in Mountjoy Prison.[191] The long detention stemmed not from the shoplifting charge, but from the British government's application for their extradition in connection with 'terrorist offences' committed by the Scottish National Liberation Army.

The SNLA announced its presence in 1982. By 1990 it had undertaken over fifty 'operations', including letterbombs targeting the Queen, Princess Diana and Margaret Thatcher.[192] The press made much of an alleged linkage with the Irish National Liberation Army;[193] a Special Branch informer alleging that the INLA financially supported its Scottish counterpart, including the funding of 'safe houses' in Dublin as an 'escape route' for SNLA fugitives.[194]

Dinsmore and Busby flew to Ireland in September 1983, but whether they used this route is unclear. Dinsmore was due to answer charges relating to the letterbombing campaign.[195] Busby faced a lesser charge: vandalisation of an army lorry at Berwick-Upon-Tweed.[196] Learning that London had filed for their extradition, the pair applied to the Irish High Court for a writ of habeas corpus under the Extradition Act (1965), on the grounds their alleged offences were political.

Busby and the political exception

As had been the case during the Emergency, the right of abode enjoyed by British subjects in Ireland allowed all parties to sidestep thorny asylum issues. In 1974, Justice Minister Patrick Cooney could explain to the Dáil why a 'British Army deserter' and 'native of Scotland' had been 'denied political asylum':

> As the man concerned is a citizen of the United Kingdom [...] he does not need any special permission to stay here, and the question of refusing political asylum does not arise.[197]

Most entanglements in Irish extradition law therefore concerned fugitives from Northern Ireland. Indeed, London expressed its concern 'about the ease with which the perpetrators of politically motivated crime have been able to resist extradition' from the Republic.[198] Busby and Dinsmore were, however, the first from a mainland British movement to employ the political exception.

In October 1984 Busby had his day in court, challenging extradition not only on the grounds that his offence was political (Scots nationalists do not recognise English sovereignty over Berwick, which is why he spraypainted slogans on army vehicles there in 1982),[199] but that the British government intended to charge him with the letterbomb offences if returned to Scotland.[200] Justice Barrington found his political beliefs 'proven' and 'granted him an order under Section 50 of the Extradition Act'.[201]

Dinsmore, whose alleged offences potentially fell outside the political exception,[202] chose instead to avoid the hearing and abscond. Rumours had him fleeing to Spain with IRA assistance, and eventually as far as Brazil.[203] He returned to face Britain's wrath in 1993: 240 hours' community service.[204]

'Relief' from extradition did not mean Busby was welcome, however. He has been closely scrutinised, and implicated in several incidents. Accompanied by a Cornish nationalist, Busby ended up in a fracas at the British embassy in 1988.[205] He was arrested in connection with the English water supply threat in 1999, and investigated over the caustic soda postal attacks in 2002.[206] He has been questioned as a suspected member of the Real IRA, and even as to his links with Islamic extremists.[207] His release without charge on these occasions fuels suspicion among Scottish groups that he is a 'pliable tool for British intelligence':

> The brits [*sic*] get criminals and […] Real IRA terrorists extradited all the time so why not Busby? The real reason is that […] [a]ny time it looks like the Nationalists are winning the 'hearts and minds' campaign, [Busby] is trotted out to create a 'Terrorist incident' in a glare of publicity.[208]

A variant of this view is reportedly shared by the British Special Branch:

> Insiders say they are now convinced Busby uses his links with other terror groups […] to feed the Irish authorities information – and as an informant he is considered too valuable to jail. One said: 'We can't see any other possible reason.'[209]

There are problems with this portrayal of Busby, however. First, his extradition to Britain was stymied by due Irish process. The British government has indeed attempted to extradite Busby, and has failed. Second, Busby is not 'too valuable to jail', as he has served a two-year prison sentence in Ireland already.

In 1995, Busby, Darin Brown, a New Zealander named Tristan Ó Cearnaigh and Hugh Smith McMahon – the SNLA's 'Dublin cell'– were arrested.[210] Smith McMahon was charged with telephoning a bomb threat to police at Inverness, for which he later received a two-year suspended sentence. He had been observed entering a callbox in the company of Busby, who was even seen, the prosecution alleged, to dial the number.[211] Smith McMahon had been in Ireland less than a year by this time, and was thought to be under the influence of this 'more dominant figure'.[212] Ironically, his defence counsel at trial was Erwan Mill-Arden, son of the Breton exile Leon who had been subjected to so much scrutiny from security services during the Emergency.

Busby was later charged by the Special Criminal Court with sending a threatening message by fax. He served two years in prison from 1997.[213] Subsequent investigations into his alleged SNLA activities have failed, reportedly owing to the Republic's lax conspiracy laws, and because no direct evidence has linked him to the incidents.[214] Busby has been the alleged mastermind, and others – 'naïve youngsters' according to the *Daily Express* – were 'incited' to carry out attacks. Paul Smith, a 15-year-old Dumbarton student, was later charged over the caustic soda packages sent to Cherie Blair and others.[215] Much of Busby's animus is however reserved for less extreme Scottish nationalists who accuse him of provocation. Evidence, in Busby's view, of their 'pro-British extremis[m]', for example, SNG 'even condemned the [7 July 2005] London bombings, [...] so this type of hysterical attack on anti-British elements is standard procedure for them'.[216]

SNLA 'actions' have continued. In January 2008 two men acting in the name of the organisation – one an Englishman, and both resident in Manchester – were jailed for mailing caustic soda concoctions to a councillor and a journalist. Busby himself was again on remand for allegedly sending bomb threats to Scottish police as this book went to press.[217]

A sympathetic haven?

What has been overlooked by movements who claim to be trained or directed from Ireland is that foreign connections are not necessarily of benefit. 'The conventional wisdom is that international connections always provide a terrorist group with enormous advantages,' writes Rapoport. 'This wisdom is deeply flawed' as this 'alienate[s] potential domestic [...] constituencies.' [218] This is especially true regarding linkage to the IRA, as for many abroad the Northern Ireland conflict represented nothing but intractable sectarian violence.

Most figures in foreign movements recognised that Ireland's circumstances were unique. 'You can't imitate the political or military method of struggle because the two societies are different,' remarked Josu Urrutikoetxea, former ETA leader, of the Irish example in 2002. 'You can only learn and show solidarity.' [219]

The connection between the Breton struggle and the IRA prompted FLB-72 to repudiate Yann Goulet, and to condemn the 'blind and inhuman terrorism practised by international groups'. Their own struggle was henceforth to remain 'profoundly rooted' in Breton soil. This it did until 2000, when a young woman, Laurence Turbec, was killed by an ARB bomb at a McDonald's in Quévert. Unleashing 'emotions and reactions without precedent in Brittany', it was a sorry end to *terrorisme souriante*.[220] Busby, for his part, has gone in the opposite direction – his 'struggle' for national liberation now entirely telecommunicated from Dublin in a way that only underscores his disconnection from contemporary Scottish concerns.

Throughout all this Ireland grew into one of the most enthusiastic members of the EU, alongside states that once opposed its independence or castigated it for its neutrality. These states regarded Irish independence with nervousness, lest the example spread to other minority regions of Europe. Alive to this perception, Dublin's support for 'fraternal' movements, if it manifested at all, remained entirely discreet and personal. The 'embarrassment' of Gwynfor Evans at the UN in 1958 was a reminder not to relax this posture, and all requests for asylum from FLB militants were firmly declined.

Setting Northern Ireland aside, Adam Busby's is therefore the only case of political asylum for a Western European minority nationalist after 1950. He furthermore represents the only Scot accorded such status. He is likely, however, to be the last. The 'Protocol on asylum for nationals of member states of the EU', part of the Amsterdam Treaty of October 1997, defines member states as 'safe countries of origin' in terms of asylum law, rendering it practically impossible for a fugitive from one EU state to gain asylum in another.[221] With each passing year and each eastward expansion of the EU, the era of the European minority nationalist exile in Ireland draws closer to its end.

CONCLUSION

Fugitive Ireland

TERRITORIAL ASYLUM IS NOW a familiar issue in Ireland. In June 2007, a refugee who fled religious persecution in Nigeria became the country's first black mayor.[1] In addition to refugee resettlements, economic development and its attractiveness to migrant labour is rapidly changing the 'imagined community' of Irishness itself.

The earlier, more secretive influx of political refugees this work has investigated did not change the face of Irishness in such visible ways, not least because of its modest numbers. Their European origins also meant the faces of minority fugitives did not stand out in an Irish crowd, although their curious accents frequently raised eyebrows and prompted enquiries. The various foreign nationalists who entered Ireland from the fall of Republican Spain did, however, assert something about their host country's contemporary identity, as much as modern immigrants testify to its economic growth. Contrary to much of the historiography that appears in Breton and other Celticist circles, this assertion did not have much to do with ethnic commonalities or solidarity with struggles of self-determination.

As the elites of movements like pan-Celticism and pan-Slavicism have learned, religion (or, more frequently, sectarianism) is a far more potent determinant of identity than ethnicity or linguistic affinity. It is perhaps no surprise that Ireland is the only Celtic nation to have regained its independence, yet even it sundered along sectarian lines. Predominantly Protestant Scotland and Wales remain in union with Protestant England, and Catholic Brittany remains within Catholic France. When invoked by Irish figures, parallels between domestic and foreign experience focused not upon Celticism, but upon a shared Catholic identity persecuted either under historic British rule or by contemporary godless communism. On this basis, diverse non-Celts from Croatia, Flanders, the Ukraine and other regions were admitted in the postwar years – or, more accurately, in the early years of the Cold War with Moscow. Although many fugitives professed an 'Irish inspiration' to their actions, it was their wartime record versus 'Red' forces that guaranteed them Irish sympathy. Provided they kept their spiritual views discreet, even the Celtic neo-pagans of the Bezen

Perrot's inner circle could obtain the same welcome in postwar Ireland as the Catholic traditionalists of the PNB.

Was Irish postwar asylum policy therefore pro-Axis? If such proclivities were held privately by Irish officials, they did not determine official policy. Willing admission of Axis figures occurred only after German defeat. Throughout the Emergency itself Ireland regarded pro-Axis or anti-British activists with extreme suspicion, and even those Scots exiles who converted to Catholicism remained under close surveillance. The burning issue for Dublin was national security, and to this end the government was committed to aiding Britain at almost every cost short of entering the war. G2 and MI5 worked closely to co-ordinate their responses to all security threats – including Celtic nationalist liaisons with German intelligence, such as Leon Mill-Arden – and the only foreign nationalist refugees welcomed by the Irish state in this period were Basques of proven anti-fascist sympathies.

It was the imminent victory of the Allies that forced Ireland to assert its sovereignty in the area of asylum. Dublin's refusal to accede to demands it harbour no 'war criminal' owed more to David Gray's 'studied affront' to Irish sovereignty than it did to any sympathy for the Axis, leavened perhaps by frustration that some five years of 'friendly neutrality' had still not granted it immunity from charges of hampering the Allies. Asylum thereby became a useful, if controversial, tool of state. The alien group used to publicly assert Irish independence in this way was, however, neither minority nationalist nor Celtic, but German.

The earliest Breton arrivals are inseparable from this German context – indeed, as the most public contest of wills between Ireland and the Allies in the asylum sphere, the German context illuminates all postwar cases. All German diplomats, spies and military personnel in Ireland were known to the Allied Control Commission, and the latter's insistence they be surrendered forced Dublin into a protracted struggle that had enduring impacts upon its reputation. When fugitive Bretons landed in Ireland at the same time, their entry was unannounced, had not been solicited nor assisted by the Irish government, and went almost entirely unnoticed. Asylum for these entrants thereby fulfilled the same psychological need to assert independence without embroiling the state in further damaging disputes.

In the absence of Gray's demands in 1944 and the dispute over the Germans, would there have been an impulse to grant asylum to any Continental fugitive at all? The fact that most came from minority regions where local nationalists had collaborated with Axis powers testifies more to the role Ireland played in their autonomist imagination than to the level of Irish awareness or support for their struggles. Yet Breton historiography is still heavy with assertions, both explicit and implicit, that Ireland was a sympathetic and 'logical' refuge. As a nation state, it could provide the protections of international law. This is all it provided, however; both fugitive Bretons, and their movement, were on their own otherwise. The projected Breton expectation of Celtic fraternity fell instead upon a state fixated with its position among European powers, leavened perhaps with that insularity Hubert Butler had identified. Yet through it all there *was* Celtic solidarity for Bretons, albeit from a source that could not itself provide asylum. Considering the energy Plaid Cymru expended in their defence, it is perhaps no surprise that many Breton fugitives preferred Wales to Ireland. Even then, Wales was but one destination among many.

De Valera chose to sacrifice good relations with the Allies in the short term in order to assert Irish sovereignty. For an old nationalist who had led his country into an 'Economic War' with Britain and still aspired to autarky, the prospect of Ireland's wartime isolation continuing into the postwar era was perhaps not entirely uncomfortable. The spectre of Soviet communism changed this outlook, and instilled a desire to repair relations with the US and contribute to the defence of 'Western civilisation'. In foreign eyes the Interparty government was less burdened by Fianna Fáil's policy of wartime neutrality, even if it, too, could not countenance allying with Britain in NATO. But this government, also, had to ensure no grist to the anti-Irish propaganda mill was handed to the American and British press. The rejection by both governments of high-profile applications for asylum are therefore as significant as the various discreet entries.

It is worth emphasising that the majority of Flemings arrived in Ireland during the first Interparty administration, and, although he entered during de Valera's premiership, Andrija Artuković left for the US with Irish documentation during Costello's, in July 1948. If there is a difference between the Fianna Fáil and Interparty approaches, it relates to the Bretons, most of whom arrived before 'Dev' lost power but were later disdained by the supposed 'pan-Celt' MacBride. For other asylees, it is difficult to describe Irish policy as 'anti-Allied', given that this secret assistance to anti-communist 'assets' was in accord with the objectives of Western security agencies.

A significant number of asylees returned to their home countries when possible, or moved on to other destinations. Among those who stayed in Ireland, the proportion for whom it was the preferred choice of refuge appears to be small. Of those who did opt for Ireland first and foremost, the largest proportion is Breton, testifying to the influence Ireland exercised upon their imagination. Although Flemings came to Ireland in similar numbers, most came only after more popular exile destinations became inaccessible, and usually then because the asylee had spent crucial months in prison. In these cases the

Church both proposed Ireland as a destination and facilitated travel. In Artuković's case, and those of the Dutch-speaking Catholics who caught *De Adelaar* to South America, Ireland was simply a stop-over *en route* to permanent sanctuary.

In all cases, however, Ireland represented a free cultural and political space. Here Flemings could fly the Leeuw van Vlaanderen or Basques the Ikurriña, and Bretons could imagine a free Brittany modelled upon their host nation, directing its energies northwestward to the Celtic world.

Yet there were no real Flemish or Breton 'communities' born of the political refugees in Ireland. Divided by their various wartime tendencies, exile exacerbated rather than eased internal tensions. Local Flemings may have been 'riven by mistrust and jealousy', but the Bretons were more divided still. Yann Goulet and Neven Henaff in time resolved many of their wartime differences, but for most of the Breton exiles the wartime split between moderate PNB and radical Bezen Perrot persisted. Armelle Goulet-Conway says she would not know a member of the Heusaff family if she passed them on the street, and there was no bridging of this political divide even on important Breton *fêtes*. 'Our saints were not their saints,' remarks Louis Feutren.[2]

Despite the fervid dreams of Ronald MacDonald Douglas, Yann Goulet, Adam Busby and the rest, Ireland was also no place to nurture a nationalist resurgence. Those unwilling to integrate and abandon plans for their home countries found Irish exile – indeed, exile in any foreign country – the 'nearest neighbour to the prison', in Albert Luykx's phrase. Even those who chose to remain still felt the loneliness and impotence of exile many years afterwards. 'I have many Irish ties here,' Seamus Reader wrote to Nan Milton in 1968, 'but it is often I sigh for my own country.'[3]

For the Irish state, however, no sentimental abstraction – whether pan-Celticism, resentment of Britain or solidarity with nationalist struggles – would determine asylum policy. Official attitudes towards the admission of exiles, and towards the national struggles of Scots, Bretons, Basques, Croats, Ukrainians, Welsh and Flemings – not to mention Germans and Austrians – were always determined by Irish *raisons d'état:* national security, sovereignty, and Catholic anti-communism. As Joseph Walshe, Secretary of the Department of External Affairs, remarked in 1941: 'Small nations like Ireland do not and cannot assume the role of defenders of just causes except their own.'[4]

APPENDIX

Foreign minority nationalists in Irish exile

BRETONS

Fugitives from custodial or capital sentences

Breton, Germain
Bourc'hiz, Yann: 'Fañch', 'Guével', 'François Ellies'
De Quelen, Jacques (& family)
Delaporte, Raymond (& wife Madeleine)
Feutren, Louis: 'Maître', 'Michel Kelleg'
Fouéré, Yann: 'Dr Mauger' (& family)
Gaonac'h, Charles
Goulet, Yann: 'Renard' (& family)
Gourlet, Joz-Yann: 'Martolod', 'Paotr ma Bro'
Guyomarc'h, Yann: 'Pipo'
Hernot, Gwion
Heusaff, Alan: 'Professeur', 'Rouat', 'Mab Ivi', 'Bernhard Heubacher'
Hirgair, Job: 'Skav', 'Christian'
Lainé, Célestin: 'Neven Henaff'
Le Boulc'h, Alphonse: 'Jan'
Lemoine, Maurice: 'Manac'h'
Le Noac'h, Youenn: 'Ruzik', 'Yann Colas'
Leroy, Anton: 'Collet'
L'Haridon, Yann

Voluntary exiles, fugitives from dégradation nationale etc.

Gallec, André
Hemon, Roparz
Legendre, Roger
Lelandais, Ernest: 'Nenesse'
Le Roux, Louis Napoléon
Mill-Arden, Leon

In Wales

Bruchet, Jacques
Helloco, Hervé: 'Bob', 'Albert Horel' (& wife Charmaine)
Jaffrennou, Gildas: 'Claude'
Perrin, Paul: 'Gwirieg'

BASQUES

Gallastegi, Eli: 'Gudari' (& family)

Ten or so others during WW2, including:

Camiña, José
Lasarte, Angel
Sasieta, Manuel

CROATS

Artuković, Andrija: 'Alois Anitch' (& family) *(thence to USA)*
Ivandić, Fr Luji *(thence to Canada)*

RUSSIAN COSSACKS

Vasileyev, Mikhail

UKRAINIANS

Turko, Josef *(thence to Canada)*
Other names unknown.

SCOTS

Busby, Adam
Dinsmore, David
Kemp Scott, George
MacClean, Colm
MacDonald Douglas, Ronald (& family)
McDougal, Duncan
Reader, Seamus
Smith McMahon, Hugh

FLEMINGS

Fugitives from custodial or capital sentences

Colen, Alexander: 'Albert Pauwels', 'Peeters'
De Rijcke, Karel
Folens, Albert (& wife Juliette)
Hollants, Achiel (& family) *(thence to Argentina)*
Luykx, Albert: 'Franciscus Josef Faes'
Op de Beeck, Edward 'Ward' (Dr)
Schotsaert, Leo (& wife Mirientje)
Smekens, Willem: 'Vink' (& family) *(thence to Argentina)*
Stassen, Nic: 'van den Brande'
Van Overveldt, Leo
Van Velthoven, Gustaaf, 'Staf': 'Michel van Houhe'
Verbruggen, Renaat
Verbruggen, Walter

Legal immigrants, and others

Callewaert, Fr L.-J.
Dehaene, Omer (& family)
Desbonnet, Joris
Hol, Jan
Mussche, Jos A.
Peeters, Jef
Seeldrayers, Karel
Smets, ?
Stevens, Gerard
Valkenborgs, ? (daughter married Albert Luykx)
Van Westreenen, Geert

Notes

Introduction

1 Skelly, *Irish diplomacy*, p. 18.
2 Fouéré, *Connemara*, p. 129.
3 McCabe, *Diplomatic history of Ireland*, pp. 92–3.
4 '[*R*]*egardant se dresser les drapeaux et défiler l'armée, écoutant sonner les cornemuses et les cuivres* […] *Je rêvais à la Place du Parlement à Rennes, à celle du château des Ducs à Nantes,* […] *également pavoisés et noirs de monde, célébrant sous nos drapeaux déployés le retour de notre liberté …*': Fouéré, *Connemara*, p. 129.
5 Butler, 'Artukovitch file'.
6 Quoted in Molohan, *Germany and Ireland*, p. 10.
7 Eoghan Harris, 'We are past masters at Nazi denial', *Sunday Independent*, 21 Jan. 2007.
8 Hull, *Irish secrets*, p. 38; Keogh, *Ireland and Europe*, p. 98.
9 Salmon, *Unneutral Ireland*, p. 138.
10 Keogh, *Ireland and Europe*, p. 164; Hull, *Irish secrets*, p. 28.
11 Lee, *Ireland 1912–1985*, p. 243. Cf. Dermot Keogh, who argues only Joseph Walshe regarded this as a possibility. See 'Eamon de Valera and Hitler', p. 69fn.
12 Lee, *Ireland 1912–1985*, p. 244.
13 Salmon, *Unneutral Ireland*, pp. 117–18.
14 Ibid., p. 219; O'Halpin, *Defending Ireland*, p. 201.
15 Dwyer, *Irish neutrality*, p. 212.
16 Dwyer, *Guests of the state*, passim; Salmon, *Unneutral Ireland*, pp. 127, 129.
17 Cited in O'Halpin, *MI5 and Ireland*, p. 31.
18 Boland to Roche, n.d., DFA P253, NAI.
19 Dwyer, *Irish neutrality*, p. 141; Keogh, *Ireland and Europe*, p. 132.
20 Dwyer, *De Valera*, pp. 288–9.
21 Lee, *Ireland 1912–1985*, p. 262.
22 Fisk, *In time of war*, p. 472.
23 *Reynolds News* clipping 31 Mar. 1946, DEA A74, NAI.
24 Molohan, *Germany and Ireland;* Davis, *Dublin's American policy.*
25 Quoted in Tabori, *Anatomy of exile*, p. 36
26 Le Mercier d'Erm quoted in Reece, *Bretons against France*, p. 83.
27 Doody, 'Brittany from the Great War'. See Chapter Eight.
28 O'Halpin, *Defending Ireland*, p. 277; Duggan, *Neutral Ireland*, pp. 62, 166.
29 'Yann Goulet', *An Phoblacht/Republican News*, 9 Sept. 1999, http://www.irlnet.com/aprn/archive/1999/September09/09obi2.html; accessed 2 July 2003.
30 Farrell, *Sheltering*, p. 37.
31 Keogh, *Jews*, p. 208.
32 Mordrel, *Breiz Atao*, p. 79.
33 *Breiz Atao* (223), 12 May 1935.
34 See Hamon, *Nationalistes*, p. 37; Le Dantec, *Bretagne*, p. 324; Brekilien, *Histoire de la Bretagne*, p. 340.
35 Lebesque, *Comment peut-on être breton?*, p. 165.
36 Ellis, *Celtic dawn*, p. 76.
37 Grahl-Madsen, *Asylum*, pp. 25, 32.
38 Constitution of Democratic Republic of Timor-Leste, Section 10 'Solidarity' (2), http://www.constitution.org/cons/east_timor/constitution-eng.htm; accessed 22 Aug. 2007.
39 Grahl-Madsen, *Asylum*, pp. 1, 2–3.
40 Augusteijn, *Public defiance to guerrilla warfare*, p. 339.
41 See Silvestri, 'Sinn Féin of India'.
42 In Agee, 'Stepinac File'.
43 Keogh, 'Ireland, the Vatican …', p. 76.

CHAPTER 1
The unwelcome brothers

1 *Evening Mail* clipping 5 July; G2 report 13 Sept. 1944, G2/2781, IMA.
2 Travel between the UK and Éire was

uncontrolled at this time. In June 1940 a British Passport Control Office was established at Dublin, and travellers to Britain were required to obtain a visa, or an exit permit from Belfast. See O'Halpin (ed.), *MI5 and Ireland,* pp. 35, 54.

3 G2 report, 13 Sep. 1944, G2/2781, IMA.

4 Archer G2 to Carroll Garda, 27 Nov. 1940, G2/2781, IMA.

5 S. & C. Gras, *La révolte des régions*, p. 161. In fact, none of the exiles was a current SNP member.

6 'Ronald MacDonald Douglas', *Siol nan Gaidheal,* http://www.siol-nan-gaidheal-usa.com/rmdoug.htm; accessed 19 August 2005.

7 'Obituary of Ronald MacDonald Douglas', *Carn: A link between Celtic nations,* 45 (Spring, 1984), p. 4.

8 Webb, *Growth of nationalism*, pp. 81, 82.

9 'Wendy Wood – patriot and nationalist', *Siol nan Gaidheal,* http://www.siol-nan-gaidheal.com/wendy.htm; accessed 21 August 2005.

10 Brown, *Hitlerism in the Highlands*, p. 1.

11 Finlay, *Independent and free*, p. 207.

12 Webb, *Growth of nationalism*, p. 82.

13 Finlay, *Independent and free*, p. 213.

14 Webb, *Growth of nationalism*, p. 82, 73.

15 Harvie, *No gods*, p. 99.

16 SNG, 'Wendy Wood'.

17 In Webb, *Growth of nationalism*, p. 78.

18 Ibid., pp. 81, 83.

19 Young was elected Party chairman in 1942, imprisoned for objection to National Service between July 1942 and March 1943, and later ran second in the Kirkcaldy Burghs by-election. See Young, *Appeal to Scots honour*, p. 1. and Finlay, *Independent and free*, pp. 229–36.

20 Pittock, *Scottish nationality*, p. 109.

21 Hanham, *Scottish nationalism*, p. 125.

22 Pittock, *Scottish nationality*, p. 105.

23 Breton militant Célestin Lainé called von Tevenar 'our great friend': *Carn,* 19 (1977), 9.

24 MI5, June 1942, KV3/7, NA.

25 MI5, KV2/303, NA.

26 Glasgow CID, 23 May 1941, HH55/558, NAS.

27 Pittock, *Scottish nationality*, p. 110.

28 MacCormick, *Flag in the wind*, pp. 96–7. The SNL was guilty of pro-fascism, in MacCormick's view.

29 Gras, *Révolte des régions*, p. 161.

30 Pittock, *Scottish nationality*, pp. 106, 107.

31 Marr, *Battle for Scotland*, p. 78.

32 Pittock, *Scottish nationality,* p. 107.

33 Zuelow, 'Scottish ethnic nationalism'.

34 Pittock, *Scottish nationality*, p. 107.

35 Marr, *Battle for Scotland,* p. 78.

36 Pittock, *Scottish nationality*, p. 110.

37 Marr, *Battle for Scotland*, p. 78.

38 In Ibid.

39 Met Special Branch, 27 July & 17 Oct.; *Smeddum*, 1:3, 12 Aug. 1933; DSSO poster, 19 Feb. 1934, HO 45/25472, NA.

40 Douglas, *Irish book*, pp. xvii–xviii, xxvi.

41 Card for SIM, 7 Nov.; Procurator-fiscal, Glasgow, 30 Oct. 1933; Met Special Branch, 8 Mar. 1934, HO 45/25472, NA.

42 *Evening Mail* cutting, 5 July 1944, G2/2781, IMA.

43 Met Special Branch, 21 Feb. 1934, HO 45/25472, NA.

44 SNG, 'Ronald MacDonald Douglas'.

45 Procurator-fiscal, Glasgow, 24 Nov.; Procurator-fiscal, Edinburgh, 8 Nov. 1933, HO 45/25472, NA.

46 SNG, 'Ronald MacDonald Douglas'.

47 Ibid.

48 'Obituary', *Carn,* 45 (1984), 3–4

49 SNG, 'Ronald MacDonald Douglas'.

50 Procurator-fiscal, Edinburgh, 24 Oct. 1933, HO 45/25472, NA

51 SNG, 'Wendy Wood'.

52 'Obituary', *Carn,* 45 (1984), 4

53 SNG, 'Ronald MacDonald Douglas'.

54 'Obituary', *Carn,* 45 (1984), 4

55 27 Nov. 1940; 11 Feb. 1941; 6 May & 13 Sept. 1944, G2/2781, IMA. G2 predicted Douglas would become even more of a 'nuisance' once these funds were exhausted.

56 In Ireland Douglas wrote *The closed door,* set in a Scottish insane asylum. It was published in 1941.

57 13 Sept. 1944, G2/2781, IMA.

58 Report Colm MacClean, 4 Jan. 1945, G2/4996, IMA.

59 'Colm MacGilleachan (Colm MacClean)', 25 May 1944. MacClean was unlikely to have been conscripted, anyway, as he was suffering from 'acute deafness' (Garda report, 5 June 1944, G2/4996, IMA).

60 14 June & 25 May 1944; 4 Jan. 1945, G2/4996, IMA.

61 13 Sept. 1944, G2/2781, IMA.

62 Smyllie, 'Unneutral neutral Éire', p. 320.

63 27 Nov. 1940, G2/2781, IMA.

64 9 Mar. 1949, DEA P168, NAI.

65 A 'Captain' Scott joined the Secret Branch of the SDF in 1933. Met Special Branch, 7 Nov. 1933, HO 45/25472, NA.

66 Hull, *Irish secrets*, p. 34.
67 Hull, 'Irish interlude', p. 710.
68 Duggan, *Herr Hempel*, p. 194.
69 Hull, *Irish secrets,* pp. 37, 29.
70 Telephone intercepts led to the arrest of Jan van Loon, a Dutchman in Royal Navy service who contacted the German legation (Hull, 'Irish interlude', pp. 710–11). The material presented here is otherwise the most detailed record known to the author of electronic surveillance upon Axis legations in Dublin.
71 Report Seamus Reader, 13 Sept. 1944, G2/2781, IMA.
72 Ellis, *Celtic dawn*, p. 82.
73 Ellis, 'John MacLean'.
74 6 May 1944, G2/2781, IMA.
75 'Na Fianna Éireann in Scotland', *Na Fianna Éireann*, http://www.fiannaeireann.com/pages/Scotland.htm; accessed 19 Aug. 2005; 'British intelligence notes on the arrest of Seamus Reader', *Na Fianna Éireann*, http://www.fiannaeireann.com/pages/SeamusReader.htm; accessed 19 Aug. 2005.
76 'Na Fianna Éireann in Scotland'.
77 See 6 May 1944, G2/2781, IMA; 'British intelligence notes'. Cf. Reader, who claimed he was arrested after the Rising and taken to Edinburgh as a 'prisoner of war': Milton, *John Maclean*, p. 129.
78 'Na Fianna Éireann in Scotland'.
79 'Ailin', 'Speech given by a representative of Republican Sinn Féin at the annual Glencoe Rally', *Republican Sinn Féin*, 18 Feb. 2003, http://www.indymedia.ie/newswire.php?story_id=29448; accessed 19 Aug. 2005.
80 Ellis, *Celtic dawn,* p. 82.
81 6 May 1944, G2/2781, IMA.
82 Milton, *John Maclean*, p. 129.
83 The SRA was a journalistic fabrication, according to Scott & Macleay, *Britain's secret war,* pp. 82, 83.
84 6 May 1944, G2/2781, IMA.
85 Molohan, *Germany and Ireland,* p. 12.
86 6 May 1944, G2/2781, IMA.
87 Secretary MacCormick 'assisted the Police in connection with enquiries regarding extreme Scottish nationalism': Glasgow CID, 24 May 1941, HH55/557, NAS.
88 26 Mar. 1943, HH55/557, NAS.
89 10 May 1941, HH55/558, NAS.
90 17 May 1941, HH55/557, NAS.
91 9 May 1941, HH55/558, NAS.
92 Finlay claims this formed following the SNP split in 1942, but NMAC pamphlets are in files from the 1941 raids: cf. Finlay, *Independent and free*, p. 224.
93 17 May 1941, 10 May 1941 & 6 May 1941, HH55/557, NAS.
94 12 May 1941, HH55/558, NAS.
95 28 May 1941, HH55/557, NAS.
96 'Scottish Nationalists', 12 May; Glasgow Police CID, 23 May 1941, HH55/558, NAS.
97 Glasgow Police CID, 23 May 1941, HH55/557, NAS.
98 Finlay, *Independent and free,* pp. 223–4.
99 Keogh, 'Eamon de Valera and Hitler', p. 72.
100 Carroll, *Ireland in the war years*, p. 69.
101 Hull, *Irish secrets,* pp. 86, 139. '[T]he Germans originally intended [...] a rising in Wales [...] but later abandoned this idea as impractical.' MI5, 'The Objectives in England [*sic*] of the German SS' (#1), 1 June 1942, KV 3/77, NA.
102 Duggan, *Neutral Ireland*, p. 166.
103 *Carn* claims he spent only six years in Ireland, and his 1967 return was from France; 'Obituary', 45 (1984), 4. SNG suggests he remained in Ireland from 1939 to 1967; *SNG*, 'Ronald MacDonald Douglas'.
104 'Ailin', 'Speech at Glencoe'.
105 O'Halpin, 'British intelligence ...', p. 119.
106 Justice Minister Gerald Boland reported only 530 foreigners entered the country between 1939 and 1945, excluding Britons. Dáil Éireann, Volume 101, 'Oral answers – Aliens entering Éire', 27 Jun. 1946, http://www.oireachtas-debates.gov.ie; accessed 10 Nov. 2006.
107 23 Dec. 1939, HO 45/25472, NA.
108 See Oswald Mosley in Chapter 3, and Chapter 8.
109 Farrell, *Sheltering,* pp. 29, 10, 48. See Chapter 7.
110 Ibid., p. 30. This was on the basis that NI did not exist in 1851.
111 Most were miners motivated by socialist solidarity. See Ellis, *Celtic dawn,* pp. 80–1.
112 Philip, *Welsh question*, p. 73.
113 See Owain Williams in Chapter 8.

CHAPTER 2
Two Bretons and a Basque

1 Mordrel, *Breiz Atao*, p. 243.
2 Hamon, *Nationalistes bretons*, p. 51.
3 Le Guennec, 'Roparz Hemon dans le Nazisme', p. 3.
4 MI5, PF600, 237 BIH To Dublin, 24 Nov. 1944, KV2/303, NA; Fant Rozec in Faligot, *Harpe*, p. 76.

5 Reece, *Bretons against France,* p. 81.
6 Caerléon, *Complots,* p. 82.
7 Reece, *Bretons against France,* p. 81.
8 Mordrel, *Breiz Atao,* p. 55.
9 In Reece, *Bretons against France,* p. 83.
10 In Mordrel, *Breiz Atao,* p. 41.
11 'Biography of Louis Napoleon Le Roux (1890–1944)', *Carn* 9 (May 1975), 21.
12 His descriptions of Ireland in 1914 lack veracity, Ó Ciosáin contends. 'La Bretagne', p. 32.
13 Faligot, *Harpe,* p. 54.
14 In Ibid., p. 76.
15 Ó Ciosáin, 'La Bretagne', p. 33.
16 *Irish Press* obituary, August 1944, KV2/303, NA.
17 Farrell, *Sheltering,* pp. 8–10.
18 Forde, *Extradition law in Ireland,* p. 60.
19 Caerléon, *Complots,* p. 94.
20 Obituary, KV2/303, NA.
21 PF600 to Dublin, KV2/303, NA; Ó Ciosáin, 'La Bretagne', p. 33.
22 Faligot, *Harpe,* p. 54.
23 'Biography of Le Roux', p. 21.
24 MI5, 24 Nov. 1944, KV2/303, NA; Ó Ciosáin, 'La Bretagne', p. 32.
25 MI5, 24 Nov. 1944; Obituary, KV2/303, NA.
26 Ó Ciosáin, 'La Bretagne', p. 32.
27 Faligot claims he was killed while writing a biography of Tom Clarke (*Harpe,* p. 54). *Tom Clarke and the Irish freedom movement* was in fact published in 1936.
28 Bryan to Minister, 11 Jan. 1945; Summary, G2/2146, IMA.
29 *Commissaire centrale de police,* Rennes, Report, members of Breiz Atao 7334, 28 Mar. 1928, F/7/13244, AN.
30 Statement Garda HQ, 5 Jan. 1945, G2/2146, IMA.
31 7334, 28 Mar. 1928, F/7/13244, AN.
32 1373/s 'Millardet (Léon Victor)', 31 Aug. 1936, F7 14686, AN.
33 1023, *Commissariat Special de Brest, 'Réunion privée autonomiste',* 19 June 1928; 911 *'Parti autonomiste breton; Rapport "secret"',* 1 June 1928, F/7/13244, AN.
34 *'Notice individuelle',* 7 Feb. 1928, F714686, AN.
35 Activities L.V. Mill-Arden, 19 Jan. 1945, G2/2146, IMA.
36 6805, *Commissariat spécial de Quimper,* 20 Aug. 1928, F/7/13244, AN.
37 Mordrel, *Breiz Atao,* p. 47.
38 See McDonald, *'We are not French!',* p. 73.
39 Frelaut, *Nationalistes bretons,* p. 11.
40 In Mordrel, *Breiz Atao,* p. 164.
41 Disillusionment with Ireland led her to write the novel *Ar follez yaouank* (The mad young woman), later produced as the film *La jeune folle.*
42 Déniel, *Mouvement breton,* p. 153.
43 Reece, *Bretons against France,* p. 113.
44 Faligot, *Harpe,* p. 82.
45 The *Bonnets Rouges* rebellion of 1675 and involvement in the Chouannerie of 1792–1815.
46 Bothorel, *Terroriste breton,* p. 75.
47 Louis Feutren, interview. Cf. Hamon, who claims that 'contrary to legend' it was Andrev Geffroy who planted the bomb. His source for this claim is not provided. *Bezen Perrot 1944,* p. 28.
48 Fouéré, *Connemara,* p. 49.
49 Report, 1 July 1942, G2/2146 SI/444, IMA.
50 Déniel, *Mouvement breton,* p. 150.
51 Hull, *Irish secrets,* p. 46.
52 Fouéré, *Connemara,* p. 49.
53 French police record Mill-Arden visiting Germany and Switzerland in 1934, as well as trips to Brittany (1373/s, 31 Aug. 1936, F714686, AN).
54 Bryan to Minister, 11 Jan. 1945, G2/2146, IMA.
55 Hull, *Irish secrets,* P.46.
56 Bryan to Minister, 11 Jan. 1945, G2/2146, IMA.
57 Aziz, *Livre noir,* p. 206. See Chapter 4.
58 Faligot, *Harpe,* p. 92.
59 Hull, *Irish secrets,* p. 86; O'Callaghan, *Jackboot in Ireland,* p. 35.
60 Report Sept. 1945, G2/2146, IMA.
61 Hull, *Irish secrets,* p. 62; Duggan, *Herr Hempel,* p. 63.
62 Stephan, *Spies in Ireland,* pp. 156–7.
63 Faligot, *Harpe,* p. 100.
64 Report 1 July 1942, G2/2146 SI/444, IMA.
65 'Mill-Arden, Leon V.'; Garda interview 18 Jan. 1945; Report Sept. 1945; Letters 7 Apr. 1940 & 15 May 1940, G2/2146, IMA.
66 Interview 'K', 2 Sept. 1942; Report 1 July 1942; G2 Southern Command, 28 Feb. 1944; Report G2, 15 Apr. 1943 S/41/160, G2/2146 SI/444, IMA.
67 Ó Ciosáin describes Millarden as a 'wholesale merchant of vegetables and potatoes' ('La Bretagne', p. 30). Fouéré acknowledges Millarden's past as a 'Breiz Atao militant' but does not explore whether he continued activities in Ireland (*Connemara,* p. 49).
68 See Hull, *Irish secrets,* p. 46.
69 English version, G2/2146, IMA.
70 Breton version, G2/2146, IMA.
71 English version, n.d., G2/2146, IMA.
72 Keogh, *Ireland and Europe,* p. 182.

73 N.d., G2/2146, IMA.
74 Fouéré, *Bretagne écartelée*, p. 45.
75 Moyse to Millarden, 17 Aug.(?) 1942, G2/2146, IMA.
76 Caerléon, *Complots*, p. 246.
77 Le Boterf, *La Bretagne sous Vichy*, p. 27. Göring confirmed at the Nuremberg Trials that a Breton state was a German war aim before 1940.
78 Ibid., p. 46.
79 N.d.; Bryan to Minister, 11 Jan. 1945; Report, Sept. 1945, G2/2146, IMA.
80 PF 600, 237/BIH to Dublin, 24 Nov. 1944, KV2/303, NA.
81 Activities L.V. Mill-Arden, 19 Jan. 1945, G2/2146, IMA.
82 Arzalier, *Les Perdants*, p. 83.
83 Bilbao fell to Franco on 19 June; the Basque army surrendered on 26 August: see Sullivan, *ETA*, p. 20.
84 Also Gallestegi, Gallestegui.
85 'Long live free Ireland!' *Aberri*, 17 Dec. 1921, in Gallastegi, *Libertad Vasca*, p. 14.
86 Iker Gallastegi, Letter, 2 May 2006.
87 Eli Gallastegi, *Libertad Vasca*, p. 9.
88 Sullivan, *ETA*, p. 3.
89 Iker Gallastegi, Letter, 2 May 2006.
90 Sullivan, *ETA*, p. 10. Carlism opposed King Fernando VII's dissolution of Salic Law, which allowed his daughter to take the throne ahead of a male heir, Don Carlos.
91 Iker Gallastegi, Letter, 2 May 2006.
92 Eli Gallastegi, *Libertad Vasca*, p. 11. Translations by Michael Leach.
93 *Aberri*, April 1923, in ibid., p. 203.
94 Ibid., p. 11.
95 Payne, *Basque nationalism*, p. 100.
96 Sullivan, *ETA*, p. 11.
97 Eli Gallastegi, *Libertad Vasca*, pp. 10, 12, 14.
98 Payne, *Basque nationalism*, p. 101.
99 Sullivan, *ETA*, p. 12. Cf. Iker Gallastegi, who claims the CNV was allowed to continue. (Letter, 2 May 2006.)
100 Iker Gallastegi, Letter, 2 May 2006.
101 Eli Gallastegi, *Libertad Vasca*, biography, n.p.
102 Iker Gallastegi, Letter, 2 May 2006.
103 Sullivan, *ETA*, pp. 5, 11–12.
104 Payne, *Basque nationalism*, p. 100.
105 Sullivan, *ETA*, pp. 14, 2, 13.
106 Eli Gallastegi, *Libertad Vasca*, pp. 186–7, 205.
107 Iker Gallastegi, Letter, 2 May 2006; 'Easter inspiration to Basque nationalists', *An Phoblacht*, 3 Apr. 1997, http:// republican-news.org/archive/1997/ April03/ 04basq.html; accessed 23 Sept. 2005.
108 Payne, *Basque nationalism*, p. 2.
109 Sullivan, *ETA*, p. 17.
110 Eli Gallastegi, *Libertad Vasca*, p. 187.
111 Payne, *Basque nationalism*, pp. 206, 221 fn.
112 Sullivan, *ETA*, p. 17.
113 Payne, *Basque nationalism*, p. 262.
114 In Keogh, *Ireland and Europe*, p. 66.
115 Manning, *Blueshirts*, p. 36.
116 Keogh, *Ireland and Europe*, p. 80.
117 Fine Gael formed from the merger of these groups and the Centre Party in September 1933.
118 '[O]ur Government […] do not want to recognise the National Government of Spain because they are sympathetic to the Red Government of Spain.' Patrick Belton TD, Dáil Éireann, 19 Feb. 1937, 'Spanish Civil War (Non-Intervention) Bill, 1937 – Second Stage (Resumed)' http://historical-debates.oireachtas.ie; accessed 19 May 2006.
119 Cooney, *Crozier and the Dáil*, p. 20.
120 *The Worker*, 23 Jan. 1937, in O'Riordan, 'Paper presented by Michael O'Riordan'.
121 'Easter Inspiration', *An Phoblacht*.
122 Dáil Éireann, 'Spanish Civil War (Non-Intervention) Bill'.
123 Iker Gallastegi, Letter, 2 May 2006.
124 External Affairs vetted applicants, but Justice could veto applications. Appeals to the Taoiseach were also possible. Fanning, *Racism*, p. 73.
125 Keogh, *Jews*, p. 116.
126 'Sounds of Basque and Irish tongues to mix at Kilberry', *Meath Chronicle*, 13 July 2002.
127 Iker Gallastegi, Letter, 2 May 2006.
128 'Sounds of Basque'; Iker Gallastegi, Letter, 2 May 2006.
129 Payne, *Basque nationalism*, p. 228.
130 Tabori, *Anatomy of exile*, p. 352.
131 Around 10,000 Spaniards of the *Maquis* were killed. Ibid., p. 204.
132 Kurlansky, *Basque history of the world*, pp. 220–3.
133 Sullivan, *ETA*, pp. 22, 31.
134 Iker Gallastegi, Letter, 2 May 2006. This was probably the Department of Justice, responsible for aliens under the 1935 Act. The Department was known as Home Affairs from 1919 to 1923.
135 Ibid.
136 Grahl-Madsen, *Territorial asylum*, p. 20.
137 Gallastegi, *Libertad Vasca*, biography, n.p.
138 Bridie Mill-Arden to Aiken, 29 Dec. 1944, G2/2146, IMA.

CHAPTER 3
Sovereignty, the Germans and the first postwar Breton arrivals

1 Fouéré, *Connemara*, p. 47.
2 Dublin had undertaken to notify London of arrivals from third countries. These were treated as entries to the UK, given the absence of border controls. MI5 however considered the Irish immigration service – with evident cause – 'not very efficient': O'Halpin (ed.), *MI5 and Ireland*, p. 35.
3 Caerléon, *Rêve fou*, p. 116.
4 'Martolod' escaped from Paris by squeezing through the barred windows of a police station, scaling the wall of Montparnasse cemetery and disappearing into the Métro. Ibid., p. 115.
5 Faligot, *Harpe*, p. 110.
6 In Molohan, *Germany and Ireland*, p. 47.
7 Bryan to Nunan, 'German-Irish Society', G2/c/540, 19 Dec. 1951, DEA P168, NAI.
8 Breton nationalists were 'granted asylum in Ireland' (Doody, 'Brittany from the Great War'), or 'chose exile in Ireland' (Hamon, *Bezen Perrot 1944*, p. 166).
9 Lebesque, *Comment peut-on être breton?*, p. 165.
10 A 'Swedish historian' in Fisk, *In time of war*, p. 475.
11 See Appendix.
12 Keogh, 'Eamon de Valera and Hitler', pp. 72, 76, 84.
13 Davis, *Dublin's American policy*, p. 13.
14 O'Halpin, 'Irish neutrality', p. 291.
15 Davis, *Dublin's American policy*, pp. 17–18, 13, 27, 19, 21.
16 In Salmon, *Unneutral Ireland*, p. 191.
17 The ministry was Foreign Affairs from 1919 to 1922; External Affairs from 1922 to 1971; and Foreign Affairs from 1971.
18 In Keogh, 'Profile of Joseph Walshe', p. 79.
19 Dwyer, *Irish neutrality*, p. 183.
20 Ibid., p. 179. Churchill found the Note 'entirely satisfactory', Letter PM to DO, A550, W2017/2017/G 7, Feb. 1944, FO 371/42679, NA.
21 Davis, *Dublin's American policy*, p. 22.
22 Lee, *Ireland 1912–1985*, p. 251.
23 Dwyer, *Irish neutrality*, p. 180.
24 O'Halpin, 'Irish neutrality', p. 295.
25 Dwyer, 'More than 60 years on'.
26 Dwyer, *Irish neutrality*, p. 193.
27 Davis, *Dublin's American policy*, p. 23.
28 Molohan, *Germany and Ireland*, p. 21.
29 'This is an ultimatum. This is an outrage,' de Valera responded. Éire Rep. to DO No.26, W3154/2017/G68, 22 Feb. 1944, FO 371/42679, NA.
30 Dwyer, *Irish neutrality*, p. 280.
31 Irish statement on war criminals, DFA P78, NAI.
32 Cable Nunan, Washington, 17 Nov. 1944, DFA P78, NAI.
33 Hansard, 'Eire (War Criminals, Right of Asylum)', 16 Jan. 1945, 116–26, excerpt in FO 898/357, NA.
34 Gray enquired if two particular Nazis had found sanctuary in Éire. Walshe was satisfied the claims were fanciful. 22 Feb. 1945, DFA P78, NAI.
35 Keogh, *Ireland and Europe*, p. 203
36 Hansard 15 May 1945 in DFA P78, NAI. Joyce was born in the USA, but claimed he was from Galway.
37 Meeting 25 Jan. 1945, FO 898/357, NA.
38 In Lee, *Ireland 1912–1985*, p. 263.
39 Dwyer, *De Valera*, pp. 288–9.
40 Dwyer, *Irish neutrality*, p. 143.
41 De Valera, *Memoir*, p. 227.
42 Davis, *Dublin's American policy*, p. 26.
43 Carroll, *Ireland in the war years*, p. 175.
44 Keogh, 'Eamon de Valera and Hitler', p. 73.
45 Speech, Commons, 13 May 1945, in Keogh, *Ireland and Europe*, p. 199.
46 Keogh, 'Eamon de Valera and Hitler', pp. 80, 77.
47 Salmon, *Unneutral Ireland*, p. 127.
48 De Valera believed Ireland would 'value material wealth only as a basis of right living'. In Lee, *Ireland 1912–1985*, p. 334.
49 UK representative Éire to Minister DEA, 30 July 1947, HO 213/2140, NA.
50 Salmon, *Unneutral Ireland*, p. 189.
51 Davis, *Dublin's American policy*, p. 26.
52 Molohan, *Germany and Ireland*, pp. 21, 23, 24.
53 Davis, *Dublin's American policy*, p. 33.
54 *Reynolds News*, 31 Mar. 1946, in DEA A74, NAI.
55 Aliens Dept., 3 July 1947, HO 213/2140, NA.
56 Molohan, *Germany and Ireland*, p. 25.
57 Ibid., pp. 20, 25.
58 'We know that the present US Minister still feels strongly on the question …' Memorandum, 30 July 1947, HO 213/2140, NA.
59 Dwyer, *De Valera*, p. 296.
60 Molohan, *Germany and Ireland*, p. 29.
61 Duggan, *Neutral Ireland*, p. 245.
62 Hull, *Irish secrets*, pp. 253, 27.

63 Molohan, *Germany and Ireland,* p. 31.
64 Hull, *Irish secrets,* p. 250.
65 Fisk, *Time of war,* p. 468.
66 Control Office to Berlin, G/255/2, 15 Apr. 1947, HO 213/2140, NA.
67 Molohan, *Germany and Ireland,* pp. 32, 45–6.
68 Duggan, *Neutral Ireland,* p. 248.
69 Hull, *Irish secrets,* p. 258.
70 *Irish Press,* 30 July 1947, HO 213/2140, NA.
71 Molohan, *Germany and Ireland,* p. 17.
72 Also, 'measures will be taken to prevent them leaving Eire clandestinely'. Commonwealth Relations Office, HO 213/2140 2, 6 Jan. 1948, HO 213/2140, NA.
73 Cremin, Sect. DEA to Berry, Sect. Justice, 11 Oct. 1961, DEA A74, NAI.
74 Molohan, *Germany and Ireland,* pp. 13–14.
75 See cuttings related to neutral attitudes to resident Germans in DEA A74 & DFA P78, NAI.
76 Dwyer, *De Valera,* p. 288.
77 Molohan, *Germany and Ireland,* p. 16.
78 Memorandum, HO 213/2140, NA.
79 Dwyer, *De Valera,* p. 288.
80 Dáil Éireann, Volume 101, 'Oral answers – Right of Asylum, 25 June 1946', http://www.oireachtas-debates.gov.ie; accessed 12 Sept. 2005.
81 Molohan, *Germany and Ireland,* p. 44.
82 Aliens Dept, 3 July 1947, HO 213/2140, NA.
83 Dominions Office, P2860/80, 2 June 1947, HO 213/2140, NA.
84 Visa application 10 Oct. 1945, DFA P253, NAI.
85 'Dr Otto Strasser', Briefing paper, DFA P253, NAI.
86 Dorril, *Blackshirt,* p. 562.
87 Memorandum 8 July 1946, DFA P253, NAI.
88 Keogh, *Jews,* p. 200.
89 Mosley would 'always be regarded by every good Irishman with appreciation and gratitude': T.P. O'Connor in Ibid., p. 61.
90 Memorandum 8 July 1946, DFA P253, NAI.
91 Dorril, *Blackshirt,* p. 553.
92 Jurado, *Foreign volunteers,* p. 5.
93 In Time-Life Editors (ed.), *Heel of the conqueror,* p. 22.
94 See Chapter 6.
95 Conway, *Collaboration in Belgium,* p. 280.
96 Boland to Duff, 3 Sept. 1946, DFA P253, NAI.
97 Roche to Boland, 11 Sept. 1946, DFA P253, NAI.
98 Boland to Roche, n.d., DFA P253, NAI.
99 Conway, *Collaboration in Belgium,* p. 281.
100 Costigan to Boland, 22 Jan. 1948; Dergent's statement, 10 Nov. 1947, DFA P253, NAI.
101 In 1955 a Belgian reporter learned Degrelle had never been to Ireland. Degrelle's Spanish supporters claimed he entered Ireland by yacht: Report Irish Legation Brussels, 14 Feb. 1955, DFA P253, NAI.
102 Fouéré, *Connemara,* p. 48.
103 'No. 395/1946: Aliens Order, 1946', *Irish statute book,* http://www.irishstatutebook.ie/ZZSI395Y1946.html; accessed 16 Nov. 2006.
104 See Fanning, *Racism,* p. 76; Keogh, *Jews,* p. 203.
105 Fanning, *Racism,* p. 76.
106 'Aliens Order, 1946'; Ministerial discretion was ruled unconstitutional in 1999.
107 Fouéré, *Connemara,* pp. 50–1.
108 Mordrel, *Breiz Atao,* p. 321.
109 Hamon, *Nationalistes bretons,* p. 172.
110 'Report on GOURLET, Joseph Jean', No. 874, 10 May 1945, KV2/303, NA; Caerléon, *Rêve fou,* p. 112.
111 This offence still forms article 88 of the French penal code. Brekilien, *Histoire de la Bretagne,* p. 330.
112 Mordrel, *Breiz Atao,* p. 424. Le Ruyet infiltrated and betrayed Resistance networks. Cadiou, *L'Hermine,* p. 201.
113 Fouéré, *Connemara,* pp. 50–1.
114 'Brother country of Brittany.' Gourlet in Ibid., p. 47.
115 Letter Defence to Mill-Arden, 15 Oct. 1945, G2/2146, IMA.
116 Gray replied, saying he respected 'old local cultures' but didn't support the 'breaking up of existing political units' in this 'over-diversified world'. Letter, 14 June 1944, G2/2146, IMA.
117 Fouéré, *Connemara,* pp. 49, 18, 50, 112.
118 Per Denez, letter, 29 April 2004.
119 Also Oscar Mac Uileas, Oscar Willis, Oscar McCarthy Willis.
120 Faligot, *Harpe,* p. 75.
121 'M. Mac Cartha Mileas [*sic*]', PA-3574/5, 18 Mar. 1939, 'Les Services de la Propagande Allemande et le Mouvement Autonomiste Breton', F7 14685, AN.
122 Hennessy, *Short biography Oscar Mac Uilis.*
123 Fouéré, *Connemara,* pp. 51, 91.
124 Molohan, *Germany and Ireland,* p. 30.

125 Transcribed letter, 10 Nov. 1948, Taoiseach S 6022 B/95, NAI.
126 See Taoiseach S 6022 B/95; DFA 96/3/98 & DFA 2000/14/176, among others.
127 See Chapter 4.
128 See Philip, *Welsh question*, p. 69; Williams, 'Welsh history'.
129 De Valera sent a recording van to Man in April 1948: Y Crearie, 'Recording Native Manx Speech', p. 315.
130 Ellis, *Celtic dawn*, pp. 88, 93.
131 This pressure forced the Interparty government into declaring the Republic, argues McCabe, *Diplomatic history of Ireland*, p. 31.
132 Mair Piette (née Phillips), interview. Piette was present at Dev's Cardiff address.
133 Ellis, *Celtic dawn*, p. 94.
134 Skelly, *Irish diplomacy*, p. 22.

CHAPTER 4
Real pan-Celticism

1 Fouéré, *Connemara*, p. 74.
2 Ibid., pp. 74, 75, 191. Fouéré occasionally spells it 'Moger' (pp. 13, 54).
3 Meeting with Roché French embassy, 29 Oct. 1947, FO371/67702, NA.
4 Sainclivier, *Bretagne de 1939*, p. 52.
5 Le Boterf, *Bretagne sous Vichy*, p. 46.
6 Sainclivier, *Bretagne de 1939*, p. 53; Le Boterf, *Bretagne sous Vichy*, pp. 160, 163, 159.
7 Nicolas, *Séparatisme en Bretagne*, p. 28.
8 Sainclivier, *Bretagne de 1939*, p. 54.
9 Le Boterf, *Bretagne sous Vichy*, pp. 81, 105.
10 Loire-Atlantique from 1957.
11 Côtes-d'Armor from 1990.
12 Le Boterf, *Bretagne sous Vichy*, p. 97.
13 *Naoned e Breizh* (Nantes in Brittany) is a nationalist slogan.
14 Raymond Delaporte in *L'Heure bretonne*, April 1943, in le Boterf, *Bretagne sous Vichy*, p. 219.
15 Fouéré, 'La politique du Comité Consultatif de Bretagne', p. 287.
16 In Le Boterf, *Bretagne sous Vichy*, p. 82.
17 Fouéré, *Écartelée*, p. 83.
18 See Chapter Five.
19 Fouéré, *Écartelée*, p. 110.
20 Doublet, *Collaboration*, p. 10.
21 The *Cour de Cassation* (France's highest court) ruled after Liberation that the Armistice of 1940 was only 'provisory' and a state of war persisted. Ibid., p. 12.
22 Minutes, 29 Oct. 1947, FO371/67702, NA.
23 Fouéré, *Écartelée*, p. 120.
24 Baudot, *Libération de la Bretagne*, p. 204.
25 Doody, 'Brittany from the Great War'.
26 Fouéré, *Écartelée*, p. 121.
27 Baudot (*Libération*, p. 207) contrasts sentences of national degradation (3,165 for Brittany) with Alsace (6,953) and Paris (8,245). He does not contrast more severe sentences.
28 Cadiou, *L'Hermine*, p. 233.
29 Capdevila, *Les Bretons*, p. 32.
30 Mordrel, *Breiz Atao*, pp. 535–7. Cf. Cadiou, *L'Hermine*, p. 234.
31 Hamon, *Nationalistes bretons*, p. 229.
32 Novick, *Resistance versus Vichy*, pp. 218–19.
33 Doublet, *Collaboration*, p. 59.
34 Not including Andrev Geffroy 'Le Grand Geff', whose death sentence was commuted. Mordrel, *Breiz Atao*, p. 535–7. Cf. Cadiou, *L'Hermine*, p. 234.
35 Fouéré, *Écartelée*, pp. 125, 129.
36 Per Denez, interview.
37 Aziz, *Livre Noir*, p. 201; 90a full report, Oct. 1944, KV2/303 NA; Pierre Hervé, Communist deputy Finistère 1945, in Cadiou, *L'Hermine*, p. 193.
38 Hamon, *Nationalistes bretons*, p. 114.
39 Mordrel, *Breiz Atao*, p. 243.
40 Fouéré, *Connemara*, p. 42.
41 Taldir edited *An Oaled* (The Foyer), and wrote of the 'new Europe' being created by 'two great soldiers: Pétain and Hitler': Caerléon, *Rêve fou*, p. 88.
42 Alan Heusaff, '1916: Ripples in the Celtic tide – Breizh', *Carn*, 76 (Winter 1991–2), 9–10: p. 9.
43 Avril, *500 Bretons*, pp. 107–8.
44 Ó Ciosáin, 'Bretagne et l'Irlande', p. 31.
45 Fouéré, *Écartelée*, p. 126.
46 Reece, *Bretons against France*, p. 171.
47 Fouéré, *Écartelée*, p. 126.
48 'Visit of Welsh delegation to Brittany', 24 Apr. 1947, FO 371/67702, NA.
49 Mordrel, *Breiz Atao*, p. 417.
50 Koreman, *Expectation of justice*, p. 97.
51 Fouéré, *Écartelée*, p. 122.
52 Doublet, *Collaboration*, p. 30.
53 Fouéré, *Connemara*, pp. 12–15.
54 Mordrel, *Breiz Atao*, p. 77.
55 In Davies, *Welsh nationalist party*, p. 38.
56 Fouéré, *Connemara*, pp. 18, 32.
57 Evans and Rhys, 'Wales', p. 257.
58 See Chapter One, and Arthur Owens, Welsh nationalist and Abwehr spy ('Johnny') who double-crossed for MI5 ('Snow'): Time-Life Editors, *Shadow war*, pp. 74–5.
59 Evans, 'History of Plaid Cymru', p. 205.

60 Ellis, *Wales*, p. 107.
61 McDonald, 'We are not French!', p. 113.
62 See 'Notes on the text'.
63 In Fouéré, *Écartelée*, p. 134.
64 Mordrel, *Breiz Atao*, p. 118.
65 Per Denez, interview; Broudic, *L'interdiction du breton*, p. 9. Three-quarters of the population of Lower Brittany communicated only in Breton in 1902 (p. 166).
66 In McDonald, 'We are not French!', p. 127.
67 Fouéré, *Écartelée*, pp. 134–5.
68 Obituary, *Carn*, 23 (Autumn 1978), 8. This claims Hemon was jailed in 1945 for presiding over the Celtic Institute. Hemon's detention was actually before trial.
69 Fouéré, *Écartelée*, p. 135.
70 McDonald, 'We are not French!', p. 124. Cf. Fouéré, who claims there was no sentence, but Hemon was unable to find work because he had been charged (*Écartelée*, p. 135). Cadiou wonders why the sentence was so 'lenient' (*L'Hermine*, pp. 229–30).
71 Fouéré, *Écartelée*, p. 135.
72 Fouéré maintains no other class of 'collaborator' was so treated (Ibid., p. 137).
73 Davies, *Welsh nationalist party*, p. 108; Fouéré, *Connemara*, p. 16.
74 Calin, *Minority literatures*, p. 104.
75 Evans, 'History of Plaid Cymru', p. 221.
76 Fouéré, *Connemara*, p. 22.
77 *Breton National News Service* (*BNNS*), 6 (May 1947).
78 *BNNS*, 12 (Jan. 1948).
79 Fouéré, *Connemara*, p. 35.
80 Piette, interview; letter, 8 March 2006.
81 Fouéré, *Connemara*, p. 42.
82 Piette and Gwennig Helloco, interviews, 26 June 2005.
83 Fouéré, *Connemara*, p. 53; Helloco, interview.
84 Alternatively *Le Helloco, An Helloko*.
85 Fouéré, *Connemara*, p. 42.
86 Henaff (Lainé), *Biographie – Memoires*, p. 60.
87 Mordrel, *Breiz Atao*, p. 229; Leach, *Bezen Perrot*, p. 9.
88 Fouéré, *Connemara*, p. 53.
89 'Breton Nationalists were instructed […] to desert to the German lines at the first opportunity': Feutren, tract for *Observer*.
90 Hamon, *Nationalistes bretons*, pp. 40–1.
91 Mordrel, *Breiz Atao*, pp. 266, 269.
92 Ibid., p. 266. See Chapter Seven.
93 Mordrel, *Breiz Atao*, pp. 266, 271.
94 Cadiou, *L'Hermine*, p. 13.
95 Hamon, *Nationalistes bretons*, pp. 40–1.
96 Mordrel, *Breiz Atao*, p. 275.
97 In Le Boterf, *Bretagne sous Vichy*, p. 131.
98 Fouéré, *Écartelée*, p. 45.
99 Aron, *Vichy regime*, pp. 72–3.
100 Brekilien, *Histoire de la Bretagne*, p. 335.
101 Hamon, *Nationalistes bretons*, pp. 51–2.
102 Wagner in Fréville, *Archives secrètes de Bretagne*, p. 40.
103 Frelaut, *Nationalistes bretons de 1939 à 1945*, p. 25.
104 In Le Boterf, *Bretagne sous Vichy*, p. 33.
105 Ousby, *Occupation*, p. 104.
106 Mordrel, *Breiz Atao*, p. 323.
107 Fouéré, *Connemara*, p. 53.
108 Mordrel, *Breiz Atao*, p. 295. See Chapter 5.
109 Ibid., p. 322.
110 Hamon, *Nationalistes bretons*, p. 149.
111 Fouéré, *Connemara*, p. 54.
112 Mordrel, *Breiz Atao*, p. 416.
113 Fouéré, *Connemara*, p. 53, 42–3.
114 *BNNS*, 2 (Jan.) & 10 (Nov. 1947).
115 *BNNS*, 9 (Sept.) & 7 & 8 (July 1947).
116 Council of the Welsh National Eisteddfod (CWNE), *Visite*, p. 21.
117 Fañch Gourvil, in '*Autonomisme breton*', Apr. 1946–Sep. 1953, Carton 39, '*Edimbourg: Consulat Général*', CADN.
118 CWNE, *Visite*, p. 21.
119 Gosling, Consulate Nantes, 'Visit of Welsh delegation to Brittany', 24 Apr. 1947, FO 371/67702, NA.
120 CWNE, *Visite*, pp. 25–7.
121 In Fouéré, *Connemara*, p. 66.
122 CWNE, *Visite*, pp. 37–8.
123 Fouéré, *Connemara*, p. 65.
124 CWNE, *Visite*, p. 26.
125 Cadiou, *L'Hermine*, p. 229 note.
126 Gosling, 24 Apr. 1947, FO 371/67702, NA.
127 Fouéré, *Connemara*, pp. 86, 87.
128 Wilson FO to Burrows Embassy Paris, 21 May 1947, FO 371/67702, NA.
129 Handwritten notation, FO 371/67702, NA.
130 Crosthwaite, minutes, 27 Oct. 1947, FO 371/67702, NA.
131 Fouéré, *Connemara.*, pp. 84, 77, 45, 70.
132 Crosthwaite, 27 Oct. 1947, FO 371/67702, NA.
133 Wilson minutes, 31 Oct. 1947, FO 371/67702, NA.
134 Handwritten note, n.d., FO 371/67702, NA.
135 Crosthwaite, 27 Oct. 1947, FO 371/67702, NA.

136 'Breton patriots sentenced for trying to fly to Ireland', *BNNS*, 7 & 8 (July 1947).
137 Richards Embassy Paris to Wilson FO, 16 June 1947, FO 371/67702, NA.
138 Circular intercepted Ille-et-Vilaine, January 1946, in '*Mouvement séparatiste breton en liaison avec le mouvement nationaliste gallois*', 23 Feb. 1946, 'Autonomisme breton', Carton 39, CADN.
139 Minutes, 17 Apr. 1947, FO 371/67702, NA.
140 Fouéré, *Connemara*, pp. 87, 88.
141 Hogg FO, note, 31 Oct. 1947, FO 371/67702, NA.
142 Fouéré, *Connemara*, pp. 88, 94.
143 Ibid., pp. 89–109.
144 Helloco, interview.
145 Caerléon, *Complots*, p. 360.
146 Fouéré, *Connemara*, p. 92.
147 Ibid., pp. 52, 116.

CHAPTER 5
Bezen Perrot

1 Feutren, interview.
2 Feutren, letter, 26 March 2006. The surname was his maternal grandmother's.
3 Feutren, interview.
4 'Radio Éireann during the Emergency: 1939–45', RTÉ Libraries and Archives, http://www.rte.ie/laweb/brc/brc_1940s.html; accessed 29 Nov. 2006.
5 Feutren, interview.
6 Lainé in Fouéré, *Écartelée*, p. 114.
7 Hull repeats the erroneous claim that the Bezen Perrot 'took part in the fighting around Hanover' in 1945. *Irish secrets*, p. 307 note.
8 'Breton armed detachment of the SS "Bezen Perrot"'.
9 In Hamon, *Bezen Perrot 1944*, p. 169.
10 In Fouéré, *Écartelée*, p. 114.
11 A Breton company of the British Loyal Emigrant Regiment supported the Chouans from 1795 to 1799: Chartrand, *Émigré & foreign troops (I)*, p. 45. Gilles Foix 'Eskob' reasoned that if Georges Cadoudal's men donned British uniform in 1795, he was justified in donning German uniform in 1944: Caerléon, *Rêve fou*, p. 139.
12 Henaff (Lainé), *Biographie – Memoires*, p. 32.
13 Lainé disavowed any relationship with an earlier group called Kentoc'h Mervel (Sooner Death). Ibid., p. 64; Leach, *Bezen Perrot*, pp. 4–5.
14 Hamon, *Nationalistes bretons*, p. 26.
15 Mordrel, *Breiz Atao*, p. 205.
16 Henaff, *Biographie*, p. 13.
17 Feutren, interview.
18 Brekilien, *Histoire de la Bretagne*, p. 338.
19 Cadiou, *L'Hermine*, p. 209.
20 McDonald, '*We are not French!*', p. 134.
21 Mordrel, *Breiz Atao*, pp. 367, 370.
22 Fouéré, *Écartelée*, p. 105.
23 Feutren, interview.
24 Ibid.
25 Mordrel, *Breiz Atao*, p. 378.
26 Feutren, interview.
27 Mordrel, *Breiz Atao*, p. 370.
28 'Eskob' in Caerléon, *Rêve fou*, p. 137.
29 Fouéré, *Écartelée*, p. 107.
30 Mordrel, *Breiz Atao*, p. 385.
31 See Hamon, *Bezen Perrot*, p. 6.
32 Feutren, letter, 7 Feb. 2006; Hamon, *Bezen Perrot*, p. 55.
33 Feutren, letter, 3 Jan. 2006.
34 Hamon, *Bezen Perrot*, pp. 8, 101, 102.
35 Alan Heusaff's memoirs in Hamon, *Bezen Perrot*, p. 128.
36 Hamon, *Bezen Perrot.*, pp. 131, 134, 137.
37 Mordrel, *Breiz Atao*, p. 373.
38 'Eskob' in Caerléon, *Rêve fou*, p. 172.
39 Alternatively Guiomarc'h, Guiomard, Guyomard.
40 Hamon, *Bezen Perrot*, p. 155.
41 'Eskob' in Caerléon, *Rêve fou*, p. 151.
42 Feutren, interview.
43 Hamon, *Bezen Perrot*, p. 64.
44 'Eskob' in Caerléon, *Rêve fou*, pp. 227, 157, 181, 228.
45 Ibid., pp. 100, 171.
46 Biddiscombe, 'Last White Terror', pp. 835, 813.
47 Capdevila, *Les Bretons*, P.108; 'Eskob' in Caerléon, *Rêve fou*, p. 173 fn.
48 Biddiscombe, 'Last White Terror', pp. 815–17.
49 'Eskob' in Caerléon, *Rêve fou*, p. 164.
50 Armelle Goulet-Conway, interview.
51 'Eskob' in Caerléon, *Rêve fou*, p. 177.
52 Feutren, interview.
53 Mordrel, *Breiz Atao*, pp. 399–400.
54 Hamon, *Bezen Perrot*, p. 159.
55 Mordrel, *Breiz Atao*, p. 400. 'Eskob' nevertheless retained respect for 'Le Grand Druide' Lainé. Caerléon, *Rêve fou*, pp. 227–8.
56 Hamon, *Nationalistes bretons*, pp. 36–7.
57 Feutren, interview.
58 Péresse in Mordrel, *Breiz Atao*, p. 400.
59 Ibid.
60 Hamon, *Bezen Perrot*, p. 161.
61 Feutren, interview.
62 CX 12799/1278, KV2/303, NA.

63 Feutren, interview.
64 Hamon, *Bezen Perrot,* pp. 45, 69.
65 Feutren, interview.
66 Hamon, *Bezen Perrot,* p. 70.
67 Feutren, interview.
68 Fouéré, *Connemara,* p. 121.
69 Feutren, interview.
70 Feutren, letter, 26 Mar. 2006.
71 Davies, *Welsh nationalist party*, p. 253 note.
72 Feutren, letter, 26 Mar. 2006.
73 Feutren, interview.
74 Ibid. 'Teil' was similarly threatened by Lainé in July 1945 for endangering *gour* in Germany: Caerléon, *Rêve fou,* p. 161.
75 Feutren, interview.
76 Mordrel, *Breiz Atao,* p. 416.
77 Feutren, letter, 2 Oct. 2005.
78 In Fouéré, *Écartelée,* p. 124.
79 Feutren, letter, 2 Oct. 2005; Fouéré, *Connemara,* p. 52.
80 Philip, *Welsh question,* p. 73.
81 Feutren, letter, 2 Oct. 2005.
82 Feutren, interview.
83 L'Haridon lived clandestinely until 1949, when he decamped for Dublin: Fouéré, *Connemara,* p. 116.
84 Feutren, letter, 2 Oct. 2005.
85 Lainé 'chose to be known by his Breton name when he came to Ireland': Feutren, letter, 7 Feb. 2006.
86 (Name withheld), e-mail, 13 Feb. 2007. Guieysse was crucial to the escape network of the Bezen, but did not go to Ireland.
87 Feutren, letter, 7 Feb. 2006.
88 (Name withheld), interview.
89 (Name withheld), e-mail, 13 Feb. 2007; Feutren, letter, 2 Oct. 2005.
90 (Name withheld), interview; Fouéré, *Connemara,* pp. 123, 90, 89; Feutren, letters, 2 Oct. 2005 & 3 Jan. 2006, and interview.
91 Goulet-Conway, interview.
92 Caerléon, *Révolution bretonne,* pp. 268–9.
93 The group actually had more than fifty members.
94 Mordrel, *Breiz Atao,* p. 270.
95 Goulet-Conway, interview.
96 '*Section Parisienne 1939–40. Autonomistes bretons, perquisitions*', F7 14686, AN.
97 Goulet-Conway, interview.
98 See Chapter Four.
99 Paul Gaignet created the organisation, Goulet claimed. Caerléon, *Rêve fou,* p. 76.
100 Feutren, interview.
101 Goulet, 'Une organisation de boy-scouts?', p. 290.
102 Goulet-Conway, interview.
103 Fouéré, *Connemara,* p. 98.
104 Goulet-Conway, interview.
105 Fouéré, *Connemara,* p. 92.
106 Feutren, interview.
107 Hamon, *Bezen Perrot,* p. 163.
108 Capdevila, *Les Bretons,* p. 374 fn. The Archives départementales d'Ille-et-Vilaine (ADIV) reports that the cited source of this information – 213W, dossier MJ – 'does not correspond [...] to any reality': Fabienne Houze, ADIV, e-mail, 27 Sept. 2007.
109 Caerléon, *Rêve fou,* pp. 184–9; Mordrel, *Breiz Atao,* p. 400.
110 Fouéré, *Connemara,* p. 57.
111 O'Halpin, '"According to the Irish minister ..."',p.95.
112 (Name withheld), interview.
113 Rigoulot, *Enfants de l'Épuration,* pp. 414–23.
114 Caerléon, *Rêve fou,* p. 112.
115 Fouéré, *Connemara,* pp. 46–7, 58; Caerléon, *Rêve fou,* p. 208.
116 Both Fouéré (*Connemara,* p. 60) and Feutren (Letter, 7 Feb. 2006) confirm Ronan Guyomarc'h settled in Spain. Feutren adds he 'never came to Ireland'. Cf. Faligot, who claims he settled at Cork. (*Harpe,* p. 108).
117 Mordrel, *Breiz Atao,* pp. 413–14.
118 Yann Fouéré, interview.
119 Caerléon, *Complots,* p. 359.
120 Hamon, *Bezen Perrot,* p. 163.
121 Fouéré, *Connemara,* pp. 124–5.
122 'Eskob' in Caerléon, *Rêve fou,* pp. 201–17.
123 Feutren, letter, 3 Jan. 2006; Fouéré, *Connemara,* p. 121.
124 Alan Heusaff, Ange Péresse obituary, *Carn,* 47–8 (Autumn-Winter 1984–5), 34.
125 Faligot, *Harpe,* p. 106.
126 'Keraudren' in Caerléon, *Complots,* pp. 340–2. He was sentenced to life in prison.
127 Fouéré, *Connemara,* p. 119. 'Nenesse' worked for the OT during the war. Among the more nonsensical claims regarding him is that he invented potato chips in packets: Faligot, *Harpe,* p. 110.
128 He preferred this form as closest to the Breton original. Other family members prefer Heussaff. (Kintilla Heussaff, interview.)
129 Broderick, 'Breton Movement', p. 1.
130 Mordrel, *Breiz Atao,* p. 223.
131 See the *symbole* used to stigmatise Breton-speaking children in McDonald, 'We are not French!', p. 76.

132 Heusaff in Broderick, 'Breton Movement', p. 4.
133 Bríd Heusaff, interview; Hamon, *Bezen Perrot,* pp. 59–60.
134 Broderick, 'Breton Movement', pp. 8, 9.
135 Hamon, *Bezen Perrot,* p. 155.
136 Broderick, 'Breton Movement', p. 9.
137 Jurado, *Foreign Volunteers*, p. 6.
138 Broderick, 'Breton Movement', p. 10.
139 Neven Henaff, review of *Fransez Debauvais et les siens* by Anna Youennou, *Carn,* (19) Autumn 1977, pp. 8–9; p. 9.
140 Bríd Heussaff, interview.
141 Hamon, *Bezen Perrot,* pp. 125–9; Bríd Heusaff, interview.
142 Caerléon, *Rêve fou,* p. 174.
143 'Targaz' was captured by the Soviets and surrendered to the French. He was judged alongside Léon Jasson 'Gouez' and received life in prison. Mordrel, *Breiz Atao*, p. 423.
144 Heusaff in Broderick, 'Breton Movement', p. 15.
145 Anna Heussaff, interview.
146 In Broderick, 'Breton Movement', p. 15.
147 (Name withheld), interview; Avril, *500 Bretons,* p. 11. 'Fañch' was Bourc'hiz's alternative *nom de guerre.*
148 Fouéré, *Connemara,* p. 125.
149 Feutren, interview.
150 Bríd Heussaff, interview.
151 'Eskob' in Caerléon, *Rêve fou,* p. 224.
152 Brian Stowell in Broderick, 'Breton Movement', p. 9.
153 Bríd Heussaff, interview.
154 Feutren, interview.
155 Garda to Bryan, 21 Aug. 1950, G2/2146, IMA.
156 (Name withheld), interview.
157 Feutren, interview.
158 Bríd Heussaff, interview.
159 Anna Heussaff, interview.
160 Keogh, 'Ireland, the Vatican ...', p. 72.
161 Ibid., p. 70.
162 Ellis, *Celtic Dawn*, p. 94.
163 Feutren, interview.
164 Feutren, letter, 26 Mar. 2006.
165 Feutren, interview.
166 'Yann Renard-Goulet', *Saoirse – Irish Freedom*, 149, 9 October 1999, http://homepage.tinet.ie/~eirenua/sep99/saoirse4.htm#2>; accessed 2 July 2003.
167 Fouéré, *Connemara*, p. 91.
168 These agents so infiltrated the Celtic Union that it became practically moribund by 1950: Ellis, *Celtic dawn*, p. 97.
169 Rugby, W1582/36/36 'Interview with the Irish Minister for Foreign Affairs', 23 Feb. 1948, FO 371/70175, NA.
170 Feutren, interview.
171 Bríd Heusaff, interview.
172 Ibid., 'Seanad Éireann – Volume 24 – 22 May, 1940; Institute for Advanced Studies Bill, 1939 – Recommittal', http://historical-debates.oireachtas.ie; accessed 31 Dec. 2006.
173 Anna Heussaff, e-mail, 4 Sept. 2007.
174 Caerléon, *Complots,* pp. 291–3.
175 Cutting 13 Sept. 1952, DFA P237, NAI.
176 WF 1653/2, 24 Nov. 1951, FO 371/96086, NA.
177 Nutting WF 1653/5; Alison WF 1653/3, FO 371/96086, NA; Mordrel, *Breiz Atao,* p. 426.
178 Review of *Au Villages des Condamnés à Mort* by Ronan Caerléon, *Breton News*, 65 (Summer 1970).
179 361/108, Nunan to Coyne, 3 Feb. 1953, DEA A74, NAI.
180 Ibid.
181 Leon Mill-Arden's *The Celtic Time* was not focused on Brittany alone. The FO dismissed it as not being 'of very great importance' (Nutting FO, WF 1653/5, 19 Dec. 1951, FO 371/96086, NA).
182 Fouéré, *Connemara,* p. 123; Caerléon, *Complots,* p. 328.
183 Issue 2 discusses Sputnik, dating it *c.*Oct. 1957 ('Spoutnik ha Breiz').
184 Nunan to Coyne, 3 Feb. 1953, DEA A74, NAI.
185 Naturalisation certificate.
186 Feutren, interview.

CHAPTER 6
A solidarity more powerful

1 The surname was probably 'Anić'. This version employed by Hubert Butler is used throughout.
2 Butler, 'Artukovitch file'.
3 Br. David of St Anthony's, Galway, in ibid.
4 Ibid.
5 Butler, 'Sub-Prefect'.
6 Dillon was expelled from Fine Gael in 1942, and served in the first IP government as an independent. He rejoined FG in 1953.
7 Butler, 'Sub-Prefect'.
8 'Oral Answers – Religious Persecution', Dáil Éireann, Vol. 103, 23 Oct. 1946, http://historical-debates.oireachtas.ie/; accessed 12 Sept. 2005.
9 Butler, 'Sub-Prefect'.
10 Agee, 'Stepinac file'.
11 At time of writing, Irish files relating to Artuković remain classified.
12 Butler, 'Artukovitch file'.

13 Ruchala, 'Andrija Artukovic'.
14 Blum, *Wanted!* (excerpt).
15 Ruchala, 'Timeline'.
16 Dedijer, *Yugoslav Auschwitz*, pp. 73, 63–9.
17 Hoare, 'Ustasha genocide'; Ruchala, 'Artukovič'.
18 Pitamitz, 'Conspirator Rediscovered'.
19 Ruchala, 'Artukovič'.
20 McAdams, 'Whitepaper on Andrija Artukovič'.
21 Butler, 'Artukovitch file'.
22 Barton, 'Croatia 1941–1946'.
23 Thomas & Mikulan, *Axis forces*, p. 15.
24 Hoare, 'Ustasha genocide'.
25 US Army Center of Military History, *German Campaigns Balkans*, 2: *Yugoslav Campaign*, http://www.army.mil/cmh-pg/books/wwii/balkan/20_260_2.htm; accessed 21 Apr. 2007.
26 Hoare, 'Ustasha genocide'.
27 O'Donoghue, *Hitler's Irish voices*, p. 52.
28 Hoare, 'Ustasha genocide'.
29 Thomas & Mikulan, *Axis forces*, pp. 4, 7.
30 Hoare, 'Ustasha genocide'.
31 *Clero-Fascist Studies Project (CFSP)*, http://web.archive.org/web/20030404022131/www.home.earthlink.net/~velid/cf/index.html; accessed 3 Aug. 2004.
32 Aarons & Loftus, *Ratlines*, p. 4.
33 *CFSP.*
34 Cooney, *Crozier and the Dáil*, p. 20.
35 O'Halpin, 'Irish neutrality', p. 284.
36 Braham, 'Vatican: remembering and forgetting', pp. 21–4.
37 Aarons & Loftus, *Ratlines*, p. 16.
38 Lituchy, 'What is the Vatican hiding?'
39 Stouffer, 'Patron saint of genocide'.
40 Dedijer, *Yugoslav Auschwitz*, pp. 75–6.
41 In Stouffer, 'Patron saint'.
42 Ibid.
43 Lituchy, 'Vatican hiding?'.
44 Stouffer, 'Patron saint'.
45 Lituchy, 'Vatican hiding?'.
46 In Stouffer, 'Patron saint'.
47 Hoare, 'Ustasha genocide'.
48 *Shoah education project*, 'Jasenovac', http://www.shoaheducation.com/camps/jasenovac.html; accessed 22 Apr. 2007.
49 Dedijer, *Yugoslav Auschwitz*, p. 270.
50 Hoare, 'Ustasha genocide'. Some estimates range to 700,000 Serbian deaths.
51 *Ireland's Nazis* (I), p. 1.
52 See Butler, 'Artukovitch file'.
53 Lituchy, 'Vatican hiding?'.
54 Ruchala, 'Artukovic'.
55 Marko Attila Hoare, e-mail, 6 Apr. 2007.
56 From *Narodne Novine*, 26 Feb. 1942, at *Jasenovac – Donja Gradina: Industry of Death 1941–1945*; http://jasenovac-info.com/cd/biblioteka/pavelicpapers/artukovic/aa0013.html; accessed 22 Apr. 2007.
57 'Government of the Independent State of Croatia (NDH)', *Axis History Factbook*, http://www.axishistory.com/index.php?id=8129;; accessed 22 Apr. 2007.
58 De Zeng, 'Ustasha Surveillance Service'.
59 Ibid.
60 Dedijer, *Yugoslav Auschwitz*, pp. 227–8.
61 De Zeng, 'Ustasha Surveillance Service'.
62 Ivo & Slavko Goldstein, *Holokaust u Zagrebu*, p. 587. Translation by Radoslav Artuković.
63 Ravnateljstvo za javni red i sigurnost: 'Directorate for Public Order and Security'.
64 De Zeng, 'Ustasha Surveillance Service'.
65 Hoare, e-mail, 10 Apr. 2007.
66 Dedijer, *Yugoslav Auschwitz*, pp. 392, 394.
67 Aarons & Loftus, *Ratlines*, pp. 17, 23.
68 Biddiscombe, *SS Hunter Battalions*, passim; Loftus, *Belarus secret*, pp. 52, 18, 44.
69 Corbett, *Guerrilla warfare*, p. 33.
70 Aarons & Loftus, *Ratlines*, p. 268.
71 See Russian Liberation Army sergeant in Tolstoy, *Victims of Yalta*, p. 53.
72 Conway, *Collaboration in Belgium*, p. 280.
73 Goñi, *Real Odessa*, p. 129.
74 AWG Randall, Copenhagen, to FO, W2723/36/38 'Argentine minister to Éire', 16 Apr. 1948, FO 371/70175, NA.
75 Goñi, *Real Odessa*, p. 132.
76 Ibid., pp. 8, 23, 63, 71.76, 129, 138.
77 Argentine Embassy, London reply Sept. 1944, quoted by Anthony Eden, Hansard 7 Mar. 1945, in DFA P78, NAI; Goñi, *Real Odessa*, p. 125.
78 'Neutrals' Replies re: Asylum to 'War Criminals", 1 Dec. 1944, DFA P78, NAI.
79 Goñi, *Real Odessa*, pp. 88–91.
80 Gordon, *Collaborationism in France*, p. 351.
81 Infield, *Skorzeny*, pp. 180–1.
82 Aarons & Loftus, *Ratlines*, p. 29.
83 Goñi, *Real Odessa*, p. 233.
84 'Alleged Vatican Protection of Jugoslav War Criminals', 12 July 1946, US State Department, at *The Pavelic Papers*, http://www.pavelicpapers.com/documents/draganovic/kd0003.html; accessed 27 July 2004.
85 See McAdams, 'Yalta and the Bleiburg tragedy'.

86 Melman, 'Tied up in the Ratlines'.
87 'FTR #532 Interview with John Loftus', *For the Record.*
88 The Americans believed the British sheltered top Ustaše in Austria for up to three months. Goñi, *Real Odessa,* p. 208.
89 Loftus, *Belarus secret,* p. 54.
90 Ruchala, 'Poglavnik's family tree'.
91 Ibid.
92 Melman, 'Tied up in the Ratlines'.
93 Aarons & Loftus, *Ratlines,* p. 24.
94 Manhattan, 'Vatican's Holocaust'.
95 'Alleged Vatican protection of Jugoslav war criminals'.
96 Dedijer, *Yugoslav Auschwitz,* p. 106; Butler, 'Artukovitch file'.
97 Lyon, 'Rat Line from Austria'.
98 Grennan, and addendum, 7–14 July 1947.
99 Loftus, *Belarus secret,* p. 113.
100 Goñi, *Real Odessa,* pp. 213, 224.
101 Lyon, 'Rat Line from Austria'.
102 Lyon, 'History Italian Rat Line'.
103 Goñi, *Real Odessa,* p. 117.
104 Hudal assisted Franz Stangl, commandant of Treblinka, escape to Syria. Aarons & Loftus, *Ratlines,* p. 27.
105 Lyon, 'History Italian Rat Line'.
106 Butler, 'Artukovitch file'.
107 Aarons & Loftus, *Ratlines,* p. 28.
108 Goñi, *Real Odessa,* p. 206.
109 "FTR#532 Interview with John Loftus", *For The Record,* 15 Nov. 2005, http://ftrsummary.blogspot.com/2005_11_15_ftrsummary_archive.html; accessed 23 Apr. 2007.
110 Goñi, *Real Odessa,* p. 137.
111 Van den Driessche, 'Emigratie', pp. 34–5.
112 Butler, 'Artukovitch file'.
113 Goñi, *Real Odessa,* p. 143.
114 Butler, 'Artukovitch file'.
115 See DFA P78, NAI.
116 'Interview with John Loftus'.
117 'Religious Persecution', Dáil Éireann, 23 Oct. 1946.
118 Duche, 'You fight your own wars', p. 11.
119 Douglas, 'Pro-Axis Underground', p. 1157.
120 'Spanish Civil War (Non-Intervention) Bill, 1937 – Second Stage (Resumed)', Dáil Éireann, 19 Feb. 1937, http://historical-debates.oireachtas.ie; accessed 19 May 2006.
121 Lorna Reid, 'State had 'go slow' policy on Jews in wake of holocaust', *Irish Independent*, 2 Jan. 2003.
122 Keogh, 'Profile of Joseph Walshe', p. 74; Keogh, *Jews*, p. 135.
123 Keogh, 'Joseph Walshe', p. 61.
124 Fisk, *Time of war*, p. 474.
125 Agee, 'Stepinac File'.
126 McCabe, *Diplomatic history of Ireland*, pp. 92–3.
127 Keogh, 'Ireland, the Vatican', pp. 68, 69–70, 73.
128 Sister Winifred Morgan, letter, 11 May 1949, Taoiseach S10739A, NAI.
129 Lee, *Ireland 1912–1985*, p. 302.
130 Butler, 'Artukovitch file'.
131 Keogh, 'Ireland, the Vatican', pp. 73, 76–7.
132 Browne, *Against the tide*, p. 141.
133 Keogh, 'Ireland, the Vatican', p. 76.
134 Einaudi, 'Constitution of the Italian Republic', p. 667.
135 Keogh, 'Ireland, the Vatican', p. 79.
136 The Soviets funded the Italian communists with 'black bags of money'. Interview F. Mark Wyatt, *CNN Cold War*, http://www.cnn.com/SPECIALS/cold.war/episodes/03/interviews/wyatt/; accessed 17 May 2007.
137 Keogh, 'Ireland, the Vatican', pp. 101, 109.
138 McCabe, *Diplomatic history of Ireland,* p. 95.
139 Abbott & Pinak, *Ukrainian armies, 1914–55*, p. 36.
140 Ibid., p. 37.
141 *UPA: Ukrainian Insurgent Army webpage*, http://hometown.aol.com/shukhevych/; accessed 13 May 2007.
142 Abbott & Pinak, *Ukrainian armies,* p. 41.
143 Aarons & Loftus, *Ratlines*, p. 139.
144 McConvery, 'Blessed Nicholas Charnetskyj'.
145 Feutren, letters, 6 Sept. & 2 Oct. 2005.
146 Translated letter, 10 Dec. 1951, FO 371/94937, NA.
147 Tolstoy, *Victims of Yalta, passim.*
148 Ward, '"Big show-off"', p. 132.
149 Prof. Zvavich described Dublin as 'an agency of the Vatican'. Keogh, *Ireland and Europe,* p. 203.
150 Keogh, *Jews*, pp. 202–3, 217.
151 Fanning, *Racism*, p. 88.
152 Ward, '"Big show-off"', p. 138.
153 Fanning, *Racism*, pp. 88, 90, 93–84.
154 Ward, '"Big show-off"', p. 131.

CHAPTER 7
'All for Flanders – Flanders for Christ'

1 Staf van Velthoven, letter, 5(?) July 2007.
2 Colen, 'Dagboek' in Van den Driessche, 'Emigratie', n.p.
3 Alexander Colen, e-mail, 25 June 2007.

4 Colen, 'Dagboek', n.p.
5 Van Velthoven, letter, 5(?) July 2007; Colen, 'Dagboek', n.p.
6 Van Haegendoren, *Flemish movement,* p. 26.
7 Gevers, 'Catholic Church and the Flemish movement', p. 110.
8 Van Haegendoren, *Flemish movement* p. 26.
9 Folens, *Aiséirí Flóndrais,* p. 15.
10 Gevers, 'Catholic and Flemish', p. 111.
11 Ibid., p. 112.
12 Mnookin & Verbeke, 'Bye bye Belgium?'.
13 Vos, 'Flemish National Question', pp. 84, 85.
14 Van Haegendoren, *Flemish movement,* p. 30.
15 Vos, 'Flemish Question', p. 87.
16 In 'Proposition de déclaration de révision de l'article 1er de la Constitution', *Sénat de Belgique,* Session de 2006–2007, http://www.senate.be; accessed 13 June 2007.
17 Hossay, *Contentions,* pp. 272, 276.
18 *Le Figaro,* 18 May 1916, p. 1.
19 Hossay, *Contentions,* p. 277.
20 Van Haegendoren, *Flemish movement,* p. 29.
21 Hossay, *Contentions,* p. 276; Folens, *Aiséirí,* p. 38.
22 Van Haegendoren, *Flemish movement,* p. 29.
23 Hossay, *Contentions,* pp. 271, 272.
24 Verschaeve, 'Flemish Nationalist's Catechism', pp. 240, 249.
25 Hossay, *Contentions,* p. 273.
26 Council of Flanders, 'Declaration of Independence, 1917', p. 238.
27 Hossay, *Contentions,* pp. 273–5.
28 Flemish Committee, 'Telegram to President Woodrow Wilson', p. 256.
29 Hossay, *Contentions,* p. 272.
30 Van Haegendoren, *Flemish movement,* p. 29.
31 Vos, 'Flemish Question', p. 89.
32 Gijsels, *Vlaams Blok,* p. 26.
33 Paul van Cauwelaert, letter, 15 Apr. 2006.
34 Frans van Cauwelaert, 'Two Contributions to a Debate', pp. 258, 260.
35 Vos, 'Flemish Question', p. 88.
36 'Jules Callewaert', *Nieuwe Encyclopedie van de Vlaamse Beweging,* http://users.pandora.be/frankie.schram/tijd/bio/callewaert.html; accessed 11 Jan. 2006.
37 Callewaert, *Ierland en het Iersche volk,* p. iv. Translation by Toos de Boer.
38 Ibid., p. iii.
39 Folens, *Aiséirí,* caption pp. 32–3.
40 Callewaert, *Ierland,* pp. iii, vi, 684, 698.
41 Folens, *Aiséirí,* pp. 37–8.
42 Belgian Minister, The Hague, '*Séjour en Hollande des activistes Belges condamnés pour crime de haute trahison,' Conseil du Cabinet,* 4 June 1923, No.76, AÉB.
43 From the medieval term for Dutch. Vos, 'Flemish Question', p. 95.
44 'Country briefings: Netherlands', *The Economist,* http://www.economist.com/countries/Netherlands/profile.cfm?folder=History%20in%20brief; accessed 18 June 2007.
45 Folens, *Aiséirí,* p. 44.
46 Gijsels, *Vlaams Blok,* pp. 31, 44, 45, 169.
47 Folens, *Aiséirí,* pp. 48–9.
48 Rich, *War aims,* p. 191.
49 Conway, *Collaboration in Belgium,* pp. 13, 16.
50 Colen, 'Dagboek', n.p.
51 Hamon, *Nationalistes bretons,* p. 40; Littlejohn, *Patriotic traitors,* p. 207.
52 In Rich, *War aims,* pp. 189, 191.
53 Conway, *Collaboration in Belgium,* pp. 27, 28, 33.
54 Time-Life eds., *Heel of the conqueror,* p. 66.
55 Gijsels, *Vlaams Blok,* pp. 78, 77.
56 Van Haegendoren, *Flemish movement,* p. 31.
57 Jurado, *Foreign volunteers,* p. 5.
58 Eric Margolis, 'Austria causes Eurohysteria', 5 Feb. 2000, *Eric Margolis: Foreign Correspondent,* http://www.ericmargolis.com/archives/2000/02/austria_causes.php; accessed 19 June 2007.
59 Jurado, *Resistance warfare,* p. 16.
60 Rich, *War aims,* p. 191.
61 Jurado, *Resistance warfare,* p. 16.
62 Gijsels, *Vlaams Blok,* p. 46.
63 Rich, *War aims,* p. 191.
64 Gijsels, *Vlaams Blok,* p. 46.
65 Gevers, 'Catholic Church', p. 116.
66 'Jules Callewaert', *Nieuwe Encyclopedie.*
67 Gordon, *Collaborationism in France,* p. 318.
68 Folens, *Aiséirí,* p. 53.
69 Conway, *Collaboration in Belgium,* p. 279.
70 'Belgian War Crimes proceedings', *Axis History Forum,* 23 Sept. 2002, http://forum.axishistory.com/viewtopic.php?p=797797#797797; accessed 11 Nov. 2005; Folens, *Aiséirí,* p. 53.
71 Gijsels, *Vlaams Blok,* p. 21.
72 Belgium 8.639m; France 41.829m

(1950). *Total Population by Country,* http://www.photius.com/rankings/world2050.html; accessed 10 May 2007. France was not '10 times bigger' as Folens claimed in *Aiséirí,* p. 53.
73 Van Haegendoren, *Flemish movement*, p. 31.
74 Folens, *Aiséirí,* p. 54.
75 In Houthaeve, *Vlamingen in Ierland*, p. 27.
76 Van den Driessche, 'Emigratie', pp. 29–30.
77 Folens, *Aiséirí,* p. 54.
78 Gijsels, *Vlaams Blok,* p. 88.
79 'Hendrik Elias', *Nieuwe Encyclopedie,* http://users.pandora.be/frankie.schram/tijd/bio/elias.html; accessed 21 June 2007.
80 Van den Driessche, 'Emigratie', p. 38.
81 Gijsels, *Vlaams Blok,* p. 89.
82 Fouéré, *Connemara,* p. 14.
83 Arzalier, *Les Perdants*, p. 221.
84 *BNNS,* (7–8) July 1947.
85 Around 150 total. Van den Driessche, 'Emigratie', p. 53.
86 Several thousand, according to Ibid.
87 Leo Poppe, 'Hier in Argentinië', *Broederband,* 11 (Dec. 1966), 49–53.
88 Gijsels, *Vlaams Blok,* p. 91.
89 Ibid., p. 88.
90 Colen, 'Dagboek', n.p.
91 Van den Driessche, 'Emigratie', p. 45.
92 Staf van Velthoven in *Ireland's Nazis* (II), p. 15.
93 Van den Driessche, 'Emigratie', p. 45.
94 Also Luyckx.
95 Colen, e-mail, 17 Nov. 2006.
96 'Nazi criminal allegations denied by Luykx', *Irish Times,* 20 Feb. 1971.
97 Bruno de Wever in *Ireland's Nazis* (II), p. 27.
98 Louis Reimis in Ibid., p. 26.
99 See Chapter Eight.
100 '[O]*verdag praatten we over de vrijheid van ons volk, doch 's nachts droomden we van onze persoonlijke vrijheid.*' Albert Luykx, 'Het Ierse volk en de bannelingen', *Broederband,* 2:11 (1966), 15–7; p. 15. Translation by author.
101 Ibid.
102 Houthaeve, *Vlamingen,* p. 27.
103 'Flemish patriot found home in Ireland', *Irish Times,* 20 Sept. 2003.
104 Ibid.; van den Driessche, 'Emigratie', p. 44; Houthaeve, *Vlamingen,* p. 27.
105 Van den Driessche, 'Emigratie', pp. 44, 68.
106 Folens interview Senan Moloney (1985), in *Ireland's Nazis* (II), p. 23.
107 Colen, e-mail, 5 Apr. 2007.
108 *Ireland's Nazis* (II), p. 23.
109 'Flemish patriot', *Irish Times.*
110 '*Oorlogsmisdadiger* honoris causa.' In Houthaeve, *Vlamingen,* p. 29.
111 'Folens family reject allegations against Albert Folens', statement to Irish media, 12 Jan. 2007.
112 *'[S]é sin, 1947, leathuair an chloig sar ar tugadh breith báis orm féin d'fhiafraigh an breitheamh díom cad a bheir dom na "cora" polaitíochta úd go léir a dhéanamh in aghaidh na Beilge. Dá mba aon tairbhe é, mar seo nó mar siúd, freagra a thabhairt, is é déarfainn: "Leon Fhlóndrais fá deara dhom é, a Thiarna"'*: Folens, *Aiséirí,* p. 24. Translation by Anna Heussaff.
113 'Flemish patriot', *Irish Times;* van den Driessche, 'Emigratie', p. 44.
114 *Ireland's Nazis* (II), p. 1; Colen, e-mail, 25 June 2007.
115 Folens' lawyers obtained a reprieve after he had absconded, Colen claims, reducing his sentence from ten to three years – the amount of time served. E-mail, 13 Apr. 2007.
116 Infield, *Skorzeny*, p. 11.
117 Vest, 'Otto Skorzeny'.
118 Infield, *Skorzeny,* pp. 151, 159–61.
119 'Wie is Willem Sassen?', *KRO-Reporter,* 11 May 2005, http://reporter.kro.nl/uitzendingen/2005/20050511willemsassen/20050511biografie.aspx; accessed 3 July 2007.
120 Lauryssens, *Eichmann diaries*, p. 10.
121 'Wie is Willem Sassen?'.
122 Lauryssens, *Eichmann diaries,* p. 5.
123 'Sassen, Willem en Alphonse na de oorlog', *Go2War2.nl,* http://www.go2war2.nl/artikel/1371/2; accessed 30 Aug. 2006. Lauryssens claims Sassen escaped from the rear of a Dutch army truck. *Eichmann diaries,* p. 9.
124 Lauryssens, *Eichmann diairies,* p. 10.
125 Van den Driessche, 'Emigratie', p. 43. This claims Smekens hid in Germany and southern France before escaping to Ireland, but doesn't specify the route taken.
126 Jurado, *Resistance warfare,* p. 16.
127 Lauryssens, *Eichmann diaries,* pp. 11, 9.
128 Van den Driessche, 'Emigratie', p. 67.
129 Houthaeve, *Vlamingen,* p. 16.
130 Ibid., pp. 15–7.
131 Lauryssens, *Eichmann diaries,* pp. 9–10.
132 Ibid., p. 10; Colen, e-mail, 26 June 2007.
133 Lauryssens, *Eichmann diaries,* p. 13.
134 Houthaeve, *Vlamingen,* p. 91.
135 Colen, 'Dagboek', n.p.

136 Folens, *Aiséirí*, caption p. 32.
137 Colen, 'Dagboek', n.p.
138 'Le père Werenfried van Straaten, le 'Père au Lard'', http://www.kirche-in-not.org/f_pw.htm; accessed 5 July 2007.
139 Colen, 'Dagboek', n.p.
140 Staf van Velthoven in *Ireland's Nazis* (II), p. 18.
141 Houthaeve, *Vlamingen*, p. 27.
142 'Flemish Patriot', *Irish Times*.
143 Houthaeve, *Vlamingen*, p. 27; 'Flemish Patriot', *Irish Times*.
144 Van Velthoven, letter, 5(?) July 2007.
145 Barry Smith, 'Baarle-Nassau/Baarle-Hertog', http://ontology.buffalo.edu/smith/baarle.htm; accessed 5 July 2007.
146 Colen, e-mail 25 June 2007.
147 Colen, 'Dagboek', n.p.
148 Colen, e-mail 25 June 2007.
149 Colen, e-mail 5 Apr. 2007.
150 Colen, e-mail 17 Nov. 2006.
151 Keogh, *Jews*, pp. 140, 207.
152 Lauryssens, *Eichmann diaries*, p. 19.
153 'The Journal: A Publication of the Australian Irish Heritage Association', http://www.irishheritage.net/2000summer.htm; accessed 5 July 2007.
154 Lauryssens, *Eichmann diaries*, p. 24.
155 Colen, e-mail, 17 Nov. 2006.
156 'Kylemore Abbey entertainment', *Connacht Tribune*, 28 Nov. 1931.
157 Colen, 'Dagboek', n.p.
158 Houthaeve, *Vlamingen*, p. 38.
159 Paul van Cauwelaert, letter, 15 Apr. 2006.
160 Cabinet Council, #29, 22 May (1941?), Belgian Government-in-Exile, AÉB.
161 Paul van Cauwelaert, letter, 15 Apr. 2006.
162 Houthaeve, *Vlamingen*, p. 105.
163 Van den Driessche, 'Emigratie', p. 67.
164 Colen, e-mail 19 Apr. 2007.
165 Dirk Folens, e-mail 27 Feb. 2006.
166 In *Ireland's Nazis* (II), p. 16.
167 Van den Driessche, 'Emigratie', p. 45.
168 Lauryssens, *Eichmann diaries*, pp. 22–3.
169 Goñi, *Real Odessa*, p. 175.
170 Van den Driessche, 'Emigratie', p. 68.
171 Jurado, *Resistance warfare*, p. 16.
172 Colen, e-mail 26 June 2007.
173 Lauryssens, *Eichmann diaries*, p. 22.
174 *Irish Independent*, 13 Apr. 1948 in 'Argentine minister to Éire', W2723/36/38, FO 371/70175, NA.
175 G2/C/233 Bryan to Boland DEA, 'Alleged Escape routes for Wanted Nazis, etc. through Ireland', 24 June 1948, DEA P168, NAI.
176 G2/C/33 22 June 1948, P168 NAI.
177 Colen, 'Dagboek', n.p.
178 Colen, e-mail, 17 Nov. 2006.
179 See the 'political exception' in Chapter Two.
180 Dirk Folens, e-mail, 27 Feb. 2006.
181 Broderick, 'Breton Movement', p. 14 fn.
182 'Extradition arrangements', Dáil Éireann, 7 Mar. 1946, http://www.oireachtas-debates.gov.ie/; accessed 12 Sept. 2005.
183 Farrell, *Sheltering*, pp. 33–4, 37.
184 O'Higgins, 'Irish extradition law', pp. 255, 251.
185 D'Udekem d'Acoz, *Voor Koning & Vaderland*, pp. 308–10. Translation by Bruno de Wever.
186 O'Higgins, 'Irish extradition law', p. 251.
187 'Addressen van Bannelingen in Ierland', 1966, 3.13 *Ierland*, AC51 *Archief Arthur de Troyer*, ADVN.
188 O'Higgins, 'Irish extradition law', p. 251.
189 Farrell, *Sheltering*, p. 38.
190 Section 5 (e), Part II, Aliens Order No. 395, 1946.
191 O'Higgins, 'Irish Extradition Act, 1965', p. 381.
192 Farrell, *Sheltering*, pp. 38, 40. See Chapter 8.
193 Salmon, *Unneutral Ireland*, p. 189.
194 Martland, *Lord Haw-Haw*, p. 39.
195 Bergmeier & Lotz, *Hitler's airwaves*, p. 93.
196 Dorril, *Blackshirt*, pp. 563–4. Dorril claims Martin Heidegger wrote *Philosophical Investigations* in Ireland. The author of this work was Ludwig Wittgenstein.
197 *Francis Parker Yockey Collection*, http://www.alphalink.net.au/~radnat/fpyockey/index.html; accessed 8 May 2006.
198 Berry, Justice, Report AK Chesterton, 18 May 1955, DFA P253, NAI.
199 Report 14 June 1955, DFA P253, NAI.
200 11 May 1955, DFA P253, NAI.
201 Report AK Chesterton, 18 May 1955, DFA P253, NAI.
202 Dorril, *Blackshirt*, p. 590; Mosley, *My life*, p. 426.
203 Confidential report 14 Apr. 1959, DFA P311, NAI.
204 Dorril, *Blackshirt*, pp. 600, 606, 610.
205 Infield, *Skorzeny*, p. 185.
206 Dáil Éireann, 12 Mar. 1963, 'Otto Skorzeny', http://historical-debates.oireachtas.ie/; accessed 9 May 2006.
207 Kim Bielenberg in *Ireland's Nazis* (II), p. 35.
208 Infield, *Skorzeny*, pp. 185–6.
209 Lauryssens, *Eichmann diaries*, p. 21.

210 Colen, e-mail, 25 June 2007.
211 Van den Driessche, 'Emigratie', p. 67.
212 Lauryssens, *Eichmann diaries,* p. 20.
213 C. Howard, Note 11 June 1960, DFA P253, NAI.
214 *Ireland's Nazis* (I), p. 35.
215 Memo: 'Grant of asylum for Señor Batista', DFA P311, NAI.
216 'Briefing document on Ireland and asylum', DFA P311, NAI.
217 Cremin to Hearne, 2 May 1959, DFA P311, NAI.
218 UN mission, 14 Apr. 1959, DFA P311, NAI.
219 16 Apr. 1959, DFA P311 NAI. Robert Briscoe TD supported Batista's application because Cuba had accepted Jewish refugees. Briscoe betrayed ignorance of asylum questions, however, by suggesting that 'the case of Oswald Mosley might furnish a very good precedent' for Batista. (Confidential Report, 14 Apr. 1959, DFA P311, NAI.)

CHAPTER 8
'Bombing Bray?'

1 Arnold Kemp, 'This way lies fascism', *The Observer*, 3 Mar. 2002.
2 Myra Philp, 'Meet the untouchable', *Daily Express* (Glasgow), 1 Aug. 2005.
3 'Arrest in water poison plot', *IPICT*, 11 July 1999, http://www.ict.org.il/spotlight/det.cfm?id=287; accessed 30 Mar. 2004.
4 'Scottish Militant Group Mails Toxic Parcels to Blair', *Islam Online*, 2002, http://www.islamonline.net/english/News/2002–03/03/article43.shtml; accessed 21 Feb. 2004.
5 'The SSG/SNLA Fiasco' *Priority Independence*, http://www.geocities.com/priority_independence/ssg.html; accessed 21 Feb. 2004.
6 Infield, *Skorzeny*, p. 237.
7 Lauryssens, *Eichmann diaries,* , p. 21.
8 Skelly, *Irish diplomacy*, pp. 86, 125.
9 Ibid., pp. 53, 68, 70.
10 28 June 1956, Taoiseach S 6022 B/95, NAI.
11 Shain, 'Governments-in-exile', p. 225; Pittock, *Scottish nationality*, p. 115.
12 31 May 1956, Taoiseach S 6022 B/95, NAI.
13 Skelly, *Irish diplomacy*, pp. 76, 98, 21–2.
14 Coogan, *Ireland since the Rising*, p. 124.
15 7 June & 28 May 1957, Taoiseach S 6022 B/95, NAI.
16 Skelly, *Irish diplomacy,* p. 87.
17 'Articulate Welshman with Tudor Flag arrives to plead for a Free Wales', *New York Times,* 11 Nov. 1958.
18 22 Mar. 1965, DFA 96/3/98, NAI.
19 28 May 1963, DFA 2001/43/86, NAI.
20 3 Sep. 1962, DFA 2001/43/86; 5 Oct. 1962, Taoiseach S6022 B/62, NAI.
21 9 Dec. 1965, DFA 96/3/98, NAI.
22 Radulescu, 'Theorising exile', p. 190.
23 De Valera, *Memoir,* p. 241.
24 Named after Perrot's resting place (*Koad-Kev* in KLTG).
25 Aidan Dunne, 'Yann Goulet, sculptor, Breton nationalist, dies', *Irish Times,* 25 Aug. 1999.
26 Goulet-Conway, interview.
27 Fouéré, *Connemara,* pp. 98–9, 268.
28 Feutren, letter, 7 Feb. 2006; Brendan Hennessy, e-mail, 20 Nov. 2003.
29 Fouéré, *Connemara,* pp. 268, 282.
30 Goulet-Conway, interview.
31 'Yann Renard-Goulet (1914–1999)', *Aosdána,* http://aosdana.artscouncil.ie/biogs/former_visarts/yannrenardgoulet.html; accessed 28 Aug. 2007.
32 Goulet-Conway, interview.
33 'Yann Renard Goulet', *Saoirse,* 9 Oct. 1999.
34 Fouéré, *Connemara,* p. 99; Letter, *Irish Times,* 19 Dec. 1972, in *'Dublin: Consulat, Légation puis Ambassade'*, Carton 205, CADN.
35 Matt Leen, 'Yann Renard Goulet', *Saoirse – Irish Freedom,* Letters, Oct. 1999, http://homepage.tinet.ie/~eirenua/oct99/letters.htm; accessed 2 July 2003.
36 De Valera, *Memoir,* p. 242.
37 'Yann Renard Goulet', *Saoirse,* 9 Oct. 1999.
38 Armelle Goulet-Conway's early school reports are in the name 'Renard'. (Interview).
39 Denez, interview.
40 See his English version of Denez's *Brezhoneg – buan hag aes* (1977).
41 *Breton News*, 12 (January 1961), 1.
42 Feutren, interview. Given the delay caused by his Belfast sojourn, it seems unlikely Feutren could have visited Brittany so many times between naturalisation (December 1952 at earliest) and the August 1953 amnesty.
43 Goulet-Conway, interview.
44 Iker Gallastegi, letter, 2 May 2006.
45 Iker Gallastegi, letter (undated), received 19 Sept. 2006.
46 Dáil Éireann, 'Expulsion of Irish Citizen from France', 8 Nov. 1962, http://historical-debates.oireachtas.ie/; accessed 12 Sept. 2005.

47 Gallastegi, letter, 19 Sept. 2006.
48 Sullivan, *ETA*, pp. 39, 40. Iker returned to Spain after the fall of Franco and today writes for the Basque newspaper *Gara*.
49 In *Celtic News*, 12 (Winter 1966), 9.
50 'Welsh boyos: more bravado than substance,' *The Age* (Melbourne), 15 June 2004.
51 Clews, *Dream of freedom*, p. 71; Ellis, *Wales*, p. 140; *Daily Sketch*, 11 Apr. 1966 & 'Welsh Army "Was 3-strong"', *Daily Telegraph*, 22 Apr. 1969, DFA 96/3/98, NAI.
52 Faligot, *Harpe*, p. 129.
53 Actually *Mec Vannin* or 'Sons of Man'.
54 Cayo Evans in Clews, *Dream of freedom*, p. 71.
55 Faligot, *Harpe*, p. 130.
56 5 Oct. 1962, Taoiseach S6022 B/62, NAI.
57 Higgins, 'Projections and Reflections', p. 18.
58 'Yann Renard-Goulet' to 1916 Committee, 24 Oct. 1965, DFA 2000/14/78, NAI.
59 Caerléon, *Révolution bretonne*, p. 276.
60 Embassy Paris to Sect. DEA, 14 Jan. 1966, DFA 2000/14/78, NAI.
61 Per Denez to Defence, 16 Oct. 1965, DFA 2000/14/78, NAI.
62 3 Mar. 1966, DFA 2000/14/78, NAI.
63 30 Nov. 1965, DFA 2000/14/78; John Murphy to DEA, 13 Mar. 1966, DFA 2000/14/78, NAI.
64 30 Nov. 1965, DFA 2000/14/78, NAI.
65 DEA to 1916 Committee, Dec. 1965, DFA 2000/14/78, NAI.
66 30 Nov. 1965, DFA 2000/14/78, NAI.
67 Chief of Protocol, 3 Dec. 1965, DFA 2000/14/78, NAI.
68 1916 Committee, 16 Mar. 1966, DFA 2000/14/78, NAI.
69 11 Jan. 1966, DFA 2000/14/78, NAI.
70 30 Nov. 1965, DFA 2000/14/78, NAI.
71 30 Aug. 1965 & 11 Jan. 1966, DFA 2000/14/78, NAI.
72 Memo 29 Nov. 1965, DFA 2000/14/78, NAI.
73 30 Nov. 1965, DFA 2000/14/78, NAI.
74 3 Mar. 1966, DFA 2000/14/78, NAI.
75 DEA to 1916 Committee, Dec. 1965, DFA 2000/14/78, NAI.
76 Faligot, *Harpe*, p. 128; Denez, interview.
77 James Nicholson, 'Free Wales Army goes marching in Ireland', *Daily Sketch*, 11 Apr. 1966, in DFA 96/3/98, NAI.
78 Op de Beeck to Minister DEA, 17 Feb. 1966, DFA 2000/14/78, NAI.
79 *Echo*, 1 (3) Dec. 1965, AC51 *Archief Arthur de Troyer*, 3.13 *Ierland*, ADVN.
80 Van den Driessche, 'Emigratie', pp. 75–6.
81 Colen, e-mail, 19 Apr. 2007.
82 Embassy Brussels to Coffey DEA, 2 Mar. 1966, DFA 2000/14/78, NAI.
83 Letter to Ronan DEA, 3 Mar. 1966, DFA 2000/14/78, NAI.
84 Houthaeve, *Vlamingen in Ierland*, p. 17.
85 Embassy Brussels to Coffey DEA, 2 Mar. 1966, DFA 2000/14/78, NAI.
86 Letter to Ronan DEA, 3 Mar. 1966, DFA 2000/14/78, NAI.
87 Higgins, 'Projections and reflections', p. 15.
88 DEA 7 Mar. 1966, DFA 2000/14/78, NAI.
89 Embassy Brussels to Coffey DEA, 2 Mar. 1966, DFA 2000/14/78, NAI.
90 Report of VCD, 1 Nov. 1966, AC51, 3.14, *Briefwisseling Ierland (Ierse bannelingen)*, ADVN.
91 *Echo, 'Een bezoek aan de Vl. bannelingen in Ierland'*, 27 July 1966, AC51, 3.13 *Ierland*, ADVN.
92 RTÉ footage at http://www.rte.ie/laweb/smil/t06/t06_19660410_glasnevin_tv.smil; accessed 16 Nov. 2006.
93 In Clews, *Dream of freedom*, p. 71.
94 'Welsh army "was 3-strong"', *Daily Telegraph*.
95 In Clews, *Dream of freedom*, pp. 69–70.
96 Scott & Macleay, *Britain's secret war*, pp. 31–2.
97 Busby in Leslie, 'Story of the SNLA'.
98 Scott & Macleay, *Britain's secret war*, pp. 12–13.
99 In Leslie, 'Story of the SNLA'.
100 Denez, interview.
101 Chartier & Cabon, *Dossier FLB*, p. 41.
102 Henry & Lagadec, *FLB-ARB*, p. 70.
103 The translation is Goulet's. 'National Committee of Free Brittany' is more accurate.
104 'Rebel sculptor warns de Gaulle', *Sunday Telegraph*, 31 Mar. 1968, in 156 EU M. Yann GOULET, 42 *Europe/Irlande* (1961–1970), EU 19-3-12/1 1967–1968, AMAÉ.
105 Transcript, 27 Jan. 1969, in #8 221/B1 Ber '*Interview de M. Jean Goulet ...*', *Serie: Europe, Sous-serie: Irlande*, 1944–1970, EU 19-3-12/1 1969, 42, AMAÉ.
106 Caerléon, *Révolution bretonne*, p. 278. There is confusion here between the IRB, which operated in Ireland and Britain, and the Fenian Brotherhood (later Clan na Gael), based in the USA.
107 John Murdoch, 'I don't trust de Gaulle', *Sunday Press* (Ireland), 1 Feb. 1969;

'Sculptor admits he leads Breton rebels', *Irish Times*, 9 Jan. 1969.
108 'Rebel Sculptor warns de Gaulle'.
109 CBL communiqués in EU 19-3-12/1 1967–1968, AMAÉ.
110 Henry & Lagadec, *FLB-ARB*, p. 48.
111 *Breton News*, 54 (Summer 1966).
112 See concern about French in the Channel Islands (#171 *la Langue francaise a Guernesey*, EU 16-3-12A, *Îles Anglo-Normandes*, 2 Dec. 1969, *Europe, Grande-Bretagne* 177, *Serie 16, sous-serie 3, dossier 12*, AMAÉ), and Louisiana; *Breton News*, 57 (Summer 1967).
113 'De Gaulle and 'Vive le Québec libre!', *The Canadian Encyclopedia*, http://www.thecanadianencyclopedia.com/PrinterFriendly.cfm?Params=A1ARTFET_E53; accessed 4 Mar. 2008.
114 Reece, *Bretons against France*, pp. 202, 213.
115 Bothorel, *Terroriste breton*, p. 98.
116 *Breton News*, 5, May 1960.
117 *Nouvel Observateur*, April 1968, in Bothorel, *Terroriste breton*, p. 94.
118 Faligot, *Harpe*, pp. 141, 127.
119 Caerléon, *Révolution bretonne*, pp. 275, 277.
120 317 EU, *Manifestation de la 'Ligue Celtique'* ..., 3 Aug. 1967, EU 19-3-12/1 1967–1968, AMAÉ.
121 CBL communiqué 24 Mar. 1968, EU 19-3-12/1 1967–1968, AMAÉ.
122 Henry & Lagadec, *FLB-ARB*, pp. 72, 109.
123 1838/1 6 Feb. 1939, *Section Parisienne 1939–40*, *Autonomistes bretons, perquisitions*, F7 14686, AN.
124 René le Vaillant, 'Le Canadien', who had been involved with Québécois nationalists.
125 Bothorel, *Terroriste breton*, pp. 120, 100–1.
126 Henry & Lagadec, *FLB-ARB*, p. 72.
127 Feutren, interview.
128 AmbaFrance Dublin, n.d., EU 19-3-12/1 1967–1968, AMAÉ. He was still forbidden to travel to Brittany.
129 Feutren, interview.
130 Julian Mounter, 'Behind the movements ...', *Irish Times*, 25 Oct. 1968, in Dublin, Carton 205, CADN.
131 'International Chieftain Commandos' manifesto 18 Oct. 1968, in EU 19-3-12/1 1967–1968, AMAÉ.
132 Mounter, 'Behind the movements'.
133 149 EU *Front de Liberation de la Bretagne*, 25 Mar. 1968, EU 19-3-12/1 1967–1968, AMAÉ.
134 Dublin to Paris, EU 19-3-12/1 1967–1968, AMAÉ.
135 AmbaFrance Dublin, n.d., EU 19-3-12/1 1967–1968, AMAÉ.
136 *Bretons réfugiés en Irlande*, 17 Oct. 1968, EU 19-3-12/1 1967–1968, AMAÉ.
137 Bitard to Minister, 28 Feb. 1969, 93 EU M/ 'Alain HEUSSAFF', EU 19-3-12/1 1969, AMAÉ.
138 Letters, *Irish Times*, 8 Jan. 1969.
139 'An Irishwoman's Diary', *Irish Times*, 22 July 1968, in DFA 2001/43/87, NAI.
140 *Irish Independent*, 5 July 1968, in DFA 2001/43/87, NAI.
141 Letter 11 June 1968, Taoiseach 99/1/42, NAI.
142 De Valera, *Memoir*, p. 279.
143 *L'Avenir de la Bretagne*, n.d., in Caerléon, *Révolution bretonne*, p. 150.
144 Henry & Lagadec, *FLB-ARB*, p. 81.
145 Fouéré, *En Prison*, p. 24.
146 'Yann Goulet is an individual of sombre memory whose extreme Rightist ideas are totally in opposition to mine and those of my comrades': 'François G.', FLB-72, in Henry & Lagadec, *FLB-ARB*, p. 127.
147 See cuttings *Sunday Press*, 12 Mar. 1972 & *Irish Times*, 18 July 1972 in Dublin, Carton 205, CADN.
148 Henry & Lagadec, *FLB-ARB*, p. 72.
149 Fouéré, *En Prison*, pp. 23–41, 181.
150 'Fianna Fáil and Gaullists to press for Fouéré trial', *Irish Times*, 7 Feb. 1976; Fouéré, *En Prison*, p. 133.
151 'EEC still refuses to act over Fouéré', *Irish Times*, 10 Feb. 1976.
152 'Fianna Fail and Gaullists', *Irish Times*, 7 Feb. 1976.
153 Fouéré, *En Prison*, p. 43.
154 Chartier & Cabon, *Dossier FLB*, pp. 45–6, 57; Cf. Rozenn Fouéré Barrett, e-mail, 26 July 2007.
155 Henry & Lagadec, *FLB-ARB*, pp. 67, 238–9.
156 Yann Fouéré, interview; Goulet-Conway, interview.
157 Anna & Kintilla Heussaff, interviews.
158 Chartier & Cabon, *Dossier FLB*, pp. 195–6, 111.
159 Jakez Bernard in ibid.; Feutren claims he encountered Lainé meeting with young Bretons in Ireland. (Interview.)
160 Chartier & Cabon, *Dossier FLB*, p. 196; Forde, *Law of extradition in the UK*, p. 119.
161 Beer, *Unexpected rebellion*, p. 22; Michael Denieffe, 'Two Bretons deny Irish threat link', *Sunday Independent*, 17 Feb. 1980.

162 Farrell, *Sheltering*, p. 48.
163 Denieffe, 'Two Bretons deny Irish threat'.
164 Chartier & Cabon, *Dossier FLB*, pp. 196–7.
165 See cuttings in DFA 96/3/98, NAI.
166 In Clews, *Dream of freedom*, p. 59.
167 'Police tell of "Guerrilla raids on Wales" plan', *Daily Telegraph*, 13 Mar. 1969, in DFA 96/3/98, NAI.
168 In Clews, *Dream of freedom*, p. 61.
169 Patrick Hannan, 'Tony Lewis: fanciful leader of the Free Wales Army', *The Guardian*, 16 Nov. 2005.
170 In Clews, *Dream of freedom*, p. 59.
171 Ibid., pp. 140–1, 172–4.
172 Van den Driessche, 'Emigratie', p. 68.
173 Ibid., p. 68; Van Velthoven, letter, n.d., received 30 Apr. 2008.
174 Kelly, *Orders for the Captain?*, pp. 22, 182.
175 O'Brien, *Arms Trial*, p. 63; Cronin, *Irish nationalism*, p. 199, among others.
176 Dáil Éireann, 'Granting of Irish Citizenship', 5 Nov. 1970, http://historical-debates.oireachtas.ie/; accessed 12 Sep. 2005.
177 Dáil Éireann, 'Granting of Irish Citizenship', 18 Feb. 1971, http://historical-debates.oireachtas.ie/; accessed 12 Sep. 2005.
178 'Nazi criminal allegations denied by Luykx', *Irish Times*, 20 Feb. 1971.
179 Kelly, *Orders for the Captain?*, p. 123.
180 In *Ireland's Nazis* (II), p. 28.
181 O'Brien, *Arms trial*, p. 197.
182 'Haughey challenges Taoiseach', *Irish Times*, 24 Oct. 1970.
183 Colen, e-mail, 17 Nov. 2006.
184 'Guns for Scots', *Irish Press*, 22 Oct. 1951 in G2/898, DEA P168, NAI.
185 Scott & Macleay, *Britain's secret war*, pp. 12, 28.
186 Letter 13 Dec. 1967, DFA 2001/43/86, NAI.
187 *Celtic News*, 27, Spring 1971.
188 Scott & Macleay, *Britain's secret war*, pp. 32, 53.
189 Harvie, *Scotland and nationalism*, p. 173.
190 Scott & Macleay, *Britain's secret war*, pp. 53, 46, 99.
191 'Bail given to wanted Scots nationalists', *Irish Press*, 18 Aug. 1984.
192 Kemp, 'This way lies fascism'.
193 Paul Cox, 'MI5 In Action: Review of "Turning Up The Heat. MI5 After The Cold War" by Larry O'Hara', *Third Way*, http://www.thirdway.org/files/reviews/mi5.html; accessed 30 Mar. 2004.
194 Scott & Macleay, *Britain's secret war*, p. 155.
195 'Judge rules Scot's crime was "political"', *Irish Press*, 17 Oct. 1984.
196 'SSG/SNLA Fiasco'.
197 Dáil Éireann, 'British Army Deserter', 23 May 1974, http://historical-debates.oireachtas.ie/; accessed 12 Sept. 2005.
198 Hogan & Walker, *Political violence and the law*, p. 279.
199 Leslie, 'Story of the SNLA'.
200 Scott & Macleay, *Britain's secret war*, p. 156.
201 'Judge rules Scot's crime was political'.
202 Dinsmore allegedly sent the letterbomb to Thatcher. Offences against heads of state are not covered by the 'political exception' (*attentat* clause). Terrorist offences also no longer qualify since the 1977 European Convention on the Suppression of Terrorism, enshrined by Dublin in 1987.
203 Leslie, 'Story of the SNLA'. *The News of the World* claimed Dinsmore was smuggled to France: Scott & Macleay, *Britain's secret war*, p. 157.
204 Cox, 'MI5 in action'. Speculation grew that Dinsmore made a 'shabby deal' with British authorities.
205 David Leslie, 'Tartan hate group links with IRA for terror plot', *News of the World* (Scotland), 23 Sept. 2001; Leslie 'Story of the SNLA'.
206 'Arrest in Water Poison Plot'; 'Parcel plot work of "sick loner"'.
207 Leslie, 'Tartan hate group'; Philp, 'Meet the Untouchable'.
208 'Niall' on *SNG* forum: 'Meet the Untouchable' thread, 1 Aug. 2005, http://www.siol-nan-gaidheal.com/phpBB2/viewtopic.php?p=20053&; accessed 16 Aug. 2005.
209 Philp, 'Meet the Untouchable'.
210 Leslie, 'Story of the SNLA'.
211 'High Court of Ireland decisions: McMahon v. Judges of the Special Criminal Court', *IEHC* 128, 30 July 1998, http://www.bailii.org/ie/cases/IEHC/1998/128.html; accessed 17 June 2005.
212 '"Tartan terrorist" admits bomb hoax role', *The Scotsman*, 19 May 1999.
213 'Police seek militant after acid parcel sent to Cherie Blair', *Irish Examiner*, 4 Mar. 2002
214 Leslie, 'Story of the SNLA'.
215 Philp, 'Meet the untouchable'.
216 Adam Busby, e-mail, 25 Nov. 2005.
217 'Pair face jail over poisoned vodka', *The Scotsman*, 28 Jan. 2008.

218 Rapoport, 'Four Waves', p. 26.
219 *La Republica* (Uruguay), 21 May 2002. Translation by Michael Leach.
220 Henry & Lagadec, *FLB-ARB*, pp. 141, 300.
221 This is possible only if the state of origin breaches EU obligations. 'Treaty of Amsterdam Protocols', pp. 12–3, http://www.eurotreaties.com/amsterdamp rotocols.pdf; accessed 6 Mar. 2008.

Conclusion

1 'Ireland elects first black mayor,' *BBC News*, 28 June 2007, http://news.bbc.co.uk/2/hi/europe/62510 94.stm; accessed 11 Aug. 2007.
2 Goulet-Conway, interview; Feutren, interview.
3 In 'Ailin', 'Speech at Glencoe'.
4 In Keogh, 'Profile of Joseph Walshe', p. 76.

Bibliography

ARCHIVES

Archief, Documentatie en Onderzoekcentrum voor het Vlaamse Nationalisme (ADVN), Antwerp

Archief Arthur de Troyer AC51

3.13 *Ierland*

3.14 *Briefwisseling Ierland (Ierse bannelingen)*

Archives de l'État en Belgique (AÉB), Brussels

Conseil du Cabinet, 4 June 1923, No. 76 *'Séjour en Hollande des activistes Belges condamnés pour crime de haute trahison'*

Conseil du Cabinet, 22 May (1941?), No. 29

Archives du Ministère des Affaires étrangères, (AMAÉ), Paris

Europe/Irlande (1961–1970)

EU 19-3-12/1 1967–1968 *'Autonomistes bretons en Irlande'*

Serie: Europe, Sous-serie: Irlande, 1944–1970

EU 19-3-12/1 1969 *'Autonomistes bretons en Irlande, Crise gaélique'*

Archives nationales (AN), Paris

Série de la police

'Autonomisme breton' F7 13244

'Autonomistes bretons' F7 14685

'Autonomistes bretons (suite)' F7 14686

Centre des Archives diplomatiques de Nantes (CADN), Nantes

Carton 39 *Edimbourg: Consulat Général*

'Autonomisme breton' Apr. 1946–Sept. 1953

Carton 205 *'Dublin: Consulat, Légation puis Ambassade'*.

Irish Military Archives (IMA), Dublin
Military Intelligence (G2)
'Douglas, Ronald Angus MacDonald' G2/2781
'MacClean, Colm' G2/4996
'Mill-Arden, Leon V.' G2/2146
'Leon V. Mill-Arden' G2/2146 SI/444

National Archives (NA), Kew, London
Foreign Office
'Andreos Geoffroy' FO 371/96086
'Breton autonomist agitation in Wales' FO371/67702
'"Casement" Plan 1944–45' FO 898/357
'Éire's diplomatic relations with Axis 1944' FO 371/42679
'Relations with Eire 1948' FO 371/70175
'Russian Cossack resident in Éire 1951' FO 371/94937
Home Office
'German agents interned in Éire, 1946–8' HO 213/2140
'Scottish National Party' HO 45/25472
Security Service (MI5)
'*Abwehr* objectives Britain II' KV 3/77
'Guy Vissault de Coëtlogon' KV2/303
'Report on *Abwehr* up to March 1942' KV3/7

National Archives of Scotland (NAS), Edinburgh
'Police action against Scottish nationalist organisations, etc. 1941' HH55/557
'SNP 1941' HH55/558

National Archives of Ireland (NAI), Dublin
Department of External Affairs/Foreign Affairs
'50th Anniversary of Easter Rising 1916. M. Per Denez, President International Celtic Congress, Proposal to bring Breton group to Ireland for 1916 Commemoration Ceremonies' DFA 2000/14/78
'Admission to Ireland of Political Refugees 1945' DFA P253
'American and British Notes on recall of German personnel here' DEA A74
'American and British Notes to Neutral Countries re. asylum for Axis leaders ('War Criminals')' DFA P78
'André Geoffroy, Breton Nationalist – Corr. Between French Minister and South Tipperary County Council' DFA P237
'Asylum for South American Refugees – General F. Batista (former President of Cuba) 1959', DFA P311

'Cornish National Movement' DFA 2000/14/176
'Correspondence with D/Defence – Intelligence Branch' DEA P168
'Press statement by Minister for Education on Scottish and Welsh nationalism' DFA2001/43/87
'Scottish Movements for Home Rule 1957-' DFA 2001/43/86
'Welsh Nationalist Movement' DFA 96/3/98

Department of the Taoiseach

'Movement for Self-Government in Scotland 1962' S 6022 B/62
'Movement for Self-Government in Scotland' S 6022 B/95
'The Movement for Self-Government in Scotland' 99/1/42
'Partition, Miscellaneous Correspondence, Resolutions, etc., 1938' S10739A

Newspapers and Periodicals

The Age (Melbourne) 2004
Argoad 1957
Breiz Atao 1935
Breton National News Service 1947–8
Breton News 1960–70
Broederband 1966
Carn: A Link Between Celtic Nations 1975–85
Celtic News 1966–71
Connacht Tribune 1931
Daily Express (Glasgow) 2005
Echo 1965–6
The Guardian 2005
Irish Independent 2003–4
Irish Examiner 2002–7
Irish Press 1953–84
Irish Times 1969–2003
La Republica (Uruguay) 2002
Le Figaro 1916
New York Times 1958
Meath Chronicle 2002
News of the World (Scotland) 2001
The Observer 2002
The Scotsman 1999–2008
Sunday Independent 1980–2007
Sunday Press 1969

Parliamentary Debates

Houses of the Oireachtas (Ireland) 1937–74 (http://www.oireachtas-debates.gov.ie)
Sénat de Belgique (Belgium) 2006–7 (http://www.senate.be)

Unpublished Primary Sources

Feutren, Louis, untitled tract composed for the *Observer*, *c.*1959–60, 2pp. (Document courtesy James McLeod.)
Henaff, Neven, (Célestin Lainé), *Biographie-Memoires* (unpublished manuscript, n.d., 65pp.)
Le Noac'h, Youenn, naturalisation certificate 1954.

Published Primary Sources

Brown, Oliver, *Hitlerism in the Highlands*, 6th ed. (London: ILP 1942).

Browne, Noël, *Against the tide* (Dublin: Gill and Macmillan, 1986).

Callewaert, Fr. Jules, *Ierland en het Iersche volk* (Leuven: Vlaamsche Boekenhalle 1923). Translation from Dutch by Toos de Boer.

Colen, Alexander, 'Dagboek uit de periode 1939–1948', in Reinout van den Driessche, 'De emigratie van Vlaamse collaborateurs na de Tweede Wereldoorlog' (MA thesis, Katholieke Universiteit Leuven, 1996).

Council of Flanders, 'Declaration of Independence, 1917', in Theo Hermans (ed.), *The Flemish movement: a documentary history, 1780–1990*, pp. 238–9 (London: The Athlone Press, 1992).

Council of the Welsh National Eisteddfod, *La visite en Bretagne: Rapport de la délégation* (Cardiff, 1947).

Delaporte, Raymond, *Brezhoneg – Buan hag aes* (Cork: CUP, 1977).

De Valera, Terry, *A memoir* (Dublin: Currach Press, 2004).

Doublet, P.H., *La collaboration: L'Épuration, la confiscation, les réparations aux victimes de l'Occupation. Exposé et commentaires suivis des principales ordonnances* (Paris: Librarie Générale de Droit et de Jurisprudence, 1945).

Douglas, Ronald MacDonald, *The Irish book: a miscellany of facts and fancies, folklore and fragments, poems and prose to do with Ireland and her people* (Dublin: Talbot Press, 1936).

Flemish Committee, 'Telegram to President Woodrow Wilson, 1919', in Theo Hermans (ed.), *The Flemish movement: a documentary history, 1780–1990*, pp. 254–7 (London: Athlone Press, 1992).

Folens, Albert, *Aiséirí Flóndrais* (An Chéad Chló: An tÚdar a Fhoilsigh, 1958). Translation from Irish by Anna Heussaff.

Folens, Juliette, 'Folens family reject allegations against Albert Folens', media release, 12 Jan. 2007.

Fouéré, Yann, *La maison du Connemara: histoire d'un Breton* (Spezet: Coop Breizh, 1995).

—— 'La politique du Comité Consultatif de Bretagne (1942–1944)', in Hervé le Boterf (ed.), *La Bretagne sous le gouvernement de Vichy*, pp. 287–93 (Paris: Éditions France-Empire, 1982).

Gallastegi, Eli, *Por la libertad Vasca*, ed. José Maria Lorenzo Espinosa (Tafalla: Txallaparta, 1996). Translation from Spanish by Michael Leach.

Goulet, Yann, 'Une organisation de boy-scouts? Les Bagadou Stourm par Yann Goulet', in Hervé Le Boterf, *La Bretagne dans la guerre,* Vol. II, *1941* (Paris: Éditions France-Empire, 1970): pp. 286–90.

Grennan, Bernard J., (Special Agent CIC), report and addendum, 7–14 July 1947, reproduced at *Jasenovac–Donja Gradina: Industry of Death*

1941–1945, http://www.jasenovac-info.com/cd/biblioteka/pavelicpapers/pavelic/ap0022.html; accessed 27 Apr. 2007.

Lyon, Paul E., (US 430th CIC), 'History of the Italian Rat Line', 10 Apr. 1950, reproduced at *The Pavelić Papers*, http://www.pavelicpapers.com/documents/army/ar0002.html; accessed 27 Jul. 2004.

——'Rat Line from Austria to South America', 12 Jul. 1948, reproduced at *The Pavelić Papers*, http://www.pavelicpapers.com/documents/army/ar0001.html; accessed 27 Jul. 2004.

MacCormick, John, *The flag in the wind: the story of the national movement in Scotland* (London: Victor Gollancz, 1955).

Mordrel, Olier, *Breiz Atao, ou histoire et actualité du nationalisme breton* (Paris: Éditions Alain Moreau, 1973).

Mosley, Oswald, *My Life* (London: Nelson, 1968).

O'Halpin, Eunan (ed.), *MI5 and Ireland, 1939–1945: the official history* (Dublin: Irish Academic Press, 2003).

Van Cauwelaert, Frans, 'Two contributions to a debate: 1919, 1921', in Theo Hermans (ed.), *The Flemish movement: a documentary history, 1780–1990*, pp. 258–61 (London: Athlone Press, 1992).

Verschaeve, Cyriel, 'The Flemish Nationalist's Catechism', in Theo Hermans (ed.), *The Flemish movement: a documentary history, 1780–1990*, pp. 240–53 (London: Athlone Press, 1992).

Young, Douglas, *An appeal to Scots honour* (Glasgow: Scottish Secretariat, 1944).

Interviews

Per Denez, St.-Benoît-des-Ondes, Brittany, 2 June 2005
Louis Feutren, Ireland, 8 June 2005
Yann Fouéré, St.-Brieuc, Brittany, 3 June 2005
Armelle Goulet-Conway, Dalkey, Ireland, 18 June 2005
Gwennig Helloco, Bow Street, Ceredigion, Wales, 26 June 2005
Anna Heussaff, Dublin, Ireland, 21 June 2005
Bríd Heussaff, Spiddal, Co. Galway, Ireland, 19 June 2005
Kintilla Heussaff, Dublin, Ireland, 21 June 2005
Mair Piette, Bow Street, Ceredigion, Wales, 26 June 2005
(Name Withheld), June 2005

Personal Correspondence

Radoslav Artukovic 2007
Adam Busby 2005
Alexander Colen 2006–7
Per Denez 2004
Louis Feutren 2005–6
Dirk Folens 2006

Rozenn Fouéré Barrett 2007
Iker Gallastegi 2006
Brendan Hennessy 2003
Anna Heussaff 2007
Marko Attila Hoare 2007
Fabienne Houze 2007
Mair Piette, 2006
Paul van Cauwelaert 2006
Staf van Velthoven 2007
(Name Withheld) 2007

SECONDARY SOURCES

Theses

Duche, Aude, 'You fight your own wars: Irish defence of the Spanish Republic at war, 1936–1939' (MA Thesis, Université de Haute Bretagne, Rennes, n.d.); PDF document, http://www.geocities.com/irelandscw/pdf-French Thesis.pdf; accessed 12 May 2007.

Van den Driessche, Reinout, 'De emigratie van Vlaamse collaborateurs na de Tweede Wereldoorlog' (MA Thesis, Katholieke Universiteit Leuven, Belgium, 1996).

Film Scripts

Farrell, Keith, *Ireland's Nazis* (Programme One), Tile Films, 14 Dec. 2006, 36pp. Document courtesy Keith Farrell.

—— *Ireland's Nazis* (Programme Two, draft 32), Tile Films, 3 Jan. 2007, 38pp. Document courtesy Keith Farrell.

Unpublished Secondary Material

Hennessy, Brendan, 'A very short biography of Oscar Mac Uilis' (unpublished document, 14 Oct. 2001, 2pp., e-mail to author).

Websites

An Phoblacht/Republican News (http://www.irlnet.com; http://republican-news.org)

Aosdána (http://aosdana.artscouncil.ie)

Axis History Factbook (http://www.axishistory.com)

Axis History Forum (http://forum.axishistory.com)

BAILII.org (http://www.bailii.org)

BBC News (http://news.bbc.co.uk)

The Canadian Encyclopedia (http://the canadianencyclopedia.com)

Clero-Fascist Studies Project (CFSP) (http://web.archive.org/web/20030404022131/www.home.earthlink.net/~velid/cf/index.html)

CNN Cold War (http:// www.cnn.com/SPECIALS/cold.war/)

Constitution.org (http://www.constitution.org)

The Economist (http://www.economist.com)

Eric Margolis: Foreign Correspondent (http://www.ericmargolis.com)
Eurotreaties.com (http://www.eurotreaties.com)
For the Record (http://ftrsummary.blogspot.com)
The Francis Parker Yockey Collection (http://www.alphalink.net.au/~radnat/fpyockey/index.html)
Go2War2.nl (http://www.go2war2.nl)
International Policy Institute for Counter-Terrorism (http://ict.org.il/spotlight)
Irish Statute Book (http://irishstatutebook.ie)
Islam Online (http://islamonline.net)
Jasenovac–Donja Gradina: Industry of Death 1941–1945 (http://www.jasenovac-info.com)
The Journal: Australian Irish Heritage Association (http://irishheritage.net)
Kirche-in-Not.org (http://www.kirche-in-not.org)
KRO-Reporter (http://reporter.kro.nl)
Na Fianna Éireann (http://www.fiannaeireann.com)
Nieuwe Encyclopedie van de Vlaamse Beweging (http://users.pandora.be/frankie.schram/tijd/bio/)
The Pavelic Papers (http://www.pavelicpapers.com)
Priority Independence (http://www.geocities.com/priority_independence)
Republican Sinn Féin (http://www.indymedia.ie)
RTÉ (http://rte.ie/)
Third Way (http://thirdway.org)
Total Population by Country (http://www.photius.com/rankings/world2050.html)
Saoirse – Irish Freedom (http://homepage.tinet.ie/~eirenua/)
Shoah Education Project (http://shoaheducation.com)
Siol nan Gaidheal (http://www.siol-nan-gaidheal.com)
UPA: Ukrainian Insurgent Army Webpage (http://hometown.aol.com/shukhevych/)
US Army Center of Military History (http://www.army.mil/cmh-pg/books/)

Books, Journal Articles and Internet Articles

Aarons, Mark & John Loftus, *Ratlines: How the Vatican's Nazi networks betrayed Western intelligence to the Soviets* (London: Heinemann, 1991).

Abbott, P. & E. Pinak, *Ukrainian armies 1914–55*, Men-At-Arms series #412 (Botley, Oxon.: Osprey Publishing, 2004).

Agee, Chris, 'The Stepinac File', *Archipelago.org*, http://www.archipelago.org/vol5–1/agee2.htm; accessed 3 Aug. 2004.

Aron, Robert, *The Vichy regime 1940–44*, translated by Humphrey Hare (London: Putnam, 1958).

Arzalier, Francis, *Les Perdants: la dérive fasciste des mouvements autonomistes et indépendantistes au XXe siècle* (Paris: Éditions de la Découverte, 1990).

Augusteijn, Joost, *From public defiance to guerrilla warfare: the experience of ordinary volunteers in the Irish War of Independence 1916–1921* (Dublin: Irish Academic Press, 1996).

Avril, Jean-Loup, *500 Bretons à connaître* (St.-Malo: Éditions l'Ancre de la Marine, 1989).

Aziz, Philippe, *Le livre noir de la trahison: Histoires de la Gestapo en France* (Paris: Éditions Ramsay, 1984).

Barton, Dennis, 'Croatia 1941–1946', *Church in History Information Centre,* http://www.churchinhistory.org/pages/booklets/croatia(n)-1.htm; accessed 21 Apr. 2007.

Baudot, Marcel, *Libération de la Bretagne* (Paris: Librairie Hachette, 1973).

Beer, William R., *The unexpected rebellion: ethnic activism in contemporary France* (New York: New York University Press, 1980).

Bergmeier, Horst J.P. & Rainer E. Lotz, *Hitler's airwaves: the inside story of Nazi radio broadcasting and propaganda swing* (New Haven, CT: Yale University Press, 1997).

Biddiscombe, Perry, 'The last White Terror: the Maquis Blanc and its impact in Liberated France, 1944–1945', *Journal of Modern History,* 73:4 (December 2001), 811–61.

—— *The SS Hunter battalions: the hidden history of the Nazi resistance movement 1944–45* (Stroud: Tempus, 2006)

Blum, Howard, *Wanted! The search for Nazis in America,* excerpt available at http://www.mosquitonet.com/~prewett/blum.html; accessed 21 Apr. 2007.

Bothorel, Jean, *Un terroriste breton* (Paris: Calmann-Lévy, 2001).

Braham, Randolph L., 'The Vatican: remembering and forgetting', in Randolph L. Braham (ed.), *The Vatican and the Holocaust: the Catholic Church and the Jews during the Nazi era*, pp. 13–46 (NY: Rosenthal Institute for Holocaust Studies, 2000).

Brekilien, Yann, *Histoire de la Bretagne* (Paris: Éditions France-Empire, 1985).

Broderick, George, 'The Breton Movement and the German Occupation 1940–1944 – Alan Heusaff and the Bezen Perrot: A case study', PDF document, *Klask online,* http://www.uhb.fr/langues/klask/documentations/bezen_perrot.pdf; accessed 13 June 2005.

Broudic, Fañch, *L'interdiction du breton en 1902: La IIIe République contre les langues régionales* (Spezet: Coop Breizh, 1997).

Butler, Hubert, 'The Artukovitch file', *Archipelago.org,* http://www.archipelago.org/vol1–2/butler.htm; accessed 3 Aug. 2004.

—— 'The Sub-Prefect should have held his tongue', *Archipelago.org,* http://www.archipelago.org/vol5–1/butler.htm; accessed 3 Aug. 2004.

Cadiou, Georges, *L'Hermine et la Croix gammée: Le mouvement breton et la collaboration* (Paris: Mango Document, 2001).

Caerléon, Ronan, *Complots pour une république bretonne: les dossiers secrets de l'autonomisme breton* (Paris: Éditions de la Table Ronde, 1967).

—— *La Révolution bretonne permanente* (Paris: Éditions de la Table Ronde, 1969).

—— *Le rêve fou des soldats de Breiz Atao* (Quimper: Nature et Bretagne, 1974).

Calin, William, *Minority literatures and modernism: Scots, Breton and Occitan, 1920–1990* (Toronto: University of Toronto Press, 2000).

Capdevila, Luc, *Les Bretons au lendemain de l'Occupation: Imaginaire et comportement d'une sortie de guerre 1944–1945* (Rennes: Presses Universitaires de Rennes, 1999).

Carroll, Joseph T., *Ireland in the war years* (Newton Abbot: David & Charles, 1975).

Chartier, Erwan & Alain Cabon, *Le dossier FLB: Plongée chez les clandestins bretons* (Spézet: Coop Breizh, 2006).

Chartrand, René, *Émigré & foreign troops in British service (I) 1793–1802*, Men-At-Arms series #328 (Botley, Oxon: Osprey, 1999).

Clews, Roy, *To dream of freedom: The struggle of MAC and the Free Wales Army* (Talybont: Y Lolfa, 1980).

Conway, Martin, *Collaboration in Belgium: Léon Degrelle and the Rexist movement 1940–1944* (New Haven, CT: Yale University Press, 1993).

Coogan, Timothy Patrick, *Ireland since the Rising* (London: Pall Mall Press, 1966).

Cooney, John, *The Crozier and the Dáil: church and state 1922–1986* (Dublin: Mercier Press, 1986).

Corbett, Robin, *Guerrilla warfare from 1939 to the present day* (London: Guild Publishing, 1986).

Cronin, Sean, *Irish nationalism: a history of its roots and ideology* (London: Pluto Press, 1980).

Davies, D. Hywel, *The Welsh nationalist party 1925–1945: a call to nationhood* (Cardiff: University of Wales Press, 1983).

Davis, Troy D., *Dublin's American policy: Irish-American diplomatic relations, 1945–1952* (Washington: The Catholic University of America Press, 1998).

Dedijer, Vladimir, *The Yugoslav Auschwitz and the Vatican: the Croatian massacre of the Serbs during World War II,* translated by Harvey L. Kendall (Buffalo, NY: Prometheus Books, 1988).

Déniel, Alain, *Le mouvement breton de 1919 à 1945* (Paris: François Maspero, 1976).

De Zeng, H.L. IV, 'Ustasha Surveillance Service and the Directorate for Public Order and Security', *Axis History Factbook,* http://www.axishistory.com/index.php?id=7257; accessed 22 Apr. 2007.

Doody, Richard, 'Brittany from the Great War to the Liberation', *The World At War,* http://worldatwar.net/article/brittany; accessed 7 July 2003.

Dorril, Stephen, *Blackshirt: Sir Oswald Mosley and British fascism* (London: Viking/Penguin, 2006).

Douglas, R.M., 'The Pro-Axis underground in Ireland, 1939–1942', *Historical Journal*, 49: 4 (2006), 1155–85.

D'Udekem d'Acoz, Marie-Pierre, *Voor Koning & Vaderland: De Belgische adel in het verzet* (Tielt: Lannoo, 2003). Translation by Bruno de Wever.

Duggan, John P., *Herr Hempel at the German Legation in Dublin, 1937–1945* (Dublin: Irish Academic Press, 2003).

—— *Neutral Ireland and the Third Reich* (Dublin: Gill and Macmillan, 1985).

Dwyer, T. Ryle, *De Valera: the man and the myths* (Dublin: Poolbeg Press, 1991).

—— *Guests of the State: the story of Allied and Axis servicemen interned in Ireland during World War II* (Dingle: Brandon, 1994).

—— *Irish neutrality and the USA, 1939–47* (Dublin: Gill and Macmillan, 1977).

—— 'More than 60 years on, the media still swallow distorted information', *Irish Examiner,* 13 Jan. 2007, http://www.irishexaminer.com; accessed 16 Jan. 2007.

Einaudi, Mario, 'The constitution of the Italian Republic', *American Political Science Review*, 42: 4 (Aug. 1948), 661–76

Ellis, Peter Berresford, 'John MacLean: in memory', *SWR*, http://srsm.port5.com/swr/memory90.html; accessed 19 Aug. 2005.

—— *The Celtic dawn: a history of pan-Celticism* (London: Constable, 1993).

—— *Wales – A nation again: the nationalist struggle for freedom* (London: Library 33, 1968).

Evans, Gwynfor, 'The history of Plaid Cymru', in *Breizh ha pobloù Europa/Bretagne et peuples d'Europe/Brittany and peoples of Europe. Articles to honour Per Denez,* Hervé ar Bihan (ed.), pp. 201–222 (Rennes: Presses Universitaires de Rennes, 1999).

—— & Ioan Rhys, 'Wales', in Owen Dudley Edwards et al. (eds.), *Celtic nationalism*, pp. 211–98 (London: Routledge & Kegan Paul, 1968).

Faligot, Roger, *La harpe et l'hermine* (Rennes: Terre de Brume, 1994).

Fanning, Bryan, *Racism and social change in the Republic of Ireland* (Manchester: Manchester University Press, 2002).

Farrell, Michael, *Sheltering the fugitive? The extradition of Irish political offenders* (Dublin: Mercier Press, 1985).

Finlay, Richard J., *Independent and free: Scottish politics and the origins of the Scottish National Party, 1918–1945* (Edinburgh: John Donald Publishers, 1994).

Fisk, Robert, *In time of war: Ireland, Ulster and the price of neutrality 1939–45* (London: Andre Deutsch, 1983).
Forde, Michael, *Extradition law in Ireland* (Blackrock, Co. Dublin: The Round Hall Press, 1995).
—— *The law of extradition in the United Kingdom* (Blackrock, Co. Dublin: The Round Hall Press, 1995).
Fouéré, Yann, *En prison pour la libération de la Bretagne,* (Paris: Nouvelles Éditions Latines, 1977).
—— *La Bretagne écartelée: Essai pour servir à l'histoire de dix ans 1938–1948,* 2nd ed. (Paris: Nouvelles Éditions Latines, 1976).
Frelaut, Bertrand, *Les nationalistes bretons de 1939 à 1945* (n.p.: Éditions Beltan, 1985).
Fréville, Henri, *Archives secrètes de Bretagne 1940–44* (Rennes: Ouest-France, 1985).
Gevers, Lieve, 'The Catholic Church and the Flemish movement', in Kas Deprez & Louis Vos (eds.), *Nationalism in Belgium: shifting identities, 1780–1995*, pp. 110–18 (Basingstoke: Macmillan, 1998).
Gijsels, Hugo, *Le Vlaams Blok* (Editions Luc Pire), translated from Dutch to French by Nadine Laurent, n.d., PDF document, http://www.lucpire.be; accessed 30 Nov. 2005.
Goldstein, Ivo & Slavko Goldstein, *Holokaust u Zagrebu* (Zagreb: Novi Liber, 2001). Translation by Radoslav Artuković.
Goñi, Uki, *The real Odessa: how Perón brought the Nazi war criminals to Argentina*, revised ed. (London: Granta Books, 2003).
Gordon, Bertram M., *Collaborationism in France during the Second World War* (Ithaca, NY: Cornell University Press, 1980).
Grahl-Madsen, Atle, *Territorial asylum* (Stockholm: Almqvist & Wiksell International, 1980).
Gras, Solange & Christian Gras, *La révolte des régions d'Europe occidentale de 1916 à nos jours* (Paris: Presses Universitaires de France, 1982).
Hamon, Kristian, *Le Bezen Perrot 1944: des nationalistes bretons sous l'uniforme allemand* (Fouesnant: Yoran Embanner, 2004).
—— *Les nationalistes bretons sous l'Occupation* (Kergleuz: An Here, 2001).
Hanham, H.J., *Scottish nationalism* (Cambridge, MA: Harvard University Press, 1969).
Harvie, Christopher, *No gods and precious few heroes: twentieth-century Scotland*, 3rd ed. (Edinburgh: Edinburgh University Press, 1998).
Henry, Lionel & Annick Lagadec, *FLB-ARB: L'histoire 1966–2005*, (Fouesnant: Yoran Embanner, 2005).
Higgins, Roisín, 'Projections and reflections: Irishness and the fiftieth anniversary of the Easter Rising', *Éire-Ireland,* 42: 3–4 (Fall-Winter 2007), 11–34.

Hoare, Marko Attila, 'The Ustasha genocide', *South Slav Journal,* 25 (1–2), Spring-Summer 2004, http://www.southslavjournal.com/mah.html; accessed 2 Apr. 2007.

Hogan, Gerard & Clive Walker, *Political violence and the law in Ireland,* (Manchester: Manchester University Press, 1989).

Hossay, Patrick, *Contentions of nationhood: nationalist movements, political conflict, and social change in Flanders, Scotland and French Canada* (Lanham, MD: Lexington Books, 2002).

Houthaeve, Robert, *Vlamingen in Ierland* (Izegem: Uitgeverij Hochepied, 1989).

Hull, Mark M., *Irish secrets: German espionage in Ireland 1939–1945* (Dublin: Irish Academic Press, 2003).

—— 'The Irish interlude: German intelligence in Ireland 1939–1943', *Journal of Military History,* 66: 3 (July 2002), 695–717.

Infield, Glenn B., *Skorzeny: Hitler's commando* (NY: St. Martin's Press, 1981).

Jurado, Carlos Caballero, *Foreign volunteers of the Wehrmacht 1941–45,* Men-at-Arms series #147 (London: Osprey Publishing, 1983).

—— *Resistance warfare 1940–45,* Men-at-Arms series #169 (London: Osprey Publishing, 1985).

Kelly, James, *Orders for the Captain?* (Dublin: James Kelly, 1971).

Keogh, Dermot, 'Eamon de Valera and Hitler: An analysis of international reaction to the visit to the German Minister, May 1945', *Irish Studies in International Affairs,* 3: 1 (1989), 69–92.

—— *Ireland and Europe 1919–1948* (Dublin: Gill and Macmillan, 1988).

—— 'Ireland, the Vatican and the Cold War: the case of Italy, 1948', *Irish Studies in International Affairs,* 3: 3 (1991), 67–114

—— *Jews in twentieth-century Ireland: refugees, anti-Semitism and the Holocaust* (Cork: Cork University Press, 1998).

—— 'Profile of Joseph Walshe, Secretary, Department of Foreign Affairs, 1922–46', *Irish Studies in International Affairs,* 3: 2 (1990), 59–80.

Koreman, Megan, *The expectation of justice: France, 1944–1946* (Durham: Duke University Press, 1999).

Kurlansky, Mark, *The Basque history of the world* (London: Jonathan Cape, 1999).

Lauryssens, Stan, *The Eichmann diaries* (MS Word document, 2002, 180pp.). Document courtesy Keith Farrell.

Leach, Daniel, '*Bezen Perrot:* The Breton nationalist unit of the SS, 1943–5', *e-Keltoi: Interdisciplinary Journal of Celtic Studies,* Vol. 4 (Nationalism), pp.1–38, http://www.uwm.edu/Dept/celtic/ekeltoi/volumes/vol4/4_1/index.html; published 6 Feb. 2008.

Lebesque, Morvan, *Comment peut-on être breton? Essai sur la democratie française* (Paris: Éditions du Seuil, 1970).

Le Boterf, Hervé, *La Bretagne sous le gouvernment de Vichy* (Paris: Éditions France-Empire, 1982).

Le Dantec, Jean-Pierre, *Bretagne: Re-naissance d'un peuple* (Paris: Éditions Gallimard, 1974).

Lee, J.J., *Ireland 1912–1985: politics and society* (Cambridge: Cambridge University Press, 1989).

Le Guennec, Pierrik, 'Roparz Hemon dans le Nazisme, trois faits', PDF document, http://membres.lycos.fr/leguenne/etudes/trois_faits/index.html; accessed 11 Feb. 2006.

'Leslie, David', 'Inside a terrorist group: The story of the SNLA', http://ssg.maoism.ru/pages/snla.html; accessed 3 Oct. 2005.

Littlejohn, David, *The patriotic traitors: a history of collaboration in German Occupied Europe 1940–1945* (London: Heinemann, 1972).

Lituchy, Barry, 'What is the Vatican hiding? The Vatican's complicity in genocide in fascist Croatia: The suppressed chapter of Holocaust history', *The Holocaust Revealed,* http://www.ccg.org/domain/holocaustrevealed.org/Church/Vatican_Hiding.htm; accessed 13 Apr. 2007.

Loftus, John, *The Belarus secret* (London: Penguin, 1983).

Manhattan, Avro, 'The Vatican's Holocaust', *Reformation.org,* Chapter 10, 'The Pope, Stepinac and Pavelić try to save Croatia', http://www.reformation.org/holoc10.html; accessed 27 Apr. 2007.

Manning, Maurice, *The Blueshirts* (Dublin: Gill and Macmillan, 1970).

Marr, Andrew, *The battle for Scotland* (London: Penguin, 1992).

Martland, Peter, *Lord Haw-Haw: the English voice of Nazi Germany* (Richmond, Surrey: National Archives, 2003).

McAdams, Michael C., 'Whitepaper on Andrija Artuković', July 1975, *Croatian Information Series Number* 4, http://www.mcadams-croatia.net/wp_on_a_artukovic.htm; accessed 12 May 2007.

—— 'Yalta and the Bleiburg tragedy', http://www.ess.uwe.ac.uk/genocide/yugoslav-hist1.htm; accessed 23 Apr. 2007.

McCabe, Ian, *A diplomatic history of Ireland, 1948–49: the Republic, the Commonwealth and NATO* (Dublin: Irish Academic Press, 1991).

McConvery, Fr. Brendan, 'Blessed Nicholas Charnetskyj', *CatholicIreland.net,* http://www.catholicireland.net/pages/index.php?nd=68&art=173; accessed 26 Mar. 2006.

McDonald, Maryon, *'We are not French!': language, culture and identity in Brittany* (London: Routledge, 1989).

Melman, Yossi, 'Tied up in the Ratlines', *Red Ice Creations,* republished from

Haaretz.com, Feb. 2006, http://www.redicecreations.com/specialreports/2006/02feb/ratlines.html; accessed 23 Apr. 2007.

Milton, Nan, *John Maclean* (London: Pluto Press, 1973).

Mnookin, Robert & Alain Verbeke, 'Bye bye Belgium?', *International Herald Tribune Opinion,* 20 Dec. 2006, http://www.iht.com/articles/2006/12/20/opinion/edmnookin.php; accessed 13 June 2007.

Molohan, Cathy, *Germany and Ireland 1945–1955: two nations' friendship* (Dublin: Irish Academic Press, 1999).

Nicolas, Michel, *Le séparatisme en Bretagne* (Brasparts: Éditions Beltan, 1986).

Novick, Peter, *The Resistance versus Vichy: the purge of collaborators in Liberated France* (New York: Columbia University Press, 1968).

O'Brien, Justin, *The Arms Trial* (Dublin: Gill & Macmillan, 2000).

O'Callaghan, Sean, *The jackboot in Ireland* (London: Allen Wingate, 1958).

Ó Ciosáin, Eamon, 'La Bretagne et l'Irlande pendant l'entre-deux guerres (première partie)', *Dalc'homp Soñj!,* (22) Spring 1988: pp.29–35.

O'Donoghue, David, *Hitler's Irish voices: the story of German radio's wartime Irish service* (Belfast: Beyond the Pale, 1998).

O'Halpin, Eunan, '"According to the Irish minister in Rome...": British decrypts and Irish diplomacy in the Second World War', *Irish Studies in International Affairs,* 6 (1995), 95–105.

—— 'British intelligence, the Republican movement and the IRA's German links 1935–45', in Fearghal McGarry (ed.), *Republicanism in modern Ireland,* pp. 108–31 (Dublin: UCD Press, 2003).

—— *Defending Ireland: the Irish state and its enemies since 1922* (Oxford: Oxford University Press, 1999).

—— 'Irish neutrality in the Second World War' in Neville Wylie (ed.), *European neutrals and non-belligerents during the Second World War,* pp. 283–303 (Cambridge: Cambridge University Press, 2002).

O'Higgins, Paul, 'Irish extradition law and practice' in Michael Forde (ed.), *Extradition law in Ireland,* pp. 228–58 (Blackrock, Co. Dublin: Round Hall Press, 1995).

—— 'The Irish Extradition Act, 1965', *International and Comparative Law Quarterly,* 15 (2), Apr. 1966: pp. 369–394.

O'Riordan, Michael, 'Paper presented by Michael O'Riordan (member of the Connolly Column and former general secretary of the Communist Party of Ireland) to the First International Forum on the International Brigades, Getafe, Spain, 12–14 November 1999', *The Irish Section of the International Brigades,* http://www.communistpartyofireland.ie/spainn-en.html#n5; accessed 19 May 2006.

Ousby, Ian, *Occupation: The ordeal of France 1940–1944* (London: John Murray, 1997).

Payne, Stanley G., *Basque nationalism* (Reno, NV: University of Nevada Press, 1975).
Philip, Alan Butt, *The Welsh question: nationalism in Welsh politics, 1945–1970* (Cardiff: University of Wales Press, 1975).
Pitamitz, Antonio, 'The conspirator rediscovered', *Jasenovac—Donja Gradina: Industry of Death 1941–1945*, http://www.jasenovac-info.com/cd/ biblioteka/pavelicpapers/pavelic/ap0038.html; accessed 21 Apr. 2007.
Pittock, Murray G.H., *Scottish nationality* (Basingstoke: Palgrave, 2001).
Rapoport, David C., 'The four waves of rebel terror and September 11', *Anthropoetics*, 8 (1), Spring/Summer 2002, pp.17–30.
Reece, Jack E., *The Bretons against France: ethnic minority nationalism in twentieth-century Brittany* (Chapel Hill, NC: University of North Carolina Press, 1977).
Rich, Norman, *Hitler's war aims: the establishment of the New Order,* Vol. II (London: Andre Deutsch, 1974).
Rigoulot, Pierre, *Les enfants de l'Épuration* (Paris: Plon, 1993).
Ruchala, Cali, 'Andrija Artukovic', *The Pavelić Papers,* http://www.pavelicpapers.com/documents.artukovic/; accessed 28 July 2004.
—— 'The Poglavnik's family tree', *The Pavelić Papers*, http://www.pavelicpapers.com/features/essays/pft.html; 27 July 2004.
—— 'Timeline: an historical overview of the Ustaše movement', *The Pavelic Papers,* http://www.pavelicpapers.com/timeline/ustasetimeline.html; accessed 27 July 2004.
Radulescu, Domnica, 'Theorising exile' in Domnica Radulescu (ed.), *Realms of exile: nomadism, diasporas, and Eastern European voices* (Lanham, MD: Lexington Books, 2002), pp. 184–204.
Sainclivier, Jacqueline, *La Bretagne de 1939 à nos jours* (Rennes: Éditions Ouest-France, 1989).
Salmon, Trevor C., *Unneutral Ireland: an ambivalent and unique security policy* (Oxford: Clarendon Press, 1989).
Scott, Andrew Murray & Iain Macleay, *Britain's secret war: Tartan terrorism and the Anglo-American State* (Edinburgh: Mainstream Publishing, 1990).
Shain, Yossi, 'Governments-in-exile and international legitimation' in Yossi Shain (ed.), *Governments-in-exile in contemporary world politics* (New York: Routledge, 1991), pp. 219–237.
Silvestri, Michael, 'The Sinn Féin of India: Irish nationalism and the policing of revolutionary terrorism in Bengal', *Journal of British Studies*, 39: 4 (October 2000), 454–86.
Skelly, Joseph Morrison, *Irish diplomacy at the United Nations, 1945–1965: national interests and the international order* (Dublin: Irish Academic Press, 1997).

Smith, Barry, 'Baarle-Nassau/Baarle-Hertog', http://ontology.buffalo.edu/smith/baarle.htm; accessed 5 July 2007.

Smyllie, Robert M., 'Unneutral neutral Éire', *Foreign Affairs*, 24: 2 (January 1946), 316–26.

Stephan, Enno, *Spies in Ireland,* translated by Arthur Davidson (London: MacDonald, 1963).

Stouffer, Bill, 'The patron saint of genocide', *Clero-Fascist Studies Project,* http://web.archive.org/web/20030415213347/www.home.earthlink.net/~velid/cf/cs/psg1.html; accessed 10 Nov. 2005.

Sullivan, John, *ETA and Basque nationalism: the fight for Euskadi, 1890–1986* (London: Routledge, 1988).

Tabori, Paul, *The anatomy of exile: a semantic and historical study* (London: Harrap, 1972).

Time-Life Editors, *The heel of the conqueror,* The Third Reich series (Alexandria VA: Time-Life Books, 1991).

—— *The shadow war,* The Third Reich series (Alexandria VA: Time-Life Books, 1991).

Thomas, N. & K. Mikulan, *Axis forces in Yugoslavia 1941–45*, Men-At-Arms series #282 (Botley, Oxon: Osprey, 1995).

Tolstoy, Nikolai, *Victims of Yalta* (London: Corgi, 1977).

Van Haegendoren, M., *The Flemish movement in Belgium* (Antwerp: Flemish Cultural Council, 1965).

Vest, Rob, 'Otto Skorzeny: The scar-faced commando', http://homepages.ius.edu/RVEST/SkorzenyDr2.htm; accessed 8 May 2006.

Vos, Louis, 'The Flemish national question', in Kas Deprez & Louis Vos (eds.), *Nationalism in Belgium: shifting identities, 1780–1995*, pp. 83–95 (Basingstoke: MacMillan, 1998).

Ward, Eilis, '"A big show-off to show what we could do": Ireland and the Hungarian refugee crisis of 1956', *Irish Studies in International Affairs*, 7 (1996), 131–41.

Webb, Keith, *The growth of nationalism in Scotland* (London: Penguin, 1977).

Williams, Peter N., 'Welsh history: Lesson 8: Modern Wales', *Suite 101,* http://www.suite101.com/lesson.cfm/17851/1278/1; accessed 8 Sep. 2005.

Y Crearie, Shorys, 'Recording native Manx speech', in Cathal Ó Luain (ed.), *For a Celtic future: a tribute to Alan Heusaff*, pp. 308–20 (Dublin: Celtic League, 1983).

Zuelow, Eric G.E., 'Towards an understanding of Scottish ethnic nationalism: The 'Watch' groups and 'Anti-Englishness' in late twentieth century Scotland', *The Nationalism Project*, http://www.nationalismproject.org/articles/zuelow1.htm; accessed 2 Aug. 2004.

Index

Compiled by Julitta Clancy